FILTERING POPULIST CLAIMS ⌐LISM

The new wave of populism that has emerged over the last five years in Europe and in the
US urgently needs to be better understood in a comparative and historical context. Using
Italy – including the experiment of a self-styled populist coalition government – as a case
study, this book investigates how populists in power borrow, use and manipulate categories of constitutional theory and instruments of constitutional law. Giuseppe Martinico
goes beyond treating constitutionalism and populism as purely antithetical to dive deeply
into the impact of populism on the activity of some instruments of constitutional
democracy, endeavoring to explore their role as possible fora of populist claims and
targets of populist attacks. Most importantly, he points to ways in which constitutional
democracies can channel populist claims without jeopardizing the legacy of post-World
War II constitutionalism. This book is aimed at academics and practicing lawyers
interested in populism and comparative constitutional law.

Giuseppe Martinico is Full Professor of Comparative Public Law at the Sant'Anna School
of Advanced Studies. Previously, he was García Pelayo Fellow at the Centre for Political
and Constitutional Studies (CEPC), Madrid, and Max Weber Fellow at the European
University Institute, Florence.

COMPARATIVE CONSTITUTIONAL LAW AND POLICY

Series Editors

Tom Ginsburg
University of Chicago

Zachary Elkins
University of Texas at Austin

Ran Hirschl
University of Toronto

Comparative constitutional law is an intellectually vibrant field that encompasses an increasingly broad array of approaches and methodologies. This series collects analytically innovative and empirically grounded work from scholars of comparative constitutionalism across academic disciplines. Books in the series include theoretically informed studies of single constitutional jurisdictions, comparative studies of constitutional law and institutions, and edited collections of original essays that respond to challenging theoretical and empirical questions in the field.

Books in the Series

Filtering Populist Claims to Fight Populism

THE ITALIAN CASE IN A COMPARATIVE PERSPECTIVE

GIUSEPPE MARTINICO

Sant'Anna School of Advanced Studies (Pisa)

CAMBRIDGE
UNIVERSITY PRESS

Shaftesbury Road, Cambridge CB2 8EA, United Kingdom

One Liberty Plaza, 20th Floor, New York, NY 10006, USA

477 Williamstown Road, Port Melbourne, VIC 3207, Australia

314–321, 3rd Floor, Plot 3, Splendor Forum, Jasola District Centre, New Delhi – 110025, India

103 Penang Road, #05–06/07, Visioncrest Commercial, Singapore 238467

Cambridge University Press is part of Cambridge University Press & Assessment, a department of the University of Cambridge.

We share the University's mission to contribute to society through the pursuit of education, learning and research at the highest international levels of excellence.

www.cambridge.org
Information on this title: www.cambridge.org/9781108791489

DOI: 10.1017/9781108866156

First published 2022
First paperback edition 2022

A catalogue record for this publication is available from the British Library

ISBN   978-1-108-49613-1   Hardback
ISBN   978-1-108-79148-9   Paperback

Contents

Introduction and Acknowledgements

*

This book is the outcome of two projects that I have coordinated over the last four years. The first one is a Jean Monnet project called *European Public Law-ius* (Eur. Publ.ius), which was funded by the Education, Audiovisual and Culture Executive Agency of the European Union. The project, which ended in 2019, was devoted to the current challenges faced by the European Union, and of course among them there is the rise of authoritarian populisms in Hungary and Poland with the well-known rule of law crisis.[1] Within the framework of this Jean Monnet project I organised an international conference devoted to the relationship between populism and political constitutionalism, which was held at the Sant'Anna School of Advanced Studies (*Scuola Superiore Sant'Anna*) in Pisa on 20 September 2019. Some of the papers presented on that occasion were later published in a volume that I edited with Giacomo Delledonne, Matteo Monti and Fabio Pacini entitled *Italian Populism and Constitutional Law: Strategies, Conflicts and Dilemmas.*[2]

In 2018, Italy witnessed the formation of a populist government, which was the result of two different populist forces (*Lega*, previously called *Lega Nord*, 'Northern League' and *MoVimento 5 Stelle*, 'Five Star Movement'), with very different agendas and voting constituencies, forming a coalition. Indeed, the results of the Italian political elections held in 2018 also represented the occasion for the second project I mentioned at the beginning of this Introduction, which is a brand new endeavour called *POP.C.CON.* ('Populism Channelled Through Constitutionalism?'). POP. C.CON. is financed by the DIRPOLIS Institute (Law, Politics and Development) of the *Scuola Superiore Sant'Anna*.

One might think that the new wave of populism in Italy would have ended after the second Conte government, created by the alliance between the *MoVimento 5*

---

[1] W. Sadursky, *Poland's Constitutional Breakdown*, Oxford University Press, Oxford, 2019; A. Jakab, D. Kochenov (eds.), *The Enforcement of EU Law and Values*, Oxford University Press, Oxford, 2017; C. Closa Montero, D. Kochenov (eds.), *Reinforcing Rule of Law Oversight in the European Union*, Cambridge University Press, 2016.

[2] G. Delledonne, G. Martinico, M. Monti, F. Pacini (eds.), *Italian Populism and Constitutional Law: Strategies, Conflicts and Dilemmas*, Palgrave, London, 2020.

Stelle and the *Partito democratico*[3], came into power, but this would probably be a mistake. Not even the advent of the Draghi government has killed the populist momentum, as the numerical strength of the populists in parliament has not changed. At the same time, it is not possible to reduce Italian populism to the success of the *Lega*. Indeed, the former Italian president of the Council of Ministers (i.e., the 'prime minister' in Italy), Giuseppe Conte, has also repeatedly defined himself as a populist,[4] so it seems that nowadays Italian political leaders do not avoid this label; on the contrary, they are happy to display it as a badge of honour. Even before Conte, Revelli[5] and Ignazi[6] considered Renzi's government to be populist in many respects. Renzi has always claimed to be an anti-populist and he was the mastermind of the political operation that led to the end of the first and the second Conte governments respectively, in August 2019 and in January 2021,[7] but the language and tone he uses create mixed feelings among scholars, as we will see. The political majority in parliament will not change in the short term, since elections will not be held in the near future (and they will not occur before the election of a new president of the Republic at the beginning of 2022), so the Five Star Movement's political agenda will not disappear. The Five Star Movement remains the party with the most seats in parliament and, paradoxically, the demise of Conte could make them even more populist in the period remaining in the legislature. Renzi has proved himself to be a demolition man, and by fostering conditions for the Draghi government he may have deprived Draghi of the possibility of being elected president of the Republic.[8] Finally, the sovereignist issue and the importance of European funds (discussed in Chapter 3) will remain central. Draghi has to decide

---

[3]   The second Conte government was also supported by a third party, *Liberi e Uguali* ('Free and Equal'), LeU.

[4]   'Conte: "Rivendico natura populista del Governo"', 28 December 2018, www.ilgiornale.it/video/politica/conte-rivendico-natura-populista-governo-1622063.html.

[5]   M. Revelli, *Populismo 2.0*, Einaudi, Turin, 2017, 135.

[6]   P. Ignazi, 'Ora il Pd pensi ai più deboli', 5 August 2019, https://rep.repubblica.it/pwa/commento/2019/08/05/news/ora_il_pd_pensi_ai_piu_deboli-232905580/?ref=nrct-1; Ignazi also had an interesting exchange on this with Renzi himself in *la Repubblica*: M. Renzi, 'Renzi: Nessun filo rosso tra me e Salvini', 6 August 2019, www.repubblica.it/politica/2019/08/06/news/nessun_filo_rosso_tra_me_e_salvini-233001980/.

[7]   G. Martinico, 'Resentment, Populism and Political Strategies in Italy', 2019, https://verfassungsblog.de/resentment-populism-and-political-strategies-in-italy/.

[8]   Unless the emergency situation ends before the end of 2021 and the Draghi government resigns at that point. Even in this scenario, however, there would be no shortage of difficulties, given the current president of the Republic's 'white semester' (the last six months of his mandate) and the impossibility for President Mattarella to dissolve the chambers according to Article 88 of the Italian Constitution. Indeed, it would be necessary to find another president of the Council supported by the political forces after Draghi's possible resignation. Technically, it would be possible for a president of the Council of Ministers to be elected president of the Republic. In practice, however, the president of the Council of Ministers would have to present his resignation immediately after the election to the current president of the Republic. Indeed, after the election by the chambers (Art. 83 of the Italian Constitution), the new president of the Council of Ministers would have to be appointed by the president of the Republic (Art. 92 of the Italian Constitution). Clearly, this would cause an interregnum of uncertain contours.

whether to use the European Stability Mechanism (opposed by the Five Star Movement and the League). Even if Salvini has decided to support the Draghi government, I am sure that the anti-European character of his party will remain relevant. The picture, in short, has not changed that much.

While, according to the polls, Conte is still very popular among Italians, his way of dealing with the COVID-19 crisis has generated harsh criticism.[9] His approach relied on a constant reference to the precautionary principle and prioritisation of the right to health over other rights (for instance the right to economic activity) as well as an interesting use of social media (in particular Facebook) to announce the contents of his decrees of the president of the Council of Ministers.[10]

Indeed, the coronavirus crisis gave new blood to the leadership of Giuseppe Conte, who decided to manage the crisis directly by communicating with Italians through Facebook instead of using traditional media.

This situation increased the protagonism and visibility of Conte and at the same time caused uncertainty, since sometimes the measures announced by the Italian premier were just part of not-yet approved drafts. The emergency has contributed to the marginalisation of the parliament.

This lack of centrality of the parliament was partly remedied later on. To a certain extent, this situation is due to the way in which the government wanted to handle the pandemic and other reasons, *in primis* the ambivalence of the opposition. On the one hand, the right-wing opposition (namely *Lega* and *Fratelli d'Italia*) avoided the parliamentary debate, leaving the Chamber of Deputies when Conte went to report back to the parliament about the measures adopted in June 2020.[11] On the other hand, *Lega* and *Fratelli d'Italia* have sometimes strategically rediscovered the importance of the parliament and have occupied the chambers to protest against the lockdown.[12]

Moreover, Conte decided to announce his government's new measures to boost economic activity in an alternative forum and format bombastically called *États généraux*[13] instead of discussing them with members of the parliament.

---

[9] For instance, Sabino Cassese, former member of the Italian Constitutional Court and eminent jurist, has written many articles in Italian newspapers to criticise the government. For instance: S. Cassese, 'Cassese: "La pandemia non è una guerra. I pieni poteri al governo non sono legittimi"', 14 April 2020, www.ildubbio.news/2020/04/14/cassese-la-pandemia-non-e-una-guerra-pieni-poteri-al-governo-sono-illegittimi/.

[10] In Italian, *decreti del Presidente del Consiglio dei ministri* (DPCM).

[11] 'Conte parla alla Camera: Fdi assente, Lega abbandona l'Aula', 17 June 2020, www.adnkronos.com/fatti/politica/2020/06/17/conte-parla-alla-camera-fdi-assente-lega-abbandona-aula_Mrt5vSvYLVP3WGfmZh18YP.html.

[12] H. Roberts, 'Salvini occupies Italian parliament in lockdown protest. Far-right leader accused of "stunt" to restore popularity which has been eclipsed by the epidemic', 30 April 2020, www.politico.eu/article/matteo-salvini-coronavirus-occupies-italian-parliament-in-lockdown-protest/.

[13] A. Le Nir, 'Italie: Giuseppe Conte ouvre des "états généraux" pour relancer le pays', 14 June 2020, www.rfi.fr/fr/europe/20200613-italie-giuseppe-conte-ouvre-etats-g%C3%A9n%C3%A9raux-relancer-le-pays.

So again, on both sides, we had a clear tendency to deprive the parliament of its role. It is difficult to imagine that parliament will play a greater role during the Draghi government, due to the (quasi) technical nature of the government, although, all the most important political parties have supported the birth of the new executive.

**

From these pages one may think that this is a parochial analysis of recent developments in Italy, but this volume aspires to do much more. Italy is a prime example of post–World War II (WWII) constitutionalism, the product of a series of fundamental choices made at the end of the awful experience of Nazi-fascism, which has inevitably reshaped the original features of constitutionalism as both a philosophical movement and set of instruments to tame political power. At the same time, the Italian experience is different from the German one (the other great example of post–WWII constitutionalism) because, among other things, it does not present itself as a militant democracy. This is an important difference because it makes the Italian case both unique (in theory at least) and very relevant to study the relationship between constitutionalism, inclusiveness, and populism. Post–WWII constitutionalism has increased the dose of counter-majoritarianism inherently present in the concept of constitutionalism and its normative dimension. It is true that even authoritarian regimes may be equipped with documents called constitutions,[14] but in these cases there will be constitutions without constitutionalism and these fundamental laws will be instruments of government only. While constitutions forged by constitutionalism are much more than this, as they tend to protect not only the power of the contingent majority to rule but also the preservation of minorities. This is after all the essence of democracy.[15] The intimate connection between pluralism and constitutionalism offers a powerful argument against those scholars who have depicted constitutionalism as holism,[16] neglecting the importance that the preservation of pluralism has in the mission of constitutionalism. Portraying constitutionalism as holism or arguing that the constitution emanates directly from a sort of a priori existing monolithic entity called 'the people' means neglecting the lesson of political history. In this sense, it is frequently the case that constitutions do not really reflect unity, they do not presume the identity of the constitutional subject; rather they are part of the process of the construction of this subject. In order to guarantee its legitimacy and effectiveness in the long run, constitutions have to create bridges connecting former enemies and contributing to the creation of a common platform of values. 'In the real world, the law cannot be

---

[14]   T. Ginsburg, A. Simpser (eds.), *Constitutions in Authoritarian Regimes*, Cambridge University Press, 2014.

[15]   H. Kelsen, *Vom Wesen und Wert der Demokratie*, Mohr, Tübingen, 1929 (Italian translation *Essenza e valore della democrazia*, Giappichelli, Turin, 2004).

[16]   N. Krisch, *Beyond Constitutionalism: The Pluralist Structure of Postnational Law*, Oxford University Press, 2010.

represented by a single figure',[17] that is why constitutions need fictions to remedy this. Fictions, and silence, are two of the greatest instruments employed by a constitution to favour integration. Constitutional silence on some sensitive issues ('elements of dormant suspension')[18] can avoid the emergence of conflicts and against this background, 'abeyances are valuable, therefore, not in spite of their obscurity, but because of it'.[19]

Fictions are also essential for the success of governments:

> The success of government thus requires the acceptance of fictions, requires the willing suspension of disbelief, requires us to believe that the emperor is clothed even though we can see that he is not [...] Government requires make-believe. Make believe that the king is divine, make believe that he can do no wrong or make believe that the voice of the people is the voice of God. Make believe that the people have a voice or make believe that the representatives of the people are the people. Make believe that governors are the servants of the people. Make believe that all men are equal or make believe that they are not.[20]

Popular sovereignty is also fiction, since 'a sovereign people is the figurative ventriloquist of our aspirations, a security blanket for our anxieties, and a projectile that we launch against those who stand between us and the horizon of our aspirations'.[21] If constitutionalism is also about the need to protect and enhance pluralism, democracy is much more than the mere rule of the majority. In enhancing democracy and the rule of law, constitutionalism inevitably clashes with the majoritarian approach to the constitution. Exploring Italy as an example of post–WWII constitutionalism, this book aims to study the tension existing between populism and constitutionalism. In particular, I shall investigate how populists in power borrow, use and manipulate categories of constitutional theory and instruments of constitutional law.[22] In so doing, my reflections will be comparative in nature and will be based on both diachronic and synchronic comparison. The importance of historical comparison is crucial to study the roots of the current new wave of populism in Italy and elsewhere. My argument is that this new round of populism has emerged because of what Umberto Eco called 'eternal fascism'.[23]

17 C. Sunstein, 'Incompletely Theorized Agreements. Commentary', *Harvard Law Review*, No. 7, 1994, 1733.
18 M. Foley, *The Silence of Constitutions: Gaps, 'Abeyances', and Political Temperament in the Maintenance of Government*, Routledge, Abingdon, 1989, 198.
19 Foley, *The Silence*, 10.
20 E. Morgan, *Inventing the People: The Rise of Popular Sovereignty in England and America*, W. W. Norton & Company, New York, 1989, 13.
21 Z. Oklopcic, *Beyond the People Social Imaginary and Constituent Imagination*, Oxford University Press, 2018, 43.
22 For a political science analysis of the populists in power, see: D. Albertazzi, D. Mcdonnell, *Populists in Power*, Routledge, Abingdon, 2015.
23 U. Eco, *Ur-Fascism*, *The New York Review of Books*, 1995, www.nybooks.com/articles/1995/06/22/ur-fascism/.

Indeed, Italy has never dealt with its own past and has treated fascism as a mere parenthesis, as an incident which will not happen again. This has created a cultural and political breeding ground that has favoured this new round of right-wing populism.

*

As for the structure, this book is divided into seven Chapters.

Chapter 1 will explore the relationship between constitutionalism and populism in theoretical terms. It will be maintained that this relationship should not be understood as if constitutionalism and populism were in perfect opposition. Populism often relies on an instrumental use of constitutional law and offers what I will call a constitutional counter-narrative. Chapter 1 will also recall the complex debate on the notion and nature of populism, but for the purpose of this volume, instead of proceeding by definitions, I will progress by identification. In other words, I shall read the latest wave of Italian populism by focusing on three emanations: politics of identity, politics of immediacy[24] and extreme majoritarianism.

Chapter 2 will explain why the Italian system is so important in examining the relationship between constitutionalism and populism. Italian history helps to explain the variety of populisms that have emerged in the country. Elements of populism can even be noted in the Italian constituent process, as we will see when recalling the experience of the *Fronte dell'Uomo Qualunque* ('The Common Man's Front'), which had thirty members at the Italian Constituent Assembly.

In Chapter 3, the concept of sovereignism ('sovranismo') will be explored to investigate 'identity politics'. Sovereignism in Italy tends to be coupled with anti-Europeanism and represents an ideal bridge connecting *Lega* and *MoVimento 5 Stelle*. Indeed populists tend to manipulate the Italian Constitution in order to portray it as if it were a sovereignist charter opposed to the EU treaties. This kind of reading neglects and denies the principle of openness, which represents a building block of post–WWII constitutionalism,[25] including its Italian version.

Chapter 4 deals with another emanation of populism, namely the politics of immediacy. In so doing it focuses on the use of the referendum. The referendum is frequently approached by constitutional law scholars with suspicion, and they usually stress both the advantages and disadvantages of its use in the context of representative democracy. Populists traditionally understand the referendum as a mantra to be used against the corruption of institutions, and this can be very dangerous, as we will see.

Chapter 5 explores the impact of populism on Italian representative democracy. I shall first illustrate how Casaleggio and the Five Star Movement (before the recent

---

[24] L. Corrias, 'Populism in a Constitutional Key: Constituent Power, Popular Sovereignty and Constitutional Identity', *European Constitutional Law Review*, No. 1, 2016, 6, 12.

[25] G. Martinico, 'Constitutionalism, Resistance, and Openness: Comparative Law Reflections on Constitutionalism in Postnational Governance', *Yearbook of European Law*, 2016, 318.

break-up) understand democracy, and then analyse the impact of the Conte governments on the legislative and non-legislative functions of the Italian parliament. As we will see, there is continuity between the pre-Conte situation and the current legislature in terms of the functioning of the institution despite the abrupt proclamations of populists. Chapter 6 analyses the impact of populism on the prohibition of the imperative mandate, a crucial component of political modernity and an element of the untouchable core of the Italian Constitution. In this analysis, I shall explore the organisation of the Five Star Movement and their internal rules, as well as the relevant case law of Italian judges. As we will see, again, despite its proclamations, the structure of the Five Star Movement resembles that of a typical political party, and all the announced transparency and horizontality do not correspond to its real course of action. In Chapter 7, building once again on the distinction between populism and populist claims, I selected some points from the populist agenda and tried to work through them. My intent was to extract and filter some normative arguments that could be reconciled with the untouchable core of post–WWII constitutionalism. The case of authoritarian populisms suggests that courts, especially constitutional courts – when present in the relevant jurisdiction – are frequently targets of populist attacks. Not by coincidence, authoritarian populists try to put pressure on courts by jeopardising their independence and reshaping them (court-packing, court-curbing).[26] Fortunately, the Italian case does not show such worrying signals although judges have frequently been attacked by Berlusconi and Salvini for instance, as we will see in the first chapters of this volume. This is also partly explicable in light of the importance that law, and in particular criminal law, has in the Five Star Movement's rhetoric and toolbox. This phenomenon can be traced back to the legacy of *Tangentopoli*, as we will see in Chapter 2. This consideration also explains why I have decided to focus on the populist impact on political actors, and in particular on the role of the parliament. This book reflects the events that took place up to 10 February 2021, with the exception of a few updates to reflect more recent developments. Renzi announced the withdrawal of the two *Italia Viva* ministers from the second Conte government in January 2021. In the eyes of many, this government crisis appeared incomprehensible. Renzi justified his choice in light of the disagreement between *Italia Viva* and the other majority forces on the Italian Recovery Plan and the Five Star Movement's refusal to use the European Stability Mechanism. On 18 and 19 January 2021, Conte went to the Houses of Parliament to see if he still had a parliamentary majority, relying on the votes of what have been called 'responsible' members of the parliament. It is worth noting that in his speech in the Chamber of Deputies on 18 January 2021 Conte described himself as anti-populist and anti-sovereignist. These are words that are difficult to reconcile

---

[26] Recently, D. Kosař, K. Sipulova, 'How to Fight Court-Packing?', *Constitutional Studies*, No. 1, 2020, 133.

with what Conte himself had advocated in 2018 and early 2019. In this sense, Giuseppe Conte has proved himself to be a true chameleon of politics.

Conte won the confidence vote in both chambers. In the Senate, however, he survived without an absolute majority of votes and thanks to the abstention of *Italia Viva*, Renzi's new party. Formally he was not required to resign, but it was clearly a difficult situation. He tried to find new votes before giving in to pressure to resign. Similar to the case of Renzi's new political force, Conte's supporters (called 'responsible' or 'Europeanists') set up a movement called *Italia23*[27] and even managed to create a new parliamentary group called *Europeisti Maie Centro democratico* (Europeanists MAIE Democratic Centre).[28] However, these efforts were not sufficient and therefore Conte went to the president of the Republic and resigned on 26 January. Once the consultations began, it was clear that the fracture between *Italia Viva* and the rest of the majority could not be mended and Mattarella decided to give the former European Central Bank (ECB) chief, Mario Draghi, the mandate to form a new government. The Draghi government is supported by all major political forces with the exception of *Fratelli d'Italia*.

*

I had intended to present different parts of this book in several conferences in the United States when the world was suddenly caught up in a pandemic. As a consequence, and like everybody else on planet Earth, I had to rethink all my plans, and those conferences became webinars or virtual workshops. I would like to thank those friends who agreed to provide comments and 'go online' with me. I probably bored them to death, but they were really kind and helpful and offered plenty of comments. My gratitude to them goes beyond the power of speech. Thanks to Antonia Baraggia, Marco Bassini, Giuseppe Bianco, Francesca Biondi Dal Monte, Paul Blokker, Edoardo Bressanelli, Andrea Buratti, Carlo Maria Cantore, Giovanni De Gregorio, Giacomo Delledonne, Cristina Fasone, Silvia Filippi, Filippo Fontanelli, Luca Gori, András Jakab, Costanza Margiotta, Matteo Monti, Matteo Nicolini, Fabio Pacini, Leonardo Pierdominici, Oreste Pollicino, David Ragazzoni, Emanuele Rossi, Robert Schütze and Rolando Tarchi. I am hugely indebted to Tom Ginsburg for supporting this project. My gratitude also goes to Zachary Elkins and Ran Hirschl, the other co-editors of this prestigious CUP series. The publication of this book is a dream, which has become reality. This book is also the outcome of a long process of growth, and sadly there are people who will not be able to read it because they passed away too soon. Paolo Carrozza and Alessandro

---

[27] *Italia23* is a movement created by some of Conte's supporters, namely by Raffaele Fantetti, a former Forza Italia senator. The website of *Italia23* can be consulted at the following URL: https://italia23.it/. Here '23' refers to 2023, when the current legislature is due to end (five years from the 2018 election).

[28] *Maie* is the group of the *Movimento Associativo Italiani all'Estero* (the Associative Movement of Italians Abroad). However, soon after the end of the second Conte government the parliamentary group, Pro-Europeans-MAIE-Democratic Centre, immediately dissolved: www.senato.it/4839.

Pizzorusso, my professors when I was a student at the University of Pisa and the *Scuola Superiore Sant'Anna* and my mentors during the first years of my academic career. I am a better person and scholar than I was when I started to teach and do research thanks to the advice I received from them, in particular about the importance of comparative law. I will be always grateful to them. This book is dedicated to my family, which is now spread between Sicily (my mum and little brother, Luca) and Tuscany (my fiancée, Lelia): I love you all. A special place in these acknowledgments is reserved for our cats: Maverick, Nino and Olmo. We fell in love with them even though they fell asleep every time I started to talk about the book. Love is asymmetrical, as are many other things in life.

1

Populist Constitutionalism: An Oxymoron?

1.1 THE MANY FACES OF THE POPULIST CHALLENGE: A CONCEPTUAL CLARIFICATION FOR THE PURPOSE OF THE BOOK

'Constitutions belong to all but are not "empty" (politically neutral)'.[1] With these words an eminent constitutional lawyer reacted to a series of attacks launched on the Italian Constitution by some political parties at the beginning of the new millennium. Indeed, the irony in this is that the new wave of populisms has been obliging constitutional lawyers to deal with some long-standing issues, including that of the neutrality of constitutions. Instead of embarking on a large-scale comparison, which may risk missing the historic roots of these phenomena, in this volume the analysis will be carried out by focusing on some important instruments of constitutional democracy – referendums and the prohibition of the imperative mandate, among others – and this will ensure consistency and coherence with the comparative law analysis carried out throughout the book. In this sense, while the present book has a precise focus on the Italian case, this does not exclude the possibility of framing this national case in a comparative perspective, as it is an ideal case study of post–World War II (WWII) constitutionalism. Building on these considerations, this book tries to address the following research question: 'How can constitutional democracies channel populist claims without jeopardising the legacy of post–WWII constitutionalism'? When dealing with this question, I shall study the impact of populism on some instruments of constitutional democracy, endeavouring to explore their role as possible fora of populist claims and targets of populist attacks.[2]

---

[1] A. Spadaro, 'Costituzionalismo versus populismo: sulla c.d. deriva populistico-plebiscitaria delle democrazie', in G. Brunelli, A. Pugiotto, P. Veronesi (eds.), *Scritti in onore di Lorenza Carlassare*, Vol. V, Jovene, Naples, 2009, 2007.

[2] It has been suggested that: 'Constitutionalists must ultimately accept that this tension cannot be resolved through legal means' (J. Scholte, 'The Complacency of Legality: Constitutionalist Vulnerabilities to Populist Constituent Power', *German Law Journal*, special issue 3, 2019, 351, 360). This point might be misleading. The effort made in this book does not necessarily lead to concluding that these post–WWII constitutional law devices will alone resist populism, or that this issue can be solved in purely legalistic terms. Here my point is that constitutional lawyers must at least try to find

Against this background, this chapter explores the relationship between constitutionalism and populism in conceptual terms. It will be argued that the relationship between populism and constitutionalism should not be seen in terms of mutual exclusion and perfect opposition.[3] Indeed, it is possible to say that populism relies frequently on concepts and categories belonging to the language of constitutionalism (majority, democracy, people), trying to reshape them to thus offer a sort of constitutional counter-narrative.[4] In this sense, the populist approach to constitutional categories can be described in light of two concepts: *mimetism* and *parasitism*. Both populism and constitutionalism are based on a profound sense of distrust of political power and refer, *prima facie*, to similar concepts, but analogies cannot be extended further, as I shall show in this chapter. In constructing a constitutional counter-narrative, populism borrows from the radical constitutional tradition, namely from the revolutionary (Jacobin)[5] one, as we will see.

This is not a book about the roots or causes of populism. Nevertheless, it is necessary to clarify what I mean by populism for the purpose of this work. The conceptualisation of populism is a matter of scholarly discourse,[6] as populism is characterised by a 'constitutive ambiguity'.[7] Similarly, Berlin once pithily said that populism suffers from a 'Cinderella complex'.[8] By that formula, Berlin meant 'that there exists a shoe – the word "populism" – for which somewhere there must exist a foot. There are all kinds of feet which it nearly fits, but we must not be trapped by these nearly-fitting feet. The prince is always wandering about with the shoe; and somewhere, we feel sure, there awaits it a limb called pure populism. This is the nucleus of populism, its essence'.[9] Far from being a mere pathological and negative fact,

---

a solution other than that suggested by a pure Schmittian perspective. On the role of constitutional law in times of erosion of democracy and the rule of law, see: A. Jakab, 'What Can Constitutional Law Do against the Erosion of Democracy and the Rule of Law? On the Interconnectedness of the Protection of Democracy and the Rule of Law', *Constitutional Studies*, special issue, 2020, 5.

3   J. W. Müller, *What Is Populism?* University of Pennsylvanian Press, Philadelphia, 2016.

4   L. Corrias, 'Populism in a Constitutional Key: Constituent Power, Popular Sovereignty and Constitutional Identity', *European Constitutional Law Review*, No. 1, 2016, 6, 25.

5   M. Fioravanti, 'Aspetti del costituzionalismo giacobino. La funzione legislativa nell'acte constitutionnel del 24 giugno 1793', *Historia del constitucionalismo*, No.1, 2016, 123.

6   M. Canovan, 'Trust the People! Populism and the Two Faces of Democracy', *Political Studies*, No. 1, 1999, 2. For a detailed analysis of the different types and outcomes of populism – agrarian populisms ('farmers', 'peasant' and 'intellectuals') and political populisms ('populist dictatorship', 'populist democracy', 'reactionary populism' and 'politicians' populism') – see: M. Canovan, *Populism*, Harcourt Brace Jovanovich, New York, 1981. On the importance of Canovan's contribution to this debate see: M. Anselmi, *Populism: An Introduction*, Routledge, Abingdon, 2018, 23.

7   Y. Mény, Y. Surel, 'The Constitutive Ambiguity of Populism', in Y. Mény, Y. Surel (eds.), *Democracies and the Populist Challenge*, Palgrave, London, 2002, 1.

8   I. Berlin, 'To Define Populism', 1967, http://berlin.wolf.ox.ac.uk/lists/bibliography/bib111bLSE.pdf.

9   Berlin, 'To Define Populism'.

populism is indeed a 'complex phenomenon'[10] and 'an essentially contested concept'.[11]

Instead of defining it, scholars have tried to capture its essence by identifying some of its ingredients.[12] As a consequence, there are different views and definitions of populism.[13] Populism and democracy are not necessarily antithetical concepts and indeed Canovan powerfully defined populism as the 'shadow' of democracy.[14] Alternatively, according to Urbinati, populism can be seen as one of the reasons for democratic disfiguration.[15]

More recently, Urbinati also clarified this transformative function carried out by populism and stressed that populism claims to determine the purposefully constitutionally inclusive notion of the people, by depicting it as a unitary and exclusionary concept,[16] used in order to create the other as the enemy.[17]

---

[10] '[P]opulism must be considered as a complex phenomenon deeply connected with democracy, while reductionist interpretations must be avoided. Populism is a modality of social expression of popular sovereignty, which acquires different forms but has some very specific traits that are determined by the social conditions of the context where it manifests itself. It is a demand for more democracy on the part of citizens; however, once it has taken hold, it can even generate an involution of democratic institutions. Therefore, I do not agree with those who describe populism as a mere phenomenon of protest or a reaction to the crisis of democracy. Although the word is the object of much polemic and criticism, it refers to a complexity of phenomena which are key to democracy and which need to be investigated', Anselmi, *Populism*, 2. He also identifies its essential traits:

'An interclass homogenous community-people who perceives itself as the absolute holder of popular sovereignty.
The community-people expresses an anti-establishment attitude.
The community-people asserts itself as an alternative to pre-existing elites, which are accused of exclusion and the decadence of the political system.
· A leader in direct connection with the community-people – with the exception of penal populism.
· A discursive, argumentative and communication style which is always Manichean, where 'us' means the community people and 'them' means all that is external to it. The discursive style is aimed at creating political polarization' (Anselmi, *Populism*, 8).

[11] C. Mudde, 'Populism: An Ideational Approach', in C. Rovira Kaltwasser, P. Taggart, P. Ochoa Espejo, P. Ostiguy (eds.), *The Oxford Handbook of Populism*, Oxford University Press, 2017, 27. He adds: 'what W. B. Gallie has called essentially contested concepts, that is, "concepts the proper use of which inevitably involves endless disputes about their proper uses on the part of their users"'; on that occasion Mudde quoted W. B. Gallie, 'Essentially Contested Concepts', *Proceedings of the Aristotelian Society*, No. 1 1956, 167, 169.

[12] P. Taggart, 'Populism and the Pathology of Representative Politics', in Y. Mény, Y. Surel (eds.), *Democracies and the Populist Challenge*, Palgrave, London, 2002, 62.

[13] For a fascinating overview, C. Rovira Kaltwasser, P. Taggart, P. Ochoa Espejo, P. Ostiguy, 'Populism: An Overview of the Concept and the State of the Art', in C. Rovira Kaltwasser, P. Taggart, P. Ochoa Espejo, P. Ostiguy (eds.), *The Oxford Handbook of Populism*, Oxford University Press, 2017, 1.

[14] Canovan, 'Trust the People!', 10. 'We should resist the temptation to write of populism in general as a pathological symptom', Canovan, 'Trust the People!', 6. See also B. Arditi, 'Populism as a Spectre of Democracy: A Response to Canovan', *Political Studies*, No. 1, 2004, 135.

[15] N. Urbinati, *Democracy Disfigured: Opinion, Truth, and the People*, Harvard University Press, Cambridge, MA, 2014.

[16] N. Urbinati, *Me the People: How Populism Transforms Democracy*, Harvard University Press, Cambridge, MA, 2019, 78.

[17] 'Constitutional democracy makes sure that no social or political actor embodies the will of the people, which must remain the permanent creation and recreation of the democratic process itself. In

In everyday language populism is normally used as a pejorative term, which 'tends to evoke the popular element as an irrational demonic force unleashed on otherwise functional liberal democracies'.[18] However, other scholars have insisted on its neutrality[19] and understood it as a logic.[20]

Two central elements of populism can be recalled among others: the centrality of 'the people' – defined in various ways[21] – and anti-elitism.[22] Populism is often associated with demagogy[23] but actually presents itself in a variety of forms, showing an incredible ideological flexibility.[24] Consequently, different approaches have been employed to study populism, which describe populism as a strategy of political mobilisation characterised by rhetoric that employs simplistic language to reach the masses.[25] Populism is also described as a 'thin-centred ideology'[26] which 'can be easily combined with very different (thin and full) other ideologies, including communism, ecologism, nationalism or socialism'.[27] Another important difference

materializing the will of the people and condensing state power into a homogeneous actor, populism attempts to resolve the "paradox" of the "empty space" of politics by "determining who constitutes the people" (Lefort, 1988: 13–20)', N. Urbinati, 'Populism and the Principle of Majority', in C. Rovira Kaltwasser, P. Taggart, P. Ochoa Espejo, P. Ostiguy (eds.), *The Oxford Handbook of Populism*, Oxford University Press, 2017, 571, 572. On that occasion Urbinati cited C. Lefort, *Democracy and Political Theory*, University of Minnesota Press, Minneapolis, 1988, 13.

[18] R. Howse, 'Epilogue: In Defense of Disruptive Democracy—A Critique of Anti-populism', *International Journal of Constitutional Law*, No. 2, 2019, 641, 643.

[19] 'Populism is also used (non-pejoratively) on the left to denote popular opposition or resistance to neoliberal political economy (Chantal Mouffe) and the opening of more egalitarian alternatives', R. Howse, 'Epilogue', 641.

[20] E. Laclau, *On Populist Reason*, Verso, London, 2005. 'For Laclau, populism is animated by a fundamental logic: an "oppositional logic" focused on constructing a unified political subject ("the people") out of a disparate set of grievances defined against the dominating power of a corrupt elite', F. Carreira da Silva, M. Brito Viera, 'Populism as a Logic of Political Action', *European Journal of Social Theory*, No. 4, 2019, 497, 500.

[21] M. Rooduijn, 'The Nucleus of Populism: In Search of the Lowest Common Denominator', *Government and Opposition*, No. 4, 2014, 573; H. Kriesi, 'The Populist Challenge', *West European Politics*, No.2, 2014, 361.

[22] M. Elchardus, B. Spruyt, 'Populism, Persistent Republicanism and Declinism: An Empirical Analysis of Populism as a Thin Ideology', *Government and Opposition*, No. 1, 2016, 111.

[23] Pazé recalls two views on the relationship between democracy and populism: a. there is no populism without democracy, and b. there is no democracy without populism, V. Pazé, 'Il populismo come antitesi della democrazia', *Teoria politica*, No. 1, 2017, 111, 112.

[24] Müller, *What Is Populism?*; L. Manucci, M. Amsler, 'Where the Wind Blows: Five Star Movement's Populism, Direct Democracy and Ideological Flexibility', *Italian Political Science Review / Rivista Italiana di Scienza Politica*, No. 1, 2018, 109.

[25] K. Abts, S. Rummens, 'Populism versus Democracy', *Political Studies*, No. 2, 2007, 405.

[26] Populism is defined as 'a thin-centered ideology that considers society to be ultimately separated into two homogenous and antagonistic groups, "the pure people" versus "the corrupt elite," and which argues that politics should be an expression of the volonté générale (general will) of the people', C. Mudde, 'The Populist Zeitgeist', *Government and Opposition*, No.4, 2004, 541, 543.

[27] B. Stanley, 'The Thin Ideology of Populism', *Journal of Political Ideologies*, No. 1, 2008, 95. More recently Tarchi has tried to define populism by relying on Linz's concept of 'mentality' (J. Linz, *Totalitarian and Authoritarian Regimes*, Lynne Rienner, Boulder, 2000), M. Tarchi, *Italia populista. Dal qualunquismo a Beppe Grillo*, Il Mulino, Bologna, 2015, 52.

is that between populism 'as a movement of opinion (critical or oppositional) and populism as a ruling power',[28] since this distinction confirms the variety of existing populisms.

More recently, constitutional lawyers have begun approaching the topic by identifying some examples of such a tension, looking at the risky use of instruments of direct democracy or at the role of some counter-majoritarian actors.[29] Indeed, populist forces (in some cases movements that explicitly define themselves as populist) have recently gained the political majority in the parliaments of some countries. In other words, some European constitutional democracies are run by populist governments today, which inevitably gives new lifeblood to the relationship between populism and constitutionalism. Corrias tried to explain the reasons why constitutional lawyers have only recently become interested in populism, going beyond a conflictual analysis and showing how – to a certain extent at least – even populism can be depicted as endowed with a kind of constitutional theory.[30]

Even more recently, Fournier defined this relationship by relying on a 'parasite analogy', saying that: 'The relation between populism and constitutional democracy is comparable to a process of parasitism in which constitutional democracy would be the host and populism would be the parasite.'[31] This book aims to explore the relationship between populism and constitutionalism, and will offer a Continental European perspective on a topic which has already been studied extensively by constitutional lawyers and political theorists in the US and the UK. However, while in Continental Europe constitutional scholars have endeavoured to reflect upon this topic, by either trying to show how irreconcilable populism and constitutionalism are[32] or attempting to present populism as a constitutional theory alternative to the traditional narrative,[33] in this book I shall adopt a different perspective, as I consider populism to be a window of opportunity to reflect on long-standing constitutional debates.

In order to understand the idea behind this book, it is necessary to introduce an important distinction between populism as such and populist claims. As political

---

[28] 'I adopt the distinction between populism as a movement of opinion (critical or oppositional) and populism as a ruling power, a perspective that allows us to face populism in its rhetorical style, its propaganda tropes, its contents, and finally its aims and achievements. This double condition mirrors the diarchic character of democracy, or citizens' equal right to participate both in the informal power of opinion-making and in the formal designation of lawmakers', Urbinati, 'Populism and the Principle of Majority', 572.

[29] C. Pinelli, 'The Populist Challenge to Constitutional Democracy', *European Constitutional Law Review*, No. 1, 2011, 5, 15. On the counter-majoritarian difficulty see: Bickel, *The Least Dangerous Branch*, Yale University Press, New Haven, CT, 1986.

[30] Corrias, 'Populism', 8.

[31] B. Arditi, 'On the Political: Schmitt contra Schmitt', *Telos*, No. 142, 2008, 7, 20; N. Urbinati, 'Democracy and Populism', *Constellations*, No. 1, 1998, 110; T. Fournier, 'From Rhetoric to Action: A Constitutional Analysis of Populism', *German Law Journal*, No. 3, 2019, 362, 364.

[32] Spadaro, 'Costituzionalismo versus populismo'; Pinelli 'The Populist Challenge', A. Voßkuhle, 'Demokratie und Populismus', *Der Staatt*, No. 1, 2018, 119.

[33] Corrias, 'Populism'.

scientists[34] have pointed out, populism does not accept the compromise on which representative democracy is based. Nevertheless, while populism does not accept mediation, this does not exclude the existence of plausible claims that can be 'filtered' and channelled through the institutions and instruments of constitutional democracy in order to improve the system without affecting its core values and principles. In Continental Europe, political scientists,[35] as well as political[36] and legal theorists[37] have already reflected on this issue by clarifying the elements that make the Continental European scenario different from the American and British scenarios,[38] where the never-ending debate between supporters of political constitutionalism and those of the so-called legal constitutionalism has offered interesting insights.[39] Of course, this does not exclude margins for comparison,[40] but the approach taken in this book differs from these scholarly pieces.

Here I shall take into account three important elements that characterise populist movements: extreme majoritarianism, 'politics of immediacy' and 'identity politics', since they are crucial to distinguishing the kind of democracy proposed by populists from that preserved by post–WWII constitutionalism.

For the purpose of this work, identity politics consists of presenting the majority as a monolithic entity vested with moral superiority, as opposed to the elite, which is frequently depicted as corrupt. 'Populists combine anti-elitism with a conviction that they hold a superior vision of what it means to be a true citizen of their nation.'[41] Here, the reductionist attitude[42] of populism, which tends to depict all those who cannot be traced back to the majority as the 'others', is once again evident. This dichotomous approach and need for an enemy has led Müller to stress the Schmittian flavour of populism.[43] Populism appeals to a 'mythical Volksgemeinschaft'[44] and constructs

---

[34] For instance, Mény, Surel (eds.), *Democracies*.

[35] Mény, Surel (eds.), *Democracies*.

[36] Laclau, *On Populist Reason*.

[37] L. Corso, 'What Does Populism Have to Do with Constitutional Law? Discussing Populist Constitutionalism and Its Assumptions', *Rivista di Filosofia del Diritto*, No. 2, 2014, 443.

[38] Corso, 'What Does'.

[39] M. Tushnet, 'Abolishing Judicial Review', *Constitutional Commentary*, No. 3, 2011, 581; J. Waldron, 'The Core of the Case Against Judicial Review', *Yale Law Journal*, No. 6, 2006, 1346. F. Michelman, 'Populist Natural Law (Reflections on Tushnet's "Thin Constitution")', *University of Richmond Law Review*, No. 2, 2000, 461. L. Kramer, *The People Themselves: Popular Constitutionalism and Judicial Review*, Oxford University Press, 2004.

[40] C. Brettschneider, 'Popular Constitutionalism contra Populism', *Constitutional Commentary*, No. 1, 2015, 81; M. Graber, S. Levinson, M. Tushnet (eds.), *Constitutional Democracy in Crisis?*, Oxford University Press, 2018.

[41] M. Marchlewska, A. Cichocka, O. Panayiotou, K. Castellanos, J. Batayneh, 'Populism as Identity Politics: Perceived In-Group Disadvantage, Collective Narcissism, and Support for Populism', *Social Psychological and Personality Science*, No. 2, 2018, 151.

[42] Mény, Surel, 'The Constitutive Ambiguity of Populism', 9.

[43] Müller, *What Is Populism?*

[44] J. Abromeit, 'A Critical Review of Recent Literature on Populism', *Politics and Governance*, No. 4, 2017, 177, 183.

'imagined communities'[45] by searching for political enemies. This also explains the bombastic approach that frequently characterises populist rhetoric. Populists need 'walls' to mark a border between what they claim to be the 'real' people and others, and construct identity by excluding political competitors from the circle of legitimacy. In other words, the kind of majority described by populists tends not to be inclusive.

Politics of immediacy[46] refers to a kind of politics which rejects the idea of mediation offered by representative institutions. This again confirms that populism aims to construct a constitutional counter-narrative by using constitutional theory concepts and reveals the anti-pluralist understanding of democracy endorsed by populist movements.[47]

1.2 CONSTITUTIONALISM AND POPULISM: BETWEEN MIMETISM AND PARASITISM

As has already been pointed out, 'Constitutional theorists have not devoted a lot of attention to the phenomenon of populism [. . .] There may be two interpretations of this silence. Either constitutional theory has nothing to say about populism, in which case the silence is justified, or constitutional theory does have something to say, in which case the silence is unjustified and (potentially) problematic'.[48] It will be argued that populists (especially when they are in government) tend to employ two strategies with regard to constitutions: mimetism (or mimesis)[49] and parasitism. Both these terms come from evolutionary biology. For the purpose of this book, mimetism refers to the 'nature that culture uses to create second nature, the faculty to copy, imitate, make models, explore difference, yield into and become Other'.[50] Parasitism instead refers to the relationship 'between two species of plants or animals

---

[45] B. Anderson, Imagined Communities: Reflections on the Origin and Spread of Nationalism, Verso, London, 1983.

[46] 'What I have called a "politics of immediacy" often shows itself in a plea for the means of direct democracy (e.g., referenda): these serve to get confirmation from "the people" for what is, according to the populist, a fortiori the only morally right political position. Again, I argue that this aspect of the constitutional theory of populism is not in accordance with contemporary constitutional theory. It fails to take into account the constitutive role of representation in a democracy', Corrias, 'Populism', 12.

[47] Spadaro, 'Costituzionalismo versus populismo'; Pinelli 'The Populist Challenge'; Voßkuhle, 'Demokratie'; I. Diamanti, M. Lazar, Popolocrazia. La metamorfosi delle nostre democrazie, Laterza, Rome, 2018.

[48] Corrias, 'Populism', 7.

[49] For the purpose of this book, mimesis and mimetism will be treated as interchangeable terms. For an analysis of the concept of mimetism in comparative studies, see: Y. Mény (ed.), Les politiques du mimétisme institutionnel: la greffe et le rejet, L'Harmattan, Paris, 1993 and L. Pierdominici, The Mimetic Evolution of the Court of Justice of the EU: A Comparative Law Perspective, Palgrave, London, 2020, 4–7. However, scholars tend to distinguish between mimesis and mimicry. For this debate in comparative literature, see for instance: M. Blanchard, 'Review: Mimesis, Not Mimicry', Comparative Literature, No. 2, 1997, 176. Nonetheless, this distinction is not relevant to the aims of this book.

[50] M. Taussig, Mimesis and Alterity, Routledge, Abingdon, 1993, xiii.

in which one benefits at the expense of the other, sometimes without killing the host organism'.[51] Mimetism, here, describes how populist leaders endeavour to present themselves as consistent and compatible with the language of constitutionalism.[52]

An example of this is the recent speech given by the Italian premier Giuseppe Conte at the United Nations, where he said:

> The Italian Government has placed these same priorities at the basis of its action. Government action that does not give due consideration to assuring that all of its citizens have equitable and fully dignified living conditions is not action that I can consider morally, much less politically acceptable.
>
> When some accuse us of souverainism or populism, I always enjoy pointing out that Article 1 of the Italian Constitution cites sovereignty and the people, and it is precisely through that provision that I interpret the concept of sovereignty and the exercise of sovereignty by the people.
>
> This approach does not modify the traditional position of Italy within the international community and consequently toward the United Nations. Security, the defense of peace and the values that best preserve it, and the promotion of development and human rights are goals that we share and shall continue to pursue with courage and conviction at the national and international levels.[53]

Here, one can see the attempt to find a reading consistent with the text of the Italian Constitution by stretching some of its key concepts and – most importantly – exercising a sort of cherry-picking approach to it.[54] Indeed, when referring to Article 1 of the Italian Constitution, populists tend to mention only a part of the relevant provision (the part recognising the principle of 'popular sovereignty') in order to find confirmation of their majoritarian approach to the fundamental charter, and to reinforce the false dichotomy between themselves (the people voted by the people) and the 'others'. In so doing, they tactically omit that the same Article 1 of the Italian Constitution subsequently clarifies that popular sovereignty should be understood as limited by the constitution itself, as the provision reads: 'Sovereignty belongs to the people and is exercised by the people in the forms and within the limits of the Constitution.'[55] This approach is very telling of how populisms try to legitimise themselves as political forces consistent with the constitution; at the same time,

---

[51] Entry 'Parasitism: biology', www.britannica.com/science/parasitism

[52] 'Mimesis is an ambiguous term. It is at the same time cognition and evaluation. Its cognitive result is imitation. There is no imitation without difference. To describe an object in terms of mimesis is to acknowledge that there is no identity. It is not the thing itself. We call toy animals realistic, but not a zoo. If mimetic imitation were to be wholly at one with what it represents, it would cease to be a representation', B. Hüppauf, 'Camouflage and Mimesis: The Frog between the Devil's Deceptions, Evolutionary Biology, and the Ecological Animal', *Paragrana Internationale Zeitschrift für Historische Anthropologie*, No. 1, 2015, 132, 134.

[53] Remarks by Giuseppe Conte to the 73rd Session of the United Nations General Assembly, 26 September 2018, www.voltairenet.org/article203153.html.

[54] This approach is not completely new in Italy. See also the examples made by M. Revelli, *Populismo 2.0*, Einaudi, Turin, 2017.

[55] Article 1 of the Italian Constitution.

when looking for such a literal link with the text of the constitution, they also advance an alternative reading of two of the constitutional concepts mentioned in that provision, 'people' and 'popular sovereignty', by relying on the constitutive ambiguity of these concepts.[56] Something similar can be found in some famous speeches given by Orbán, like that given at the 25th Bálványos Summer Free University and Student Camp in 2014, where an alternative understanding of democracy (a non-liberal one) was advanced:

> Honorable Ladies and Gentlemen
>
> In order to be able to do this in 2010, and especially these days, we needed to courageously state a sentence, a sentence that, similar to the ones enumerated here, was considered to be a sacrilege in the liberal world order. We needed to state that a democracy is not necessarily liberal. Just because something is not liberal, it still can be a democracy. Moreover, it could be and needed to be expressed, that probably societies founded upon the principle of the liberal way to organise a state will not be able to sustain their world-competitiveness in the following years, and more likely they will suffer a setback, unless they will be able to substantially reform themselves.[57]

The concept of democracy is stretched to advance a possible constitutional counter-narrative according to a dynamic similar to what we saw in the Italian case. In this sense, Blokker argued that, 'while populism ought to be understood as a rejection of liberal constitutionalism, it equally constitutes a competing political force regarding the definition of constitutional democracy.'[58] He identified four pillars of what he calls 'populist constitutionalism':[59]

> I propose to 'unpack' the populist constitutional approach by analysing four of its critical components. These components can be understood as distinctive parts of the populist critique on liberal or legal constitutionalism. First, populists emphasise the people and popular sovereignty. This reference to the people provides the main normative justification for the populist constitutional programme. Second, the

---

[56] On 'popular indeterminacy' and populism see: P. Ochoa Espejo 'Populism and the Idea of The People', in C. Rovira Kaltwasser, P. Taggart, P. Ochoa Espejo, P. Ostiguy (eds.), *The Oxford Handbook of Populism*, Oxford University Press, 2017, 607, 610.

[57] V. Orbán's speech at the 25th Bálványos Free Summer University and Student Camp, 26 July 2014, Băile Tuşnad (Tusnádfürdő), https://budapestbeacon.com/full-text-of-viktor-orbans-speech-at-baile-tusnad-tusnadfurdo-of-26-july-2014/. On the crisis of European integration from an Eastern European perspective see: I. Krastev, *After Europe*, University of Pennsylvania Press, Philadelphia, 2017.

[58] P. Blokker, 'Populism as a Constitutional Project', *International Journal of Constitutional Law*, No.2, 2019, 537. On populist constitutions, see D. Landau, 'Populist Constitutions', *The University of Chicago Law Review*, No. 5, 2018, 521.

[59] This formula is also used by Corso in her work. Looking at populism as thin ideology, she distinguishes between two dimensions of populism – the anti-pluralistic dimension, which inevitably conflicts with constitutionalism and perceives populism as leading to authoritarian results, and its anti-elitist nature and defensive character. Corso connects populist constitutionalism to popular constitutionalism: L. Corso, 'Populismo, limiti al potere e giudici costituzionali. Una lezione americana', *Ragion pratica*, No. 1, 2019, 211, 215.

populist project is based on an extreme form of majoritarianism, which is the core of the populist mode of government, or the way in which populists imagine their project politically. Third, the populists' practical approach to the law is based on instrumentalism, which mobilises the law in the name of a collectivist project. Fourth, the populist attitude towards the law, or its main prescriptive and evaluative judgments of the law, consists of a critical, emotional stance, or what I call 'legal resentment'.[60]

While this way of studying populism is interesting, as it looks at the content of populist movements to identify some of the flaws of current constitutional democracies, as we will see in the final section, this approach risks creating conceptual confusion, since it results in neglecting the counter-majoritarian – and to certain extent also the pluralist[61] – dimension of constitutionalism as such (especially of post–WWII constitutionalism in Europe). The second approach normally followed by populists has been called 'parasitism'.[62] In fact, one could say that the real aim of populist movements is to alter the axiological hierarchies that characterise constitutional democracies, for instance by presenting democracy (understood as the rule of majority) as a kind of 'trump card' which should prevail over other constitutional values.[63]

If the majority is 'the people',[64] its will must thus prevail at all costs and immediately. Against this background, it has been correctly said:

> Populism understands liberal democracy and the rule of law as a historical interruption and aberration. It rejects the idea of the legal-constitutional order because, according to populists, it produces or favours inequalities (e.g., between the haves and have-nots, between cosmopolitans and locals, or between foreigners and nationals), as well as, more importantly, because it leads to the erosion of the

---

[60] Blokker, 'Populism as a Constitutional Project', 540–1.

[61] Interestingly, Blokker makes a distinction between left-wing and right-wing populisms in this respect: 'A more complete, historical discussion would need to take due account of cases in Latin America, as well as left-wing populism more in general [...] Both left- and right-wing populism tend to deny a strong separation of politics and law and endorse a stronger link between constitutions and the people. And while arguably left-wing manifestations of populism (as in Latin America) have shown a more direct engagement with genuinely participatory projects of constitutionalism (in the form of, e.g., constituent assemblies), both forms of populism tend to suffer from an exclusionary tendency, which results from the quest for an authentic people, and in practice risk sliding into either authoritarian or "leaderist"–plebiscitarian modes, ultimately denying their democratic thrust', Blokker, 'Populism as a Constitutional Project', 537.

[62] Parasitism has already been employed in studies on populism. See: Arditi, 'On the Political', 20; Urbinati, 'Democracy'; Fournier, 'From Rhetoric'.

[63] 'The populist rhetoric manipulates the rule of law and the majoritarian pillars of constitutional democracy by convincing a fictional majority that constitutional democracy gives rise to a tyranny of minorities. Populism in action represents the second facet of the populist strategy. It corresponds to a specific constitutional strategy of legal and constitutional reforms aiming at disrupting constitutional democracy', Fournier, 'From Rhetoric', 363.

[64] In similar terms: 'As the only subject that deserves representation is a unified people, which is equated with the majority, there is no need for a higher law that mediates between and integrates different social forces that compete for political power', Blokker, 'Populism as a Constitutional Project', 544.

historical nation. The hierarchy of the legal–constitutional order is not to be replaced by an inclusive, more universalistic order, but rather by a return to, or realisation of, the past, that is, of a traditional order, based on 'natural' hierarchies related to ethnicity, family, and tradition.[65]

I shall come back to these points throughout the book, and explain why populism rejects one of the most important aspects of constitutionalism: its counter-majoritarian nature.

1.3 THE CONSTITUTION AS A STRAITJACKET

As scholars have pointed out, populists do not normally acknowledge the distinction between constitutional and non-constitutional politics, since they do not conceive the constitution as neutral. This reveals a sort of legal scepticism that can be traced back to what Blokker calls 'legal resentment'.[66] This element is connected to what Arato calls the 'regeneration of the people'[67] and to populism's tendency 'to occupy the space of the constituent power'.[68] In other words: 'Most importantly, populists implicitly claim that there is an absolute primacy of constituent power vis-à-vis the constitution and the rules and powers derived from it. The people as constituent power is ultimately not bound by constitutional constraints because it is the source from which the constitution receives its legitimacy'.[69]

This also explains why populists tend to perceive limits and procedures as obstacles in the path of establishing the democratic principle. Moreover, populists depict courts and independent agencies as biased and non-neutral since 'independent judges and courts are understood as an illegitimate constraint on majority rule, and hence legal means are to be employed to counter this situation'.[70] These

---

[65] Blokker, 'Populism as a Constitutional Project', 541. On the relationship between liberal democracy and populism see: S. Rummens, 'Populism as a Threat to Liberal Democracy', C. Rovira Kaltwasser, P. Taggart, P. Ochoa Espejo, P. Ostiguy (eds.), *The Oxford Handbook of Populism*, Oxford University Press, 2017, 554.

[66] 'Legal resentment, so I argue, is a crucial dimension of the populist constitutional programme, and comes forth out of a distinctive populist reading of liberal constitutionalism. The populist approach regards liberal constitutionalism as both a mindset and a practice. The latter could be aptly described as the post–Second World War "default design choice for political systems across Europe and North America", in the form of a constitutionalism that "typically hinges on a written constitution that includes an enumeration of individual rights, the existence of rights-based judicial review, a heightened threshold for constitutional amendment, a commitment to periodic democratic elections, and a commitment to the rule of law". In this, the populist criticisms are not unlike those that have emerged in academic debates on "new constitutionalism" and judicial review. Populists tend to be critical about the strong and independent nature of apex courts, the role and form of judicial review, and the extensive and entrenched nature of individual rights', Blokker, 'Populism as a Constitutional Project', 549.

[67] A. Arato, 'Political Theology and Populism', *Political Theology*, No. 1, 2013, 143, 143.

[68] A. Arato, 'How We Got Here? Transition Failures, Their Causes, and the Populist Interest in the Constitution', 2017, https://papers.ssrn.com/sol3/papers.cfm?abstract_id=3116219, 6.

[69] Corrias, 'Populism', 9.

[70] Blokker, 'Populism as a Constitutional Project', 547.

considerations clarify why populists seem to be on a permanent political campaign. The Italian case is particularly emblematic of this trend, as the (former) Italian Deputy Prime Minister and Interior Minister, Matteo Salvini, has been responding to critics with the same mantra – 'you should first resign and run for election instead of doing politics from the judicial bench'[71] – but this was a rhetorical element already present in the approach endorsed by the Berlusconi government.[72] Against this background, contemporary populisms do not emerge completely out of the blue, since they are the consequences of long-standing issues that have characterised the political contexts in which they operate. Building on these ideas, some scholars have drawn a parallel between political constitutionalism and populism:

> A particularly manifest populist form of legal–instrumental action regards judicial independence and judicial review [...] This critique can be understood as a populist version of the theoretical critique raised against legal constitutionalism in the form of a 'political constitutionalism', as endorsed, for instance, by Jeremy Waldron and Richard Bellamy, inter alia in its questioning of the political engagement of unaccountable constitutional courts and the status of judicial review.[73]

Nevertheless, important differences exist between political constitutionalism and populism, as the latter is deeply rooted in a kind of pre-political understanding of the 'People',[74] seen as the direct and automatic source of political truth, and this inevitably results in questioning representative institutions as well.[75] This is an element that does not necessarily characterise political constitutionalism as such.

Other authors who have been working on this kind of partial convergence between populism and popular constitutionalism have pointed this out.[76] For instance, Alterio recalled three important differences: '(i) the notion of the people they support, (ii) how they propose to mediate the popular will, and (iii) how the framers of the constitution conceive the idea of popular participation'.[77]

With regard to the first point, she clarified that 'the "people" for popular constitutionalists do not dissolve into a whole, but eventually express themselves when faced with specific conflicts and issues'.[78] The second point insists upon the politics of immediacy recalled at the beginning of this work, in the sense that, unlike populists, popular constitutionalists 'plead for a strengthened form of representative and social

---

[71] 'Salvini come Berlusconi: "Io ministro eletto dal popolo, i magistrati non lo sono"', 2018, www
.ilfattoquotidiano.it/2018/09/07/salvini-come-berlusconi-io-ministro-eletto-dal-popolo-i-magistrati-
non-lo-sono/4611540/.
[72] D. Nelken, 'Legitimate Suspicions? Berlusconi and the Judges', *Italian Politics*, No. 1, 2002, 112.
[73] Blokker, 'Populism as a Constitutional Project', 547–8.
[74] Actually, on this point my feeling is that populisms vary.
[75] R. Brubaker, 'Why Populism?', *Theory and Society*, 2017, No. 5, 357, 365.
[76] A. M. Alterio, 'Reactive vs Structural Approach: A Public Law Response to Populism', *Global Constitutionalism*, No.2, 2019, 270, 283.
[77] Alterio, 'Reactive', 283.
[78] Alterio, 'Reactive', 283–4.

institutions'[79] instead of proposing the emptying or overcoming of representative democracy. The third point brings to the table the importance of instruments of direct democracy, *in primis* the referendum. Indeed, frequently, the attack on representative institutions and the emphasis on referendums are taken as two sides of the same coin, since they are both emanations of that lack of mediation that political scientists frequently portray as one of the pillars of populism.[80] As Canovan pointed out, 'New Populists often call for issues of popular concern to be decided by referendum, bypassing professional politicians and leaving decisions to the people'.[81] Referendums also galvanise the dichotomous approach frequently endorsed by populists in their constant appeals to the people understood as a monolithic entity, in the sense that they tend to designate a portion of the people as the people.[82]

1.4 SOME GUIDELINES TO CHALLENGE THE POPULIST CONSTITUTIONAL COUNTER-NARRATIVE

Populism questions liberal constitutional democracy from many perspectives. It also contributes to a sort of alternative 'constitutional imaginary',[83] drawing on aspects from different traditions – it has a Schmittian flavour while also borrowing some points from political and popular constitutionalism – and coming up with a sort of theoretical syncretism. Although it fails as an alternative constitutional project, populism represents an interesting test for constitutional democracy, which undoubtedly has some flaws.[84]

However, my point is that populist constitutionalism is an 'oxymoron',[85] a category whose analytical validity should be questioned. The risk is indeed one of stretching the concept of constitutionalism too far. In order to explain this point, I will rely on the lesson provided by comparative constitutional law, which offers a number of arguments to question the populist counter-narrative.

---

[79] Alterio, 'Reactive', 284.

[80] Y. Mény, Y. Surel, *Populismo e democrazia*, Il Mulino, Bologna, 2004.

[81] M. Canovan, *The People*, Polity, Oxford, 2005, 76.

[82] The Brexit saga is very telling of this approach. See: M. Freeden, 'After the Brexit Referendum: Revisiting Populism as an Ideology', *Journal of Political Ideologies*, No. 1, 2017, 1, 7; 'Brexiters, too, invoke the referendum as the "will of the people", a phrase understood as a singular homogeneous monolith, conveniently ignoring that 62.5% of the electorate ("remainers", and those who abstained from participating) did not vote to leave the EU but are "automatically" included in that will. That discursive populism has been voiced not only by UKIP members but by UK government ministers and governing party M.P.s; thus Priti Patel, Secretary of State for International Development, insisted in an interview on 16 October 2016 that "the British people have spoken and we will deliver for them"'.

[83] On constitutions and social imaginary, see: Z. Oklopcic, *Beyond the People: Social Imaginary and Constituent Imagination*, Oxford University Press, 2018.

[84] Blokker, 'Populism as a Constitutional Project'.

[85] G. Halmai, 'Is There Such Thing as "Populist Constitutionalism"? The Case of Hungary', *Fudan Journal of the Humanities and Social Sciences*, No. 3, 2018, 323, 329.

The obsession of populist movements with the 'politics of immediacy'[86] inevitably results in questioning many of the instruments of representative democracy and in emphasising the importance of instruments of direct and participatory democracy.

As it will be argued throughout the book, it is possible to sum up the anti-populist potential of the comparative law lesson in four points: 1) its understanding of democracy; 2) its view on the relationship between democracy and other constitutional values; 3) the 'contextualisation' of the referendum; and 4) the way in which it framed the relationship between constitutionalism and democracy. Starting with the first point, one of the greatest lessons of comparative law[87] consists in accepting a complex (i.e., non-reductionist)[88] vision of democracy, which is crucial to finding objections to the constitutional counter-narrative advanced by populists. Concerning the second point, comparative legal studies have also clarified that democracy cannot be used as a trump card[89] which always prevails over other constitutional values. On the contrary, democracy should be understood as a star in a broader constellation of constitutional goods. This argument is crucial in order to challenge what we called parasitism, that is, the alteration of the axiological hierarchies of democracies,[90] as we will see later on.

---

[86] Corrias, 'Populism', 12.

[87] Starting with the debate on the idea of a concurrent majority as opposed to the 'numeral majority' in Calhoun (J. C. Calhoun, *A Disquisition on Government*, 1849, http://praxeology.net/JCC-DG.htm). For Calhoun, 'A concurrent majority consists of voices from each of the conflicting interests in society, which are given veto powers against each other in a way that incorporates qualitative as well as quantitative features. Hence, any government action can only be taken with widespread consent across all sectors and strata of the community. Calhoun asserted that this "organism" can more fully "collect the sense of the community" and therefore "aid and perfect" the right of suffrage'. A. Loo, *John C. Calhoun's Concurrent Majority*, 2016, http://theprincetontory.com/john-c-calhouns-concurrent-majority/.

On the relationship between democracy and majority see: H. Kelsen, *Vom Wesen und Wert der Demokratie*, Mohr, Tübingen, 1929, Italian translation *Essenza e valore della democrazia*, Giappichelli, Turin, 2004; G. Zagrebelsky, *Il 'Crucifige!' e la democrazia. Il processo di Gesú Cristo come paradigma dei diversi modi di pensare la democrazia*, Einaudi, Turin, 1995, 10; M. Salvadori, *Democrazia. Storia di un'idea tra mito e realtà*, Donzelli, Rome, 2016, 483; C. Closa, 'A Critique of the Theory of Democratic Secession', in C. Closa, C. Margiotta, G. Martinico (eds.), *Between Democracy and Law: The Amorality of Secession*, Routledge, Abingdon, 2019, 49, 51; M. Wind, *The Tribalization of Europe – A Defense of Our Liberal Values*, Espasa Calpe, Madrid, 2019.

[88] On complexity and reductivism, see: J. Mittelstraß, 'Complexity, Reductionism, and Holism in Science and Philosophy of Science', in V. Hösle (ed.), *Complexity and Analogy in Science: Theoretical, Methodological and Epistemological Aspects*, Acta 22, Pontifical Academy of Sciences, Vatican City, 2014, www.pas.va/content/dam/accademia/pdf/acta22/acta22-mittelstrass.pdf.

[89] '[A]lthough ingrained in the ideology of the people and the language of democracy, populism as a ruling power tends to give life to governments that stretch the democratic rules toward an extreme majoritarianism', Urbinati, 'Populism and the Principle of Majority', 572.

[90] 'The Hungarian case can be used to argue that the collapse of the distinction between populism as a movement and populism as a ruling power corresponds to the collapse of the distinction between ordinary political and constitutional politics; it corresponds to the transformation of ordinary "changeable" policy into relatively immutable constitutional provisions. This change is for the sake of freezing the new majority into a permanent one, and thereby undermining the most basic of the democratic principles: majority rule within a political pluralistic environment in which any majority

The third point is particularly topical nowadays and tries to impede an instrumental use of the referendum, and I will come back to that in Chapter 4, which is devoted to the use of this instrument by populists to delegitimise parliaments. The fourth point has to do with the alleged tension between constitutionalism and democracy. As suggested by the Canadian Supreme Court in its powerful Reference Re Secession of Quebec, from which a priceless mine of arguments against the constitutional counter-narrative advanced by populists can be borrowed:

> It might be objected, then, that constitutionalism is therefore incompatible with democratic government. This would be an erroneous view. Constitutionalism facilitates – indeed, makes possible – a democratic political system by creating an orderly framework within which people may make political decisions. Viewed correctly, constitutionalism and the rule of law are not in conflict with democracy; rather, they are essential to it. Without that relationship, the political will upon which democratic decisions are taken would itself be undermined.[91]

This passage is a powerful argument against those who consider constitutions and constitutionalism as 'straitjackets'[92] and obstacles for the realisation of the will of the people. It is interesting to compare these lines with the considerations made by Colón-Ríos, according to whom constitutionalism should open up to the claims of constituent power instead of posing limits on it.[93]

This radical openness characterises what he calls 'weak constitutionalism':

> Weak constitutionalism does not maintain the precedence of a constitution that is presumed to rest in the correct abstract principles over the constituent power of the people. Instead of privileging the supremacy of the former through a constitution that is difficult or impossible to change or of privileging the supremacy of the legislature by allowing it to alter the constitution by simple majority rule, it seeks to leave the door open for future constituent activity.[94]

---

is presumed temporary and changeable. Populism in power makes democracy an extreme majoritarianism', Urbinati, 'Populism and the Principle of Majority', 585.

[91] Canadian Supreme Court, Reference Re Secession of Quebec [1998] 2 SCR 217, para. 78.

[92] This is an element that both popular constitutionalism and populism have in common as suggested by Corso, 'What Does', 450.

[93] 'In practical politics, a test for determining whether a party's or a movement's view of "the people" is compatible with democratic legitimacy is seeing whether politicians or movements that invoke the people are self-limited [...]. If they represent the people, but they consider the people to be open to change, then the movement or party will acknowledge the possibility of defeat and will be open to incorporate disagreement, or accept other views as legitimate contestants. In contrast, the view of the people that populists often adopt leads them to say that the people is unlimitable. Populists claim that the people is always right and, thus, complete and absolute', Ochoa Espejo 'Populism and the Idea of The People', 622–3.

[94] J. Colón-Ríos, *Weak Constitutionalism: Democratic Legitimacy and the Question of Constituent Power*, Routledge, Abingdon, 2012, 11. Other scholarship looks at constituent power as a 'capacity': 'Understood as a capacity that, in principle, may momentarily be exercised by any entity, constituent power theory explains how a new constitution can unlawfully replace a pre-existing constitution yet come to have lawful authority itself, without implying the diachronic existence of the constituent

These lines seem to advocate a clear departure from the legacy of post–WWII constitutionalism and lead us back to a sort of Jacobin understanding of constituent power, something which makes this concept operative on a permanent basis and without constraints. Additionally, as Negri underlined, the Jacobin understanding of constituent power was also characterised by a strong moralistic approach which can also be found – as we have seen – in the populist rhetoric.[95] This idea of constituent power also creates a false dichotomy, that between constitutionalism and democracy. In this respect, as we will see in the book, comparative law clarifies the relationship between democracy and majority, implying the necessity to understand democracy as a mosaic, where the will of the majority cannot be treated as a trump card against other constitutional values. Therefore, pluralism is a crucial aspect that still divides populism and constitutionalism,[96] since populists start with the 'unity and undivided nature of the People' whose will is seen as 'indivisible'.[97] My argument is that this is not consistent with the very idea of constitutionalism, which is inherently based on the attempt to limit political power.[98] In other words, 'the populist reading of constituent power displays a strong preference of the rule of men over the rule of law and, as a consequence, a general distrust of law and procedures'.[99] Against this background, my claim is that populism struggles not

power as an entity', O. Doyle, 'Populist Constitutionalism and Constituent Power', *German Law Journal*, special issue 2, 2019, 161, 162.

[95] 'Now, the problem is not at all felt in its intensity by the Jacobins. They make an already resolved problem out of it: for them equality is given as continuity of freedom, and political rights are the substratum of the social ones. In the Jacobins there is not the sense of the puzzle that keeps these terms really separated: they are, through a somersault of reason, linearly taken into consideration and unified. For Robespierre and Saint-Just constituent power is a direct expression of the social, which, without contradiction, is embodied in the political. It is not strange that Robespierre thinks of himself as "anti-Machiavellian," by sustaining that morals fully identify with the political, and that one single politics of virtue and the heart exists! This is not odd, because, in moralistic terms, here they say exactly what had been proposed in logical terms: the normal continuity of freedom and equality [...] They are convinced that the political and social exigencies expressed in the course of the revolution are part of only one design', A. Negri, *Insurgencies: The Constituent Power and the Modern State*, University of Minnesota Press, Minneapolis, 1999, 210–11.

[96] On populism as anti-pluralism, see: W. Galston, *Anti-Pluralism: The Populist Threat to Democracy*, Yale University Press, New Haven, CT, 2018.

[97] 'Populists criticize the liberal understanding of the rule of law for its emphasis on individualism and hence its eroding effect on unity, as an obstacle to achieving political unity or to protect the long-term existence of the collectivity. The liberal rule of law erodes unity, because it divides the polity (in its emphasis on political competition, different interests to be safeguarded, and individual rights), it weakens its decision-making powers (through a hierarchy of legal rules and constraints), and through its opening up of the polity to international influence (e.g., through its universalistic rationality and design, and its disregard for local mores)', Blokker, 'Populism as a Constitutional Project', 549–50.

[98] 'Populism rejects the emphasis on the limitation of political power through legal norms and the subjection of power to higher norms as in legal constitutionalism, while it promotes a constitutional order that puts popular sovereignty and constituent power upfront. It denounces the rule of law and the constitutional state as vehicles that promote the interests of minorities (elites) against the well-being of the people and claims to build a new constitutional order that will promote the common good against partial interests', Blokker, 'Populism as a Constitutional Project', 539.

[99] Corrias, 'Populism', 10.

only with what Blokker calls 'legal constitutionalism', but also with constitutionalism as such. As we will see in Chapter 2, constitutionalism is based on both anthropological and 'potestative pessimism'.[100] Evidence of a certain degree of anthropological pessimism can be found in the reflection of Hobbes[101] and in Federalist 51,[102] which is emblematic of this. Potestative pessimism refers to the fact that constitutionalism does not trust political power and, because of that, it has traditionally been described as a philosophical movement aimed at limiting it and governing its exercise. As we will see in Chapter 2, emotions are important in the constitution-making processes and have been crucial in the rise of post–WWII constitutionalism. Post–WWII constitutions understand democracy as a system where contingent majorities are prevented from deciding vis-à-vis some fundamental goods, as the spread of counter-majoritarian devices such as the judicial review of legislation or the eternity clauses show. The increase of the counter-majoritarian component of constitutionalism has posed new barriers to a sort of permanent constituent power.[103]

1.5 FINAL REMARKS

In this chapter I tried to offer a conceptual overview of the issue of the relationship between constitutionalism and populism. It is possible to identify at least three approaches.

The first approach is that endorsed by authors such as Voßkuhle and Spadaro.[104] For them, there is a conflictual relationship between these two concepts which are depicted as antithetical categories. This is evident even from the title of an article written by Spadaro more than ten years ago: *Costituzionalismo versus populismo* ('Constitutionalism versus Populism').[105] This first view corresponds, to a certain

---

[100] D. Zolo, 'Teoria e critica dello Stato di diritto', in P. Costa, D. Zolo (eds.), *Lo Stato di diritto. Storia, teoria, critica*, Feltrinelli, Milan, 2003, 17, 35.

[101] On anthropological pessimism in Hobbes and other authors, see: C. Heydt, *Moral Philosophy in Eighteenth-Century Britain: God, Self, and Other*, Cambridge University Press, 2017, 158.

[102] 'The interest of the man must be connected with the constitutional rights of the place. It may be a reflection on human nature, that such devices should be necessary to control the abuses of government. But what is government itself, but the greatest of all reflections on human nature? If men were angels, no government would be necessary. If angels were to govern men, neither external nor internal controls on government would be necessary. In framing a government which is to be administered by men over men, the great difficulty lies in this: you must first enable the government to control the governed; and in the next place oblige it to control itself. A dependence on the people is, no doubt, the primary control on the government; but experience has taught mankind the necessity of auxiliary precautions', 'Federalist 51', 1788, https://billofrightsinstitute.org/founding-documents/primary-source-documents/the-federalist-papers/federalist-papers-no-51/.

[103] '[T]he idea of the popular will embodied in a leader or a group is inconsistent with any genuine separation or division of powers. Where populists came to power under constitutions that had such elements, these had to be eliminated or vitiated. This was above all a matter of diminishing the power and independence of apex courts', A. Arato, 'How We', 7.

[104] Voßkuhle, 'Demokratie'; Spadaro, 'Costituzionalismo versus populismo'.

[105] Spadaro, 'Costituzionalismo versus populismo'.

extent, to the idea endorsed by political scientists such as Mény and Surel[106] that constitutionalism is inevitably at odds with populism because of its 'institutional' and pro-rule of law nature.[107] As a consequence, populism is seen as a challenge and a threat to the values of constitutionalism. According to a second approach, it is possible to say that constitutionalism and populism share something,[108] in the sense that they are both based on a profound sense of distrust towards political power. Back in 2016, Corrias suggested that it is possible to say that populists use categories belonging to a particular constitutional tradition, namely the revolutionary one.[109] These considerations inevitably make the chemistry between populism and constitutionalism more difficult to read in antithetical terms. This is an idea that can be related to the important studies made by Müller.[110] This view is close to mine, with a significant difference. According to Corrias it is possible to argue that 'populism contains a (largely implicit) constitutional theory'.[111] In my opinion, there is no populist constitutional theory at all;[112] that is why I prefer the formula constitutional counter-narrative to describe the instrumental and cherry-picking approach to the constitution endorsed by populists, as we will see throughout the book.

Finally, there is a third strand in the literature, propounded by authors who write of 'populist constitutionalism' or 'constitutional populism'. There may be different reasons for employing these formulae. Blokker, for instance, denotes 'populist constitutionalism'[113] as the constitutional project of illiberal democracies, while Corso employs 'populist constitutionalism'[114] to refer to some views present in the

---

[106] Mény, Surel, 'The Constitutive Ambiguity of Populism', 9. When commenting on their thoughts, Anselmi argued that 'While in the former it acquires institutionalized and mediating modalities, in the latter it finds a direct expression through a powerful capacity to delegitimize the status quo', Anselmi, *Populism*, 6. 'Constitutionalism is the dimension of protection and limitations to any discretionality of power, and is based on the defence of the rule of law and checks and balances. Populism, on the other hand, is characterized by the call to the power of the people in search of direct, top-down and leader-focused modalities of consensus and legitimization. It simplifies and erodes mediation systems, delegitimizes the rule of law, produces radical and maximalist perspectives based on overpromising', Anselmi, *Populism*, 36.

[107] On illiberal democracies and the rule of law, see: G. Palombella, 'Illiberal, Democratic and Non-Arbitrary? Epicentre and Circumstances of a Rule of Law Crisis', *Hague Journal on the Rule of Law*, No. 1, 2018, 5.

[108] For a similar view, see: R. Chiarelli, 'Il populismo nella Costituzione italiana', in R. Chiarelli (ed.), *Il populismo tra storia, politica e diritto*, Rubettino, Soveria Mannelli, 2015, 177. However, the conclusions by Chiarelli are different from those advanced in this work.

[109] Corrias, 'Populism', 8.

[110] Müller, *What Is Populism?*

[111] Corrias, 'Populism', 8.

[112] '[C]ontemporary populism does not follow a single constitutional theory, but a pragmatic approach varying from country to country, and because the challenges it poses should be viewed as dependent from a malaise that affects the practice of democracy within European countries not less than the EU', C. Pinelli, 'The Rise of Populism and the Malaise of Democracy', in S. Garben, I. Govaere, P. Nemitz (eds.), *Critical Reflections on Constitutional Democracy in the European Union*, Hart, Oxford, 2019, 27, 29.

[113] Blokker, 'Populism as a Constitutional Project', 540–41.

[114] Corso, 'Populismo', 215.

American debate, which can be traced back to what we call 'popular constitutional-ism'. Finally, for Alterio 'constitutional populism'[115] means the attempt made to constitutionalise some of the claims, especially in terms of direct or participatory democracy, made by populists in Latin America. While I understand the idea of these authors who view populism not as a mere threat but as a symptom of a broader crisis of constitutional democracy, and thus see a window of opportunity to change and reinforce it, I still tend to consider these formulae as oxymoronic. As Müller said, accepting the idea of populist constitutionalism implies losing the normative dimension of constitutionalism as such. I fully agree.

One can now draw some conclusions on the analogies and differences existing between populism and constitutionalism. They share at least two elements: emo-tions are crucial for both populism and constitutionalism, and, to a certain extent, both are based on a profound sense of distrust towards political power.[116] However, these analogies cannot be extended further. As I wrote when referring to political constitutionalism, constitutionalism as such also concurs with the institutionalisa-tion of power and inevitably considers the institutional framework as a part of the constitutional safeguards enshrined in the fundamental law. When doing so, con-stitutionalism tends to limit sovereignty and to reject the idea of an unbound, permanent and Jacobin constituent power.[117] If populism ultimately does not accept any form of limitation of power, this makes its constitutional counter-narrative a misleading, tricky and very dangerous misrepresentation. Accepting populist constitutionalism would also risk reducing constitutions to mere instruments of government, thus losing the primary functions served by constitutionalism, namely, that of limiting and shaping political power.[118]

---

[115] Alterio, 'Reactive', 273. See also D. Landau, 'Populist Constitutions', *The University of Chicago Law Review*, No. 5, 2018, 521, 523.

[116] 'Populism describes the faith in grassroots organizations, in ordinary people's wisdom and a deep distrust of elite's values', Corso, 'What Does', 446. P. Rosanvallon, *Counterdemocracy: Politics in an Age of Distrust*, Cambridge University Press, 2008; for Rosanvallon, populism is a sort of degeneration of counterdemocracy.

[117] 'This is the important difference with the democratic rule of majority, and the reason why democracy and demagoguery (or populism) are not the same, although they both make appeal to the people and the majority principle, and although they belong to the same genre', Urbinati, 'Populism and the Principle of Majority', 582.

[118] F. Rubio Llorente, *La forma del poder: estudios sobre la constitución*, CEPC, Madrid, 2013.

2

Italy and Post–World War II Constitutionalism

2.1 ITALY AND POPULISM(S)

For research like that carried out in this book, diachronic comparison and historical research are essential to show why some of the ambiguities that remained after World War II favoured the emergence of different waves of populism in Italy. The aim of this chapter is twofold: on the one hand, I shall clarify why the Italian case is so important to study the relationship between constitutionalism and populism. On the other hand, Italian political culture partly explains the variety of populisms experienced in the country.

Italian populism is interesting to comparative lawyers for many reasons. First, the country has a long-lasting tradition of anti-parliamentarism over the course of its history as a unitary state. After the end of World War II, populism characterised many of the new parties and movements that came to the forefront in Italian politics. In fact, members of the *Fronte dell'Uomo Qualunque* ('Common Man's Front founded by Guglielmo Giannini'), the first populist movement in Italy, participated in the work of the national Constituent Assembly. Second, as written in the Introduction, after the 2018 general election, Italy became the first European country in which two self-styled populist forces (*MoVimento 5 Stelle* and *Lega*), with very different agendas and voting constituencies, formed a coalition government which then ended in September 2019. However, in the wake of this government experience, in September 2019 *MoVimento 5 Stelle* formed a new coalition with the *Partito democratico* (a non-anti-establishment party) and a third party, *Liberi e Uguali* ('Free and Equal'), without abandoning its populist features. In this respect, Italy has not only been marked by populist politics for many decades –right now, it is the set of an experiment of a self-styled populist coalition government.

Third, the Italian case is of great interest because the country is a founding member of the European Communities (now European Union). Therefore, the constitutional implications of populist politics have to be considered not only within the national framework but also in the wider context.

In this respect, this volume will offer the perspective of a constitutional lawyer from Continental Europe. While political scientists and sociologists have already explored Italian populism,[1] constitutional lawyers have approached the topic by focusing on other jurisdictions.[2] For instance, scholars from Eastern Europe have devoted attention to the rule-of-law crisis in Poland and Hungary,[3] but do not offer a comprehensive analysis of the relationship between constitutionalism and populism. There is another strand of literature that has dealt with this issue, but it mainly consists of collective volumes[4] or symposia published in legal blogs.[5]

Going beyond Europe, it is possible to find interesting evidence in the literature regarding authoritarian and illiberal constitutions,[6] or what Landau called 'abusive constitutionalism',[7] but all these publications present a broader perspective and deal only incidentally with the constitutional consequences of the populist challenge. Latin America is another fascinating area from this point of view.[8] However, Italy, for different and sometimes obvious reasons (not being an illiberal democracy, at least not yet), has not been covered in these important publications.

2.2 CONSTITUTIONALISM AND MEMORY OF HORROR

World War II incisively shaped European constitutionalism and represents an evident turning point that fed the anthropological pessimism characterising the history of constitutionalism.[9] 'Fed' because, after all, horror and fear lie at the basis of the constitutional compact as has been theorised since Hobbes:

[1]   M. Tarchi, *Italia populista. Dal qualunquismo a Beppe Grillo*, Il Mulino, Bologna, 2015. I. Diamanti, M. Lazar, *Popolocrazia: La metamorfosi delle nostre democrazie*, Laterza, Rome, 2018. P. Blokker, M. Anselmi (eds.), *Multiple Populisms Italy as Democracy's Mirror*, Routledge, Abingdon, 2019. E. Bressanelli, D. Natali (eds.), *Contemporary Italian Politics*, special issue on Italian politics, No. 3, 2019.

[2]   M. Graber, S. Levinson, M. Tushnet (eds.), *Constitutional Democracy in Crisis?*, Oxford University Press, 2018; T. Ginsburg, A. Huq, *How to Save a Constitutional Democracy*, Chicago University Press, 2018.

[3]   C. Closa, D. Kochenov (eds.), *Reinforcing the Rule of Law Oversight in the European Union*, Cambridge University Press, 2016; A. Bogdandy, P. Sonnevend (eds.), *Constitutional Crisis in the European Constitutional Area: Theory, Law and Politics in Hungary and Romania*, C. H. Beck-Hart-Nomos, Oxford, 2015.

[4]   G. Mesežnikov, O. Gyárfášová, D. Smilov (eds.), *Populist Politics and Liberal Democracy in Central and Eastern Europe*, Institute for Public Affairs, Bratislava, 2008.

[5]   M. Hailbronner, D. Landau (eds.), 'Constitutional Courts and Populism', 2018, www .iconnectblog.com/2017/04/introduction-constitutional-courts-and-populism/; A. Baraggia (ed.), 'The Aftermath of the Italian General Election of March 4, 2018', https://bit.ly/3gLwjQK; C. Grabenwarter, 'Constitutional Resilience', 2018, https://verfassungsblog.de/constitutional-resilience/.

[6]   T. Ginsburg, A. Simpser (eds.), *Constitutions in Authoritarian Regimes*, Cambridge University Press, 2013.

[7]   D. Landau, 'Abusive Constitutionalism', *UC Davis Law Review*, No. 1, 2013, 189.

[8]   R. Gargarella, *Latin American Constitutionalism, 1810–2010. The Engine Room of the Constitution*, Oxford University Press, 2013.

[9]   'The "concreteness" of the former vis-à-vis ordinary citizens, namely the public power's capability of blurring the public/private divide by interfering with the conscience of individuals, was of course the main threat to be avoided. But this was not a good reason for reviving the "abstract" version of

There are two feelings at the root of modern constitutionalism: horror and fear. It is the horror of anarchy and of the massacres of civil and religious wars that give rise to the need for peace and order and which calls for the investiture of a pacifying and ordering power that puts an end to anarchy and eliminates the massacres.[10]

The 'post–World War II Constituent Assemblies were therefore confronted with the issue of how to reverse the premises of totalitarianism without returning to the old Rechtsstaat'.[11]

While scholars tend to read constitutionalism and constitutions as an attempt to rationalise power, this should not be understood as excluding any type of role of emotions in constitutional law. On the contrary, emotions, especially fear, have played a key role.[12] In identifying the emotions affecting the content of national constitutions, a key role is, of course, played by the history of each legal system: the horror, the conflicts, the past – in other words, everything that has led to the rupture with the previous legal regime and to the creation of the new system of norms. Post-totalitarian constitutions believe in democratic systems in which contingent major-ities are prevented from making decisions vis-à-vis some fundamental goods, as shown by the 'eternity clause'[13] in the German Basic Law and the 'republican

sovereignty which characterized the pre-totalitarian tradition. If the Assemblies took the path of conceiving the constitution, as superimposed on the other sources of law, as the highest expression of the state's will, the ultimate ends of the national community would lie wholly in the hands of the state. At the same time, if they intended both the entrenchment of the constitution's amending procedure and the establishment of constitutional review over legislation as merely formal devices, the substance of political power would remain unchallenged. In the post-totalitarian perspective, to the contrary, whatever subject, including the state, is prevented from determining the community's ultimate ends, while these are expressed as substantive principles enshrined in the constitution. In the meanwhile, the state itself ceases to be viewed as a monolithic subject; rather it is viewed as a set of public institutions whose constitutional legitimacy does not depend on a pre-determined hierarchical position, but varies according to their respective functions', C. Pinelli, 'The Formation of a Constitutional Tradition in Continental Europe since World War II', *European Public Law*, No. 2, 2016, 257, 263.

[10] M. Luciani, 'L'antisovrano e la crisi delle costituzioni', *Rivista di diritto costituzionale*, No. 1, 1996, 124, 131 (my own translation).

[11] Pinelli, 'The Formation of a Constitutional Tradition', 263.

[12] 'For rationalism, emotions are separate from reason; the passions' interference in reasoning, even if irresistible, is only a troubling external nuisance. Law is described as a mechanism to counter such interference, institutionally reinforcing reason's shelter. This isolationist position, based on the reason-emotion divide, is unsustainable. Emotions participate in building a constitution and a culture of constitutionalism, and then these creatures of constitutional sentiment patrol emotion display [. . .] How do constitutional sentiments (the specific constitutional and public affairs-oriented part of public sentiments) contribute to constitution building? There are several models for this relationship, beginning with theories that advocate that law should follow emotions and moral intuitions, in particular. I argue that modern societies are emotionally and morally divided, and that constitutions approach public sentiment in a selective way', A. Sajó, 'Emotions in Constitutional Design', *International Journal of Constitutional Law*, No. 3, 2010, 354, 354–5.

[13] 'Perhaps the most famous example of constitutional unamendability is Article 79(3) of the German Basic Law (Grundgesetz) of 1949. Written against the background of the experience of the Weimar Constitution and the Holocaust, Article 79(3) prohibits constitutional amendments affecting the division of the Federation into states (Länder), human dignity, the constitutional order, and basic

form' clause[14] in the Italian Constitution. The existence of these ultimate barriers inevitably represents a limit to permanent constituent power.[15]

Some years ago, Elster reflected upon the importance of fear and violence in constitution making, starting with the premise that: 'contrary to a traditional view, constitutions are rarely written in calm and reflective moments. Rather, because they tend to be written in period of social unrest, constituent moments induce strong emotions and, frequently, violence'.[16] In his essay, Elster analysed the cases of the American and French revolutions, but these considerations can also be applied to other experiences that are rich in provisions aimed at dispelling the fear of the past, for instance, to what Mortati called constitutions 'born from the Resistance'.[17] In this sense, post–WWII constitutionalism, in its attempt to establish the 'forms' and 'limits' of the exercise of popular sovereignty – according to the terminology used by the Italian Constitution – emphasised its counter majoritarian character. In this way, it identified some untouchable core whose alteration could lead to a revolution understood in a technical sense, that is, to a break in the chain of validity.[18]

This is true with regard to human rights that are the product of history, as Bobbio[19] recalled, but this can also be said about all those expedients that any legal system

institutional principles describing Germany as a democratic and social federal state. This provision is commonly referred to as "the Eternity Clause" (die Ewigkeitsklausel), and following the German jargon, the terminology of "eternity" to describe such protected provisions spread in the constitutional literature', Y. Roznai, 'Negotiating the Eternal: The Paradox of Entrenching Secularism in Constitutions', *Michigan State Law Review*, No. 2, 2017, 253, 255–6. Article 79(3) of the German Basic Law: 'Amendments to this Basic Law affecting the division of the Federation into Länder, their participation in principle in the legislative process, or the principles laid down in Articles 1 and 20 shall be inadmissible'.

[14]   Article 139 of the Italian Constitution: 'The republican form shall not be a matter for constitutional amendment'.

[15]   '[T]he idea of the popular will embodied in a leader or a group is inconsistent with any genuine separation or division of powers. Where populists came to power under constitutions that had such elements, these had to be eliminated or vitiated. This was above all a matter of diminishing the power and independence of apex courts', A. Arato, 'How We Got Here? Transition Failures, Their Causes, and the Populist Interest in the Constitution', 2017, https://papers.ssrn.com/sol3/papers.cfm?abstrac t_id=3116219, 7.

[16]   J. Elster, 'Constitution-making and violence', *Journal of Legal Analysis*, No. 1, 2012, 7, 7. Building on Elster, Choudhry added that: 'Theorists who explain and justify constitutional practice through historical examples deploy an account of a pristine past. Bruce Ackerman's theory of "constitutional moments," which is a leading account of the phenomenology of extra-legal constitutional change in the United States, is an illuminating illustration [. . .] we should revisit Ackerman's historical account. Ackerman claims that the Civil War amendments were produced through this special, and peaceful, constitutional process. But entirely absent from his analysis is that these amendments were adopted in the immediate aftermath of what remains the bloodiest war in American history', S. Choudhry, 'Civil War, Ceasefire, Constitution: Some Preliminary Notes', *Cardozo Law Review*, No. 5, 2012, 1907, 1908.

[17]   C. Mortati, *Lezioni sulle forme di governo*, Cedam, Padua, 1973, 222. For a critical approach see: M. Cartabia, 'The Italian Constitution as a Revolutionary Agreement', in R. Albert (ed.), *Revolutionary Constitutionalism: Law, Legitimacy, Power*, Hart, Oxford, 2020, 313, 321.

[18]   H. Kelsen, *General Theory of Law and State*, Russell and Russell, New York, 1945, 115.

[19]   N. Bobbio, 'Sul fondamento dei diritti dell'uomo', in N. Bobbio, *L'età dei diritti*, Einaudi, Turin, 1997, 5.

designs to deal with the challenges posed by the context. In this respect, constitutions are risk-management devices, as has been suggested, for instance, by Vermeule, according to whom 'constitutions and public law generally are best understood as devices for regulating and managing political risks'.[20] It is no coincidence that when presenting his theory this author started with the Madisonian concerns expressed in Federalist no. 10.[21] After all, constitutionalism is, in its simplest version, also based on what Zolo called 'potestative pessimism',[22] as it does not trust political power, and that is why it was born – as a philosophical movement[23] – with the aim of limiting (first) and shaping (later) political power. In this respect, it has been said that the 'memory of evil'[24] is one of the reasons why some factors are perceived by constitutions as potentially risky. This confirms that emotions matter even in constitution-making processes. All these considerations converge to explain why 'fear is part of social cognition in that it warns others of nearby danger and solicits help. Emotions function as "commitment devices" in situations where the temptations of defection are high, which makes signalling to others credible. Because of the commitment signalled by intensive emotions, people can count on others in future cooperation'.[25]

Post–WWII constitutions confirm this; it suffices to think of three fundamental devices that have been incorporated into almost all post–WWII constitutions: constitutional rigidity requiring a supermajority to amend constitutional provisions; judicial review of legislation frequently entrusted to centralised bodies, normally called constitutional courts; and unamendability clauses. All these instruments have increased the counter-majoritarian flavour of constitutionalism.

Besides these, it is possible to mention other provisions that make sense from a legal point of view only if contextualised in the particular atmosphere characterising that period. I am referring, in particular, to Article 21 of the German Basic Law, a provision admitting the possibility of banning unconstitutional political parties.[26]

Two features make the German experience a special case of post–WWII constitutionalism: the importance of the principle of dignity and the concept of militant democracy. It is no coincidence that the preamble of the German Basic Law opens by referring to the 'responsibility before God and man', and Article 1 of the same text

---

[20] A. Vermeule, *The Constitution of Risk*, Cambridge University Press, 2013, 10.

[21] Vermeule, *The Constitution*, 60.

[22] D. Zolo, 'Teoria e critica dello Stato di diritto', in P. Costa, D. Zolo (eds.), *Lo Stato di diritto. Storia, teoria, critica*, Feltrinelli, Milan, 2003, 17, 35.

[23] Bobbio, 'Sul fondamento dei diritti dell'uomo', 5.

[24] T. Todorov, *Memory as a Remedy for Evil*, Seagull Books, Kolkata, 2010; S. Veca, *La priorità del male*, Feltrinelli, Milan, 2012.

[25] Sajó, 'Emotions', 358.

[26] See also Article 18 of the German Basic Law: 'Whoever abuses the freedom of expression, in particular the freedom of the press (paragraph (1) of Article 5), the freedom of teaching (paragraph (3) of Article 5), the freedom of assembly (Article 8), the freedom of association (Article 9), the privacy of correspondence, posts and telecommunications (Article 10), the rights of property (Article 14), or the right of asylum (Article 16a) in order to combat the free democratic basic order shall forfeit these basic rights. This forfeiture and its extent shall be declared by the Federal Constitutional Court'.

is devoted to dignity, defined as 'inviolable'. Dignity is a keyword in the text of the Basic Law adopted after World War II. Article 21 of the German Basic Law instead recalls the debate of militant democracy. Originally, the concept of militant democracy was coined by Loewenstein in two articles published in the *American Political Science Review*[27] devoted to the necessary counter-limits to the rise of Nazifascism.[28] According to the original concept, 'democracy stands for fundamental rights, for fair play for all opinions, for free speech assembly, press'[29] and, if this is true, it must be ready to fight in order to protect its very untouchable core against those forces which could destroy 'the very basis of its existence and justification'.[30] This concept has been used extensively by scholars in comparative constitutional law and political science. Militant democracy seems to look at problematic conflicts between the protection of two constitutional goods (freedom of speech or political association versus democracy), embodying a real 'constitutional dilemma', that is, 'a choice between two separate goods (or evils) protected by fundamental rights; a fundamental loss of a good protected by a fundamental right no matter what the decision involves'.[31]

In his seminal articles, Loewenstein connected this concept to the necessity for democracies to protect their fundamental values from actors who are ready to deny them by relying both on coercion and on what he called emotionalism.[32] It is in these cases that democracy must renounce tolerance in order to fight against the emergence of authoritarian forces. As Sajó pointed out: 'Within the framework of the democratic process, using the mechanisms of democracy (free speech, assembly,

---

[27] K. Loewenstein, 'Militant Democracy and Fundamental Rights, I', *American Political Science Review*, No. 3, 1937, 417; K. Loewenstein, 'Militant Democracy and Fundamental Rights, II', *American Political Science Review*, No. 4, 1937, 638.

[28] 'Fascist propaganda has succeeded in instilling this belief in the masses and, like any belief, it cannot be argued. On the other hand, if fascism is not a spiritual flame shooting across the borders, it is obviously only a technique for gaining and holding power, for the sake of power alone, without that metaphysical justification which can be derived from absolute values only. If this hypothesis is realized, the answer is equally inescapable. If democracy is convinced that it has not yet fulfilled its destination, it must fight on its own plane a technique which serves only the purpose of power. Democracy must become militant', Loewenstein, 'Militant Democracy and Fundamental Rights, I', 422–3.

[29] Loewenstein, 'Militant Democracy and Fundamental Rights, I', 430.

[30] Loewenstein, 'Militant Democracy and Fundamental Rights, I', 431.

[31] L. Zucca, Conflicts of Fundamental Rights as Constitutional Dilemmas, STALS (Sant'Anna Legal Studies) Research Paper 16/2008, 2008, www.stals.santannapisa.it/sites/default/files/stals_Zucca.pdf.

[32] 'General characteristics and special features of dictatorial and authoritarian government are too well known to be repeated here. Expressed in an empirical formula, such government is a super-session of constitutional government by emotional government. Constitutional government signifies the rule of law, which guarantees rationality and calculability of administration while pre-serving a definite sphere of private law and fundamental rights. Dictatorship, on the other hand, means the substitution for the rule of law of legalized opportunism in the guise of the raison d'etat [...] Since, in the long run, no government can rely only on force or violence, the cohesive strength of the dictatorial and authoritarian state is rooted in emotionalism, which thus has supplanted the element of legal security in the last analysis determining constitutional government', Loewenstein, 'Militant Democracy and Fundamental Rights, I', 418.

elections), a regime may be established that dissolves democracy. As Goebbels observed, "[i]t will always remain one of the best jokes of democracy that it provides its own deadly enemies with the means with which it can be destroyed". Tolerance might become suicidal in certain political circumstances'.[33]

Militant democracy thus implies the existence of a sort of untouchable core of values relied on by a given legal order to justify the compression of other constitutional principles. In this sense, it is a selective concept, since it implies the existence of a hierarchy or elite of principles whose threat may justify and trigger a counter-reaction. Militant democracy has become very popular within the social sciences and has been referred to as one of the main paradigms to study the relationship between law and emergency in counter-terrorism policies.[34] When reading Loewenstein, it is clear that fundamental rights and the rule of law are at the heart of this concept; their preservation is thus crucial to avoid a dictatorial drift.

Article 21 of the German Basic Law is a clear post-totalitarian norm that codifies the possibility of a very rigid sanction – the ban. This can, of course, be explained in light of the fear and memory of horror. As such, the option underlying Article 21 of the German Basic Law has always been seen as an *extrema ratio* to be activated only in extraordinary circumstances. Until 2017, Article 21 had been applied twice by the German Constitutional Court when it was asked to rule on the unconstitutionality of two parties: the *Sozialistische Reichspartei* and the *Kommunistische Partei Deutschlands*. The first judgment, given in 1952, was a pretty obvious one given the continuity between the Nazi ideals and that party.[35] It was more complicated for the German Constitutional Court to ban the *Kommunistische Partei Deutschlands* in 1956.[36] This judgment also confirmed that the anti-totalitarian rationale of the norm was not solely characterised by an anti-Nazi purpose. After a long period in which Article 21 was seen as a sort of sleeping giant, in 2017 the German Constitutional Court delivered a fundamental judgment about the *Nationaldemokratische Partei Deutschlands* (NPD),[37] in which it 'concluded that the NPD is anti-constitutional (*verfassungsfeindlich*)', but, 'at the same time, the Court held that the NPD was too insignificant to constitute a serious threat to German democracy, and therefore is not unconstitutional (*verfassungswidrig*)'.[38] First, the Court confirmed that Article 21 is not a transitional provision or a sleeping giant. It also questioned the argument of the respondent according to

[33] A. Sajò, 'From Militant Democracy to the Preventive State', *Cardozo Law Review*, No. 5, 2006, 2255.

[34] S. Tyulkina, *Militant Democracy: Undemocratic Political Parties and Beyond*, Routledge, Abingdon, 2015, 123–166.

[35] BVerfGE 2, 1, at 12 (1952).

[36] BVerfGE 5, 85, at 140 (1956).

[37] 2 BvB 1/13 (2017).

[38] G. Molier, B. Rijpkema, 'Germany's New Militant Democracy Regime: National Democratic Party II and the German Federal Constitutional Court's "Potentiality" Criterion for Party Bans: Bundesverfassungsgericht, Judgment of 17 January 2017, 2 BvB 1/13, National Democratic Party II', *European Constitutional Law Review*, No. 2, 2018, 394, 394–395.

which Article 21 was unconstitutional. In so doing, it tried to adapt the meaning of Article 21 in light of the new political context in Germany by accepting the risk of involving these forces in the political process instead of banning them. This also made Article 21 a last resort device that can be applied only when the potentiality criterion is satisfied. The Court came to this conclusion also because of the influence exercised by the case law of the Strasbourg Court. In this way, the German Constitutional Court transformed a very rigid mechanism into a kind of proportionality exercise:

> In accordance with the exceptional character of the prohibition of a political party as the preventive prohibition of an organization and not a mere prohibition of views or of an ideology, there can, however, be a presumption that the criterion of 'seeking' has been met only if there are specific weighty indications suggesting that it is at least possible that a political party's actions directed against the goods protected under Article 21(2) GG may succeed (potentiality).[39]

On that occasion, the Court also listed some factors that should be considered when assessing the threat represented by a political party.[40] This judgment was harshly criticised[41] and de facto induced a constitutional amendment which introduced 'a new instrument to the German militant democracy arsenal: ending state funding for a political party'.[42] The historical argument was a key one in the reasoning of the Court; since Germany had become a mature democracy, it was necessary to preserve the principle of political openness rather than impeding the participation of a party, which is not yet a clear threat to democracy, in the democratic process. In so doing, the Court tried to compensate for the emotional rationale that had forged Article 21:

> Therefore, in relation to Article 21(2) GG, it must be taken into account that the provision is, above all, based on the historical experience of the rise of the Nazi party in the Weimar Republic and efforts to prevent recurrence of such incidents by means of early intervention against totalitarian political parties. Against that background, the notion that the prohibition of a political party should only be considered when a political party has become so strong that, if events are allowed to take their course, undermining or abolition of the free democratic basic order does not

---

[39] 2 BvB 1/13 (2017), para. 585.

[40] See para. 587: '(1) "the situation of the political party" when it comes to "membership numbers", finances, and such; (2) the "impact" it has on society, in terms of "election results, publications, alliances and supporter structures"; (3) "its representation in public offices and representative bodies"; (4) "the means, strategies and measures it deploys"; and (5) "all other facts and circumstances" that might indicate if the party can achieve its aims', Molier, Rijpkema, 'Germany's New Militant Democracy Regime', 398.

[41] 'The NPD II decision also introduces a degree of uncertainty that, up to now, was absent from the German militant democracy regime. All militant democracies that incorporate a "risk calculation" test are affected by the question: how does one establish whether the danger a party poses to democracy is concrete enough? At which exact moment in time, in terms of the FCC, is the "potentiality" threshold met?', Molier, Rijpkema, 'Germany's New Militant Democracy Regime', 409.

[42] Molier, Rijpkema, 'Germany's New Militant Democracy Regime', 398.

merely seem possible but is in fact probable, is incompatible with such efforts. In that respect, the determination in Article 21(2) first sentence GG of an early timing for the prohibition of a political party that does not require waiting for a specific threat to the free democratic basic order to emerge is the result of the specific historical experience of the establishment of the tyrannical and despotic rule of the National Socialists.[43]

As mentioned earlier, in contextualising Article 21, the German Constitutional Court was greatly influenced by the case law of the Strasbourg Court, and this is a confirmation of another pillar of post–WWII constitutionalism:[44] the principle of constitutional openness to international law, as we will see in Chapter 3. Article 21 has been very influential over other post-totalitarian experiences, especially in Eastern Europe, where similar provisions have been flourishing as a reaction to the communist past.[45] On a different note, it is also interesting to look at Article 20(4) of the German Basic Law which codifies the right to resist,[46] a choice which is also present in some constitutions in Europe (Portugal, Art. 21;[47] the Czech Republic, Art. 23;[48] Slovakia, Art. 32[49]) and which has rediscovered importance in many Latin American Countries. Provisions codifying such a right are exposed to the risk of interpretative abuses, as has been pointed out by Ginsburg, Lansberg-Rodriguez, and Versteeg.[50] While Article 20(4) of the German Basic Law cannot be described as a post-totalitarian provision, since it was introduced in 1968, in some cases the codification of the right of resistance is clearly a reaction to the abuses created by a totalitarian (or authoritarian) regime which had passed laws that were in clear contrast to justice and dignity.

---

43 2 BvB 1/13 (2017), para. 621.

44 On post–WWII constitutionalism: Pinelli, 'The Formation of a Constitutional Tradition'.

45 M. Steuer, 'Militant Democracy on the Rise: Consequences of Legal Restrictions on Extreme Speech in the Czech Republic, Slovakia and Hungary', *Review of Central and East European Law*, 2019, No. 2, 162.

46 Article 20(4) of the German Basic Law: 'All Germans shall have the right to resist any person seeking to abolish this constitutional order if no other remedy is available'.

47 Article 21 of the Portuguese Constitution: 'Everyone has the right to resist any order that infringes their rights, freedoms or guarantees and, when it is not possible to resort to the public authorities, to use force to repel any aggression'.

48 Article 23 of the Czech Constitution: 'Citizens have the right to put up resistance to any person who would do away with the democratic order of human rights and fundamental freedoms established by this Charter, if the actions of constitutional institutions or the effective use of legal means have been frustrated'.

49 Article 32 of the Slovak Constitution: 'The citizens shall have the right to resist anyone who would abolish the democratic order of human rights and freedoms set in this Constitution, if the activities of constitutional authorities and the effective application of legal means are restrained'.

50 'Constitutions are typically adopted to bind the future on behalf of the present. Yet our findings show that they, at least in some cases, also have the important purpose of interpreting, and in some cases justifying, the past. Finally, the conclusion explores the possible consequences of the right to resist in actual constitutional practice', T. Ginsburg, D. Lansberg-Rodriguez, M. Versteeg, 'When to Overthrow your Government: The Right to Resist in the World's Constitutions', *UCLA Law Review*, No. 5, 2013, 1184–1260.

2.3 ITALY AND POST–WORLD WAR II CONSTITUTIONALISM

The Italian constitutional experience is another important example of post–WWII constitutionalism and had a certain influence over other constitutional processes. It is said that the Italian Constitution is the result of a political compromise among the three most important forces that acted as the engine of the constituent phase: the liberal, the Christian democratic and the Socialist–Communist (left-wing) traditions. These traditions came together in the National Liberation Committee (*Comitato di Liberazione Nazionale* (CLN)), and the 'glue' of this compromise was their shared anti-fascism. The Italian Resistance began after the announcement of the armistice of Cassibile on 8 September 1943 (declaring the end of hostilities between the Italian Kingdom and the Anglo-American Allies), and it ended in May 1945, after Italy's 'liberation day' on 25 April 1945. The activity and the personalities of those who worked at the CLN had a fundamental impact on the Italian Constituent Assembly.

In the Italian case, constitutional openness is understandable as a product of that anti-fascism[51] that had a crucial role in unifying the leading forces of the CLN. The fascist era[52] resulted in a crisis in the most profound sense of the term, as it implied an important moment of reflection regarding the very nature of the whole constituent process. Unlike the case of Germany, the Italian constituent experience is less known abroad and, at the same time, it is probably a more genuine example of a constituent phase because of the lesser impact of foreign influences. This does not mean that there was no foreign influence on the Italian constituent process,[53] but

---

[51]   M. Luciani, 'Antifascismo e nascita della costituzione', *Politica del diritto*, No. 2, 1991, 191. See also G. Delledonne, 'La Resistenza in Assemblea costituente e nel testo costituzionale italiano del 1948', *Historia Constitucional*, No. 1, 2019, 217.

[52]   On fascism as a mere 'parenthesis' in Italian history see: B. Croce, *Per una nuova Italia. Scritti e discorsi (1943-44)*, Ricciardi, Naples, 1944. 'The idea that Fascism, to quote Benedetto Croce, was a mere "parenthesis" in Italian history has a persistent and obvious appeal. There is a powerful human urge to remember happy episodes and repress or forget those that are less pleasant. The urge is compounded by the fact that many post-war Italian institutions – perhaps more than in other European countries – were to a large degree continuations of their Fascist predecessors. The legitimacy of the post-war Italian order, together with the sense of moral superiority reflected in the "Good Italian" (*italiani brava gente*) myth, thus to some degree requires the minimisation of the preceding era and its influence on later events. The problem of collective amnesia is especially powerful in the legal field. Even more so than other areas, the Italian legal system was largely continuous before and after 1945. A substantial portion of the country's laws, including both its criminal and civil codes, were written during the Fascist period', A. Livingston, 'Was the Fascist Era Really a "Parenthesis" for the Italian Legal System?', in S. Skinner (ed.), *Fascism and Criminal Law: History, Theory, Continuity*, Hart, Oxford, 2015, 85.

[53]   See, for instance, the activity of the Postwar planning committee of the Interdivisional committee. See also the document entitled: Italy: 'Reconstruction of Local Government – views of the interdivisional committee', PWC, 25 Sept. 1944 (RG 59, Box 144) cited by S. Volterra, 'La Costituzione italiana e i modelli anglosassoni con particolare riguardo agli Stati Uniti' in U. De Siervo (ed.), *Scelte della Costituente e cultura giuridica. I: Costituzione italiana e modelli stranieri*, Il Mulino, Bologna, 1980, 117, 224. See also D. W. Ellwood, *L'alleato nemico. La politica dell'occupazione*, Feltrinelli, Milan, 1977, 263.

scholars have shown that the Italian Constituent Assembly was genuinely free to write a new constitution that was its 'autogenous product'.[54]

Moreover, despite the existence of a Ministry for the Constituent Assembly, the Government never submitted a draft of a constitution or a detailed text to the Assembly, but limited itself to some preparatory documents that were important, but not crucial, to the work of the sub-committees of the Assembly.[55] It is necessary to dwell on the origin of the Constituent Assembly at this point. After the liberation of Rome, the Legislative Decree of the Lieutenant of the Realm no. 151 dated 25 June 1944 stated that the choice between a republic and a monarchy had to be made by a Constituent Assembly. This Constituent Assembly was tasked with giving a new constitution to the country. Later, with the Legislative Decree of the Lieutenant of the Realm no. 98 of 16 March 1946, the first decree was amended, and the form of the state was entrusted to a popular vote. Finally, the Legislative Decree of the Lieutenant of the Realm no. 99 of 16 March 1946 proclaimed that both the referendum and the elections of the Constituent Assembly would take place on 2 June 1946. The Italian People opted for the Republic and elected the Constituent Assembly, which was composed of 556 members. A committee of 75 deputies (chosen among the members of the Constituent Assembly and chaired by Meuccio Ruini) had a primary role in preparing and writing the constitutional text.[56] The Committee was divided into three sub-committees: the first was chaired by Umberto Tupini and worked on the 'rights and duties of the citizens'; the second was chaired by Umberto Terracini and worked on the 'constitutional organization of the State'; and, the third was chaired by Gustavo Ghidini and worked on 'economic and social relationships'. Another committee ('Committee of 18') drafted the constitution in accordance with the activity of these three sub-committees. The Italian Constitution came into force on 1 January 1948. The members of the Constituent

---

[54] F. Bruno, 'I giuristi alla Costituente: l'opera di Costantino Mortati', in U. De Siervo (ed.), *Scelte della Costituente e cultura giuridica. II: Protagonisti e momenti del dibattito costituzionale*, Il Mulino, Bologna, 1980, 59. On the contrary, there was evident American influence in subsequent years which generated the beginning of what Elia called the 'conventio ad excludendum', a non-written practice which excluded the Communist party from government and which made alternation impossible. L. Elia, entry 'Governo (forme di)', *Enciclopedia del Diritto*, Vol. XIX, Giuffré, Milan, 1970, 657. As Olivetti wrote: 'On the whole, the influence of foreign models operated through Italian political parties and the personal beliefs and expertise of the members of the Constitutional Assembly and did not take the form of a direct foreign imposition of constitutional solutions, as happened to the other defeated States in World War II (the case of Japan is the more evident in this sense, but also the influence of the Allied Powers on the framing of the German fundamental Law of 1949 was far larger than the "direct" influence on the Italian Constitutional Assembly)', M. Olivetti, 'Foreign influences on the Italian Constitutional System', paper submitted to the 6th World Congress of the International Association of Constitutional Law, on Constitutionalism: Old Concepts, New Worlds, Santiago, 12–16 January 2004, for workshop no. 2 on Foreign Influences on National Constitutions, available at: www.giurisprudenza.unifg.it.

[55] Bruno, 'I giuristi', 60.

[56] On this, see L. Elia, 'La commissione dei 75, il dibattito costituzionale e l'elaborazione dello schema di costituzione', in AA.VV., *Il parlamento italiano 1861-1988*, Vol. XIV, Nuova Cei, Milan, 1989, 128.

Assembly were outstanding:[57] some of them were lawyers (Piero Calamandrei, Costantino Mortati), some were politicians (e.g., Palmiro Togliatti, Sandro Pertini) and some of them had a mixed background (Vittorio Emanuele Orlando, the father of Italian studies in public law, and former prime minister and important statesman). These figures, with such different cultural and political backgrounds, gathered together around the memory of the past.[58]

The Italian Constitution belongs to the group that Mortati called 'constitutions born from the Resistance',[59] as they were forged with the clear intent of denying and overcoming the entirety of 'values' (or anti-values) that had characterised the fascist era.

'Resistance' here refers to the activity of those movements that fought against the occupation in many countries during World War II. In Italy, Resistance is a sort of umbrella concept employed to refer to 'a heterogeneous and temporary coalition of networks and individuals that fought against the German and Fascist troops between September 1943 and April 1945'.[60]

By 'constitutions born from the Resistance', Mortati also referred to other documents, for instance, the French (IV Republic) and the German constitutional texts. As Carrozza[61] noticed, by stretching the concept of Resistance one could include within this group the Portuguese, Spanish and Greek constitutions that were drafted during the 1970s.

2.4 THE RESISTANCE AS A CONSTITUENT MOMENT

Frequently depicted as a unitary genetic moment, the 'resistance soon became a political myth of the new democratic Italy: a "Republic founded on the Resistance", as a common expression went'.[62] This has created an ideal resistance–constitution continuum.[63] The constitution is understood as having been forged by the Resistance which stemmed from a whole people:

---

[57]   E. Cheli, 'Il problema storico della Costituente', *Politica del diritto*, No. 4, 1973, 485.

[58]   As Calamandrei recalled: 'If you want to go in pilgrimage to the place where your constitution was born, you should go to the mountains where the resistance fighters were killed, to the prisons where they were jailed, to the fields where they were hanged. Wherever an Italian died trying to win back the freedom and dignity of our nation, there you should go, young Italians, because it was there that your constitution was born', P. Calamandrei, 'Discorso sulla Costituzione', 1955, www.calamandrei-vc.it /web/index.php?option=com_content&task=view&id=233&Itemid=124.

[59]   Mortati, *Lezioni*, 222.

[60]   A. Varriale, 'The Myth of the Italian Resistance Movement (1943–1945). The Case of Naples', *Kirchliche Zeitgeschichte*, No. 2, 2014, 383, 383.

[61]   P. Carrozza, 'Constitutionalism's Post-modern Opening', in M. Loughlin, N. Walker (eds.), *The Paradox of Constitutionalism: Constituent Power and Constitutional Form*, Oxford University Press, 2007, 169, 180.

[62]   Varriale, 'The Myth of the Italian Resistance', 383.

[63]   G. E. Rusconi, *Resistenza e postfascismo*, Il Mulino, Bologna, 1995.

This moral and psychological dimension enabled a whole people, not just the few who actively resisted, to claim that they were not passive objects of history, first enslaved by the Nazis and fascists then liberated by others, but that they deserved their freedom because they had fought for it.[64]

Actually, as historians have shown, the Resistance was far from unitary, as there were evident differences behind the front and anti-fascism was the only glue. This also explains why the Resistance was initially treated as a taboo not to be mentioned, as well as why legal scholars emphasised the continuity between the *Statuto Albertino* (the previous *octroyée* fundamental charter) and the new constitution. Only in the sixties did the Resistance acquire a mythical aura which served as the constituent moment, as recently stressed by Filippetta,[65] who undertook a comparison of the academic production published immediately after the end of World War II. An important book, which offers a comprehensive view on this debate, is, of course, *Civil War: A History of the Italian Resistance* by Pavone.[66] The starting assumption is that 'the traditional depiction within Italy of the conflict as one of national liberation of all Italians against the Nazis and their fascist allies was reductive and one-sided'.[67] Far from corresponding to a 'revisionist reduction',[68] this book was written by a man who joined the Resistance and fought against Nazi-fascism.

In this book, Pavone distinguished among three dimensions of the Resistance, which was simultaneously a patriotic war of national liberation against German occupation, a class war fought mainly by communists, and a civil war between partisans ('partigiani') and fascists.

He also made another fundamental distinction, between 'the military resistance of the few partisans, and a wider resistance of hearts and minds, which involved all those who supported anti-fascism and looked forward to a democratic Italy. For them, the Resistance was a great moral quest, a way of redeeming Italy from the stigma of having allowed the establishment of fascism'.[69] It has been argued that, 'in no other country in Europe has national identity been so closely bound to memories

---

[64] D. Sassoon, 'Claudio Pavone Obituary', *The Guardian*, 22 December 2016, www.theguardian.com /books/2016/dec/22/claudio-pavone-obituary.

[65] G. Flippetta, *L'estate che imparammo a sparare. Storia partigiana della Costituzione*, Feltrinelli, Milan, 2018. On the constitutional history of Italy, see also: L. Paladin, *Per una storia costituzionale dell'Italia repubblicana*, Il Mulino, Bologna, 2004; C. Ghisalberti, *Storia costituzionale d'Italia 1848–1994*, Laterza, Rome, 2020; B. Pezzini, S. Rossi (eds.), *I giuristi e la Resistenza: Una biografia intellettuale del Paese*, FrancoAngeli, Milan, 2016; A. Buratti, M. Fioravanti (eds.), *Costituenti ombra Altri luoghi e altre figure della cultura politica italiana (1943–48)*, Carocci, Rome, 2010.

[66] C. Pavone, *A Civil War: A History of the Italian Resistance*, Verso, London, 2013.

[67] D. Sassoon, 'Claudio Pavone Obituary'.

[68] D. Shonfield, 'Claudio Pavone's classic history rescued the real history of the Italian resistance, and is still an essential counter to revisionist narratives, argues David Shonfield', 2014, www.counterfire.org /articles/book-reviews/16985-a-civil-war-a-history-of-the-italian-resistance.

[69] Sassoon, 'Claudio Pavone Obituary'.

of the war. Italy's Republic was born of World War II, its constitution defined by anti-Fascism, its parties self-identified with national Resistance'.[70]

Resistance was also a moment of division, and there are important novels that have challenged its rhetorical representation.[71] Historians are split as to how to describe Italy's fascist era,[72] and this fracture has paved the way for historical revisionism.[73] Scholars in political theory and comparative history have debated the nature of the fascist regime and the possibility of tracing it back to the notion of totalitarianism.[74] Umberto Eco, in his lectures on fascism delivered at Columbia University, argued:

> In my country today there are those who are saying that the myth of the Resistance was a Communist lie. It is true that the Communists exploited the Resistance as if it were their personal property, since they played a prime role in it; but I remember partisans with kerchiefs of different colors. Sticking close to the radio, I spent my nights – the windows closed, the blackout making the small space around the set a lone luminous halo – listening to the messages sent by the Voice of London to the partisans. They were cryptic and poetic at the same time (The sun also rises, The roses will bloom) and most of them were 'messaggi per la Franchi'. Somebody whispered to me that Franchi was the leader of the most powerful clandestine network in northwestern Italy, a man of legendary courage. Franchi became my hero. Franchi (whose real name was Edgardo Sogno) was a monarchist, so strongly anti-Communist that after the war he joined very right-wing groups, and was charged with collaborating in a project for a reactionary coup d'état. Who cares? Sogno still remains the dream hero of my childhood. Liberation was a common deed for people of different colors.[75]

---

[70]   T. Cragin, L. A. Salsini, *Resistance, Heroism, Loss World War II in Italian Literature and Film*, Rowman and Littlefield, Lanham, 2018.

[71]   For instance: B. Fenoglio, *Johnny the Partisan*, Quartet Books, London, 1995.

[72]   See the works by R. De Felice, especially the multi-volume work on Mussolini: R. De Felice, *Mussolini il rivoluzionario, 1883–1920*, Einaudi, Turin, 1965; R. De Felice, *Mussolini il fascista. Vol. I: La conquista del potere, 1921–1925*, Einaudi, Turin, 1966; R. De Felice, *Mussolini il fascista. Vol. II: L'organizzazione dello stato fascista, 1925–1929*, Einaudi, Turin, 1968; R. De Felice, *Mussolini il duce. Vol. I: Gli anni del consenso, 1929–1936*, Einaudi, Turin, 1974; R. De Felice, *Mussolini il duce. Vol. II: Lo stato totalitario 1936–1940*, Einaudi, Turin, 1981; R De Felice, *Mussolini l'alleato. Vol. I. L'Italia in guerra, 1940–1943. Tomo I: Dalla guerra «breve» alla guerra lunga*, Einaudi, Turin, 1990; R. De Felice, *Mussolini l'alleato. Vol. II. L'Italia in guerra 1940–1943. Tomo II: Crisi e agonia del regime*, Einaudi, Turin, 1990; R. De Felice, *Mussolini l'alleato. Vol. III. La guerra civile 1943–1945*, Einaudi, Turin, 1997. On De Felice, see: B. W. Painter Jr., 'Renzo De Felice and the Historiography of Italian Fascism', *American Historical Review*, 1990, 391; M. Ledeen, 'Renzo De Felice and the Controversy over Italian Fascism', *Journal of Contemporary History*, 1976, 269.

[73]   G. Pansa, *Il sangue dei vinti*, Sperling & Kupfer, Milan, 2003.

[74]   On totalitarianism, see: H. Arendt, *The Origins of Totalitarianism*, Harcourt, Brace and Co., New York, 1951. On fascism and totalitarianism, see: A. J. Gregor, *The Ideology of Fascism: The Rationale of Totalitarianism*, Free Press, New York, 1969; D. E. Germino, *The Italian Fascist Party in Power: A Study in Totalitarian Rule*, University of Minnesota Press, Minneapolis, 1959. On Arendt's reflections on fascism and totalitarianism, see: E. Gentile, 'Le silence de Hannah Arendt: L'interprétation du fascisme dans Les origines du totalitarisme', *Revue d'histoire moderne et contemporaine*, No. 3, 2008, 11.

[75]   U. Eco, *Ur-Fascism, The New York Review of Books*, 1995, www.nybooks.com/articles/1995/06/22/ur-fascism/.

These lines are very telling and reveal the never-ending discourse on fascism in Italy, a formula which at a certain point became a catch all term; indeed, on that occasion, Eco listed fourteen elements that are at the heart of what he called eternal fascism:[76] 1. 'the cult of tradition';[77] 2. 'the rejection of modernism';[78] 3. 'the cult of action for action's sake';[79] 4. 'disagreement is treason';[80] 5. 'fear of difference';[81] 6. 'appeal to a frustrated middle class';[82] 7. 'the obsession with a plot';[83] 8. 'the enemies are at the same time too strong and too weak';[84] 9. 'pacifism is trafficking with the enemy';[85] 10. 'contempt for the weak';[86] 11. 'everybody is educated to become a hero';[87] 12. 'machismo';[88] 13. 'selective populism';[89] and 14. 'Ur-Fascism speaks Newspeak'.[90]

I shall come back to these points when analysing the new wave of populism in Italy. Make no mistake, populist movements should not be conflated with far-right forces,[91] but it is indisputable that sometimes they share certain elements with them,

---

[76] 'Fascism became an all-purpose term because one can eliminate from a fascist regime one or more features, and it will still be recognizable as fascist. Take away imperialism from fascism and you still have Franco and Salazar. Take away colonialism and you still have the Balkan fascism of the Ustashes. Add to the Italian fascism a radical anti-capitalism (which never much fascinated Mussolini) and you have Ezra Pound. Add a cult of Celtic mythology and the Grail mysticism (completely alien to official fascism) and you have one of the most respected fascist gurus, Julius Evola. But in spite of this fuzziness, I think it is possible to outline a list of features that are typical of what I would like to call Ur-Fascism, or Eternal Fascism. These features cannot be organized into a system; many of them contradict each other, and are also typical of other kinds of despotism or fanaticism. But it is enough that one of them be present to allow fascism to coagulate around it', Eco, *Ur-Fascism*.

[77] 'One has only to look at the syllabus of every fascist movement to find the major traditionalist thinkers. The Nazi gnosis was nourished by traditionalist, syncretistic, occult elements', ibid.

[78] 'The Enlightenment, the Age of Reason, is seen as the beginning of modern depravity. In this sense Ur-Fascism can be defined as irrationalism', ibid.

[79] 'Action being beautiful in itself, it must be taken before, or without, any previous reflection. Thinking is a form of emasculation', ibid.

[80] 'The critical spirit makes distinctions, and to distinguish is a sign of modernism. In modern culture the scientific community praises disagreement as a way to improve knowledge', ibid.

[81] 'The first appeal of a fascist or prematurely fascist movement is an appeal against the intruders. Thus Ur-Fascism is racist by definition', ibid.

[82] 'One of the most typical features of the historical fascism was the appeal to a frustrated middle class, a class suffering from an economic crisis or feelings of political humiliation, and frightened by the pressure of lower social groups', ibid.

[83] 'The followers must feel besieged. The easiest way to solve the plot is the appeal to xenophobia', ibid.

[84] 'By a continuous shifting of rhetorical focus, the enemies are at the same time too strong and too weak', ibid.

[85] 'For Ur-Fascism there is no struggle for life but, rather, life is lived for struggle', ibid.

[86] 'Elitism is a typical aspect of any reactionary ideology', ibid.

[87] 'In Ur-Fascist ideology, heroism is the norm. This cult of heroism is strictly linked with the cult of death', ibid.

[88] 'Machismo implies both disdain for women and intolerance and condemnation of nonstandard sexual habits, from chastity to homosexuality', ibid.

[89] 'There is in our future a TV or Internet populism, in which the emotional response of a selected group of citizens can be presented and accepted as the Voice of the People', ibid.

[90] 'All the Nazi or Fascist schoolbooks made use of an impoverished vocabulary, and an elementary syntax, in order to limit the instruments for complex and critical reasoning', ibid.

[91] C. Mudde, *The Far Right Today*, Polity Press, Cambridge, 2019.

such as the myth of the strong man, the obsession with conspiracy theory, the fear of difference and the need for enemies. When examining the Italian context, one of the points argued throughout the book is that at least a part of this new wave of Italian populism has built upon the ambiguities that Italian culture has always had with Ur-fascism. This does not mean concluding that *Lega* and *MoVimento 5 Stelle* are fascists; rather my point is that they have flourished due to the persistence of this silent post-war legacy. This leads me to the next point: the truth is that Italy has never seriously dealt with its past, the country has never had anything comparable to the Nuremberg trials.[92] We can trace the current debate about the return of fascism in Italian politics back to this cultural atmosphere. For some authors, fascism is not back[93] or cannot come back[94] because of the changed context that would provide sufficient guarantees against it; for others, the inexistence of a clause comparable to Article 21 of the German Basic Law (providing for the political ban on anti-democratic parties that aim to undermine the basic foundations of German democracy) has inevitably favoured the emergence of (self-declared) neo-fascist parties, such as *CasaPound Italia* (CPI) and *Forza Nuova*.[95] 'The Missing Italian Nuremberg', as Battini called it, is perhaps the most important difference between the Italian and German strands of post-war constitutionalism. More recently, as we will see, some aspects of the Resistance have been questioned as one-sided and biased. Far-right parties have attacked many of the icons of the Resistance. For instance, Salvini, the leader of the *Lega* who previously served as interior minister (and deputy prime minister) during the first Conte government, refused to participate in the official celebration of 25 April, Italy's Liberation Day, and this was seen as a very dangerous signal considering the strong anti-fascist character of the Italian Constitution.

---

[92] M. Battini, *The Missing Italian Nuremberg*, Palgrave, London, 2007. See also: F. Focardi, *La rimozione delle colpe della seconda guerra mondiale*, Rome, Laterza, 2013.

[93] E. Gentile, *Chi è fascista? Gli italiani stanno tornando a essere fascisti? Laterza*, Rome, 2019.

[94] B. Vespa, *Perché l'Italia diventò fascista*, Mondadori, Milan, 2019.

[95] 'The name CasaPound had a great symbolic meaning, with a clear reference to the American poet and modernist Ezra Pound, who wrote extensively during the war against housing rent as usury, as well as anti-Semitism. Pound was the incarnation of the ideal fascist revolution, meaning by that the struggle against plutocracy. The symbol of the party is a stylized turtle, embodying the right to housing. The turtle carries its own home and is among the animals that live longest. But this symbol also refers to the Roman formation called Testudo, the army of Rome that, in the words of CPI, showed the greatness and force of the Empire, which emerged "from a vertical order and from a hierarchical principle," Contextually, the octagonal shape is reminiscent of the historical monument Castel del Monte, built by the "last Cesare" in Italy, the emperor Federico II. The arrow is the same we find in other far-right movements' flags in Europe, such as that of The Nordic Resistance Movement (nrm) in Scandinavia [...] The Forza Nuova party (FN) was founded in September 1997, two years after Fiuggi, and was meant to be a new reference point for both the youth fringes of the Italian radical right and conservative right-wing traditionalists; a party for parliamentary deputies, autonomous groups and skinheads', E. Cassina Wolff, 'CasaPound Italia: "Back to Believing. The Struggle Continues"', *Fascism*, No. 1, 2019, 61, 61 and 82.

In actual fact, there is a provision similar to that of Article 21 of the German Basic Law; I am referring to one of the final provisions, namely provision XII of the Italian Constitution, which reads: 'It shall be forbidden to reorganize, under any form whatsoever, the dissolved Fascist party. Notwithstanding Article 48, the law has established, for not more than five years from the implementation of the Constitution, temporary limitations to the right to vote and eligibility for the leaders responsible for the Fascist Regime'.[96]

While the second paragraph of provision XII was a transitional provision, the first part is still in force. It does not give the Italian Constitutional Court a power like that of the German Constitutional Court. The content of provision XII was meant to be implemented by a statute passed in 1952 by the Italian Parliament, law 645/1952, also known as 'Legge Scelba', after Mario Scelba, the former Italian minister of, inter alia, the interior. This law provided for the criminalisation of apology (here understood as public defence of a crime) of fascism in Article 4, but as the courts have clarified, its application is understood as an exceptional sanction. The Italian Constitutional Court was also asked to rule on the constitutionality of this law for an alleged breach of free speech guaranteed by Article 21 of the Italian Constitution, but the *Corte costituzionale* rescued its provisions.[97] In judgment 1/1957, the *Corte costituzionale* clarified that apology of fascism, in order to be considered a crime, 'must consist not in a laudatory defense, but in an exaltation that could lead to the reorganisation of the fascist party. This means that it must be considered not in itself, but in relation to that reorganisation, which is prohibited by the 12th provision'.[98] This interpretation is confirmed, from a systematic point of view, by the fact that Article 1 of Legge Scelba defines what is understood as 'reorganization of the Fascist party' for the purpose of the law.

But the Italian case is not isolated; even in France, the Resistance has played the role of an important laboratory for the development of political and social ideals[99] forged in opposition to those of the occupying forces.

It is possible to find this element in many constitutions born from the Resistance which were the product of a political compromise among very different democratic forces. These forces had, as their only common point, the rejection of the totalitarian experiences. This explains why these constitutions are inspired by the sincere denial of the features of the previous regime and by the need for an entirely different

---

96 A. Pizzorusso, 'Disp. XII', in G. Branca-A.Pizzorusso (eds.) *Commentario della Costituzione*, Zanichelli, Bologna, 1995, 198; G. E. Vigevani, 'Origine e attualità del dibattito sulla XII disposizione finale della Costituzione: i limiti della tutela della democrazia', 2019, www.medialaws.eu/rivista/origine-e-attualita-del-dibattito-sulla-xii-disposizione-finale-della-costituzione-i-limiti-della-tutela-della-democrazia/.

97 Corte costituzionale, decision 1/1957 and decision 74/1958. See also Corte costituzionale, decision 15/1973 and decision 254/1974. Available at: www.cortecostituzionale.it.

98 Corte costituzionale, decision 1/1957 and decision 74/1958, available at: www.cortecostituzionale.it. My own translation.

99 H. Michel, B. Mirkine-Guetzévitch, *Les idées politiques et sociales de la Résistance*, Presses universitaires de France, Paris, 1954.

society. Some of these constitutions (including the Italian one) claimed the need for new societal models and were very rich in declarations of principle, reflecting a wish to produce a break with the past. In some cases, these so-called promised revolutions[100] have remained solely on paper, as one of the most influential members of the Italian Constituent Assembly, Piero Calamandrei, bitterly acknowledged with regard to many provisions of the Italian Constitution a few years after it came into force.[101] Denying the features of the previous regime also implies the impossibility of amending some parts of the constitution and, in this respect, the Italian Constitution has its own eternity clause. The constitutional amendment[102] offers a privileged perspective to explore the impact of populism over constitutional democracy, as it inevitably leads to the idea of constitutional rigidity as one of the most important counter-majoritarian devices of post–WWII constitutionalism. Against this background, focusing on the defence of some supreme principles of (democratic) organisations means recognising that each political regime presents inevitable organisational and procedural 'survival conditions'. These conditions are indeed functional for the preservation of the untouchable constitutional core guaranteed by the eternity clauses. Limits of the constitutional amendment are generally linked to fundamental structural choices, like the republican form of the state, and safeguards for fundamental rights. The unamendability of some provisions of the constitution is related to the lack of neutrality of the Italian Constitution, to the rejection of the totalitarian past that has been codified in Article 139, the so-called 'republican form'. It reads: 'The republican form shall not be a matter for a constitutional amendment'. As Faraguna pointed out: 'The formulation of the unamendability clause of the Italian Constitution is rather short and vague when compared with the formulation of unamendability clauses of the same generation. In fact, unamendable provisions grew not only numerically, but also in length and complexity, increasingly covering more and more protected values'.[103] While, at first glance, this provision seems to limit the amendment to the impossibility of transforming the Italian Republic into a monarchy, the hostility against monarchy (rejected in the institutional referendum held on 2 and 3 June 1946) is not the

---

[100] Calamandrei wrote about a 'promised revolution' in exchange for the failed revolution that had been sought by the Leftist forces, that is, a rupture with the past that was supposed to be even more radical than it was at that time. P. Calamandrei, 'Cenni introduttivi sulla Costituente e i suoi lavori', in P. Calamandrei, A. Levi (eds.), *Commentario sistematico alla Costituzione italiana*, G. Barbèra, Florence, 1950, now in P. Calamandrei, *Scritti e discorsi politici*, La Nuova Italia, Florence, Vol. II, 1966, 421.

[101] P. Calamandrei, 'La Costituzione e le leggi per attuarla', in AA.VV., *Dieci anni dopo: 1945–1955*, Laterza, Rome, 1955, now in *Opere giuridiche*, Vol. III, Morano, Naples, 1965, 553.

[102] R. Albert, X. Contiades, A. Fotiadou (eds.), *The Foundations and Traditions of Constitutional Amendment*, Hart, Oxford, 2017; R. Albert, *Constitutional Amendments: Making, Breaking, and Changing Constitutions*, Oxford University Press, 2019. Y. Roznai, *Unconstitutional Constitutional Amendments: The Limits of Amendment Powers*, Oxford University Press, 2017.

[103] P. Faraguna, 'Unamendability and Constitutional Identity in the Italian Constitutional Experience', *European Journal of Law Reform*, No. 3, 2019, 329, 333.

only rationale of the provision. The king and the royal family had a huge responsibility for the advent of Mussolini. King Vittorio Emanuele III, in particular, did not sign the state of siege requested by Prime Minister Luigi Facta to tackle the 'March on Rome' organised by Mussolini in 1922. He also appointed Mussolini as prime minister on 29 October 1922. Hostility to the royal family is confirmed by another transitional and final provision, namely provision XIII, which condemned the royal family to exile.[104] This provision was later amended by constitutional law 1/2001 and since 2002 members of the Savoia family have been allowed to enter and live in Italy.

Article 139 of the Italian Constitution has been traced back to a broader trend of comparative law:[105]

> However, even if the unamendable clause of the 1948 Italian Constitution does not represent a significant novelty in the comparative scenario, its historical premises are worthy of attention. In fact, its inclusion in the last article of the constitution is due to a peculiar limitation of the primary constituent power of the Constituent Assembly, whose election was contextual to the referendum on the form of the state. Since the Constituent Assembly had no power to review the decision of the people on the form of state, it decided to eternally bind the constitutional amendment powers on this point.[106]

Both constitutional openness – which will be analysed in Chapter 3 – and the unamendability clause can be seen as the direct offspring of the rejection of the legal nationalism that had characterised the fascist phase in Italy. They are both functional to the preservation of some higher goods that cannot be affected by the choices of the contingent majority in office. As such, these higher goods are beyond the political process and are intangible. However, as the Italian Constitutional Court clarified in 1988, by republican form one should understand something more, that is, the entirety of supreme principles that represent the essence of the post–WWII constitutional experience.

---

[104] Provision XIII: 'The members and descendants of the House of Savoy shall not be voters and may not hold public office or elected offices.

Access and sojourn in the national territory shall be forbidden to the ex-kings of the House of Savoy, their spouses and their male descendants.

The assets, existing on national territory, of the former kings of the House of Savoy, their spouses and their male descendants shall be transferred to the State. Transfers and the establishment of royal rights on said properties which took place after 2 June 1946, shall be null and void'.

[105] 'Coming back to Article 139 Const. It., the inclusion of an unamendability clause in the 1948 Italian Constitution is not particularly innovative in comparative terms. In fact, the idea of entrenched constitutional laws dates back to the eighteenth century in its very first epiphanies. Constitutional norms providing for the unamendability of the republican form of state already existed in the nineteenth century. In the twentieth century, explicit unamendability has become a popular constitutional design: in the post-war constitutional wave, almost one third of the newly adopted constitutions included one or more unamendable clauses. In the post-cold war constitutional wave, this figure staggered to 50 per cent approximately', Faraguna, 'Unamendability', 333.

[106] Faraguna, 'Unamendability', 333.

Indeed, with judgment 1146/1988, the Italian Constitutional Court partly remedied this ambiguity by clarifying that the concept of 'republican form' had to be interpreted broadly as it includes the supreme principles codified in the first part of the constitution:

> The Italian Constitution contains some supreme principles that cannot be subverted or modified in their essential content, either by laws amending the Constitution, or by other constitutional laws. These include both principles that are expressly considered absolute limits on the power to amend the Constitution, such as the republican form of State (Art. 139) as well as those principles that even though not expressly mentioned among those principles not subject to the procedure of constitutional amendment, belong to the essence of the supreme values upon which the Italian Constitution is founded.
>
> This Court, furthermore, has already recognised in numerous decisions how the supreme principles of the constitutional order prevail over other laws or constitutional norms, such as when the Court maintained that even the prescription of the Concordat, which enjoy particular 'constitutional protection' under Article 7, paragraph 2, are not excluded from scrutiny for conformity to the 'supreme principles of the constitutional order' (see Judgments 30/1971, 12/1972, 175/1973, 1/1977, 18/1982), and also when the Court affirmed that the laws executing the EEC Treaty may be subject to the jurisdiction of this Court 'in reference to the fundamental principles of our constitutional order, and to the inalienable rights of the human person'.[107]

In the first part of this chapter, I clarified what I mean by post–WWII constitutionalism, trying to stress the increase of counter-majoritarian components added to the techniques employed by constitutionalism. Constitutionalism also endorsed a substantive notion of democracy. As has been recalled: 'The post-war European Constitutions, the German and the Italian above all, rest on the assumptions that a procedural concept of democracy is incompatible with liberalism and human rights. The more hidden (and therefore rooted) precommitment, however, does not relate to the institutional setting, but on a vision of the common man'.[108] Against this background, post–WWII constitutions are not only risk management devices, but they also become pluralism-enabling and pluralism-preserving tools.[109] In its normative sense, constitutionalism is inherently pluralistic and this is an important detail that already explains the tension between constitutionalism and populism, which was analysed in Chapter 1. The memory of horror and evil was fundamental

---

[107] Corte costituzionale, decision 1146/1988, www.cortecostituzionale.it. Translation quoted by Faraguna, 'Unamendability', 336.

[108] L. Corso, 'What Does Populism Have to Do with Constitutional Law? Discussing Populist Constitutionalism and Its Assumptions', *Rivista di Filosofia del Diritto*, No. 2, 2014, 443, 464.

[109] 'I conclude that populists can write constitutions that do offer genuine constraints, but populism and normative constitutionalism — understood as pluralism-preserving and rights-guaranteeing — do not go together', J. W. Müller, 'Populism and Constitutionalism', in C. Rovira Kaltwasser, P. Taggart, P. Ochoa Espejo, P. Ostiguy (eds.), *The Oxford Handbook of Populism*, Oxford University Press, 2017, 590, 591–2.

in shaping the contents of post–WWII constitutions, as we have seen when recalling some provisions of the German Basic Law. Italy definitely belongs to post–WWII constitutionalism, but also shows some important differences to the German case.

This chapter builds upon this and underlines that, in spite of the important novelties introduced by the 1948 Italian Constitution, Italy has never completely dealt with its fascist past, and this has resulted in the creation of a context which has favoured the emergence of this new wave of populism as we will see in the second part of this chapter.

2.5 ITALIAN POPULISMS: AN OVERVIEW

The context discussed above has facilitated the emergence of different waves of populism in Italy. Famously, Tarchi, one of the most important voices in this debate on Italian populism, has defined Italy as a laboratory[110] for those who are interested in studying these phenomena. As recalled in the Introduction, germs of populism can even be found in the Italian constituent process. The 'Common Man's Front' was a political movement born out of a weekly magazine (*L'Uomo qualunque*, started in 1944), which achieved critical success in the elections of 1946 and had thirty members in the Constituent Assembly, the majority of whom were lawyers. Before the end of fascism, Giannini also wrote a short book, *La folla* ('The Crowd'), where he described the Crowd as 'a peaceful and laborious majority, a Crowd, is an irresistible force that all [rulers] have to be prepared to face. On the surface easy to be dominated and ruled, the Crowd is instead always in charge of its will and its energies; and no hero or minority, no matter how intelligent, is capable of containing the impetus [of the Crowd] in decisive moments'.[111]

The histrionic figure of Guglielmo Giannini brought together all the ambiguities of this movement, which rapidly collapsed. The aim of this section is not to provide an exhaustive history of the 'multiple populisms'[112] that have characterised Italy since World War II. The goal of this section is instead to present some common traits that characterise the latest wave of populist movements in order to prepare the terrain for the juridical reflection advanced in this book. In his *Italia populista*, Tarchi wrote of a 'Fascist populism' that insisted on the need for 'going towards the people', reclaiming the myth of the people and the controversy surrounding 'parliamentary cretinism', bureaucrats and intellectuals,[113] an evident dose of demagoguery and

[110] M. Tarchi, 'Italy: The Promised Land of Populism?', *Contemporary Italian Politics*, No. 3, 2015, 273.

[111] G. Giannini, *La folla. Seimila anni di lotta contro la tirannide*, Il Faro, Rome, 58, cited and translated by N. Urbinati, 'Anti-party-ism as a Structural Component of Italian Democracy', in P. Blokker, M. Anselmi (eds.), *Multiple Populisms: Italy as Democracy's Mirror*, Routledge, Abingdon, 2020, 67, 74.

[112] P. Blokker, M. Anselmi (eds.), *Multiple Populisms: Italy as Democracy's Mirror*, Routledge, Abingdon, 2020.

[113] Tarchi, *Italia populista*, 172. Tarchi also quotes P. Milza, 'Mussolini entre fascisme et populisme', *Vingtième Siècle. Revue d'histoire*, No. 56, 1997, 115, at 118. This connecting thread between fascism

indeed not by coincidence Eco included, as we saw, populism in the essence of eternal fascism. Scholars have identified signs of populism in the rhetoric of Nenni and Togliatti,[114] respectively leaders of the Italian Socialist Party and the Italian Communist Party but as has been noted, they cannot be compared to the *Fronte dell'uomo qualunque* ('Common Man's Front', mentioned previously, created by Guglielmo Giannini, an Italian journalist, writer, and director born in Pozzuoli, close to Naples), which was able to merge libertarian aspects and individualism, making the defence of the common people the essential feature of its propaganda machinery. This resulted in a constant controversy and mobilisation against the 'partitocrazia' (particracy)[115] seen as the 'sworn enemy of the political restoration of the parties in Italy'.[116] *Qualunquismo* was the word coined to portray the approach endorsed by this political force:

'Qualunquismo' presented itself as the voice of ordinary people, those excluded from the division of power, fed up with greedy and corrupt politicians, indifferent to ideologies they saw as a mere cover for elite ambitions for domination, sceptical of any programme and mistrustful of electoral promises they expected to be systematically broken by those elected. Declaring its aversion to both fascism and anti-fascism, to the monarchist, clerical or conservative Right and to the Republican, Socialist or Communist Left, the UQ [Uomo Qualunque] focused on the unbridgeable gap between the people on the one hand – united in their desire to be 'left in peace', and to get on with life in the wake of the bloody passions that had for years divided the peninsula – and the professional politicians on the other [. . .]. Giannini's rhetoric counterposed the idea of a government made up of technicians and neutral administrators competent in public affairs to that of the hegemony of the 'parasites' and their natural allies, the plutocrats. It is this extreme simplification of politics and the offer of 'easy, ready-made solutions', identified 50 years later by analysts as pivots of the argumentative structure, that allows us to place Le Pen and Tapie (Saussez 1992), Bossi and Berlusconi, Haider, Blocher, De Winters, Glistrups

and populism is explored by F. Finchelstein, *From Fascism to Populism in History*, University of California Press, Oakland, 2018.

[114] Tarchi, *Italia populista*, 174. Starting with his idea of populism as a logic, Laclau famously defined Togliatti as a populist leader, E. Laclau, *On Populist Reason*, Verso, London, 2005, 182.

[115] 'In the political history of modern Italy, "partitocrazia" was used for the first time on 12 February 1946. Its paternity belongs to Roberto Lucifero d'Aprigliano (1903– 1993), a liberal monarchic who employed it during the XXIII plenary session of the Kingdom of Italy's National Council (Consulta) precisely to describe the effects of party-list proportional representation. However, he had previously used the same term in the last chapter of a short book he had published in 1944 on the philosophical and political implications of the electoral systems – Introduzione alla libertà ("Introduction to Freedom"). These two expressions of his antipartyism – the one running through his political writings and the one fueling his political action – resorted to very similar arguments and were constitutive of the same intellectual project. As a political theorist, Lucifero attacked the "dishonest behavior of parties" as the outcome of the "increasing power of minorities" through the proportional system', D. Ragazzoni, '"Particracy": The Pre-populist Critique of Parties and Its Implications', in P. Blokker, M. Anselmi (eds.), *Multiple Populisms: Italy as Democracy's Mirror*, Routledge, Abingdon, 2020, 86, 88.

[116] Tarchi, *Italia populista*, 175.

and the leader of the Rumanian Populists, Tudor, in the same family. It is precisely this simplification which was used as an effective instrument to gain consensus by the UQ in 1945.[117]

In Giannini's speeches one can find an evident anti-party-ism[118] and a moralistic attack against corrupt politicians, two elements that go on to inspire the other waves of Italian populisms. All these elements make the *qualunquismo* a prototype of populism in Europe.

Anti-party-ism and particracy are autonomous concepts, to a certain extent even competing notions:

> Anti-partyism consists of a distinctive interpretation of democracy, which can take more individualist-liberal forms as well as more organic or corporate ones. Anti-partyist views imagine democracy in a depoliticised manner, in which conflict is deflated and partisanship less prominent. Anti-partyism is then not merely about a critique on 'particracy', and its malfunctioning – corrupt parties that fail to promote the common good – but it equally points to an alternative vision, intrinsic in democracy, rooted in a desire to make the 'people' the only ruling party.[119]

Particracy instead refers to the excessive power of political parties, which are able to dominate the political life of the country, by managing appointments, moving votes and using vetoes. Before the advent of Sartori's study,[120] the formula remained elusive since 'the various partisans of antipartyism in Italy resorted to the label of "particracy"[121] (or "esecracy" or "party mania") to evoke a polemical target with no clearly defined identity'.[122] With Labriola and above all Maranini, the critique of parties related to closed party lists and the power acquired by the mass parties and their secretariats. Maranini and Labriola were two eminent intellectuals of that period and this again shows how widespread this anti-party sentiment was. Of course, in this case the roots of their critiques are grounded in reasons other than Giannini's, but their ideas also contributed to creating a cultural atmosphere that has always characterised Italian politics. In particular, according to Maranini, political parties have deprived the people of their sovereignty because of the way in which they select candidates:

---

[117] M. Tarchi, 'Populism Italian Style', in Y. Mény, Y. Surel (eds.), *Democracies and the Populist Challenge*, Palgrave, London, 2002, 120, 122.

[118] N. Urbinati, 'Anti-party-ism as a Structural Component of Italian Democracy', in P. Blokker, M. Anselmi (eds.), *Multiple Populisms: Italy as Democracy's Mirror*, Routledge, Abingdon, 2020, 67. It is correct to say that in Italy there have been different forms of anti-party-ism, M. Gregorio, *Parte totale. Le dottrine costituzionali del partito politico in Italia tra Otto e Novecento*, Giuffrè, Milan, 2013, 125.

[119] P. Blokker, M. Anselmi, 'Introduction', in P. Blokker, M. Anselmi (eds.), *Multiple Populisms: Italy as Democracy's Mirror*, Routledge, Abingdon, 2020, 1, 7.

[120] G. Sartori, *Parties and Party Systems. A Framework for Analysis*, Cambridge University Press, New York, 1976.

[121] *Partitocrazia* in Italian. In English, 'partitocracy' is also used.

[122] Ragazzoni, 'Particracy', 91.

The people is called periodically to cast their ballot, but they are not allowed to choose which candidate to vote for; the most they can do is determine the proportion of the elected officials based on the lists that parties' ruling committees propose. As you can tell, the people's sovereignty is thus completely undermined; it survives, to a minimal extent, only where parties are democratically organised. Unfortunately, though, little to no democracy exists within parties; all of them tend to give all powers to a restricted number of party bureaucrats – a tendency that was a defining feature of fascism and remains a staple of all sorts of totalitarianism.[123]

However, these two concepts share the idea of parties as elements of fragmentation in the attempt to give a unitary notion of the people. In this sense they are both expressions of a sort of *odium partium*,[124] which characterises the history of Italian democracy, as they both precede the introduction of parliamentary democracy.[125] Moreover, the origins of 'party criticism' began even earlier, at the end of the XIX century in Italy.[126] *Qualunquismo* benefitted from this cultural and political atmosphere in which one can see how these two seminal elements of populism (anti-politics and anti-party sentiment) became vehicles of 'depoliticisation'.[127] The contribution of the Common Man's Front to the Constituent Assembly is traditionally seen as almost irrelevant, but actually many of its elected members were lawyers who frequently intervened in the debate, adopting a variety of positions. Generally speaking, they were in favour of what they called an 'administrative state',[128] based on the separation of powers and resembling the myth of the night watchman state. They constantly fought against the intrusiveness of state action, consistent with the liberal paradigm of impermeability between civil society and the state. They also pushed for

[123] G. Maranini, 'Totalitarismo dei partiti', *L'Arno*, II, 28 July 1946, 45, cited and translated by Ragazzoni, 'Particracy', 93, 69. Ragazzoni also points out that 'It is worth underlining that Maranini's critique of Italian parties did not entail the rejection of parties tout court. What he feared in the upcoming age of party democracy was their oligarchic involution – in other words, the dissolution of the link between parties and democracy and the institutionalization of a political oligopoly dominated by party leaders and bureaucrats', Ragazzoni, 'Particracy', 93. See also G. Maranini, *Governo parlamentare e partitocrazia: lezione inaugurale dell'anno accademico 1949–1950*, Editrice Universitaria, Florence, 1950.

[124] Urbinati, 'Anti-party-ism'.

[125] 'The Italian case is an eloquent example of the fact that the political practice in the age of democracy has generated and generates party-ism and anti-party-ism ceaselessly', Urbinati, 'Anti-party-ism', 69.

[126] Urbinati finds the germs of this mistrust of political parties in Marco Minghetti and Benedetto Croce. '[W]ith the collapse of fascism, the Italian political spectrum was split into two parts: the party side, which was the strongest and best organized (it included the Communist Party, the Democratic Christians, the Socialist Party, the Republican Party and the Party of Action) and the anti- or/and critical-of-party side, which was a weaker group and made up of essentially two components: the liberal party and the Everyman Front. The liberal party was older, and its more authoritative members, Croce among them, were somehow nostalgic of pre-fascism liberal parliamentarianism and in this sense inimical of mass parties rather than of parties', Urbinati, 'Anti-party-ism', 75.

[127] F. De Nardis, 'Depoliticization, Anti-politics and the Moral People', in P. Blokker, M. Anselmi (eds.), *Multiple Populisms: Italy as Democracy's Mirror*, Routledge, Abingdon, 2020, 49, 51.

[128] T. Forcellese, 'L'uomo qualunque. L'idea dello "Stato amministrativo" alla Costituente', in A. Buratti, M. Fioravanti (eds.), *Costituenti ombra Altri luoghi e altre figure della cultura politica italiana (1943–48)*, Carocci, Roma, 2010, 445.

a state with minimal intervention in the economy and tried to introduce a prohibition of strikes. Their positions were mainly neglected or defeated in the Assembly, but they also raised interesting points, like those connected to the openness to Europe of the Italian post-war system (they were in favour of the United States of Europe). Moreover, they also supported the idea of a Constitutional Court.[129] Finally, another good intuition they had was to support the nomination of a woman, Ottavia Penna Buscemi, as president of the Republic. However, this attempt was not successful and Buscemi only obtained thirty-two votes.[130] Later, for other reasons, she decided to distance herself from the Front.

The other important populist force that is necessary to recall in this overview[131] is the *Lega*, previously called *Lega Nord*.[132] I shall come back to some of its current features in Chapter 3; here I shall limit myself to some general considerations. The *Lega* has been a chameleonic force that transformed from an ethno-regional force into an anti-establishment force. It was created between 1989 and 1991 and originally stemmed from the merger of some autonomist groups present in some regions in the north of Italy (mainly Piedmont, Veneto, Liguria, Tuscany and Lombardy). It became a secessionist force, which initially claimed to fight for the independence of Padania[133] and benefitted from the political earthquake represented by *Tangentopoli* (Bribesville):

> In a context marked by the destabilisation of the party system and the end of international bipolarism, the Lega Nord appeared as a cross-cutting party, charac-
> terised by antiparty protest and the mobilisation of cleavages that would have been
> unusual in the political competition of the post-war period, such as the one between

[129] On their contribution in the Constituent Assembly see: M. Cocco, *Qualunquismo. Una storia politica e culturale dell'uomo qualunque*, Le Monnier, Florence, 2018, 137.

[130] The first president of the Italian Republic was Enrico De Nicola.

[131] In his studies Tarchi also takes into account a number of other figures or movements: Achille Lauro, Leoluca Orlando's party, *la Rete* (the Network) and even the *Partito radicale*. The *Partito radicale*, however, has given an important contribution to the fight for civil rights in Italy. Pannella, the historical leader of the *radicali*, launched a series of tough attacks on institutions, including the *Corte costituzionale* once defined as 'the supreme dome [i.e., echelon] of the particracy mafiosity', my own translation: 'Radicali e referendum: "Grande mobilitazione"', 14 January 2005, www.corriere.it /Primo_Piano/Politica/2005/01_Gennaio/14/Radicali.shtml. Here mafiosity (*mafiosità*) refers to mentality which in his view made the particracy similar to the mafia due to the way in which establishment parties controlled the country. On that occasion Pannella attacked the Constitutional Court for its case law on the referendum, which as we will see in Chapter 4, has traditionally been used by *radicali* for their political battles. Their language somehow anticipated Berlusconi's rhetoric. For a complete overview, see: Tarchi, *Italia populista*, 195 et seq.

[132] For a detailed analysis of the Lega Nord in English, see: D. Albertazzi, 'Going, Going, ... Not Quite Gone Yet? Bossi's Lega and the Survival of the Mass Party', *Contemporary Italian Politics*, No.2, 2016, 115. D. McDonnell, 'A Weekend in Padania: *Regionalist Populism and the Lega Nord*', *Politics*, No. 2, 2006, 126. G. Passarelli, D. Tuorto, *Lega & Padania: storie e luoghi delle camicie verdi*, Il Mulino, Bologna, 2012.

[133] *Lexico* defines Padania as a 'A term for the Po Valley area of northern Italy, suggested by the Italian political party Lega Nord (Northern League) as a name for a proposed independent state', www .lexico.com/definition/padania.

centre and periphery. Therefore, the Lega did not mobilise a class fracture, or a religious one, as used to be the case for the First Republic parties, but rather a territorial one.[134]

Initially the *Lega Nord* was 'a populist movement of protest and identity'[135] and its historical leader, Umberto Bossi entered the political scene by attacking establishment parties and depicting the state as the Mafia and Rome as a corrupt capital, 'thieving Rome' (*Roma ladrona*). Padania does not exist; it is a fiction created by a series of symbols, conventions and rituals invented by the *Lega Nord*.[136] The anti-establishment party nature of the *Lega Nord* did not impede collaboration with some eminent intellectual figures, like Gianfranco Miglio, who worked hard on the idea of a northern secession. The construction of the alleged identity of Padania occurred by identifying a common enemy, which was originally the South, portrayed as lazy in opposition to the rich, productive and allegedly exploited North. Noteworthy are the frequent attacks on *Terroni* (which is what the people from the south of Italy are contemptuously called).[137] Bossi created his leadership by breaking some taboos in the political scene – his language, for instance, was an innovation which directly questioned the political jargon widespread at that time:

> Using direct, crude, sarcastic expressions, and not infrequently violent in its polemics, the *Lega* broke the symbolic codes to which voters had been accustomed by the traditional political forces, broke through the barrier of ideologies and made the appeal for a return to genuine communitarian traditions – away from planetary horizons to concentrate on the prime needs of territory, family and work – more credible. While the politicos' jargon is a synonym for hypocrisy and division, and bureaucratic verbiage gives an impression of abstractness and remoteness from the real problems of everyday life, the language used by Lega leaders is that of common

---

[134]   C. Biancalana, 'Four Italian Populisms', in P. Blokker, M. Anselmi (eds.), *Multiple Populisms: Italy as Democracy's Mirror*, Routledge, Abingdon, 2020, 216, 217.

[135]   Tarchi, 'Populism Italian Style', 129. 'The message expressed in the first Lega manifestos and documents was summary, basic and aimed at the man in the street; it appealed to local identity as the basis for reconstructing homogeneous, solid, secure communities free of class discrimination, and with clear, undisputed acknowledgement of a number of interests (and values) common to all their members. The proposal to revive the various Northern dialects as means of daily communication and to make their use legal in institutional contexts, from administrative offices to local council chambers, was designed to emphasise the links that ensure solidarity amongst ordinary people, and at the same time indicated their distance from the "legal country" (pays légal) of the elites. When this claim was dropped, the attempt to create a unitary local popular consciousness found other instruments: slogans stressing a strong aversion to the exploiting centralised state', ibid.

[136]   Biancalana, 'Four Italian Populisms', 219. 'It organised regular propaganda days, called "Padania days", to emphasise the main themes tackled in its programme. It also created a large number of "Padanian" occupational, cultural, sporting, recreational and voluntary work associations, designed to compete with those of the Italian state. It founded a Padanian National Guard', Tarchi, 'Populism Italian Style', 130.

[137]   Etymologically speaking, the word *terrone* comes from *terra* (land) and denotes a person that farms the land. For instance, the present author is a proud *terrone* since he is from Sicily, the most beautiful island on planet Earth.

sense, as spoken at home, in the bar, or in the street among friends: the language that unites, homogenises and allows frank communication. The fact that the main person speaking on public occasions is the man who personifies the movement – Umberto Bossi – is manifest proof of the leader's availability to openness to a direct relationship with the people. As Bossi repeats on every possible occasion, the Lega is not just popular but also and especially of the common people. The choice of a more 'vernacular' language helps reinforce the theme presented in the Lega's propaganda – that is, the rejection of intellectual, political and cultural mediation, mistrust of representation, and the demand for autonomy in local communities.[138]

Over the years, with the transformation of the *Lega Nord* into the *Lega* and with its new nature of national party, the other/enemy has become the immigrant. The structure of the party has changed significantly and a further acceleration in this direction has been given by the rise of Salvini. Although the roots of this change grew gradually, an important moment in this shift is represented by the fall of Umberto Bossi, who was overwhelmed by a series of scandals (inter alia, appropriation of party funds for personal use).

Salvini became the leader of the party in 2013 and led the *Lega* to the successful electoral results obtained in 2018. Salvini and Bossi have some common traits: the use of informal outfits, direct appeals to the people, charismatic leadership and attacks on institutions.[139] However, while the *Lega Nord* originally defined itself as anti-fascist, the *Lega* has more recently become a right-wing party with close connections to the far right as we will see in Chapter 3.[140]

Tangentopoli was a turning point in the history of Italian politics and another wave of populism was fed by this big scandal. The roots of the Five Star Movement's approach to the relationship between politics and justice can be found therein and this also applies to the debate about the judicialisation of politics, with the alleged instrumental use of criminal law and justice as a strategy to influence politics.

Some traditional parties (for instance, the *Democrazia cristiana* and Bettino Craxi's *Partito socialista italiano*) were overwhelmed by this scandal. *Forza Italia* was a product of that time and was created in 1993 when Silvio Berlusconi decided to enter politics by announcing it on his TV channels.[141] On Berlusconi and *Forza Italia*, I shall limit this overview to stressing just some of their relevant aspects for the purpose of this book. *Forza Italia* did not define itself as a political party

---

[138] Tarchi, 'Populism Italian Style', 127.

[139] 'Salvini is similar to Bossi in some traits: he presents himself as a man of the people, who says things as they are and values common sense (the "buonsenso"; see Passarelli and Tuorto 2018). Like Bossi, he uses his clothing to communicate closeness to the people and informality, in opposition to traditional politicians (Salvini uses tracksuit tops instead of vests)', Biancalana, 'Four Italian Populisms', 222.

[140] For an account of this transformation under Salvini, see: D. Albertazzi, A. Giovannini, A. Seddone, '"No Regionalism Please, We Are Leghisti!" The Transformation of the Italian Lega Nord under the Leadership of Matteo Salvini', *Regional and Federal Studies*, No. 5, 2018, 645.

[141] On 26 January 1995. The video can be found here: www.youtube.com/watch?v=UpXOAlFFpBQ. G. Mazzoleni, 'Populism and the Media', in D. Albertazzi, D. McDonnell (eds.), *Twenty-First Century Populism: The Spectre of Western European Democracy*, Palgrave, London, 2008, 49, 53.

initially[142] but managed to benefit from the crisis of the former governing parties thanks to the image of outsider that Berlusconi gave himself: he depicted himself as a self-made man who managed to create his own business and success in the north of Italy.[143] He also adopted direct and frank language, attacked corrupt parties and identified the 'communists' (the leftist forces) as the enemy. He claimed he had 'come on the pitch' (employing soccer metaphors)[144] to challenge and defeat them for the sake of Italy.[145] He has also been accused of and prosecuted for several crimes as well as convicted of fraud. After the conviction he was barred from public office until 2018, when he came back in a coalition with *Fratelli d'Italia* and *Lega*. He has always claimed to be 'the most persecuted man in the entire history of the world'.[146] He also attacked the judges seen as partisans and non-neutral actors intent on affecting the political equilibria of the country.

He has been a populist pioneer in many respects: when deciding on any course of action (including his entry into politics) he has always consulted with communication experts and carried out surveys and opinion polls. He has used his experience in the world of business and the media to innovate[147] the style of political communication:

> He is the archetypal self-made man who has not cut his ties with his social hinterland, and who, despite his enormous wealth, tries to seem like the man in the street: more able, more fortunate, but of the same mettle. 'I am one of you' is the phrase he frequently adopts in dialogue with the public. The charisma his supporters rapidly acknowledge in him is not natural, but situational [...]; it is based not on a halo of personal qualities, but on his followers' desire to imitate, fed by an efficient alternation of demagogic attitudes, that simultaneously narrow his distance from rank-and-file followers, and claims to assume the indispensable role as leader, that reinstate it. Paternalist and reassuring, Berlusconi proclaims himself as the interpreter and defender of the popular will, but his ideal rostrum is not a soapbox at a public meeting but the small screen of television – as the owner of the three most-watched private networks, he knows the medium to perfection. His model is not that of the mob orator, but the proprietor of a firm trying to straighten out the accounts,

---

[142] E. Poli, s, Il Mulino, Bologna, 2001.

[143] G. Orsina, *Il berlusconismo: nella storia d'Italia*, Marsilio, Venice, 2013.

[144] 'Berlusconi, in his speech, also made ample use of football metaphors, both due to the huge popularity of this sport and because he himself was the president of a football team. As in the case of other populist leaders, the language and attitudes that are unusual in the political realm (such as the jokes and the gaffes during important institutional occasions) were used by Berlusconi to underline the difference with the political and party élite', Biancalana, 'Four Italian Populisms', 224.

[145] 'He was able to present himself to anti-Left voters as the "man of providence" who had entered the lists at precisely the right time to prevent the country's government ending up in the hands of the ex-communists', Tarchi, 'Populism Italian Style', 132.

[146] 'The many trials of Silvio Berlusconi explained', 9 May 2014, www.bbc.com/news/world-europe -12403119.

[147] 'Against these enemies, Berlusconi proposed a profound renovation of politics, both in terms of the people involved in it (who needed to be outsiders of politics) and in terms of modalities of action, oriented towards the efficiency that is typical of entrepreneurs. There was therefore a supremacy of the private over the public', Biancalana, 'Four Italian Populisms', 225.

to distribute responsibilities and to guarantee the collaboration of all his employees.[148]

Forza Italia originally distanced itself from the traditional parties not only by adopting a flexible and light structure, but also by employing language to connect with the electors. It is no coincidence that *Forza Italia* immediately won the political elections in 1994. His charismatic traits inaugurated a season of personalisation of politics. Although in Italy the people do not elect the president of the Council of Ministers directly, with Berlusconi the debate about constitutional reforms and the introduction of a presidential form of government got a renewed boost. The political system had to adapt to his persona and received a decisive input towards bipolarism: '[t]he 2005 electoral reform reinforced the tendency towards personalisation by requiring parties to identify who their prime ministerial candidate was. In the 2006 elections, coalitions backing either Prodi or Berlusconi won 98.9 percent of the vote. Italy was not going to become, as many feared, a system hegemonized by the media magnate. Prodi's presence at any rate guaranteed "bi-leaderism"'.[149]

Calise famously called *Forza Italia* the 'personal party'[150] to emphasise not only the importance that the personality of Berlusconi has had for his party, but also his unwillingness to be replaced. Not by coincidence, all aspiring successors have been challenged and then humiliated by Berlusconi himself before leaving the party. This is the case of Angelino Alfano, for instance, who left politics after creating his own party *Nuovo Centrodestra*, which supported the Letta, Renzi and Gentiloni governments. Alfano also served as minister in these governments.

Insisting on the rhetoric of the ordinary man, Berlusconi always accuses his rivals of not having done much in their lives, of being professionals of politics, since they 'have always "lived off politics", making careers as party officials, without ever demonstrating they could do anything else'.[151]

Indeed, the importance of the media has been crucial to his success. In fact, scholars have written of 'audience democracy'[152] or 'tele-populism'.[153] His jokes and non-politically correct style have also induced scholars to speak of 'macho populism'.[154] He also tries to reinforce his image as ordinary man by insisting on personal and family anecdotes, and in 2001, just before the elections, he also

---

[148] Tarchi, 'Populism Italian Style', 133.

[149] M. Donovan, M. Gilbert (eds.), 'Silvio Berlusconi and Romano Prodi', in E. Jones, G. Pasquino (eds.), *The Oxford Handbook of Italian Politics*, Oxford University Press, 2015, 394, 398.

[150] M. Calise, *Il partito personale. I due corpi del leader*, Laterza, Rome, 2007. F. Raniolo, 'Forza Italia: a leader with a party', *South European Society and Politics*, Nos. 3-4, 2006, 439; D. McDonnell, 'Silvio Berlusconi's Personal Parties: From Forza Italia to the Popolo della Libertà', *Political Studies*, 61 No.1 suppl., 2013, 217.

[151] Tarchi, 'Populism Italian Style', 133.

[152] B. Manin, *The Principles of Representative Government*, Cambridge University Press, 1997, 218.

[153] P. A. Taguieff, *L'illusion populiste*, Berg International, Paris, 2002, 27.

[154] F. Finchelstein, *From Fascism*, 242.

distributed by mail a short pamphlet titled *Una storia italiana* ('An Italian Story') to feed this narrative.[155]

Once he became president of the Council he obtained control of all the main TV channels[156] (RAI, the national public broadcasting company of Italy, and *Fininvest*, a holding he created in 1975), and not even the left-wing parties – when they subsequently had the possibility to govern the country – managed to come up with a legislative solution to solve this conflict of interests.[157]

His entry into politics was viewed with suspicion by many intellectuals, including Norberto Bobbio[158] and once in office he broke a taboo by labelling many provisions of the Italian Constitution as leftist:

> [T]he unprecedented concentration of massive political, economic, and mediatic power in the hands of the same individual made Berlusconi a closeted 'despot' rather than an outspoken 'liberal,' posing a potentially serious threat to the foundational logic of constitutional democracy. Berlusconi's impatience with the institutions and procedures of modern representative politics – legitimate opposition, rotation in office, party government, rule of law, checks and balances – was evident at multiple levels [...] He frequently resorted to decrees to quickly pass laws favoring his own interests and skillfully bypass parliamentary deliberation. He attempted to increasingly empower the executive over the legislative and thus redesign Italy's Constitution along semi-presidential lines.[159]

Berlusconi launched a new series of attempts to reform the constitution, which he frequently criticised as being non-neutral. For instance, in 2003 he attacked Article 41 of the Italian Constitution,[160] concerning the right to economic initiative, maintaining that it is Soviet inspired:

---

[155] G. Mola, 'Berlusconi: "La mia biografia in tutte le famiglie italiane"', 11 April 2001, www.repubblica.it/online/politica/campagnacinque/libro/libro.html.

[156] 'At this level, Berlusconi's experience represents an early case of proto-populism in power that skillfully exploited the political potential of the media—a topic that has generated an endless literature over the past few years across a variety of fields—and managed to be, at once, antipartisan (against previous parties and current antagonists) and hyper-partisan (stretching the identification between his holistic "non-party" party, its leader, and the nation as much as he could)', D. Ragazzoni, 'The Populist Leader's Two Bodies: Bobbio, Berlusconi, and the Factionalization of Party Democracy', *Constellations*, No. 3, 2020, 213, 225.

[157] A. Pertici, 'L'etica pubblica e la riforma sempre in-attesa del conflitto di interessi', 2016, www.gruppodipisa.it/8-rivista/1-andrea-pertici-l-etica-pubblica-e-la-riforma-sempre-in-attesa-del-conflitto-di-interessi.

[158] Ragazzoni, 'The Populist Leader's Two Bodies', 220. See Bobbio's articles on *La Stampa* and then collected in a volume: N. Bobbio, *Contro i nuovi dispotismi: scritti sul berlusconismo*, Dedalo, Rome, 2008.

[159] Ragazzoni, 'The Populist Leader's Two Bodies', 218.

[160] Article 41, Italian Constitution: 'Private economic enterprise is free.
      It may not be carried out against the common good or in such a manner that could damage safety, liberty and human dignity.
      The law shall provide for appropriate programmes and controls so that public and private-sector economic activity may be oriented and coordinated for social purpose'.

I have also repeatedly publicly complained that our Basic Law gives little room for companies [. . .] The wording of Article 41 et seq. is affected by the Soviet implications which refer to the Soviet culture and constitution.[161]

In 2009, he publicly asserted that 'the Charter is a law made many years ago under the influence of the end of a dictatorship and with the presence at the [drafting] table of ideological forces that considered the Russian Constitution a model from which to take numerous indications'.[162] These are just examples of the systematic attacks made by Berlusconi on the constitution.[163] This also prepared the basis for a new round of mega-constitutional politics striving for a vast reform of the constitution, which was rejected by a referendum held under Article 138 of the Italian Constitution in 2006:

> In the last decade of the past century, a wind of 'constitutional newism' was blowing, which ranged from proposals that intended to ameliorate the functioning of the system to a comprehensive criticism, if not a real and full-blown denigration, of the Republican Constitution – seen as a product from another 'era' and party system (the antifascist parties that had supported Italy from 1944 onwards) that were supposed to be overcome – and therefore as an 'old' and inadequate instrument for new times and new necessities.[164]

Some of these features were later retrieved by Renzi who, in fact, has been defined as a 'Leftist Berlusconi'.[165] Renzi himself has been defined a populist, an anti-populist populist *à la* Macron.[166] I think one can find some populist claims and images in his behaviour, but I would not define Renzi as a pure populist leader, partly because of the influence that the Democratic Party structure has had in taming his populist traits.

---

[161] 'La Costituzione è di ispirazione sovietica', 12 April 2003, www.repubblica.it/online/politica/berlu parla/torino/torino.html.

[162] 'Berlusconi: "Costituzione ideologizzata"', 7 February 2009, www.corriere.it/politica/09_febbraio_07/ berlusconi_costituzione_bd1e8990-f53f-11dd-a70d-00144f02aabc.shtml. My own translation.

[163] On Berlusconi's approach to constitutional politics, see: A. Pizzorusso, *La Costituzione ferita*, Laterza, Rome, 1999.

[164] V. Onida, *La Costituzione. La legge fondamentale della Repubblica*, Il Mulino, Bologna, 2007, 125, cited and translated by P. Blokker, 'Populism and Constitutional Reform. The Case of Italy', in G. Delledonne, G. Martinico, M. Monti, F. Pacini (eds.), *Italian Populism and Constitutional Law. Strategies, Conflicts and Dilemmas*, Palgrave, London, 2020, 11, 19.

[165] F. Bordignon, 'Matteo Renzi: A "Leftist Berlusconi" for the Italian Democratic Party?', *South European Society and Politics*, No. 1, 2014, 1.

[166] 'Renzi's leadership, on the other hand, presents features similar to those described by Mair (2000, 2002) for Blair's New Labour, as well as aspects similar to the "anti-populist populism" of Macron in France, starting from the personalization of leadership, radical change in the organisational and planning structure of the political party and culture, and, finally, progressively overcoming the party as a place for political decision-making and responsibility', L. Viviani, 'Populist Anti-party Parties', in P. Blokker, M. Anselmi (eds.), *Multiple Populisms: Italy as Democracy's Mirror*, Routledge, Abingdon, 2020, 106, 117. Viviani refers to P. Mair, 'Partyless Democracy', 2000, https://newleftreview .org/issues/II2/articles/peter-mair-partyless-democracy.

He finally left the Democratic Party after having fought for its internal renewal, insisting on the need for a generational change, by defying the long-standing members of the secretariat of the party. In order to do that he contributed to the creation of an 'open party',[167] with the use of the primaries for the selection of the party leader, a model later followed even by *Lega* and *Fratelli d'Italia*. Renzi is evidence of the 'populist contagion'[168] which has affected the mainstream political class. There are also important differences: he is not an outsider; he is a pure politician and does not have the economic power of Berlusconi. He also failed to transform the *Partito democratico* into a personalistic party. Finally, his approach to mega-constitutional politics is clearly majoritarian and looks at the constitution as a piece of legal machinery whose second part, at least, risks reducing the efficiency and the speed of the system.[169]

Returning to Berlusconi, it is possible to say that *Tangentopoli* also paved the way for the entry to the scene of another populist character, Antonio Di Pietro, a former prosecutor in the *Tangentopoli* trials and probably the most famous protagonist of that season. After leaving the judiciary, he became minister for public works during the Prodi government. He later created his own political party, *Italia dei Valori* (Italy of Values), whose name refers to the moral superiority of his fight against corruption.[170] Although he has never become a relevant figure in Italian politics, his decision to move from the judiciary to politics revamped the controversy about the politicised judiciary in Italy and was only the first of several cases of former judges entering the political arena.

Finally, the Five Star Movement. I am going to analyse many of its traits over the course of this book, so in this section I will mention just three elements. The first one has to do with the history of this political force, which does not define itself as a party but as a movement and, so far, it has renounced public funding reserved for Italian political parties. It was created in 2009, but its roots can be traced back to 2005. It was born as a form of protest and post-ideological movement.

Initially, the Five Star Movement avoided debates on TV and tried to connect directly to the people by using public squares and the internet.[171] It is no coincidence

---

[167]	S. Vassallo, G. Passarelli, 'Centre-left prime ministerial primaries in Italy: the laboratory of the "open party" model', *Contemporary Italian Politics*, No. 1, 2016, 12.

[168]	Biancalana, 'Four Italian Populisms', 233. 'Renzi's case shows how the populist style has also "infected" traditional and ruling political actors', Ibid., 238.

[169]	Bordignon, 'Matteo Renzi'.

[170]	'His movement, the newly-founded "L'Italia dei valori", tries to recreate the psychological climate of the years of "Tangentopoli", to set themes of illegality at the centre of political discourse, and to incite a new, strong anti-partitocratic reaction among ordinary people. Yet he lacks the essential ingredient for the success of populist recipes: a serious economic and/or moral system crisis such as that which occurred in the early 1990s', Tarchi, 'Populism Italian Style', 135.

[171]	'From the start, therefore, the M5S combined online mobilisation on the web with the offline version, in local contexts and in the squares. In 2007 and 2008, two big street demonstrations were organised, the "V-days", dedicated to gathering signatures for a popular legislative initiative that would block the eligibility to parliament for convicted people, fix a limit of two terms in office for parliamentarians, and abolish public financing for publishing as well as the professional category of journalists. So we can see that from the very start, typical traits of populist phenomena emerged – such as the importance of the

that the start of this movement is due to the launch of the blog of its charismatic leader, the comedian Beppe Grillo. Grillo was supported by *Casaleggio Associati*, a company founded and run by Gianroberto Casaleggio, an entrepreneur, who also co-founded the Five Star Movement and edited Beppe Grillo's blog. The Five Star Movement presents both continuity and discontinuity with the tradition of the Italian populist past. On the one hand, its approach to reality is dichotomous and majoritarian and, on the other hand, like Berlusconi, it relies on mass media to connect to the people by going beyond the idea of audience democracy. Indeed, the people here are not only the audience, which passively attends the show, but they can actively participate in the selection of candidates via online ballots and in deciding the most important choices to be made by the Five Star Movement. So, the *MoVimento 5 Stelle* is both an example of pure populism in the words of Tarchi[172] and a manifestation of techno-populism[173] at its best.

While the *Lega* has more to do with identity politics, the Five Star Movement is interesting from the perspective of the politics of immediacy:

First, M5S cannot be strongly characterised as being 'of the people'. Nationalism, traditional values, and communitarian identity are marginal to its political dis-course. The people to whom M5S's representatives seem to refer are similar to the participants in a class action against the previous ruling elites; their main bond is a claim for damages against past governments. Second, it endorses some kind of technological utopianism, whereby digital platforms are envisaged as gradually replacing political action. Third, M5S has maintained a strong anti-corruption posture which is grounded in its suspicion of the very essence of political power, no matter which political group is in charge of ruling the country. These three features serve to explain why M5S's political discourse is heavily oriented towards dispelling any risk of factionalism, to remain faithful to the ambition of radically purging public choices subject to any private (elitist) influence.[174]

---

leader's figure, the aversion towards the political class and journalists, both seen as useless intermediaries – but also some specific traits of the M5S, such as the importance of the Internet.
  As mentioned, the M5S was officially founded in 2009. It was a top-down foundation, and the analysis of party documents [...] indicates that the fate of the party was strictly linked to the leader, who was the owner of the symbol, which was granted from time to time to the lists and candidates who wanted to take part in the election with the M5S. The M5S rejected the label of party, defining itself as Movement or Non-party, and presented a different organizational structure from traditional parties, which combined the typical horizontal structure of social movements with a strong central-isation', Biancalana, 'Four Italian Populisms', 227–8.

172 'Populismo allo stato pure', Tarchi, *Italia populista*, 333.
173 E. De Blasio, M. Sorice, 'Technopopulism and direct representation', in P. Blokker, M. Anselmi (eds.), *Multiple Populisms: Italy as Democracy's Mirror*, Routledge, Abingdon, 2020, 127. Gerbaudo defined the Five Star Movement as an example of a digital party: P. Gerbaudo, *The Digital Party: Political Organisation and Online Democracy*, Pluto Press, London, 2019.
174 L. Corso, 'When Anti-Politics Becomes Political: What Can the Italian Five Star Movement Tell Us about the Relationship Between Populism and Legalism', *European Constitutional Law Review*, No. 3, 2019, 462, 464.

The Five Star Movement's obsession with transparency and direct involvement later led to the introduction of a series of reforms on the referendum and on questioning the free parliamentary mandate. A very telling example is the negotiation with the *Partito democratico* led by Bersani in 2013. Those negotiations – that eventually failed[175] – were broadcast online to guarantee transparency and offered a very humiliating view of the leader of the *Partito democratico*.[176] Over the years the Movement has changed.[177] Di Maio resigned as its leader but he was still minister for foreign affairs in the second Conte government, and Grillo is still influential,[178] but there are other potential members of the Movement who are tempted to run for the leadership, like Alessandro Di Battista.[179] Finally, and this is very interesting for comparative lawyers, the Five Star Movement also retrieved some aspects of post-*Tangentopoli*, some points highlighted by Di Pietro, for instance, and made law, especially criminal law, part of their arsenal to target the enemy[180] (unlike Berlusconi and Renzi, who have consistently been against the judicialisation of politics). In other words, in the *MoVimento 5 Stelle*'s rhetoric the law became part of a strategy, 'a way of concealing political behaviour'.[181]

[175] F. Grandesso, 'Black Smoke for Bersani, Dangerous Games for Italy!', 7 March 2013, www .neweurope.eu/article/black-smoke-bersani-dangerous-games-italy/.

[176] M. Musso, M. Maccaferri, 'At the origins of the political discourse of the 5-Star Movement (M5S): Internet, direct democracy and the "future of the past"', *Journal Internet Histories: Digital Technology, Culture and Society*, Nos. 1–2, 2018, 98.

[177] F. Tronconi, The Italian Five Star Movement during the Crisis: Towards Normalisation? *South European Society and Politics*, Vo. 23, No. 1, 2018, 163. C. Biancalana (eds.), *Disintermediazione e nuove forme di mediazione. Verso una democrazia post-rappresentativa?*, Feltrinelli, Milan, 2018.

[178] 'The Movimento 5 Stelle, despite the strong relevance of Grillo's figure, initially opposed any form of personalisation: the rhetoric of the Movement states that inside the M5S there are no leaders and "one equals one". However, from 2013 onwards, some parliamentarians have acquired visibility, starting to erode Grillo's media-wise and organisational hegemony', in P. Blokker, M. Anselmi (eds.), *Multiple Populisms: Italy as Democracy's Mirror*, Routledge, Abingdon, 2020, 229.

[179] However, Di Battista recently announced his intention to leave the Five Star Movement after the Movement's decision to support the Draghi government.

[180] 'Whereas with the term "populism" we qualify the ideology of a political movement, its "penal" qualification should correspond to a populist political movement whose main political programme is the achievement of justice through punishment and sanctions, which would be absurd even in the worst dystopian world. Criminal law and its use are indeed contents with a high symbolic value; however, they remain instruments, not objectives, of any idea of justice', S. Anastasia, M. Anselmi, 'Penal Populism in the Multi-populist Context of Italy', P. Blokker, M. Anselmi (eds.), *Multiple Populisms: Italy as Democracy's Mirror*, Routledge, Abingdon, 2020, 164, 166. See also N. Selvaggi, 'Populism and Criminal Justice in Italy', in G. Delledonne, G. Martinico, M. Monti, F. Pacini (eds.), *Italian Populism and Constitutional Law: Strategies, Conflicts and Dilemmas*, Palgrave, London, 2020, 291 and, from a different perspective, L. Manconi, F. Graziani, *Per il tuo bene ti mozzerò la testa. Contro il giustizialismo morale*, Einaudi, Turin, 2020.

[181] Corso, 'When Anti-Politics Becomes Political', 466.

3

Mimetism and Parasitism in Action: Sovereignism and Identity Politics versus Post–World War II Constitutional Openness

In this chapter, I will analyse a case study that is crucial to exploring the way in which populists understand identity politics, while in subsequent chapters, I will investigate the perspective of politics of immediacy. The concepts of mimetism and parasitism presented in Chapter 1 will be tested, and the notion of sovereignism ('sovranismo') – frequently alluded to in the Italian debate and elsewhere – will be used as a case study. This combination between populism and sovereignism[1] has been labelled 'PopSovism':

> The populist component of PopSovism [populist sovereignism] puts itself on the side of 'the people', defined as a country's native ethno-cultural group(s), which must be defended against both national and transnational 'elites' and against other 'outsiders' such as immigrants. Its sovereignist component advocates a return to an international order in which the nation-state, guided by the self-identified interests of the native ethno-cultural population, maintains or re-asserts sovereign control over its laws, institutions, and the terms of its international interactions. Supra- or inter-national actors and global market forces are seen as restrictions on the nation-state that should be reduced and/or opposed.[2]

One of the few elements that *Lega* and *MoVimento 5 Stelle* share is an evident anti-Europeanism that presents itself in different forms. Sovereignism is one of these forms.[3] For the purpose of this chapter, I shall briefly recall the roots of the debate on

---

[1] On the broader issue of the relationship between populism and nationalism see: Benjamin de Cleen, 'Populism and Nationalism' in C. Rovira Kaltwasser, P. Taggart, P. Ochoa Espejo, P. Ostiguy (eds.), *The Oxford Handbook of Populism*, Oxford University Press, 2017, 342.

[2] S. De Spiegeleire, C. Skinner, T. Sweijs, *The Rise of Populist Sovereignism: What It Is, Where It Comes From and What It Means for International Security and Defense*, The Hague Centre for Strategic Studies (HCSS), 2017, https://bit.ly/3gFmMMg.

[3] The success of sovereignism in Italy can be partly explained in light of the links allegedly existing between Russia and the *Lega* and due to the key role played by Gianluca Savoini, who is the former spokesperson of Matteo Salvini and is involved in the Russiagate scandal that exploded in 2019. Savoini is frequently accused of having fed the racist extremism within the *Lega*, due to his close connection

sovereignism and subsequently identify analogies in the Hungarian and Italian contexts. Finally, I will look at how populists manipulate the relevant provisions of the Italian Constitution and combine this mimetism and parasitism to construct a dichotomous relationship between the constitution and the EU treaties. Vladislav Yuryevich Surkov is commonly referred as the mastermind behind the invention and dissemination of the concept of sovereignism. Make no mistake, when developing his argument, he built upon a longer debate in Russia; although the starting point of this discussion is frequently dated back to 2006,[4] he actually did not use 'sovereignism' in his interventions at that time.[5] Rather, he adopted the concept of sovereign democracy[6] that later inspired the Christian democracy employed by the Hungarian Prime Minister Orbán.[7]

In 2009, Surkov wrote an article in English where he outlined the pillars of his thinking.[8] It is interesting to note that one of the first arguments he mentioned was the consistency of his concept with the constitutional wording:

> The idea of sovereign democracy in Russia is consistent with the provisions of the Constitution, according to which: first, 'the bearer of sovereignty and the sole source of power in the Russian Federation shall be its multiethnic people'; second, 'no one may usurp power in the Russian Federation'.[9]

On this basis, he defined sovereign democracy as 'a mode of the political life of society in which the state authorities, their bodies and actions are elected, formed, and directed exclusively by the Russian nation in all its unity and diversity for the sake of achieving material well-being, freedom, and justice for all the citizens, social groups, and peoples that constitute it'.[10]

---

with Maurizio Murelli, former neo-fascist who spent eleven years in jail and later founded Orion, a far-right think tank. On this story, see: C. Gatti, *I demoni di Salvini. I postnazisti e la Lega Milano*, Chiarelettere, Milan, 2019. To respond to the allegations concerning this connection between post-Nazisim and the *Lega*, Murelli himself and Rainaldo Graziani, the son of Clemente Graziani (founder of *Ordine Nuovo*, an extreme right-wing organisation involved in some terrorist activities in the 1970s) released a series of interviews in 2019. They are available on YouTube at the following link: www.youtube.com/watch?v=-ozKImwqybY&feature=emb_title. Murelli has openly admitted to looking at the *Lega* as the ideal lab to develop his ideas.

4 V. Zorkin, 'Bukva i duch Konstitucii, in Rossijskaja Gazeta', 9 October 2018, www.rg.ru/2018/10/09/zorkin-nedostatki-v-konstitucii-mozhno-ustranit-tochechnymi-izmeneniiami.html, cited by A. Di Gregorio, 'La Russia e le elezioni europee', 2019, www.federalismi.it/nv14/articolo-documento.cfm?Artid=38721.

5 Di Gregorio, 'La Russia e le elezioni europee'.

6 I. Krastev, '"Sovereign Democracy", Russian-Style', *Insight Turkey*, No. 4, 2006, 113.

7 F. Delfino, 'La democrazia "illiberale": il modello di democrazia "sovrana" in Russia e di democrazia "Cristiana" in Ungheria. Origini, similitudini e divergenze', *Nuovi Autoritarismi e Democrazie* (NAD), No. 2, 2019, 1.

8 V. I. Surkov, 'Nationalization of the Future: Paragraphs pro Sovereign Democracy', *Russian Studies in Philosophy*, No. 4, 2009, 8. On the concept of illiberal democracy, see F. Zakaria, 'The Rise of Illiberal Democracy', No. 6, *Foreign Affairs*, 1997, 22, 3.

9 Surkov, 'Nationalization', 8–9.

10 Surkov, 'Nationalization', 9.

Against this background, globalisation[11] is seen as a threat, since: 'The global fruits of enlightenment (economic, informational, and military instruments of globalisation), by their very existence, produce not only the hope of universal prosperity but also the temptation of global domination'.[12]

Surkov went on to attack the European Union. It is convenient to quote this passage as it was recalled by Italian sovereignists:

> People cite the European Union as an example of giving up sovereignty for the great virtues. They forget the hitch about the European Constitution (which assumedly can be overcome). They also overlook that what is involved is either the establishment of a stable association of sovereign states or (in the boldest dreams) the synthesis of a multiethnic European nation and its, so to say, all-union sovereignty, by whichever politically correct euphemisms it may be designated.[13]

For Surkov, Putin has managed to ensure stability against international pressures and centrifugal forces thanks to a direct relationship with the Russian people[14] and to the hierarchical system inherited from the Soviet tradition.[15] Another key figure is that of Aleksandr Dugin, author of an influential book in this debate in which he argued that 'Social justice, national sovereignty and traditional values are the three main principles of the Fourth Political Theory'.[16] By fourth political theory, he refers to a theory that recalls and goes beyond what he calls 'three main political theories of the past – liberalism, Marxism (socialism) and fascism (National Socialism)'.[17] His theory combines Heidegger, esoterism and a strong criticism of Western universalism. His thinking reveals an important element shared by populists, namely the need to go beyond the distinction between right and left. Apart from that, Dugin[18] is also among the first members of the National Bolshevik Party founded by Eduard Limonov. His relationship with Putin is not clear; in the past, he criticised Putin but currently he is seen as one of the main ideologists supporting him. He left the National Bolshevik Party before the party was banned. Putin is frequently portrayed as the strong man who has impeded the rise of the oligarchs. Putin himself, in a famous interview released to the *Financial Times*, has defined liberalism as

---

[11] On the relationship between globalisation and populism, see: D. Rodrik, 'Why Does Globalization Fuel Populism? Economics, Culture, and the Rise of Right-Wing Populism', 2020, https://drodrik .scholar.harvard.edu/publications/why-does-globalization-fuel-populism-economics-culture-and-rise-right-wing.

[12] Surkov, 'Nationalization', 11.

[13] Surkov, 'Nationalization', 12.

[14] Di Gregorio clearly explains the use of the notion of 'deep people' as opposed to 'deep state' in Surkov: Di Gregorio, 'La Russia e le elezioni europee', 12–13. On this see also: L. Bershidsky, 'Putin Ally's "Deep State" Twist Is Deep Russian People', 12 February 2019, www.bloomberg.com/opinion/articles/ 2019-02-12/russia-has-its-own-deep-state-it-s-called-deep-people.

[15] Delfino, 'La democrazia "illiberale"', 8.

[16] A. Dugin, *The Fourth Political Theory*, Arktos, London, 2012, 196.

[17] Dugin, *The Fourth Political Theory*, 35.

[18] On Dugin see: F. Veiga, C. González-Villa, S. Forti, A. Sasso, J. Prokopljevic, R. Moles, *Patriotas indignados*, Alianza, Madrid, 2019, 107.

obsolete. To his mind, instead of reassuring citizens, liberal governments have denied traditional values, insisting too much on multiculturalism and sexual diversity, and in his view, 'this must not be allowed to overshadow the culture, traditions and traditional family values of millions of people making up the core population'.[19]

Putin has many followers in Italy. Diego Fusaro, a philosopher, has described Putin as a positive figure struggling to resist the Western turbo-capitalistic and imperialistic view of the world, as an emblematic character necessary to regain multipolarity and diversity against 'the thalassocratic monarchy of the dollar' (*monarchia talassocratica del dollaro*).[20]

3.2 THE EU AND THE NEW WAVE OF POPULISMS

For sovereignists, the EU is the emblem of a post-sovereign power that should be avoided and of which Russia is a competitor; it is an obstacle in the path towards the emergence of a Russian international leadership. It is also a 'civilian power',[21] which is not compatible with the idea of sovereign democracy that emphasises the importance of military power, especially in Putin's rhetoric. For Hungarian and Italian sovereignists, the EU is also the source of a dangerous homogenisation that affects traditional values and national identity. The Hungarian scenario is very telling of this. Scholars have stressed the ambivalent relationship between Viktor Orbán and Russia, making a distinction between the pre- and post-2010 re-election.[22] Indeed, their view on Russia is probably one of the most evident differences between Poland and Hungary. To understand Orbán's view on Christian democracy and on the role of the EU, it is useful to analyse the text of a speech he gave in 2019:

> International interpretation can best be summed up in the claim that what must operate in the world are liberal democracies – especially in Europe. These must construct and implement a kind of liberal internationalism, from which a liberal empire must emerge. The European Union is none other than an embodiment of

---

[19] L. Barber, H. Foy, A. Baker, 'Vladimir Putin: Liberalism Has "Outlived Its Purpose"', *Financial Times*, 28 June 2019, www.ft.com/content/670039ec-98f3-11e9-9573-ee5cbb98ed36. For an idea of how Putin understands international law, see: V. Putin, 'Speech and the Following Discussion at the Munich Conference on Security Policy', given in Munich in 2007, http://en.kremlin.ru/events/president/transcripts/24034.

[20] D. Fusaro, *Glebalizzazione. La lotta di classe al tempo del populismo*, Rizzoli, Milan, 2019, 7, my own translation.

[21] M. Telò, *Europe: A Civilian Power? European Union, Global Governance*, World Order, Palgrave, London, 2006.

[22] Delfino, 'La democrazia "illiberale"', 12–13.

this; but under the Democrats, under President Obama, the United States conceived of something like this on a global scale. Seen from here it is obvious that what is happening in Hungary is very different: it is something else. Hungary is doing something different, creating something different [. . .] liberal democracy was viable up until the point when it departed from its Christian foundations. For as long as it protected personal liberty and property it had a beneficial effect on humanity. But the content of liberal democracy changed radically when it began to break the bonds that bind people to real life: when it questioned the identity of a person's sex, devalued people's religious identity, and deemed people's national affiliation superfluous. And the truth is that in Europe over the past twenty or thirty years this has become the spirit of the age.[23]

According to these lines, liberalism undermines traditional values, in particular Christian ones, and the EU has become part of this plot. Hungary must preserve its special nature and culture; in other words, its identity.[24] With regard to Russia, Di Gregorio[25] interestingly pointed out that this is a concept frequently recalled by the president of the Russian Constitutional Court, Valery Dmitrievich Zorkin, who has stressed the democratic deficit of international organisations, including the Council of Europe, and the need to preserve national sovereignty. Recently, constitutional courts have come under siege, with scholars criticising them for their abuse of the national (or, according to another terminology, constitutional)[26] identity argument. In this sense, Halmai[27] has also blamed the German *Bundesverfassungsgericht* (German Constitutional Court) for providing other constitutional courts (namely the Hungarian one) with a problematic series of techniques by provoking a worrying (even dangerous in his mind) escalation of constitutional conflict. Moreover, constitutional pluralists have been accused of offering arguments to autocrats and populists to justify violations of the values set out in Article 2 of the Treaty on European Union

[23] Prime Minister Viktor Orbán's speech at the 30th Bálványos Summer Open University and Student Camp, 28 July 2019, in www.kormany.hu/en/the-prime-minister/the-prime-minister-s-speeches/prime-minister-viktor-orban-s-speech-at-the-30th-balvanyos-summer-open-university-and-student-camp.

[24] 'Populists, too, understand constitutional identity in the sense of sameness. However, they do not only claim that both authors and addressees of the constitution should be understood as one and the same (which is something most democrats also do). Instead, the populist understanding of the identity of the people is reductive in the sense that it tends to narrow down identity to sameness and radicalise this notion', L. Corrias, 'Populism in a Constitutional Key: Constituent Power, Popular Sovereignty and Constitutional Identity', *European Constitutional Law Review*, No. 1, 2016, 6, 23.

[25] Di Gregorio, 'La Russia e le elezioni europee'. She commented upon an interview given by Zorkin. The interview in Russian can be found at the following link: 'Bukva i duch Konstitucii', 9 October 2018, www.rg.ru/2018/10/09/zorkinnedostatki-v-konstitucii-mozhno-ustranit-tochechnymi-izmeneniiami.html.

[26] For instance, E. Cloots, National Identity in EU Law, Hart, Oxford, 2015, 163 and G. Di Federico, *L'identità nazionale degli stati membri nel diritto dell'Unione europea. Natura e portata dell'art. 4, par. 2, TUE*, Editoriale Scientifica, Naples, 2017, 15.

[27] G. Halmai, 'Abuse of Constitutional Identity. The Hungarian Constitutional Court on Interpretation of Article E (2) of the Fundamental Law', *Review of Central and East European Law*, No. 1, 2018, 23.

(TEU).[28] It is interesting to see how the Hungarian Constitutional Court manipulated the concept of national identity stemming from Article 4 TEU by reading it as an isolated concept, and how it construed it in light of its own concept of constitutional identity. This case is a perfect example of how mimetism and parasitism have been employed to justify a claim that is against the very essence of the EU treaties:

> According to Article 4 (2) TEU, 'the Union shall respect the equality of Member States before the Treaties as well as their national identities, inherent in their fundamental structures, political and constitutional, inclusive of regional and local self-government.' The protection of constitutional identity should be granted in the framework of an – informal cooperation with EUC based on the principles of equality and collegiality, with mutual respect to each other, similarly to the present practice followed by several other Member States' constitutional courts and supreme judicial bodies performing similar functions. The Constitutional Court of Hungary interprets the concept of constitutional identity as Hungary's self-identity and it unfolds the content of this concept from case to case, on the basis of the whole Fundamental Law and certain provisions thereof, in accordance with the National Avowal and the achievements of our historical constitution – as required by Article R) (3) of the Fundamental Law. The Constitutional Court establishes that the constitutional self-identity of Hungary is a fundamental value not created by the Fundamental Law – it is merely acknowledged by the Fundamental Law. Consequently, constitutional identity cannot be waived by way of an international treaty – Hungary can only be deprived of its constitutional identity through the final termination of its sovereignty, its independent statehood. **Therefore the protection of constitutional identity shall remain the duty of the Constitutional Court as long as Hungary is a sovereign State. Accordingly, sovereignty and constitutional identity have several common points, thus their control should be performed with due regard to each other in specific cases** [emphasis added].[29]

Here, the Hungarian Constitutional Court first started with Article 4.2 TEU (which employs the concept of national identity). Second, it used the concept of constitutional identity, coupling it with the preservation of sovereignty (a term which is not used in Art. 4.2 TEU). Third, it read the concept of constitutional identity in light of Article R.3, thus offering an alternative reading of the same concept.

In so doing, the Hungarian Constitutional Court completely disregarded the fact that in Article 4 TEU, national identity must be read in system with the concept of loyal cooperation stemming from paragraph 3. In other words, the alternative reading of constitutional identity offered by the Hungarian Constitutional Court is in patent conflict with the meaning of Article 4.2 TEU invoked by the Hungarian

---

[28] R. D. Kelemen, L. Pech, 'Why Autocrats Love Constitutional Identity and Constitutional Pluralism. Lessons from Hungary and Poland', *Reconnect Working Paper* No. 2, 2018, https://reconnect-europe.eu/wp-content/uploads/2018/10/RECONNECT-WorkingPaper2-Kelemen-Pech-LP-KO.pdf.

[29] Hungarian Constitutional Court, Decision 22/2016, https://hunconcourt.hu/dontes/decision-22-2016-on-joint-excercise-of-competences-with-the-eu/, paras. 62–6, emphasis added.

judges. This example shows how instrumental and selective the populist under-standing of the relevant EU law provision is.

After the judgment, the notion of constitutional identity was codified in the Hungarian Constitution in 2018 with the approval of the seventh amendment. Now Article R.4 reads: 'The protection of the constitutional identity and Christian culture of Hungary shall be an obligation of every organ of the State.'[30] The latest developments and the reaction to the spread of the COVID-19 virus have reinforced the authoritarian nature of the Hungarian system, making the picture even more complex.[31]

Orbán has often been seen as a role model by Salvini, and there are similarities, especially looking at their migration policy and the way the EU is blamed for migration flows. It is, however, interesting to look at three Italian intellectual figures who have championed sovereignism: Paolo Becchi, Luciano Barra Caracciolo and Giuseppe Valditara. A premise is necessary: we are in a phase characterised by a return of sovereignty as a general category, as the recent works by Carlo Galli,[32] among others, show.[33] Galli himself, at a certain point in his book, argues that the search for sovereignty is both a reaction against an economy that brings crisis and an attempt to build a new order.[34]

Before moving ahead, it is worth underlining the strange absence of the concept of 'motherland' (*patria*) – also invoked by Article 52 of the constitution – in Italian populist discourse. A partial exception is represented by the reference to Article 52 of the constitution[35] made by Salvini and Meloni with regard to the burning issue of migration, in particular before and after the Senate's decision to allow the prosecution of Salvini over a migrant ship blockade[36] he orchestrated when he served as interior minister. The argument here is that populists have the duty to protect their homeland and identity against the alleged threats posed by immigrants. Of course, this kind of approach completely neglects the duties that the Italian Republic has under international law.[37]

[30]   Article Q.4 of the Hungarian Constitution, www.kormany.hu/download/f/3e/61000/ TheFundamentalLawofHungary_20180629_FIN.pdf.
[31]   Starting with Act XII of 2020 of March 31, 2020, 'On Protecting Against the Coronavirus', https://drive .google.com/file/d/1GQjupog_8x5YwG9ARZ9ZV3GVawvp6Zqd/view; K. Scheppele, 'Orban's Emergency', 2020, https://verfassungsblog.de/orbans-emergency/; L. Livingston, 'Understanding Hungary's Authoritarian Response to the Pandemic', 2020, www.lawfareblog.com/understanding-hungarys-authoritarian-response-pandemic.
[32]   Carlo Galli is an eminent Professor of History of Political Thought at the University of Bologna.
[33]   C. Galli, *Sovranità*, Il Mulino, Bologna, 2019.
[34]   Galli, *Sovranità*, 128.
[35]   Article 52 of the Italian Constitution: 'Defence of the motherland is a sacred duty for every citizen. Military service is obligatory within the limits and in the manner set by law. Its fulfilment shall not prejudice a citizen's job, nor the exercise of their political rights.
      The organisation of the armed forces shall be based on the democratic spirit of the Republic'.
[36]   'Salvini per difendersi cita a sproposito la Costituzione: "La difesa della Patria è sacro dovere di ogni cittadino"', 4 February 2020, https://bit.ly/3gL1qMm.
[37]   A. Palm, L. Barana, 'Italy's Migration Policy: A Self-Defeating Approach Spells Marginalisation in Europe', 2019, www.iai.it/en/pubblicazioni/italys-migration-policy-self-defeating-approach-spells-marginalisation-europe; S. Penasa, 'The Italian Way to Migration: Was It "True" Populism? Populist

3.3 EUROPEAN LAW IN SOVEREIGNIST TIMES

Sovereignism implies a sharp critique of the European project and the current economic paradigm but risks not delivering when it comes to proposing an alternative plan.[38] Having clarified this, the first author I will mention is Paolo Becchi, Professor of Legal Philosophy at the University of Genova. Becchi has authored different works devoted to sovereignism,[39] and has been very close to the *MoVimento 5 Stelle* first, and more recently, to the *Lega*.[40] Becchi wrote, among other things, a volume entitled *Manifesto Sovranista* ('Sovereignist Manifesto'), in which one can find all the recurring elements of Italian sovereignism, including its evident anti-EU flavour. The EU is portrayed as a part of that homogenising globalisation that we have already seen when analysing the Russian context. It is often defined as an expression of a 'global elite' against the peoples.[41] According to this reconstruction, the EU has enslaved the European peoples. Becchi's sovereignism is different from the old sovereignism because it is not nationalist.[42] Indeed, his sovereignism is described as pro-European, since it stands for a Europe which should be understood as different from the European Union.[43] The subtitle of his book is 'For the liberation of the European peoples' and he drafted a charter of the rights of the European peoples[44] in one of the chapters. Another important element is the obsession with plot and conspiracy that characterises the whole book. According to Becchi, the euro was the product of a *coup d'état*; Becchi himself wrote a book entitled *Colpo di Stato permanente* ('Permanent coup d'état'[45]) in which he argues that Italian membership of the EU was based on a manipulation of Article 11 of the Italian Constitution. Becchi entitles the last part of his *Manifesto* 'The European Union and Italy: the legal reconstruction of an enslavement'[46] in which he denounces the alleged misinterpretation of Article 11 of the Italian Constitution. In his view, compared to the mechanisms envisaged by countries such as Germany, Italy had one main issue, which was the absence of an explicit clause devoted to its relationship with the EU.[47] For Becchi, it is possible to argue from the preparatory works of the Constituent Assembly that the founding fathers wanted to explicitly exclude membership of the European integration

Policies as Constitutional Antigens' in G. Delledonne, G. Martinico, M. Monti, F. Pacini (eds.), *Italian Populism and Constitutional Law. Strategies, Conflicts and Dilemmas*, Palgrave, London, 2020, 255.

[38] Galli, *Sovranità*, 144.
[39] P. Becchi, *Italia sovrana*, Sperling & Kupfer, Milan, 2018; P. Becchi, *Manifesto sovranista: per la liberazione dei popoli europei*, Giubilei Regnani, Cesena, 2019.
[40] Matteo Salvini himself authored the preface to a volume that Becchi wrote with Giuseppe Palma: P. Becchi, G. Palma, *Dalla Seconda alla Terza Repubblica. Come nasce il governo Lega-M5S*, Paesi edizioni, Rome, 2018.
[41] Becchi, *Manifesto sovranista*, 9, 19.
[42] Becchi, *Manifesto sovranista*, 8–9.
[43] Becchi, *Manifesto sovranista*, 21.
[44] Becchi, *Manifesto sovranista*, 31–39.
[45] Becchi, *Colpo di Stato permanente: Cronache degli ultimi tre anni*, Marsilio, Venice, 2014.
[46] Becchi, *Manifesto sovranista*, 101.
[47] Becchi, *Manifesto sovranista*, 111.

project from the scope of Article 11.[48] He derives this interpretation from the exchange between two members of the Constituent Assembly, Emilio Lussu and Aldo Moro.[49] This reading of the Italian Constitution is manipulative and historically and profoundly wrong. First of all, when the European Coal and Steel Community (ECSC) was set up, there were no explicit constitutional provisions in the founding Member States devoted to it. As in Italy, the German Constitutional Court admitted direct effect and primacy on the basis of constitutional provisions generally devoted to the international community. In this sense, the only difference between Italy and Germany is that Germany was faster in amending its Basic Law to include an explicit reference to the European Communities (now Art. 23 of the German Basic Law) as it did in 1992, while Italy did so in 2001. But in both countries, the local constitutional courts accepted the structural principles of Community law much earlier by reading their constitutional clauses devoted to the international community broadly (in Germany Art. 24, in Italy Art. 11). This happened because of the simple fact that the entry into force of the European Treaties happened later than the entry into force of these two national constitutions. The same thing happened in other Member States. The second erroneous point in Becchi's reconstruction regards the exchange between Lussu and Moro, a brief exchange in which Moro clarified that there was no need to include Europe in the wording of Article 11 because it was too early to constitutionalise a reference to a possible European federation or confederation, and because the wording of Article 11 was already broad enough to cover it.[50] Here, one can find the cherry picking and manipulative approach that characterises the mimetic strategy employed by populists.

The point that membership of the Eurozone can be seen as a possible *coup d'état* deserves further discussion, since it is shared by Barra Caracciolo.[51] Becchi recalls an old academic article written by an eminent public law scholar and former minister for finance, Giuseppe Guarino.[52] In his article, Guarino argued that the entry into force of the euro was based on an invalid regulation, namely regulation 1466/1997, which was in conflict with the European Treaties, namely with Article 104C of the Treaty of the European Union (TEU).[53] This regulation governed the strengthening

---

[48] Becchi, *Manifesto sovranista*, 126.

[49] Becchi, *Manifesto sovranista*, 126.

[50] Here you can find the mini-report of the relevant working session of the Constituent Assembly held on 24 January 1947: www.nascitacostituzione.it/01principi/011/index.htm?art011-003.htm&2.

[51] As we will see, this is an idea present even in the thinking of left-wing sovereignists, see for instance: M. Rizzo, *Il golpe europeo. I comunisti contro l'Unione*, Baldini Castoldi Dalai, Milan, 2012.

[52] Becchi, *Manifesto sovranista*, 132.

[53] 'The 60% debt rule and the 3% deficit rule are long established. They constitute one of the four "Convergence Criteria" contained in the Maastricht Treaty, which came into effect on 1 November 1993. The Convergence criteria are criteria that European Union Member States have to fulfill in order to adopt the euro as their currency. Article 104c of the Maastricht Treaty also states "Member States shall avoid excessive government deficits". The Maastricht Treaty also requires that Member States exercise "compliance with budgetary discipline on the basis of the following two criteria: (a) whether the ratio of the planned or actual government deficit to gross domestic product

of the surveillance of budgetary positions and the surveillance and coordination of economic policies. The argument is very technical, but it can be summed up as follows: Regulation 1466/1997 is a legal source that may not breach the EU treaties which represent 'the basic constitutional charter'[54] of the EU. For Guarino 'the rules laid down in the Regulation are different from, indeed opposed to, those of the Treaty',[55] because 'the Treaty sets an objective for growth in accordance with Article 2, whose attainment is entrusted to the economic policies of the individual member states, each of which was to take account of the concrete, specific conditions of its own economy'.[56] According to Guarino 'the regulation abolishes all this. The Member State's economic policies are cancelled. As a consequence, every possible contribution by Member States is cancelled'.[57] On this basis, Guarino concluded that this regulation suppressed democracy by producing a 'coup d'état'.[58]

This debate has had no echo beyond Italy[59] and, in spite of this theory, Regulation 1466/1997 has never been declared invalid despite the fact that EU law gives remedies to challenge it. This thesis has been retrieved to attack the so-called

exceeds a reference value [...] (b) whether the ratio of government debt to gross domestic product exceeds a reference value [...] The reference values are specified in the Protocol on the excessive deficit procedure annexed to this Treaty". The reference values are the 60% debt rule and the 3% deficit rule. These rules were further advanced four years later in the Stability and Growth Pact (SGP). The SGP was a set of agreements made in 1997 between the Member States of the EU. It has since been substantially developed. The aim of the SGP was to ensure that the economies of the EU remained in healthy fiscal positions. It was believed that this was necessary for the stability of the Euro, which was to be introduced two years later. The two main provisions of the SGP were, once again, that countries should have a budget deficit no higher than 3% of GDP and a debt to GDP ratio no higher than 60% of GDP. The SGP was set out in a European Council resolution in June 1997 and in two major pieces of legislation: regulations[ii] 1466/1997 and 1467/1997. Regulation 1466/1997 is known as the Stability and Growth Pact's "preventative arm" because it sets out a multilateral surveillance system through which a country's budgetary positions are observed in order to prevent countries from developing deficits greater than 3% of GDP or debt to GDP ratios greater than 60%. A significant part of this is that it requires each country to specify a medium term budgetary objective. Regulation 1467/1997 is known as the Stability and Growth Pact's "corrective arm" because it sets out how a country should correct their fiscal position if they have deficits greater than 3% of GDP or debt to GDP ratios greater than 60%. It provides for an "excessive deficit procedure" that should be implemented if countries are not achieving the aims of the SGP', O. Gilmore, 'Ratification of ESM Treaty Moves One Step Closer', 2012, http://oisingilmore.com/tag/iiea/.

[54] CJEU, 294/83, Les Verts ECLI:EU:C:1986:166, para. 23.
[55] G. Guarino, 'The "Truth" About Europe and the Euro. A Second Essay', *Nomos. Le attualità del diritto*, No. 2, 2014, 25, 32.
[56] Guarino, 'The "Truth" About Europe and the Euro', 33.
[57] Guarino, 'The "Truth" About Europe and the Euro', 33.
[58] 'Technically speaking, the suppression of democracy can be termed "the de facto installation of a new regime," which is an even graver violation than what we call a "coup d'état". To deprive a complex community of its democratic regime is a hazardous, perilous operation. Regulation 1466 managed the trick in a simple if unforeseeable manner', Guarino, 'The "Truth" About Europe and the Euro', 37.
[59] For a synthesis of this debate, see: M. Baldassarri, 'The Resilient Governance of the EU: Towards a Post-democratic Society' in M. Baldassarri, E. Castelli, M. Truffeli, G. Vezzani, *Anti-Europeanism Critical Perspectives Towards the European Union*, Springer, Berlin, 2020, 77.

'Fiscal Compact', formally called the Treaty on Stability, Coordination and Governance in the Economic and Monetary Union (TSCG).

A premise should be made for non-European readers. At the beginning of March 2012, twenty-five European leaders signed the new TSCG – which represents just one of the links in a longer chain of measures adopted to fight the EU crisis. These measures include the creation of the European Financial Stability Facility (EFSF), the European Financial Stabilisation Mechanism (EFSM), the Euro Plus Pact, the amendment of Article 136 of the TFEU, the European Stability Mechanism (ESM) and the so-called six and two packs,[60] among others.[61] With these measures, the EU intended to deal with different aspects of the crisis and tried to establish a new integrated surveillance system for budgetary and economic policies and a new budgetary timeline. The surveillance system calls for clearer rules and better coordination of national policies and allows for swifter sanctions. All of the measures run in parallel. Some of them are part of the EU legal order (e.g., six pack, two pack), while others are external to it; some of them are interdependent (in some aspects, the six pack and the TSCG), while others are not (for instance, generally speaking, the Euro Plus Pact is more about competitiveness, while the TSCG is more about austerity). This explains why some Member States participate in some of these actions without necessarily taking part in the others. This emphasis on austerity has indirectly been feeding sovereignism.[62]

Article 3.2 of the 'Fiscal Compact' (TSCG) provides for the necessity of States to codify the budget rule in national law 'through provisions of binding force and permanent character, preferably constitutional, or otherwise guaranteed to be fully respected and adhered to'. From a formal point of view external to EU law, since it is a treaty signed by some of the EU Member States, it is an *inter-se agreement*, an instrument frequently used in European law.[63] Its nature does not exclude the need for compatibility with EU law and, indeed, soon after the entry into force of this treaty there was a debate on whether this last provision (Art. 3.2) is inconsistent with Article 4.2 of the TEU, which states – as we saw while dealing with the Hungarian

---

[60] The so-called six pack is composed of five Regulations (Regulations 1173/2011, 1174/2011, 1175/2011, 1176/2011 and 1177/2011) and one Directive (Directive 2011/85). The two pack is composed of two Regulations (Regulation 472/2013 and 473/2013).

[61] On this 'jungle' of measures, see: G. Bianco, 'The New Financial Stability Mechanisms and Their (Poor) Consistency with EU Law', EUI RSCAS 2012/44, 2012, http://cadmus.eui.eu/handle/1814/23428.

[62] On this, see: F. Bignami, *EU Law in Populist Times*, Cambridge University Press, 2019. In particular, the Introduction (F. Bignami, 'Introduction. EU Law Sovereignty and Populism', 3); the chapter by R. Dehousse, 'The Euro Crisis and the Transformation of the European Political System', 134; and the chapter by B. Bugarič, 'The Populist Backlash against Europe', 477. For an influential and critical evaluation of austerity, see W. Streeck, *Buying Time: The Delayed Crisis of Democratic Capitalism*, Verso Books, London, 2014.

[63] B. De Witte, 'Using International Law in the Euro Crisis: Causes and Consequences', ARENA Working Paper, 4/2013 Oslo, 2013, www.sv.uio.no/arena/english/research/publications/arena-working-papers/2013/wp4-13.pdf.

case – the necessity to respect the national identity and constitutional structure of EU Member States. Note that Article 2 of the TSCG concerns the relationship with EU law and reaffirms the precedence of EU law over the treaty, a point which is present in many other parts of the treaty.[64] However, the fact that only a minority of Member States have amended their constitution to codify such a rule shows that this was only a theoretical debate.[65]

The argument made by Professor Guarino was also brought to the attention of the European parliament and the Commission by Claudio Morganti, then a member of the European parliament (for *Lega Nord* at that time), who recalled the essays by Guarino in two written questions.[66] The president of the Commission officially responded on 6 February 2013 by saying:

The main contention of the essay quoted by the Honorable Member is that the preventive part of the SGP and the Fiscal Compact, by introducing the obligation for MS to attain and maintain a medium-term budgetary objective (MTO), in principle more demanding than the deficit reference value of 3%, exceed what could be legally required. The Commission does not share this assessment. The balanced budget rule provides for a balanced medium term budgetary objective to guarantee the 3% limit *ex ante*. The first aim of the MTO is thus precisely that of providing an adequate safety margin against the breaching of the deficit reference value. In other words, and consistent with the wording of the Treaty, the deficit reference value should not be intended as an objective but a limit that should not be trespassed under normal cyclical fluctuations. This demands that MS pursue an objective that, taking into account normal cyclical fluctuations, should be more

---

[64] For instance, Article 3 of the TSCG reads that the Fiscal Compact is to be applied 'Without prejudice to the obligations derived from European Union law'; Article 7 of the TSCG, concerning sanctions for states in excessive deficit procedure, is applicable 'while fully respecting the procedural requirements of the European Union Treaties'. A similar reference to EU law contained in Article 10 on enhanced cooperation applies 'In accordance with the requirements of the European Union Treaties'. In this respect one should also take into account Article 5.2 TEU: 'the Union shall act only within the limits of the competences conferred upon it by the Member States in the Treaties to attain the objectives set out therein' and Article 13.2 TEU: 'Each institution shall act within the limits of the powers conferred on it in the Treaties, and in conformity with the procedures, conditions and objectives set out in them'.

[65] 'Article 3.2. of the Treaty on Stability, Coordination and Governance in the Economic and Monetary Union, (hereinafter, Fiscal Compact) creates an obligation, at least for the Contracting Parties within the Euro area, to adopt a balanced budget rule "through provisions of binding force and permanent character, preferably constitutional, or otherwise guaranteed to be fully respected and adhered to throughout the national budgetary processes", by one year after its entry into force on 1 January 2013. However, only a minority of eurozone countries (like Italy and Spain) have constitutionalised the balanced budget clause, which means that a constitutional reform was an option but was not mandatory', C. Fasone, 'Constitutional Courts Facing the Euro Crisis. Italy, Portugal and Spain in a Comparative Perspective', Max Weber Programme MWP 2014/25, 2014, cadmus.eui.eu/bitstream/handle/1814/33859/MWP_WP_2014_25.pdf.

[66] See the written questions presented by Hon. Member Claudio Morganti available at the following links: www.europarl.europa.eu/sides/getDoc.do?pubRef=-//EP//TEXT+WQ+E-2012-010892+0+DOC+XML+V0//EN and www.europarl.europa.eu/sides/getDoc.do?pubRef=-//EP//TEXT+OQ+O-2013-000075+0+DOC+XML+V0//EN.

demanding than the reference value. Otherwise, at least in the negative phase of the cycle, it could be expected that MS would breach the reference value, which is clearly in contradiction with the Treaty.[67]

This debate confirms the particular nature of this new wave of populism in Europe as compared to what is happening elsewhere. The financial crisis and the response of the EU (by means of both EU law measures and international treaties signed by some of its Member States) has favoured the success of these movements and has made the EU an easy target for them, facilitating, among other things, the emergence of sovereignism.

This idea of 'stolen democracy' has become very influential due to this group of authors. A similar conclusion[68] can be found in work by Giuseppe Valditara,[69] Professor of Roman Law at the University of Turin and very close to the group *Noi con Salvini* ('We with Salvini'). His book *Sovranismo*[70] also has a preface written by Thomas Williams, Breitbart Rome Bureau Chief. In 2018, he was also appointed head of department at the Ministry for Education, University and Research. For him, sovereignism is a reaction to progressivism.

Germany is the other recurrent protagonist of the sovereignist plot. On this basis, the only way for the Italian people to be emancipated is to leave the European Union, but in Italy, a referendum such as the one that was held in the UK is not possible,[71] as we will see in Chapter 4. According to this approach, there is an 'impossible coexistence' between the EU treaties and the Italian Constitution.[72] One of the champions of Italian sovereignism is Barra Caracciolo. Barra Caracciolo is a member of the Italian State Council – the supreme administrative law court in Italy – and former under-secretary (*sottosegretario*) for European affairs. In his books, he has openly challenged the principle of primacy of EU law, which is a bit weird if one considers that he is also a member of the State Council. He also runs a blog, called *orizzonte48*, where he frequently publishes very harsh posts against the EU.[73]

---

[67] 'Answer given by Mr Barroso on behalf of the Commission', 6 February 2013, Official Journal of the European Union, https://eur-lex.europa.eu/legal-content/IT/TXT/HTML/?uri=OJ:C:2013:339E: FULL&from=MT.

[68] For an overview, see F. Giubilei, 'Oggi tutti parlano di "sovranismo" ma (quasi) nessuno spiega che cosa sia', 11 December 2018, www.ilgiornale.it/news/spettacoli/oggi-tutti-parlano-sovranismo-quasi-nessuno-spiega-che-cosa-1614631.html.

[69] G. Valditara, *Sovranismo. Una speranza per la democrazia di Valditara*, Book Time, Milan, 2017.

[70] Valditara, *Sovranismo*.

[71] More recently, Gianluigi Paragone, a journalist and former member of the Five Star Movement, created a party called *No Europa per l'Italia – ItalExit con Paragone*. Here is the party's website: https://italexit.it/.

[72] L. Barra Caracciolo, *Euro e (o?) democrazia costituzionale. La convivenza impossibile tra costituzione e trattati europei*, Dike Giuridica Editrice, Rome, 2013.

[73] http://orizzonte48.blogspot.com/.

Leaving an analysis of EU austerity policies aside, it is interesting to note there have also been attempts to present a left-wing version of sovereignism. An example is the so-called 'democratic sovereignism'[74] presented by Somma, Professor of Comparative Law at the La Sapienza University, Rome. According to him, we need a new type of Europe that must depart from the neoliberal orthodoxy that characterises the EU: the 'United Europe does not promote peace and justice, nor does it respect equality between States'.[75] This arrangement does not respect social rights and solidarity and has been secured by the principle of primacy of EU law, which does not have 'a constitutional basis'.[76]

This argument is tricky for at least two reasons. First of all, the Italian Constitutional Court itself has accepted the principle of primacy of EU law, making it conditional upon the respect of the supreme principles, called counter-limits (*controlimiti*).[77] Second, it could be replicated for all the other Member States that did not have a constitutional basis when the Court of Justice delivered *Costa/Enel*.[78] Third, it is questionable whether certain aspects of the principle of primacy are also recognised by Article 117 of the Italian Constitution after the 2001 constitutional reform.

The solution, according to Somma, consists in the re-nationalisation (defined as 'inevitable')[79] of economic policies understood as an 'essential prerequisite for reactivating popular sovereignty and social conflict as the foundations of economic democracy'.[80] In his view, if this does not happen and if what he calls 'ideological Europeanism' does not cease, identitarian sovereignism (as opposed to what Somma calls democratic sovereignism) will prevail. For Somma the 'EU has developed as an institution devoted to depoliticizing markets through a neoliberal federalist approach, thus becoming an institution which has denied the reasons for its own existence'.[81]

All of these authors frequently invoke the principle of popular sovereignty but, as happened with the speech given by Prime Minister Conte at the UN referred to in Chapter 1, they tend to invoke only the sentence stating that 'Sovereignty belongs to the people', always omitting the part in which Article 1 of the constitution reads that

---

[74]   A. Somma, 'Un sovranismo democratico per un nuovo europeismo', *MicroMega*, 2018, http://temi.repubblica.it/micromega-online/un-sovranismo-democratico-per-un-nuovo-europeismo/.

[75]   Somma, 'Un sovranismo democratico', my own translation.

[76]   Somma, 'Un sovranismo democratico', my own translation.

[77]   Corte costituzionale, decision 183/1973, *Frontini*: [1974] 2 CMLR 372. However, Somma defines this doctrine and the counter-limits as 'opiates' capable of reassuring legal practitioners of the existence of an emergency brake. The same definition can be found in A. Guazzarotti, 'Sovranità e integrazione europea', 2017, www.rivistaaic.it/it/rivista/ultimi-contributi-pubblicati/andrea-guazzarotti/sovranit-e-integrazione-europea.

[78]   CJEU, C-6/64 Flaminio Costa v E.N.E.L. ECLI:EU:C:1964:66.

[79]   Somma, 'Un sovranismo democratico', my own translation.

[80]   Somma, 'Un sovranismo democratico', my own translation.

[81]   A. Somma, 'Europa, sovranità e ordine economico nel prisma delle teorie federaliste', *DPCE online*, No. 1, 2020, 427, 427.

sovereignty 'is exercised by the people in the forms and within the limits of the Constitution'. In the next section I will clarify why neither right-wing nor left-wing sovereignism belongs to the wording and spirit of the Italian Constitution and of post–WWII constitutionalism.

3.4 OPENNESS AND ITALIAN CONSTITUTIONAL LAW

Openness is one of the pillars of post–WWII constitutionalism. As written in Chapter 2, in the Italian case constitutional openness is understandable as a product of the anti-fascism[82] that had a crucial role in unifying the leading forces of the *Comitato di Liberazione Nazionale*. The constitutional provisions that govern the foreign relations of the Italian Republic are the direct offspring of this idea. Italy is usually seen as a country characterised by a strong dualist tradition, according to which the international and national legal systems are conceived of as autonomous. There are two fundamental provisions in the Italian Constitution regarding the relationship between international and domestic law; Article 10[83] and Article 11.[84] These two articles provide the first important distinction between the general rules of international law and international treaties in Italy. As for the former, Article 10 provides for an automatic procedure of adoption, in the sense that such norms are directly incorporated into the Italian system. According to Italian scholars, the general rules of international law (which would correspond to customary international law) belong to the constitutional level.[85]

As for international treaties, it is necessary for there to be a national act to transform the international act into national law. The intervention of the national legislature is not required for all treaties, since Article 80 provides for the necessity of legislation enabling the ratification only with reference to some treaties.[86] The procedure of ratification is also governed by Article 87, which empowers the president of the Republic to ratify international treaties. When the intervention of

---

[82] M. Luciani, 'Antifascismo e nascita della costituzione', *Politica del diritto*, No. 2, 1991, 191. See also G. Delledonne, 'La Resistenza in Assemblea costituente e nel testo costituzionale italiano del 1948', *Historia Constitucional*, No. 1, 2009, 217.

[83] 'The Italian legal system conforms to the generally recognised principles of international law.
    The legal status of foreigners is regulated by law in conformity with international provisions and treaties.
    A foreigner who, in his home country, is denied the actual exercise of the democratic freedoms guaranteed by the Italian constitution shall be entitled to the right of asylum under the conditions established by law.
    A foreigner may not be extradited for a political offence'.

[84] 'Italy rejects war as an instrument of aggression against the freedom of other peoples and as a means for the settlement of international disputes. Italy agrees, on conditions of equality with other States, to the limitations of sovereignty that may be necessary to a world order ensuring peace and justice among the Nations. Italy promotes and encourages international organisations furthering such ends'.

[85] G. de Vergottini, *Diritto costituzionale*, Cedam, Padua, 2004, 32.

[86] 'Parliament shall authorise by law the ratification of such international treaties as have a political nature, require arbitration or a legal settlement, entail change of borders, spending or new legislation'.

parliament is required, it intervenes with a normal legislative statute. According to the majority of scholars, this confers a primary force in the national hierarchy of law to norms derived from international treaties. Despite this, the Italian Constitution recognises a particular force to laws related to international obligations. Article 75(2) (devoted to the referendum), states: 'No referendum may be held on a law regulating taxes, the budget, amnesty or pardon, or a law ratifying an international treaty'.

Apart from Articles 10 and 11, another fundamental provision is entrenched in Article 117,[87] which will be discussed below. What I would like to stress here is that, because of the dualist tradition, international treaties acquire the strength of the domestic statute adopted for their incorporation. This explains why, at the beginning, both the Convention for the Protection of Human Rights and Fundamental Freedoms (ECHR) and EU law were considered primary sources in the Italian legal system.

Another important feature of the Italian legal order is that, unlike in other countries like Portugal and Spain, no specific status is accorded to treaties devoted to human rights. This is another key point to be kept in mind when analysing the Italian Constitutional Court's judicial developments in this field. However, the main example of Italian constitutional openness is given by Article 11, which is devoted to the rejection of 'war as an instrument of aggression against the freedom of other peoples and as a means for the settlement of international disputes'. Article 11 also agrees 'on conditions of equality with other States, to the limitations of sovereignty that may be necessary to a world order ensuring peace and justice among the Nations'. However, if we look at the Italian Constitution one can perceive a sort of tension between its constitutional openness and the choice in favour of the dualist paradigm. The Italian Constitution is based on an evident parallelism between the values inspiring the domestic activity of the Italian Republic and those inspiring the external dimension. This double orientation (internal and external) of the constitutional project was crystal clear to the members of the Italian Constituent Assembly.[88]

There are at least three reasons for the codification of the pacifist principle in the Italian Constitution. The first is connected to political realism: Italy could not be considered a military power, so the constitutionalisation of an imperialistic foreign policy was not an option.[89] The second reason was, in a manner of speaking, ethical, and finds expression in the words used, among others, by Don Luigi Sturzo, who defined war as 'immoral, illegitimate and prohibited'.[90] But the main reason for it

---

[87]   Another relevant provision in this field is Article 26 of the Italian Constitution: 'Extradition of a citizen may be granted only if it is expressly envisaged by international conventions. In any case, extradition may not be permitted for political offences'.

[88]   See for instance, T. Perassi, *La Costituzione e l'ordinamento internazionale*, Giuffrè, Milan, 1952.

[89]   See P. Nenni, *Una battaglia vinta*, Edizioni Leonardo, Rome, 1946, 104.

[90]   L. Sturzo, 'La guerra, l'Italia e l'intervistato', in L. Sturzo, *Politica di questi anni. 1957–1959*, Zanichelli, Bologna, 1954, 144.

was the intent 'to transfer, onto the international level, those principles of freedom, equality and substantive respect for the human person' that were to be affirmed and implemented in the domestic order.[91]

Insisting on this last point Cassese traced the Italian example back to a broader trend present at a comparative level,[92] as we will see in the next section. That said, due to the dualist tradition, the Italian Constitutional Court has only recently relied on external sources (primarily the ECHR and EU law) to review the constitutionality of domestic norms.

In terms of protection of fundamental rights, the ECHR has by far been the international agreement with the biggest impact over the Italian national system and this has also created tensions and disagreements between the *Corte costituzionale* and the European Court of Human Rights (ECtHR). If this openness (understood as friendliness towards the international community) gives us the idea of the axiological continuity between the domestic and the external dimension, the choice made in favour of dualism seems to emphasise, on the contrary, the discontinuity, the impermeability between the internal and the external spheres. Further developments (especially concerning the application of EU law and of the ECHR) have radically questioned the validity of the traditional dualist category. With regard to EU law, the position of the Italian Constitutional Court is emblematic of a broader trend. With regard to the ECHR, it is necessary to briefly recall its case law to appreciate the departure from the original dualism.

The original position of the *Corte costituzionale* (also called *Consulta*)[93] reflected a dualist conception of the relationship between the ECHR and domestic law. Since the accession of the Italian legal order to the ECHR was the result of an ordinary law,[94] the Italian Constitutional Court considered, for a long time and with certain exceptions,[95] that the ECHR was a source of law endowed with primary force, which explains the consequent application of the *lex posterior derogat legi priori* rule in case of conflict between a law covered by the ECHR and another Italian norm. This situation persisted until the 1990s, when the *Corte costituzionale*, seemingly changing its mind, began to draw a distinction between the content and the form of the laws giving effect to international treaties.[96] In other words, since, from a material point of view, the content of the ECHR aims to protect rights codified in the Italian Constitution, it seemed necessary to rethink the previous case law.

[91] A. Cassese, 'Politica estera e relazioni internazionali nel disegno emerso alla Assemblea Costituente' in U. De Siervo (ed.), *Scelte della Costituente e cultura giuridica. I: Costituzione italiana e modelli stranieri*, Il Mulino, Bologna, 1980, 505, 519, my own translation.

[92] See: A. Cassese, 'Modern Constitutions and International Law', *Collected Courses of the Hague Academy of International Law*, 1985, 331.

[93] This is taken from the name of the building where the Constitutional Court is based: *Palazzo della Consulta*, www.cortecostituzionale.it/jsp/consulta/istituzioni/palazzo_en.do.

[94] Law 848/1955.

[95] See, for instance, Corte costituzionale, decision 10/1993, whereby the *Consulta* described the ECHR as an 'atypical source of law'.

[96] Corte costituzionale, decision 388/1999, www.cortecostituzionale.it.

Another turning point was the constitutional reform of 2001, by which a new version of the first paragraph of Article 117 was adopted. It reads: 'Legislative powers shall be vested in the State and the Regions in compliance with the Constitution and with the constraints deriving from EU legislation and international obligations'.[97] Since 2007, in the wake of decisions 348 and 349/2007 of the Corte costituzionale, the ECHR has been viewed as a super-legislative source that could occasionally be used to review the constitutionality of domestic legislation even though it cannot be traced back to the realm of constitutional sources.

Initially and for a long time, the Italian Constitutional Court used Article 11 in order to cover the necessary limitations of sovereignty requested by the European integration process. This happened until 2001 when the first important amendment concerning European integration was introduced by codifying the duty to exercise legislative power in compliance with Community law (now in the already cited Art. 117 of the Italian Constitution). Since some champions of sovereignism frequently attack the Italian Constitutional Court for its case law on EU law and for the way in which it justified the (alleged) *coup d'état* represented by European integration, it is helpful to recall the main points of this case law. The Italian Constitution's new Article 117(1) expressly codifies the limit that supranational obligations represent for domestic law. Looking at the judicial parameter, it is evident that this provision led to interesting innovations in the Italian Constitutional Court's case law. Soon after the reform, the interpretation of this provision created a division among scholars.[98] According to some, Article 117(1) simply codified the pre-existing situation: it granted a sort of *a posteriori* assent to European primacy[99] as it was developed by the Court of Justice and accepted across the European Community. Other scholars, instead, emphasised the importance of the constitutional status given to European primacy, and asserted that Article 117 paved the way for the acceptance of the Italian monist thesis.[100] Apart from the amendment of 2001, which modified Article 117, other amendments to the Italian Constitution, namely Article 81, were introduced in 2012 to constitutionalise the so-called budget rule requested by the 'Fiscal Compact'.

---

[97]   F. Biondi Dal Monte, F. Fontanelli, 'The Decisions No. 348 and 349/2007 of the Italian Constitutional Court: The Efficacy of the European Convention in the Italian Legal System', *German Law Journal*, No. 7, 2008, 889; O. Pollicino, 'The Italian Constitutional Court at the Crossroads between Constitutional Parochialism and Co-operative Constitutionalism. Judgments No. 348 and 349 of 22 and 24 October 2007', *European Constitutional Law Review*, No. 2, 2008, 363.

[98]   For an overview, see A. Ruggeri, 'Riforma del titolo V e giudizi di "comunitarietà" delle leggi', 2007, www.associazionedeicostituzionalisti.it/dottrina/ordinamentieuropei/ruggeri.html.

[99]   C. Pinelli, 'I limiti generali alla potestà legislativa statale e regionale e i rapporti con l'ordinamento comunitario', *Foro italiano*, No. 5, 2001, 194.

[100] F. Paterniti, 'La riforma dell'art. 117, 1°Co. della Costituzione e le nuove prospettive dei rapporti tra ordinamento giuridico nazionale e Unione Europea', *Giurisprudenza costituzionale*, No. 3, 2004, 2101; A. Pajno, 'Il rispetto dei vincoli derivanti dall'ordinamento comunitario come limite alla potestà legislativa nel nuovo Titolo V della Costituzione', *Le Istituzioni del federalismo*, No. 5, 2003, 813.

The Constitutional Court originally established the basis for accepting EU law as a supranational law with primacy and direct effect in Article 11 of the Italian Constitution. This acceptance, however, did not come about immediately. On the contrary, it was the result of a long series of judgments. One reason for this can be attributed to the original absence of an explicit European clause in the Italian Constitution. As a matter of fact, as aforementioned, Article 11 was originally conceived to deal with Italian membership of organisations like the United Nations rather than to justify the consequence of supranationalism (a phenomenon that was unknown when the Italian Constitution came into force).

Another feature of the approach of the Italian Constitutional Court to EU law is given by the counter-limits doctrine, devised by the *Consulta* in 1973 soon after the well-known judgment of the Court of Justice in *Internationale Handesgesellschaft*.[101] In this judgment, the Court of Justice pointed out the primacy of EU law over national law, including national constitutional principles.[102] In this respect the Italian position – along with the German one – is relevant for a complete understanding of the reasons for the 'resistance'. Constitutional courts have claimed to maintain their own role (the role of guardians of national constitutional identity) without exceptions. They have denied the acceptance of dangerous (in their view) monist visions in order to preserve the constitutional identity of their legal orders. Contrary to what sovereignists argue, they have raised some barriers against the penetration of EU law in order to define the fundamental principles of the legal orders of which they are the guardians. Hypothetically, if an EU provision conflicted with the fundamental principles of the national legal order, the constitutional court could strike down the national statute executing the EU treaties, thus causing a 'rupture' between the national and supranational legal orders. Constitutional courts in fact normally have jurisdiction over national legislation (including the legal source of execution of treaties) but not over EU law provisions: the latter are beyond their jurisdiction because, in their argumentation, they belong to another legal order.

Starting with this approach, one can understand why constitutional courts have refused the possibility of striking down EU law provisions, since the acceptance of this option would have implied adhesion to the monist theory of the Court of Justice. It is a legal fiction that makes it possible to defend the untouchable core of constitutional legal orders by preserving the formal autonomy of the national and supranational orders and the jurisdiction of the Court of Justice. The identification

---

[101] CJEU, 11/70, Internationale Handelsgesellschaft ECLI:EU:C:1970:114 1125.

[102] 'Therefore the validity of a Community measure or its effect within a Member State cannot be affected by allegations that it runs counter to either fundamental rights as formulated by the constitution of that State or the principles of its constitutional structure', CJEU, 11/70, Internationale Handelsgesellschaft ECLI:EU:C:1970:114 1125.

of these barriers to European integration represents the essence of the counter-limits doctrine (*dottrina dei controlimiti*), devised by the Italian Constitutional Court in case 183/73, the *Frontini* judgment[103] (but see also case 170/84, the *Granital* judgment).[104] The consequence of a possible declaration of invalidity could spell Italy's withdrawal from the EU: according to Cartabia,[105] in these two cases, in fact, the counter-limits test was conceived as a way to carry out an exceptional check on the respect of the conditions of constitutionality of Italian accession to the European Communities.

Following this reconstruction, the counter-limits worked as conditions for evaluating the legitimacy of the limitations of sovereignty accepted by Italian accession to the European venture. Later on (with the decision 232/1989, the *Fragd* judgment),[106] the nature of the counter-limits doctrine changed, transforming itself from an exceptional check into a 'simple' check of compatibility of EC law with the Constitution which could not threaten Italy's membership of the European Communities (now the EU).

Because of the 'transformation' of this doctrine, the counter-limits have worked as a limitation to European primacy: that is why, according to the same scholarship, since the *Fragd* judgment, the Italian Constitutional Court has implicitly admitted that any possible conflict with the Constitution would not cause invalidity of the statute of execution of the EC (at that time) Treaty, but just the non-applicability of the EU law norm.[107]

Concerning the possibility of overcoming such limitations of sovereignty by referendum, it is necessary to recall what the Italian Constitutional Court pointed out in *Frontini*:

> The doubt that the limitations of sovereignty consequent upon the signature of the Rome Treaty and the entry of Italy into the EEC could require the use of the procedure of constitutional amendment for approval of the ratification and implementation Bill has its exact equivalent in the analogous doubt already expressed in 1951 on the occasion of the approval of the Treaty instituting the European Coal and Steel Community: a doubt correctly resolved by the Italian Parliament deciding that the ratification and implementation of that Treaty could be made by means of an ordinary statute. In truth, as this Court has already stated in COSTA v. ENEL, Article 11 means that, when its pre-conditions are met, it is possible to sign treaties

---

[103] Corte costituzionale, decision 183/1973, *Frontini*: [1974] 2 CMLR 372.

[104] Corte costituzionale, decision 180/1974, *Granital*: [1984] CMLR 756. On this, see M. Cartabia, *Principi inviolabili e integrazione europea*, Giuffrè, Milan, 1995.

[105] Cartabia, *Principi inviolabili*, 110.

[106] Corte costituzionale, decision 232/1989, www.cortecostituzionale.it. In English: *Fragd* (1990) 27 CML Rev 93.

[107] See M. Cartabia, J. H. H. Weiler, *L'Italia in Europa*, Il Mulino, Bologna, 2000, 171–2. A similar adaptiveness has been shown with regard to the changed approach towards the preliminary ruling mechanism. While initially the *Corte costituzionale* refused to consider itself as a judge under EU law, in the wake of decisions 102 and 103/2008 it has accepted referring preliminary questions to the CJEU.

which involve limitation of sovereignty and to agree to make them executory by an ordinary statute. The provision would finish emptied of its specific normative content if it were held that for every limitation of sovereignty covered by Article 11 recourse had to be had to a constitutional statute. It is clear that it has not only a substantive but also a procedural value, in the sense that it permits such limitations of sovereignty, on the conditions and for the ends therein set out, releasing Parliament from the necessity of making use of its power of constitutional amendment.[108]

Nevertheless, more recently, with particular regard to the Treaty establishing a Constitution for Europe, the former president of the Italian Constitutional Court, Marta Cartabia, inter alia, advocated the possibility of 'covering' the reform of the EU treaties by means of a constitutional law.[109] As discussed in Chapter 2, according to the case law of the Italian Constitutional Court, the 'republican form' formula used in Article 139 of the Italian Constitution corresponds to the supreme principles included in the first part of the Italian Constitution. This means that, if there is a correspondence between the content of the counter-limits doctrine and that of the republican form, no referendum may be used to surpass these limits. Finally, it is useful to mention that, according to Fabbrini and Pollicino, the 'limitations of sovereignty' enshrined in Article 11 of the Italian Constitution constitute a core element of the state's constitutional purpose and are part of the republican form clause, thus they are unamendable.[110]

I have insisted on including this excursus because it shows some important elements that can serve as powerful arguments to challenge the constitutional counter-narrative advanced by populists.[111]

To recap, it is possible to make three conclusive points. First, recall how the Italian Constitution understands the role of the Italian Republic in the international and European arena, noting particularly the difficulties encountered by the Italian Constitutional Court in concretising the difficult balance struck by the Constituent Assembly, where sovereignty (not sovereignism) should be read in light of the new constitutional values stemming from post–WWII constitutionalism. Second, against this background, in order to guarantee some higher goals, the national legal system

---

[108] Corte costituzionale, decision 183/73, www.cortecostituzionale.it. On this point, see: C. Fasone, 'Quale è la fonte più idonea a recepire le novità del Trattato di Lisbona sui parlamenti nazionali?', *Osservatorio sulle Fonti*, No. 3, 2010, 1.

[109] M. Cartabia, 'La ratifica del trattato costituzionale europeo e la volontà costituente degli Stati membri', *Forum di Quaderni Costituzionali*, available at: www.forumcostituzionale.it.

[110] F. Fabbrini, O. Pollicino, 'Constitutional Identity in Italy: Institutional Disagreements at a Time of Political Change', in C. Calliess, G. van der Schyff (eds.), *Constitutional Identity in a Europe of Multilevel Constitutionalism*, Cambridge University Press, 2019, 201.

[111] Previously, in Chapter 1, I mentioned the speech given by the Italian Prime Minister Giuseppe Conte at the United Nations in which he argued that: 'When some accuse us of souverainism or populism, I always enjoy pointing out that Article 1 of the Italian Constitution cites sovereignty and the people, and it is precisely through that provision that I interpret the concept of sovereignty and the exercise of sovereignty by the people' ('Remarks by Giuseppe Conte to the 73rd Session of the United Nations General Assembly', 26 September 2018, www.voltairenet.org/article203153.html).

benefits from coordination with international public and EU laws. In this sense, although the EU or the Council of Europe does not correspond to features embodied by state constitutionalism in the national arena, they do have a role in preserving and safeguarding some of the constitutional goods protected by national constitutions.[112] Third, in spite of what sovereignists argue, the Italian Constitutional Court has not given up sovereignty, constitutional identity and national democracy as if it were an accessory to the alleged European and global *coup d'état*. On the contrary, the Italian Constitutional Court has frequently threatened to use the counter-limits doctrine, not only with regard to the Court of Justice of the EU[113] but also against the International Court of Justice.[114] Similar dynamics of resistance occurred with regard to the case law of the Strasbourg Court.[115] These episodical disagreements show that the Italian Constitution is acquainted with some limits to this constitutional openness when fundamental principles are at stake, and is a confirmation of the difficult equilibrium reached by the Constituent Assembly. As we will see, similar disagreements can be found elsewhere and show that post–WWII constitutionalism has tried to favour international openness without renouncing state sovereignty,[116] but this has nothing to do with the nostalgic sovereignism that characterises populists in Italy[117] who conceive the Italian legal system as self-referential and disconnected from the international community and its international obligations. Sovereignists tend to invoke a plot in which Italy is the constant victim of an international conspiracy guided by a global elite, of which the EU is a manifestation. In this scenario, the euro and EU membership are based on a *coup d'état* accepted by supranational and national elite, without any possibility of

---

[112] This point has been developed by Maduro who, among others, radically challenges the argument of those who deny the existence or possibility of a supranational constitutionalism by making a distinction between the idea of constitutionalism as such and state constitutionalism, which is understood as a particular historical experience and not as the paradigm of constitutionalism as such. Maduro does not even argue that supranational constitutionalism is constitutionalism as such, but argues that the interaction between these two constitutionalisms (i.e., the state–national and the supranational) might represent an approach to the ideals of constitutionalism, M. Maduro, 'Three Claims of Constitutional Pluralism', in M. Abvelj, J. Komárek (eds.), *Constitutional Pluralism in the European Union and Beyond*, Hart, Oxford, 2012, 67.

[113] More recently, see Taricco: CJEU, C105/14 Taricco and Others ECLI:EU:C:2015:555; Corte costituzionale, decision 24/2017, www.cortecostituzionale.it; CJEU, C-42/17, M.A.S. and M.B. ECLI:EU: C:2017:936; Corte costituzionale, decision 115/2018, www.cortecostituzionale.it. See also, Corte costituzionale, decision 269/2017 and its aftermath; on this, see: G. Martinico, G. Repetto, 'Fundamental Rights and Constitutional Duels in Europe: An Italian Perspective on Case 269/2017 of the Italian Constitutional Court and Its Aftermath', *European Constitutional Law Review*, No. 4, 2019, 731.

[114] Corte costituzionale, decision 238/2014, www.cortecostituzionale.it.

[115] For instance, Corte costituzionale, decision 49/2015, www.cortecostituzionale.it.

[116] G. Martinico, 'National Courts and Judicial Disobedience to the ECHR. A Comparative Overview', in O. M. Arnardóttir, A. Buyse (eds.), *Shifting Centres of Gravity in Human Rights Protection: Rethinking Relations between the ECHR, EU, and National Legal Orders*, Routledge, Abingdon, 2016, 59.

[117] D. Amoroso, 'Italy', in F. Palombino (ed.), *Duelling for Supremacy International Law vs. National Fundamental Principles*, Cambridge University Press, 2019, 184.

preserving national constitutional identity[118] due to a Europeanisation that undermines the basis of national democracy. In light of this, they frequently argue that coexistence between the EU treaties and the Italian Constitution is not possible.[119] As is evident from this overview, this dichotomy is built on the basis of a mimetic and manipulative reading of the constitution.

The COVID-19 pandemic has given a new boost to Euroscepticism.[120] The European Union has discovered that it is divided about how to challenge the next economic crisis, especially with regard to the possible inclusion of loans, and even grants, in the Recovery Fund proposed by Germany and France. This proposal has worsened the existing fracture between the so-called frugal countries (Austria, Denmark, the Netherlands and Sweden)[121] and those most affected by COVID-19.

The anti-Europeanism present in some components of the Five Star Movement and the unclear destiny of conditionality in the ESM Pandemic Crisis Support (PCS)[122] induced Conte to hesitate on the ESM. The ESM issue was also at the basis of the failure of the plan for a possible third Conte government, due to the opposition of the Five Star Movement.[123] Despite its support for the Draghi government, the *Lega*'s sovereignism has not magically disappeared.

Europe has been attacked by sovereignists for not having done much to tackle the health crisis, even though the EU has limited competences in this field.[124] In spite of the original ambiguity of President Lagarde[125] and the European Central Bank

---

[118] Becchi, *Manifesto sovranista*, 8–9.

[119] Barra Caracciolo, *Euro*.

[120] 'The issue of Euroskepticism has been a hardy perennial for populist parties in Western Europe. While UKIP and the Alternative for Germany are relatively recent phenomena, the issue of Europe has always been on the agenda of populist forces — even if it has been rather low down. The French National Front has always maintained a hostile position as the EU has been seen to compromise national identity. The reason for the common advocacy of Euroskepticism by populists lies in the nature of the integration process itself: a project of elites that is, at best, complex and remote and, at worst, democratically deficient is too easy a target for populists. It is not a coincidence that it is hard to think of a contemporary West European populist party that does not exhibit a degree of Euroskepticism. For very few it is the primary focus but for almost all it is one part of their armory of issues', P. Taggart, 'Populism in Western Europe', in C. Rovira Kaltwasser, P. Taggart, P. Ochoa Espejo, P. Ostiguy (eds.), *The Oxford Handbook of Populism*, Oxford University Press, 2017, 248, 257.

[121] See the piece by Austrian premier, S. Kurz, 'The "frugal four" advocate a responsible EU budget', 16 February 2020, www.ft.com/content/7faae690-4e65-11ea-95a0-43d18ec715f5.

[122] M. Dani, A. Menéndez, 'Soft-conditionality through soft-law: le insidie nascoste del Pandemic Crisis Support', 2020, www.lacostituzione.info/index.php/2020/05/10/soft-conditionality-through-soft-law-le -insidie-nascoste-del-pandemic-crisis-support/.

[123] The end of the second Conte government has further fuelled this controversy, especially for the Five Star component led by Alessandro Di Battista, Di Maio's old rival for the leadership of the movement. In fact, Di Battista defined Draghi as an 'apostle of the elite', 'Governo: Di Battista contro Draghi, "l'apostolo delle élite"', 2 February 2021, www.affaritaliani.it/notiziario/governo_di_battista_contro_ draghi_lapostolo_delle_elite-182844.html.

[124] See Article 168 TFEU.

[125] Her declarations boosted another round of anti-Europeanism: 'Italy furious at ECB's Lagarde "not here to close spreads" comment', 13 March 2020, www.reuters.com/article/us-ecb-policy-italy-minister/italy-furious-at-ecbs-lagarde-not-here-to-close-spreads-comment-idUSKBN20Z3DW.

(ECB), however, the EU has promised a lot and done much. The ECB has confirmed the 'whatever it takes approach',[126] 'firing its bazooka'[127] with new bond purchases. The escape clause (so-called suspension) of the Fiscal and Growth Pact has been activated,[128] the ESM has been reshaped,[129] the European instrument for temporary Support to mitigate Unemployment Risks in an Emergency (SURE) was launched[130] and above all a fight for a bigger European budget to sustain the new European Recovery Fund has started. Finally, the Board of Directors of the European Investment Bank agreed a 25 billion Euro Pan-European Guarantee Fund to respond to the COVID-19 crisis on 26 May 2020.[131] This perhaps falls a good deal short of creating a robust European solidarity, but it is a big move if compared to the status quo. Moreover, the debate on the mutualisation of sovereign debt has resumed[132] and if the battle over the budget is well managed, it could be a game changer.

It is no coincidence that some have evoked the need for a European Hamiltonian[133] (or Madisonian?)[134] moment. The tip of the iceberg was reached

---

[126]   'Within our mandate, the ECB is ready to do whatever it takes to preserve the euro. And believe me, it will be enough', 'Speech by Mario Draghi, President of the European Central Bank at the Global Investment Conference in London 26 July 2012', 2012, www.ecb.europa.eu/press/key/date/2012/html/sp120726.en.html.

[127]   B. Hall, M. Arnold, S. Fleming, 'Coronavirus: Can the ECB's "Bazooka" Avert a Eurozone Crisis?', 23 March 2020, www.ft.com/content/a7496c30-6ab7-11ea-800d-da70cff6e4d3; T. Fairless, 'After Firing Its Bazooka, ECB Could Reload to Fight Coronavirus', 29 April 2020, www.wsj.com/articles/after-firing-its-bazooka-ecb-could-reload-to-fight-coronavirus-11588155329.

[128]   'Statement of EU Ministers of Finance on the Stability and Growth Pact in Light of the COVID-19 Crisis', 23 March 2020, www.consilium.europa.eu/en/press/press-releases/2020/03/23/statement-of-eu-ministers-of-finance-on-the-stability-and-growth-pact-in-light-of-the-covid-19-crisis/.

[129]   'Finance ministers agreed on the features and standardised terms for euro area countries to access the European Stability Mechanism (ESM) Pandemic Crisis Support. Member states can borrow up to 2% of their GDP to finance direct and indirect healthcare, cure and prevention related costs due to the COVID-19 pandemic', 2020, www.consilium.europa.eu/en/policies/coronavirus/timeline/.

[130]   *Report on the comprehensive economic policy response to the COVID-19 pandemic*, 9 April 2020, www.consilium.europa.eu/en/press/press-releases/2020/04/09/report-on-the-comprehensive-economic-policy-response-to-the-covid-19-pandemic/; 'The Commission's SURE initiative provides funding to Member States of up to €100 billion by covering part of the costs related to the creation or extension of national short-time work schemes', 'ESM Pandemic Crisis Support', 2020, www.esm.europa.eu/content/europe-response-corona-crisis.

[131]   'EIB Board approves €25 billion Pan-European Guarantee Fund in response to COVID-19 crisis', 2020, www.eib.org/en/press/all/2020-126-eib-board-approves-eur-25-billion-pan-european-guarantee-fund-to-respond-to-covid-19-crisis.htm.

[132]   A. Steinbach, 'The Mutualization of Sovereign Debt: Comparing the American Past and the European Present', *Journal of Common Market Studies*, No. 5, 2015, 1110.

[133]   S. Capooer, 'This Isn't Europe's "Hamilton" Moment', 2020, www.politico.eu/article/this-isnt-europes-hamilton-moment/; G. Calhoun, 'Europe's Hamiltonian Moment – What Is It Really?', 26 May 2020, www.forbes.com/sites/georgecalhoun/2020/05/26/europes-hamiltonian-moment–what-is-it-really/; A. Kaletsky, 'Europe's Hamiltonian Moment', 2020, www.project-syndicate.org/commentary/french-german-european-recovery-plan-proposal-by-anatole-kaletsky-2020-05.

[134]   E. Jones, 'Not Hamilton but Madison: Diversity Makes for a Better Union', 2020, www.iiss.org/blogs/survival-blog/2020/05/europe-diversity-politics-covid-19.

in the decision on the Public Sector Purchase Programme (PSPP),[135] when the German Constitutional Court declared that the CJEU had acted ultra vires because of the way in which the Luxembourg Court had exercised the proportionality review in the *Weiss* case.[136] Even before this decision, scholars[137] had warned about the 'bad example'[138] offered by the German judges, especially since in 2012, the Czech Constitutional Court[139] declared the CJEU's judgment in C-399/09 *Landtová* ultra vires.[140] The Czech case represents the first example of the application of the ultra vires doctrine. However, the situation is different now because of the prestige and charisma of the German Constitutional Court and indeed the risk of a domino effect is very high. In fact, the judgment found the Court of Justice decision in the *Weiss* case[141] to be ultra vires and thus considered the German institutions to be unbound by any of the relevant effects. This decision has triggered a very interesting debate in legal journals and blogs. In particular, the German Constitutional Court somehow questioned the way in which the CJEU had carried out the proportionality test in *Weiss*.[142] In the German Constitutional Court's words:

> The specific manner in which the CJEU applies the principle of proportionality in the case at hand renders that principle meaningless for the purposes of distinguishing, in relation to the PSPP, between monetary policy and economic policy, i.e. between the exclusive monetary policy competence conferred upon the EU (Art. 3(1) lit. c TFEU) and the limited conferral upon the EU of the competence to coordinate general economic policies, with the Member States retaining the competence for economic policy at large (Art. 4(1) TEU; Art. 5(1) TFEU).[143]

---

[135] German Constitutional Court, 5 May 2020: 2 BvR 859/15 – 2 BvR 1651/15 – 2 BvR 2006/15 – 2 BvR 980/16. For some comments, see M. Poiares Maduro, 'Some Preliminary Remarks on the PSPP Decision of the German Constitutional Court', 2020, https://verfassungsblog.de/some-preliminary-remarks-on-the-pspp-decision-of-the-german-constitutional-court; M. Avbelj, 'The Right Question about the FCC Ultra Vires Decision', 2020, https://verfassungsblog.de/the-right-question-about-the-fcc-ultra-vires-decision; T. Marzal, 'Is the BVerfG PSPP Decision "Simply Not Comprehensible"? A Critique of the Judgment's Reasoning on Proportionality', 2020, https://verfassungsblog.de/is-the-bverfg-pspp-decision-simply-not-comprehensible/.

[136] C-493/17, Weiss and Others ECLI:EU:C:2018:1000.

[137] G. Halmai, 'Abuse of Constitutional Identity. The Hungarian Constitutional Court on Interpretation of Article E) (2) of the Fundamental Law', *Review of Central and East European Law*, No. 1, 2018, 23.

[138] O. Pollicino, 'Metaphors and Identity Based Narrative in Constitutional Adjudication: When Judicial Dominance Matters', 2019, https://blog-iacl-aidc.org/2019-posts/2019/2/27/metaphors-and-identity-based-narrative-in-constitutional-adjudication-when-judicial-dominance-matters.

[139] Pl. ÚS 5/12, www.usoud.cz/en/decisions/2012-01-31-pl-us-5-12-slovak-pensions.

[140] C-399/09, Landtová ECLI:EU:C:2011:415.

[141] CJEU, C-493/17, ECLI:EU:C:2018:1000.

[142] C-493/17, Weiss and Others ECLI:EU:C:2018:1000. Before Weiss, the CJEU has given another important case in the field of economic governance, the Pringle case. CJEU, C-370/12, Thomas Pringle/Government of Ireland, Ireland, The Attorney General ECLI:EU:C:2012:756.

[143] 2 BvR 859/15, para. 127, https://bit.ly/3qLWKKv. On this, see: Marzal, 'Is the BVerfG PSPP Decision "Simply Not Comprehensible"? A Critique of the Judgment's Reasoning on Proportionality', 2020, https://verfassungsblog.de/is-the-bverfg-pspp-decision-simply-not-comprehensible/#comments.

In a nutshell, the German Constitutional Court gave the ECB Governing Council a three-month ultimatum to adopt 'a new decision that demonstrates in a comprehensible and substantiated manner that the monetary policy objectives pursued by the ECB are not disproportionate to the economic and fiscal policy effects resulting from the programme'.[144] While the tone of the German Constitutional Court is shocking and perhaps also a bit arrogant, scholars have already stressed that there are many ways of overcoming the impasse.[145] Moreover, as the German Constitutional Court explicitly stated, this decision does not affect the new Pandemic Purchasing Program of the ECB.

This judgment confirms a recent trend in which courts have been eager to intervene, despite the technicalities of the question, by making a series of important decisions concerning European economic governance.[146]

Despite this decision, the ECB confirmed its intention to insist on its expansive monetary policy approach, and a press release following the judgment of the German Constitutional Court of 5 May 2020 was published on the website of the Court of Justice stating:

> In general, it is recalled that the Court of Justice has consistently held that a judgment in which the Court gives a preliminary ruling is binding on the national court for the purposes of the decision to be given in the main proceedings. In order to ensure that EU law is applied uniformly, the Court of Justice alone – which was created for that purpose by the Member States – has jurisdiction to rule that an act of an EU institution is contrary to EU law. Divergences between courts of the Member States as to the

[144] 'Following a transitional period of no more than three months allowing for the necessary coordination with the ESCB, the Bundesbank may thus no longer participate in the implementation and execution of Decision (EU) 2015/774, the amending Decisions (EU) 2015/2101, (EU) 2015/2464, (EU) 2016/702 and (EU) 2017/100, and the Decision of 12 September 2019, neither by carrying out any further purchases of bonds nor by contributing to another increase of the monthly purchase volume, unless the ECB Governing Council adopts a new decision that demonstrates in a comprehensible and substantiated manner that the monetary policy objectives pursued by the ECB are not disproportionate to the economic and fiscal policy effects resulting from the programme. On the same condition, the Bundesbank must ensure that the bonds already purchased under the PSPP and held in its portfolio are sold based on a – possibly long-term – strategy coordinated with the ESCB', German Constitutional Court, 5 May 2020: 2 BvR 859/15 –2 BvR 1651/15 –2 BvR 2006/15 –2 BvR 980/16.

[145] 'I don't think the ECB can and will directly comply with the German Court's judgment. To do so would open the door to multiple national legal challenges, placing it under the jurisdiction of all national high courts, with disastrous consequences for the ECB and its role under the Treaties. But, without directly addressing the German Constitutional Court demand, the ECB may adopt a new decision with a more in depth justification of the program. This justification will likely mostly pay lip service to the arguments on proportionality raised by the Constitutional Court. But that may be sufficient to provide the justification needed by German authorities, that are the actual addressees of the judgment, to say that the requirement the Court has imposed has been fulfilled by the ECB and the problem is therefore solve. Naturally, those that brought this case will argue otherwise but that will have to be done through a new case: time will be gained (and the composition of the Court will also partly change)', Poiares Maduro, 'Some Preliminary Remarks on the PSPP Decision of the German Constitutional Court'.

[146] Fasone, 'Constitutional Courts Facing'.

validity of such acts would indeed be liable to place in jeopardy the unity of the EU legal order and to detract from legal certainty. Like other authorities of the Member States, national courts are required to ensure that EU law takes full effect. That is the only way of ensuring the equality of Member States in the Union they created. The institution will refrain from communicating further on the matter.

Scholars have asked for the activation of a procedure of infringement against Germany, which is possible under Article 258 TFEU,[147] but politically difficult not just because this would involve a national constitutional court.[148] However, on 9 June 2021, the Commission sent letter of notice to Germany.[149] This move was surprising since it came only a few days after a decision of the German Constitutional Court in which the *Bundesverfassungsgericht* dismissed two applications for an order of execution that had been lodged after the BVG's judgment of 5 May 2020 on the PSPP.[150] More generally, the current phase seems to confirm the persistent weaknesses affecting European economic governance and the protagonism of the ECB[151] in this phase. In this sense, the EU's economic architecture is still paying the price of the choices made by the Maastricht Treaty, which identified four main pillars at its basis: 1) Coordination of economic policy making between Member States; 2) coordination of fiscal policies, notably through limits on government debt and deficit; 3) a centralised monetary policy with a European Central Bank; and 4) the creation of a single currency (euro).[152] In particular, the persistent asymmetry between the monetary union (centralised) and the economic union (based on a mere coordination of national economic policies), the incomplete (if compared to a fully fledged federal central bank) mandate of the European Central Bank, the limited budget of the EU and the uncertainty surrounding budgetary

---

[147] Article 258 TFEU: 'If the Commission considers that a Member State has failed to fulfil an obligation under the Treaties, it shall deliver a reasoned opinion on the matter after giving the State concerned the opportunity to submit its observations.

  If the State concerned does not comply with the opinion within the period laid down by the Commission, the latter may bring the matter before the Court of Justice of the European Union', F. Fabbrini, 'Suing the BVerfG', 2020, https://verfassungsblog.de/suing-the-bverfg/#comments.

[148] The infringement procedure is per se a procedure giving the EU Commission discretion about whether or not to bring the case before the CJEU: D. Chalmers, G. Davies, G. Monti, *European Union Law: Cases and Materials*, Cambridge, 2010, 399. In theory the CJEU already clarified that it is possible to activate a procedure like this in case of breach of EU law caused by judicial actors: CJEU, C-224/01, Köbler ECLI:EU:C:2003:513; CJEU, C-173/03 Traghetti del Mediterraneo ECLI:EU:C:2006:391.

[149] June infringements package: key decisions, 9 June 2021, https://ec.europa.eu/commission/presscorner/detail/en/inf_21_2743.

[150] German Constitutional Court, 2 BvR 1651/15, 2 BvR 2006/15.

[151] N. Scicluna, 'Politicization without Democratization: The Impact of the Eurozone Crisis on EU Constitutionalism', 2013, www.carloalberto.org/assets/working-papers/no.341.pdf; N. Scicluna, *European Union Constitutionalism in Crisis*, Routledge, Abingdon, 2015.

[152] C. Degryse, 'The New European Economic Governance', *Working Paper European Trade Union Institute* 2012/14, 2012, www.etui.org/Publications2/Working-Papers/The-new-European-economic-governance.

policies in the Union together with the weaknesses of the Stability and Growth Pact[153] have been identified as some of the main anomalies of the system.[154]

However, after this decision of the German Constitutional Court on the PSPP, the scholarly debate in Italy and elsewhere has mirrored the political one. Scholars have accused the German Constitutional Court of pushing for an ordo-liberal understanding of the European Union[155] and have written about the end of the law;[156] others have again insisted on a German driven conspiracy.[157]

3.5 OPENNESS AND POST–WORLD WAR II CONSTITUTIONALISM

Openness and Resistance are essential keywords to understand the essence of so-called post–WWII constitutionalism. Indeed, according to scholars, there are at least three central points in the evolution of Western constitutionalism: the distinction between constituent power and constituted power, the affirmation of the idea of the constitution as 'higher law' and its combination with the discovery of the judicial review of legislation and, finally, the tension between universal

---

[153] J. V. Louis, 'The Review of the Stability and Growth Pact', *Common Market Law Review*, No. 1, 2006, 85.

[154] P. Krugman, *End This Depression Now!*, W. W. Norton & Company, New York, 2012, Chapter 10.

[155] 'Probably the GCC, reflecting part of the German public opinion, considers perfectly legitimate the phenomenon – described by Giacché as "monetary annexation" – by which control of production within a monetary union must be given to the "more deserving" actors. Once again, a Darwinian perspective which ignores the notion that diverging yield spreads will make access to credit prohibitive to businesses situated in peripheral Member States, negating the concept of fair competition versus "more deserving" businesses situated in the stronger Member States', A. Guazzarotti, 'Very Unkind Things about the German Constitutional Court's Rebellion against the ECJ in the Quantitative Easing Case', 2020, https://verfassungsblog.de/very-unkind-things-about-the-german-constitutional-courts-rebellion-against-the-ecj-in-the-quantitative-easing-case/. Guazzarotti referred to a book by V. Giacché, ANSCHLUSS. L 'annessione: L'unificazione della Germania e il futuro dell'Europa, Imprimatur, Reggio Emilia, 2013. Giacché is also author of another book titled *Costituzione italiana contro trattati europei. Il conflitto inevitabile*, Imprimatur, Reggio Emilia, 2015, where he writes of an 'unavoidable conflict' between the Italian Constitution and the EU treaties.

[156] M. Dani, J. Mendes, A. J. Menéndez, M. Wilkinson, H. Schepel, E. Chiti, *At the End of the Law: A Moment of Truth for the Eurozone and the EU*, 2020, at https://verfassungsblog.de/at-the-end-of-the-law. This approach forgets that things like these have happened even in fully fledged federal systems: A. Baraggia, G. Martinico, *Who Is the Master of the Treaties? The Compact Theory in Karlsruhe*, 2020, www.diritticomparati.it/who-is-the-master-of-the-treaties-the-compact-theory-in-karlsruhe/;
S. J. Boom, *The European Union after the Maastricht Decision: Will Germany be the Virginia of Europe*, in *American Journal of Comparative Law*, No. 2, 1995, 177; T. Dumbrovsky, *Federal Solution to the EU Internal Sovereignty Conundrum: The European Doctrine of the Czech Constitutional Court and the U.S. Compact Theory*, in L. Tichy, T. Dumbrovsky (eds.), *Sovereignty and Competences of the European Union*, Prague, 2010, 80; R. Schütze, *Federalism as Constitutional Pluralism: 'Letter from America'*, in M. Avbelj, J. Komárek (eds.), *Constitutional Pluralism in the European Union and Beyond*, Hart, Oxford, 2012, 185.

[157] See the interview given by Becchi: F. Provenzani, '"La trappola della Germania per far accettare il MES all'Italia" (Paolo Becchi)', 7 May 2020, www.money.it/Piano-Germania-MES-Italia-Paolo-Becchi.

aspiration (inherited from the rationalism of the Enlightenment) and national – territorial identity.[158]

In this section I shall examine openness understood as one of the building blocks of post–WWII constitutionalism. By openness, I mean the constitutionally established friendliness ('Freundlichkeit') towards legal sources that are, from a formal point of view, external to those governed by the national system, or, in other words, that are not produced by national actors (and, as such, are not traceable to the general will of the people) in charge of the law-making functions according to the constitution. As recalled, openness is one of the most evident features characterising these texts, and it is possible to find the roots of this phenomenon even earlier, looking back at what Mirkine-Guetzévitch called the 'internationalization of modern constitutions',[159] in the 1930s. In other words, openness seems to belong within the core of the 'nouvelles tendances du droit constitutionnel'.[160] Something similar might be argued with regard to the connection between adaptiveness and constitutionalism, as I have tried to show elsewhere (especially looking at what scholars term 'evolutionary constitutionalism').[161]

This kind of openness might present different forms: it can be limited to what we call general public law (international customary law) or even extended to international treaties. Within this last group, there are constitutions that present a wider openness with regard to human rights treaties because of the similarity existing between their provisions and the substance of these treaties. Spain and Portugal, as we will see, are good examples. This kind of openness, as has been studied by several scholars,[162] performs a double function of constitutional relevance: on the one hand, it reinforces the original pact codified in the constitution, for example by providing new instruments to guarantee those rights enshrined in the *Verfassung*. The Dutch case is emblematic of this; there, the constitutional reform of 1953 introduced, among other things, Article 94[163] of the *Grondwet*, which empowers national judges to disapply national law in conflict with international treaties, primarily the ECHR. This is what

[158] P. Carrozza, 'Constitutionalism's Post-modern Opening', in M. Loughlin, N. Walker (eds.), *The Paradox of Constitutionalism: Constituent Power and Constitutional Form*, Oxford University Press, 2007, 169, 182.

[159] B. Mirkine-Guetzévitch, *Les Nouvelles tendances du droit constitutionnel*, Giard, Paris, 1931, 48.

[160] Mirkine-Guetzévitch, *Les Nouvelles tendances*.

[161] G. Martinico, *Lo spirito polemico del diritto europeo. Studio sulle ambizioni costituzionali dell'Unione*, Aracne, Rome, 2011, 27.

[162] A. Peters, 'Compensatory Constitutionalism: The Function and Potential of Fundamental International Norms and Structures', *Leiden Journal of International Law*, No. 3, 2006, 579.

[163] 'Statutory regulations in force within the Kingdom shall not be applicable if such application is in conflict with provisions of treaties that are binding on all persons or of resolutions by international institutions'. On constitutional openness in the Netherlands, see: B. Oomen, 'Strengthening Constitutional Identity Where There Is None: The Case of the Netherlands', *Revue interdisciplinaire d'études juridiques*, No. 2, 2016, 235; G. Betlem, A. Nollkaemper, 'Giving Effect to Public International Law and European Community Law before Domestic Courts: A Comparative Analysis of the Practice of Consistent Interpretation', *European Journal of International Law*, No. 3, 2003, 569.

I mean by providing new instruments to guarantee constitutional rights. On the other hand, constitutional openness also performs a transformative function, by giving new blood to the constitutional text (for instance, serving to update the list of rights included in the original text) and by making it more adaptive to the new needs of society. Again, the Dutch example is crucial and the openness of the *Grondwet* has been invoked to justify the lack of necessity for new amendments to its first part.[164]

This adaptiveness of the original text has some limitations, of course, because many of these constitutions are also characterised by the existence of a group of principles that must not be jeopardised, because their violation would imply the denial of the axiological bases on which their legal orders are founded. As we saw in Chapters 1 and 2, constitutional law scholars describe this set of principles in different ways, for example, the 'republican form' ('forma repubblicana')[165] in Italy and the eternity clause ('Ewigkeitsklause')[166] in Germany.[167]

This openness is represented by constitutional provisions that govern not only the effects of external norms in the local territory, but also national participation in and contribution to the international community. All of these norms are based on the existence of an axiological continuity between the principles and values that govern the life of a given polity within its own boundaries and those that should characterise the international community. In other words, these constitutions have never accepted the limitation of the promotion of their values to domestic boundaries, and indeed, even when the wording of their provisions refers to 'citizens', their constitutional courts have frequently extended the substance of these norms to non-citizens, at least in the field of fundamental rights.[168] These constitutions seek to govern the activity of domestic actors even beyond the national territory, promoting their values even in the postnational arena. The Italian experience is emblematic from this point of view, but is also part of a broader trend.[169]

Today, national constitutions do not provide an exhaustive list of fundamental rights as a consequence of that constitutional openness, which, according to Saiz Arnaiz,[170] causes these constitutions to make reference to international and supranational law to ensure the protection of certain constitutional goods. For instance, with regard to the Italian case, it is said that the general clause of protection of fundamental rights

---

[164]   See Oomen, 'Strengthening Constitutional', 245 and J. Gerards, 'The Irrelevance of the Netherlands Constitution, and the Impossibility of Changing It', *Revue interdisciplinaire d'études juridiques*, No. 2, 2016, 207.

[165]   Article 139 of the Italian Constitution.

[166]   Article 79(3) of the Basic Law (Grundgesetz-GG) for the Federal Republic of Germany.

[167]   For an overview of these clauses, see F. Palermo, *La forma di stato dell'Unione europea. Per una teoria costituzionale dell'integrazione sovranazionale*, Ceda m, Padua, 2005.

[168]   This is the Italian case, for instance, see Corte costituzionale, decision 432/2005, www .cortecostituzionale.it.

[169]   See: Cassese, 'Modern Constitutions', 331.

[170]   A. Saiz Arnaiz, *La apertura constitucional al derecho internacional y europeo de los derechos humanos. El artículo 10.2 de la Constitución Española*, Centro de Estudios Políticos y Constitucionales, Madrid, 1999.

contained in Article 2 of the constitution is to be considered an open norm.[171] This reading of Article 2 has allowed the Constitutional Court to recognise and guarantee the so-called new rights (the right to knowledge, the right to privacy, environmental rights) and to keep the constitution up-to-date with respect to the need to protect the 'person' (*principio personalista*).

In the 1990s, when commenting upon some of the provisions of Central and Eastern European constitutions, Eric Stein stressed the existence of a 'paradigm of progressive internationalisation of constitutions':[172] however, those provisions represented only a fifth stage[173] of this process that was connected, in that case, with a broader phenomenon of mixed or (partially) guided domestic constituent processes due to the influence of the international community.[174]

The case of Central and Eastern European constitutions and the cases of the German and Italian constitutions share the same spirit of openness, as recalled by Cassese and Stein,[175] among others. In this process of internalisation of modern constitutions, the Republic of Weimar represents an important starting point. The Weimar Constitution originated from the acknowledgment of the atrocities of World War I, as can be inferred from the wording of its preamble[176] and Article

---

[171] Article 2 of the Italian Constitution: 'The Republic recognizes and guarantees the inviolable rights of the person, both as an individual and in the social groups where human personality is expressed'.

[172] E. Stein, 'International Law in Internal Law: Toward Internationalization of Central-Eastern European Constitutions?' *American Journal of International Law*, No. 3, 1994, 427, 429.

[173] Stein, 'International Law in Internal Law'.

[174] A. Lollini, F. Palermo, 'Comparative Law and the "Proceduralization" of Constitution-Building Processes', in J. Raue, P. Sutter (eds.), *Facets and Practices of State-building*, Martinus Nijoff, Leiden, Boston, 2009, 301.

[175] Cassese, 'Modern Constitutions', 351. In the words of Stein: 'Antonio Cassese conjures up another, related correlation between the efforts to establish democracy following the defeat of an authoritarian system in a war and revolution, on the one hand, and what he terms "the opening of state constitutions" to the international community generally and international law in particular, on the other. Writing in 1985, he perceived four historic stages: the first extending from 1787 to World War I; the second, from the Weimar Constitution of 1919 to World War II; the third, from the French Constitution of 1946 to the late 1950s; and the fourth starting in the early 1960s. The United States Constitution of 1789, written after a revolutionary war against a monarchy, was the first milestone on this historic continuum [...] After more than a century, and another war and revolution against a monarchy the short-lived democratic Weimar Constitution of 1919 made "generally recognized rules of international law" a part of federal law. This formula was extended (after still another war) in the 1949 Basic Law of the Federal Republic of Germany so as to make general international law superior to legislation and directly invocable by individuals [...]The 1931 Constitution of the democratic, socialist Spanish Republic took the lead by establishing for the first time in history the precedence of treaties over ordinary legislation, enforceable by a Constitutional Court-a solution embraced in substance after almost half a century of war and dictatorship by the new Spanish Constitution of 1978. The Constitutions of 1946 and 1958 restructuring post–World War II democratic France carried on the idea of treaties' superiority over legislation, subject, however, to the perplexing new requirement of reciprocity – a pattern followed by the Francophone countries of Africa', Stein, 'International Law in Internal Law', 427–9.

[176] 'The German people, united in its tribes and inspired by the will to renew and strengthen its Reich in liberty and justice, to serve peace inward and outward and to promote social progress, has adapted this constitution'.

227 of the Treaty of Versailles, which references 'a supreme offence against international morality and the sanctity of treaties'.[177]

This combination of factors generated a series of norms aimed at bringing the internal and external dimensions together in the constitutional discipline. Article 4 of the Weimar Constitution acknowledged that 'the generally recognised rules of international law are valid as binding elements of German Reich law'. Another relevant provision is its Article 162 stating that: 'the Reich advocates an international regulation of the rights of the workers, which strives to safeguard a minimum of social rights for humanity's working class'. Provisions such as Article 162 are based on the attempt to create a parallelism of values between the domestic and international spheres. Another important novelty, which was later adopted by the Spanish Constitution of 1931, was the progressive involvement of the parliament in foreign affairs.[178]

Indeed, the Spanish Constitution of 1931 contained a number of interesting provisions, starting with Article 7 ('The Spanish State shall abide by the universal norms of international law, including them in its positive law')[179] and, above, all Article 65, which considered 'all international conventions ratified by Spain and registered in the League of Nations and in the nature of international law' as 'a constitutive part of Spanish legislation'. This way, the Spanish Constitution created a clear obligation for the national legislature to act in compliance with international law and this resulted, as Cassese stressed,[180] in transforming a possible violation of international law into a breach of the constitution (a constitution guaranteed by the establishment of a constitutional adjudicator, the *Tribunal de Garantías Constitucionales*). Finally, another series of provisions accorded an important set of competences to the Spanish parliament in the field of foreign affairs (authorisation of ratification of international treaties, declaration of war).[181]

The German Basic Law is another example of the external openness of modern constitutions. Its preamble opens by acknowledging the responsibility of the German people 'before God and man' and affirming 'the determination to promote world

---

[177]   The Versailles Treaty June 28, 1919: Part VII, Article 227, text available at: avalon.law.yale.edu/imt/partvii.asp.

[178]   A. Cassese, 'Politica estera e relazioni internazionali nel disegno emerso alla Assemblea Costituente', in U. de Siervo (ed.), *Scelte della Costituente e cultura giuridica. I: Costituzione italiana e modelli stranieri*, Il Mulino, Bologna, 1980, 505, 519. See Article 35 of the Weimar Constitution: 'Reichstag establishes a standing committee for foreign affairs, which also meets when Reichstag is not in session, after the term is expired or after Reichstag has been dissolved, until a new Reichstag meets for the first time. Their sessions are not public, unless two thirds of its members vote to hold a public session. Reichstag furthermore establishes a standing committee to safeguard the rights of parliament juxtaposed Reich government, for the time when parliament is not in session [or], after a term has expired or Reichstag has been dis-solved, until a new Reichstag has assembled. These committees have the status of inquiry committees'.

[179]   Spanish Constitution of 1931. An English version is available here: https://bit.ly/3q5uX02.

[180]   Cassese, 'Politica estera e relazioni internazionali', 510–11.

[181]   See Article 77 of the Spanish Constitution of 1931.

peace as an equal partner in a united Europe',[182] and its Article 25 recognises the primacy and precedence of the general rules of international law over national norms. Also, in practice, thanks to techniques like the famous 'Völkerrechtsfreundliche Auslegung',[183] the German legal system has shown itself to be very open to the influence of international law.

A third wave of constitutional internationalisation is represented by the Spanish and Portuguese constitutions. These constitutions introduced a fundamental distinction between the general category of international treaties and the particular group of international treaties devoted to human rights. As for Portugal, the fundamental provision is Article 16 of the Constitution[184] which recognises that international human rights treaties have a complementary role to the Constitution. This provision accords an interpretative role to the Universal Declaration of Human Rights, seemingly excluding other conventions like the ECHR, but the Portuguese Constitutional Court has often used the ECHR as an important auxiliary hermeneutic tool for interpreting the constitution, leaving the matter unresolved.[185] A similar provision is Article 20(1) of the Romanian Constitution: 'Constitutional provisions concerning the citizens' rights and liberties shall be interpreted and enforced in conformity with the Universal Declaration of Human Rights, with the covenants and other treaties Romania is a party to'. Finally, the most important confirmation of human rights treaties' special ranking in Spain is Article 10(2),[186] acknowledging that they provide interpretive guidance in the application of human rights-related constitutional clauses (even if the Constitutional Court specified that this does not implicate that human rights treaties have a constitutional status[187]). An example that is particularly interesting in studying the openness of these constitutions to international human rights treaties is the Czech case. Before the Czech Euro amendment,

---

[182] German Basic Law, Preamble: www.btg-bestellservice.de/pdf/80201000.pdf.

[183] 'According to this technique, any German law should be construed as far as possible in conformity with international law, parallel to the established method of interpretation to comply with EU law ("Europarechts konforme Auslegung"). This mode concerns any norm in national law, since any norm must be in conformity with the international law obligations of Germany', P. Dann, M. Engelhardt, 'The Global Administrative Order Through a German Lens: Perception and Influence of Legal Structures of Global Governance in Germany', *German Law Journal*, No. 7, 2011, 1371, 1386.

[184] Article 16 of the Portuguese Constitution: '1. The fundamental rights enshrined in this Constitution shall not exclude such other rights as may be laid down by law and in the applicable rules of international law. 2. The provisions of this Constitution and of laws concerning fundamental rights shall be interpreted and construed in accordance with the Universal Declaration of Human Rights'.

[185] On Portugal, see: F. Pereira Coutinho, 'Report on Portugal', in G. Martinico, O. Pollicino (eds.), *The National Judicial Treatment of the ECHR and EU Laws: A Comparative Constitutional Perspective*, Europa Law Publishing, Groningen, 2010, 351, 360.

[186] Article 10 of the Spanish Constitution: '2. The norms relative to basic rights and liberties which are recognized by the Constitution shall be interpreted in conformity with the Universal Declaration of Human Rights and the international treaties and agreements on those matters ratified by Spain'.

[187] Tribunal Constitucional, sentencia 30/1991, available at www.tribunalconstitucional.es.

Articles 10 and 87 of the constitution[188] distinguished between international treaties in general and international human rights treaties, giving the latter a super-primary rank and leaving the question of whether international human rights treaties belonged to the constitutional block unanswered. At the same time Article 87(1),[189] of the constitution empowered the Constitutional Court to declare the unconstitutionality of laws conflicting with the Constitution but also those conflicting with international human rights treaties. After the Czech Euro amendment,[190] the new Article 10 of the constitution abandoned such a distinction and now grants all international treaties a super-primary but still sub-constitutional rank,[191] at least from a formal point of view. The Czech Constitutional Court has also adopted a very broad reading of the ECHR and considers it, and other human rights treaties, as different and superior to other international treaties.[192]

In fact, the Czech Constitutional Court has given a very creative reading to new constitutional provisions, de facto rewriting them, since it considers itself empowered to review the validity of national legislation in light of the ECHR[193] in spite of the new text of the Constitution. In 2002 the Czech Constitutional Court said that: 'The inadmissibility of changing the substantive requirements of a democratic state based on the rule of law also contains an instruction to the [CCC], that no amendment to the Constitution can be interpreted in such a way that it would result in limiting an already achieved procedural level of protection for fundamental rights and freedoms'.[194] This way, therefore, the Constitutional Court concluded that 'the international human rights treaties have retained their constitutional status'.[195]

The constitutional openness described by Cassese has produced a turning point, even in the way it conceives the function of the general principles in these legal orders.

In comparative law the idea of general principles is frequently associated with that of openness, since general principles are open norms in at least three ways. First, principles are characterised by what Betti defined a 'surplus of axiological meaning'

---

[188]   Article 10 (previous version) of the Czech Constitution: 'Ratified and promulgated international accords on human rights and fundamental freedoms, to which the Czech Republic has committed itself, are immediately binding and are superior to law'.

[189]   Article 87 (previous version) of the Czech Constitution: '1. The Constitutional Court resolves: (a) the nullification of laws or their individual provisions if they are in contradiction with a constitutional law or an international agreement under Article 10 [international human rights treaties]'. On this: O. Pollicino, *L'allargamento ad est dell'Europa e rapporti tra Corti costituzionali e Corti europee. Verso una teoria generale dell'impatto interordinamentale del diritto sovranazionale?*, Giuffrè, Milan, 2010, 104.

[190]   Constitutional Act 395/2001 Coll.

[191]   See M. Bobek, D. Kosař, 'Report on the Czech Republic and Slovakia', in G. Martinico. O. Pollicino (eds.), *The National Judicial Treatment of the ECHR and EU Laws: A Comparative Constitutional Perspective*, Europa Law Publishing, Groningen, 2010, 133.

[192]   Judgment of 15 April 2003 (I. ÚS 752/02).

[193]   Judgment of the CCC of 30 November 2004, Pl. ÚS 15/04; Judgment of the CCC of 22 March 2005, Pl. ÚS 45/04.

[194]   Judgment of the CCC of 25-06-2002, Pl. ÚS 36/01, www.usoud.cz/en.

[195]   Bobek, Kosař, 'Report on the Czech Republic', 135.

[*eccedenza di contenuto assiologico*],[196] because of their *vis expansiva* and their indefinite content when compared to other norms. Second, principles are also open since they often act as a bridge between two different normative systems (law and morality) by connecting positive law and natural law.[197] Finally, they are open because they connect domestic and international legal systems, especially after World War II. However, if general principles have been traditionally connected with the idea of openness, comparative law shows that this has not always been the case.[198] The debate on codifications in Continental Europe clearly shows that there was a period when the general principles were associated with the necessary closure of a legal system, especially in those systems where the civil codes were conceived as an expression of legal nationalism.[199] The debate on the general principles of law in the Italian Civil Code (dated 1942 and passed under the fascist regime) is emblematic from this point of view.[200]

Article 12 of the preliminary provisions to the Italian Civil Code (listing the interpretative criteria available to the interpreter) was drafted to impede a reference to the principles of natural law.[201] When commenting on this provision Guastini argued that the role originally reserved to systematic interpretation was very limited for the interpreter.[202] Thus, systematic interpretation was seen as a sort of *extrema ratio*, that is, exploitable only in exceptional cases. Scholars have also said that according to the original scheme of the Italian Civil Code, systematic interpretation was seen as an act of integration rather than as an act of interpretation *stricto sensu* understood.[203] After entry into force of the Italian Constitution, many of the provisions of the same Civil Code (including Art. 12 of its preliminary provisions) were interpreted in light of the new constitutional principles,[204] and this has changed the role of the general principles as well.[205] If once they were seen as the moment of closure for a legal system (nothing out of the Code, no reference to natural law was allowed), today, the principles are perceived as the moment of openness for a legal order that connects domestic and international law and systematic interpretation

---

[196] E. Betti, *Teoria generale della interpretazione*, II, Giuffrè, Milan, 1955, 850.

[197] On this debate, see R. Dworkin, *Taking Rights Seriously*, Harvard University Press, Cambridge, MA, 1977.

[198] G. Del Vecchio, 'Les bases du droit comparé et les principes généraux du droit', *Revue internationale de droit comparé*, No. 3, 1960, 493.

[199] P. Grossi, *A History of European Law*, Blackwell, Malden, 2010, 154.

[200] L. Paladin, 'Costituzione, preleggi e codice civile', *Rivista di diritto civile*, No. 1, 1993, 19, 23.

[201] Paladin, 'Costituzione, preleggi'.

[202] R. Guastini, *Le fonti del diritto. Fondamenti teorici*, Giuffrè, Milan, 2010, 347.

[203] Guastini, *Le fonti del diritto*.

[204] M. Ruotolo, 'L'incidenza della Costituzione repubblicana sulla lettura dell'art. 12 delle preleggi', in D. M. Cananzi, R. Righi (eds.), *Ontologia e analisi del diritto. Scritti per Gaetano Carcaterra*, Giuffrè, Milan, 2012, 1297; A. Giuliani, 'Le disposizioni sulla legge in generale. Gli articoli da 1 a 15', in P. Rescigno (ed.), *Trattato di diritto privato 1, Premesse e disposizioni preliminari*, UTET, Turin, 1999, 379.

[205] Paladin, 'Costituzione, preleggi'.

(often combined with consistent interpretation)[206] which is no longer seen as a last resort for the interpreter. If this is true, constitutionalism has favoured the emergence of a kind of 'osmotic law'[207] or, as I have tried to explain elsewhere, 'complex' law.[208] Against this background, principles serve as channels of openness by securing the axiological (desired) continuity that exists between the domestic and the international levels and that is functional to the efforts made to project the values of constitutionalism beyond the national dimension. As has been happening in Italy and elsewhere, this constitutional openness has not excluded margin for conflicts and disagreements between national constitutional or supreme courts and international judges[209] who have, to borrow the title of an interesting book, been 'duelling for supremacy'.[210] This confirms that, by opening up to the law of the international community, EU post–WWII constitutions have not renounced sovereignty. On the contrary, they have tried to come up with a balance between sovereignty and openness which enables international and EU law to participate in the historical mission developed by constitutionalism. This explains the growing success of the ECHR and EU law that has given an added value to the protection of fundamental rights at the national level.[211] If this is true, post–WWII constitutionalism has certainly rejected the nationalist flavour that sovereignists claim to find in the wording of these constitutional documents.

---

[206]   R. Bin, 'L'interpretazione conforme. Due o tre cose che so di lei', 2015, www.rivistaaic.it/it/rivista/ultimi-contributi-pubblicati/roberto-bin/l-interpretazione-conforme-due-o-tre-cose-che-so-di-lei.

[207]   A. Ruggeri, 'Dimensione europea della tutela dei diritti fondamentali e tecniche interpretative', 2009, www.federalismi.it/nv14/articolo-documento.cfm?Artid=14806.

[208]   G. Martinico, *The Tangled Complexity of the EU Constitutional Process: The Frustrating Knot of Europe*, Routledge, Abingdon, 2012.

[209]   M. Breuer (ed.), *Principled Resistance to ECtHR Judgments – A New Paradigm?* Springer, Berlin, 2019; P. Popelier, S. Lambrecht, K. Lemmens (eds.), *Criticism of the European Court of Human Rights*, Intersentia, Antwerp, 2016.

[210]   Palombino (ed.), *Duelling for Supremacy*.

[211]   H. Keller, A. Stone Sweet (eds.), *A Europe of Rights: The Impact of the ECHR on National Legal Systems*, Oxford University Press, Oxford, 2009; G. Martinico, O. Pollicino, *The Interaction between Europe's Legal Systems: Judicial Dialogue and the Creation of Supranational Laws*, Elgar, Cheltenham, 2012.

4

Mimetism and Parasitism in Action: Politics of Immediacy and the Case of the Referendum

In this chapter, I shall investigate the aspect of the politics of immediacy, exploring how populists understand the referendum. Following an idea endorsed by Davide Casaleggio, the mastermind of the Rousseau platform,[1] former Minister Riccardo Fraccaro[2] denounced the insufficiency of classic representative democracy and stressed the need for more direct democracy, especially with the advent of new technologies. These are important considerations that deserve attention and should not necessarily be seen as populist. However, Davide Casaleggio also said that 'the overcoming of representative democracy is inevitable'[3] and in light of these declarations, one may express concerns, especially regarding the maximum dose of direct democracy that a system of representative democracy can tolerate. Not by coincidence, Bobbio warned that 'nothing threatens to kill democracy more than excess of democracy',[4] stressing the risk of immediacy. If democracy is essentially 'the time that gives us detachment from problems and their solutions',[5] the politics of immediacy could kill the quality of our democracy and destroy the time factor, which is essential in building political compromise. This is even more evident in light of the

---

[1] Rousseau is The Five Star Movement's online platform, where the registered users of the Movement discuss issues and vote. It is understood as a tool of direct democracy. Davide Casaleggio is the son of Gianroberto Casaleggio, the late guru of the Five Star Movement.

[2] 'Riccardo Fraccaro: meno onorevoli e più referendum. In cinque leggi il piano di riforme', 11 September 2018, https://bit.ly/3gDm56c; see also R. Fraccaro, 19 June 2018, https://ricerca .repubblica.it/repubblica/archivio/repubblica/2018/06/19/la-democrazia-integrale32.html.

[3] 'Davide Casaleggio: "Il Parlamento? In futuro forse non sarà più necessario"', 23 July 2018, https://bit.ly /2UjK7tW.

[4] N. Bobbio, *Il futuro della democrazia*, Einaudi, Turin, 1984, 14, my own translation. 'Representative democracy is the true target, as the populist critique of parliamentary politics translates into a call for an unmediated relation of the leader to the people en masse', N. Urbinati, 'Populism and the Principle of Majority', in C. Rovira Kaltwasser, P. Taggart, P. Ochoa Espejo, P. Ostiguy (eds.), *The Oxford Handbook of Populism*, Oxford University Press, 2017, 571, 575.

[5] G. Zagrebelsky, 'Una riflessione sulla democrazia', in Gruppo di Resistenza Morale (ed.), *Argomenti per il dissenso. Costituzione, democrazia, antifascismo*, Celid, Turin, 1994, 24–5 also cited by F. Pallante, *Contro la democrazia diretta*, Einaudi, Turin, 2020, 111, my own translation.

acceleration produced by new technologies,[6] which has led to a new form of populism:

> [T]he link between politicians and the people becomes one of not only directness but also immediacy thanks to the innovation of social media. Taken together, the age of social media redefines political temporality by accelerating the tempo of democratic processes, heralding the arrival of instantaneous democracy. [. . .] new populism and instantaneous democracy do not result from the lack of information or the people's loss of the desire for knowledge. The question is how the learning function of constitutional democracy can continue to work in the face of the relentless pursuit of instantaneousness. As discussed above, the fundamental challenge from new populism is its unmaking the structure of articulated politics in constitutional democracy as it rides the wave of instantaneous democracy to displace the deliberative political tempo. That suggests that the multistage process of constitutional governance and its embedded function of democratic learning operate on a particular political temporality.[7]

Davide Casaleggio constantly refers to the potential of new technologies for the life of contemporary democracies, especially in terms of participation in political life.

New technologies also offer exciting ideas for rethinking the relationship between democracy and constitutionalism, and perhaps even for overcoming that noble but ambiguous concept of constituent power.[8] In this respect, new technologies also risk changing the balance between direct and representative democracy achieved by contemporary constitutions. In this chapter, I shall look at the how the Italian Constitution tries to manage the risks connected with the referendum. As always in this book, Italy will be treated as the product of a broader comparative constitutional trend. I shall recall how populists understand the referendum by introducing some general elements that will be expanded upon in subsequent chapters. While referendums are normally seen by populist movements as a kind of 'catch-all' appeal to the people used to react against the corruption or passivity of institutions,

---

[6] On populism and the media, see: L. Manucci, 'Populism and the Media', in C. Rovira Kaltwasser, P. Taggart, P. Ochoa Espejo, P. Ostiguy (eds.), *The Oxford Handbook of Populism*, Oxford University Press, 2017, 467. On the Italian case: M. Monti, 'Italian Populism and Fake News on the Internet: A New Political Weapon in the Public Discourse', in G. Delledonne, G. Martinico, M. Monti, F. Pacini (eds.), *Italian Populism and Constitutional Law Strategies, Conflicts and Dilemmas*, Palgrave, London, 2020, 177.

[7] M. S. Kuo, 'Against instantaneous democracy', *International Journal of Constitutional Law*, No. 2, 2019, 554, respectively at 561 and 571. The author adds that: 'The democracy of instantaneousness brings about a new political landscape. On the one hand, it releases the untapped political energy in democratic societies, suggesting a more responsive and unmediated form of politics. On the other hand, instantaneousness unleashes the spell of authenticity. In the eyes of populists, this appears to be a democratic dream come true. The feature of instantaneousness breathes new life to populism. New populism points in the direction of unmediated politics', Kuo, 'Against instantaneous democracy', 561.

[8] H. Landemore, 'We, All of the People. Five Lessons from Iceland's Failed Experiment in Creating a Crowdsourced Constitution', 2014, https://slate.com/technology/2014/07/five-lessons-from-icelands-failed-crowdsourced-constitution-experiment.html.

constitutional lawyers tend to handle referendums with care,[9] looking upon them as noble instruments whose compatibility with representative democracy must be guaranteed. I will also discuss how constitutional lawyers have traditionally looked at the referendum with suspicion, stressing both the pros and cons of its use in the context of representative democracy. In so doing, I shall emphasise the chameleonic nature of this instrument and the variety of solutions that have been devised in comparative law[10] to deal with the risks of abuse. In closing, I shall review the constitutional frame characterising the Italian context and the critical role played by the Italian Constitutional Court in 'rationalising' this instrument; and finally, I shall look at comparative constitutional law in order to prove how artificial the concept of majority endorsed by populists is, and to identify some solutions to preserve constitutional democracy from excessive use of the referendum.

4.2 THE REFERENDUM AND CONSTITUTIONAL LAW: AN INSTRUMENT TO HANDLE WITH CARE

It has been said that 'referendums do not automatically improve the democratic process. Instead, they often function as a substitute for a comprehensive discussion on the merits of vital policy issues'.[11] These lines say a lot about the constitutive ambiguity of referendums: on the one hand, they have entered the toolbox of post-totalitarian democracies; on the other hand, the idea that they represent a window of opportunity to discuss the merits of some fundamental political choices may introduce risks for the entire system. As political scientists and historians recall, referendums were frequently employed by authoritarian leaders in the past,[12] which is why they are still seen today with suspicion and permitted with varying levels of freedom by different countries' constitutional provisions.[13] Scholars have also identified reasons why excessive use of this instrument may be problematic:

---

[9] R. Carré de Malberg, 'Considérations théoriques sur la question de la combinaison du referendum avec le parlementarisme', *Annuaire de l'Institut international de droit public*, Vol. II, 1931, PUF, Paris, 272; B. Mirkine Guetzévitch, 'Le référendum et le parlementarisme dans les nouvelles constitutions européennes', *Annuaire de l'Institut international de droit public*, Vol. II, PUF, Paris, 1931, 285; M. Volpi, 'Referendum (dir. cost)', *Digesto delle discipline pubblicistiche*, Vol. XII, UTET, Turin, 1997, 434.

[10] D. Butler, A. Ranney (eds.), *Referendums Around the World: The Growing Use of Direct Democracy*, AEI press, Washington, 1994; Matt Qvortrup, *A Comparative Study of Referendums: Government by the People*, Manchester University Press, 2002.

[11] L. Topaloff, 'The Rise of Referendums: Elite Strategy or Populist Weapon?', *Journal of Democracy*, No. 3, 2017, 127.

[12] 'Here popular votes have – as the case of Napoleon Bonaparte shows – been used as a topdown device to acquire legitimacy for a decision made by a more or less autocratic ruler', M. Qvortrup, 'Introduction: Theory, Practice and History', in Qvortrup (ed.), *Referendums around the World*, Palgrave, London, 2018, 1, 10.

[13] Butler, Ranney (eds.), *Referendums*; Qvortrup, *A Comparative Study*.

Referendums are also poor tools for addressing complex questions that cannot be posed in a straightforward yes-or-no manner. The 'Oxi' referendum, initiated by Greece's populist ruling party Syriza, contained 68 words and name-checked four international institutions. It also asked citizens to give their opinion on an EU and IMF proposal whose deadline had already passed by the time of the vote. In holding this referendum, Greece's leaders seemed to be interested more in rallying support that might aid them at the international negotiating table than in setting the actual policy options clearly and honestly before the voters. The 2016 Brexit referendum also failed to offer clear options [. . .] In fact, referendums are a highly problematic mechanism for channeling the people's voice in representative democratic systems. Referendums raise difficult questions concerning the nature of legitimacy within these systems. They also often fail to allow for adequate public debate, as the recent experiences of the 'Oxi' and Brexit referendums have revealed.[14]

As noted above, scholars have traditionally pointed out the ambiguities of referendums and the risks connected to appropriate use of the instrument. More recently, the possibility of distinguishing between referendums and plebiscites[15] has seemed to become more problematic,[16] although scholars continue to use this distinction by arguing that a 'plebiscite is a populist device through which the people are treated by a government as a manipulable mass rather than a reasoning public'.[17] Although the use of referendums is a relatively recent phenomenon,[18] this debate has been going on for a long time.[19] Max Weber, for instance, recalled such risks and stressed that it can be used to relieve political forces of responsibility:

> The referendum does not know the compromise, upon which the majority of all laws is based in every mass state with strong regional, social, religious and other cleavages [. . .] Moreover, the plebiscitary principles weaken the autonomous role of the party leader and the responsibility of the civil servants. A disavowal of the leading officials through a plebiscite which rejects their proposals does not and

[14] Topaloff, 'The Rise', 138.

[15] F. Biagi, 'Plebiscite', *The Max Planck Encyclopedia of Comparative Constitutional Law*, 2017, https://oxcon.ouplaw.com/view/10.1093/law-mpeccol/law-mpeccol-e414.

[16] Butler, Ranney (eds.), *Referendums*.

[17] 'Two criteria allow us to identify which phenomenon we are facing. Who initiates the proposal on which the people vote and who phrases the question? What is the issue to be settled?' Jack Hayward, 'The Populist Challenge to Élitist Democracy in Europe', in J. Hayward (ed.), *Elitism, Populism, and European Politics*, Oxford University Press, 10, 15.

[18] 'According to the Center for Research on Direct Democracy, a total of only fourteen national referendums took place worldwide between the years 1700 and 1800. All of these fourteen votes took place after 1792, and six of them occurred in France. In the course of the next century, this number went up to 140. In both the nineteenth and the twentieth centuries, the majority of referendums took place in a single country—Switzerland, which introduced the referendum as a national political institution with its 1848 constitution and has since held more nationwide referendums than all other countries combined', Topaloff, 'The Rise', 128.

[19] M. Luciani, 'Il referendum: questioni teoriche e dell'esperienza italiana', *Revista catalana de dret públic*, No. 2, 2008, 157; M. Luciani, 'Introduzione', in M. Luciani, M. Volpi (eds.), *Referendum*, Laterza, Rome, 1992, 3; A. Di Giovine, 'Referendum e responsabilità politica', *Diritto Pubblico Comparato ed Europeo*, No. 3, 2005, 1214.

cannot enforce their resignation, as does a vote of no-confidence in parliamentary states, for the negative vote does not identify its reasons and does not oblige the negatively voting mass, as it does a parliamentary majority voting against a government, to replace the disavowed officials with its own responsible leaders.[20]

These are considerations that have inspired generations of social scientists and that are dramatically topical nowadays. The debate on the noble and yet complex instrument of the referendum has been given new lifeblood by the British events connected to the Brexit vote held on 23 June 2016, the consequent request for a new referendum on Scottish independence and the burning Catalan question. There are different explanations for this: the crisis of traditional political parties, since referendums have increasingly been called 'at the time when the relationship between "aggregators" and "articulators" broke down; at the time when the frozen party system began to thaw, and at the time when the number of party-identifiers began to drop'.[21] These considerations do not exclude the possibility that referendums can also give an added value to representative democracy. Scholars have dealt extensively with this subject,[22] and there are also mature democracies that have inherited, and to a certain extent, constitutionalised some plebiscitary elements. Such is the case of the French Fifth Republic, for instance. Article 3 of the French Constitution reads: 'National sovereignty belongs to the people who shall exercise it through their representatives and by means of referendum'. Tierney has dealt with this provision, showing how it responds to a certain constitutional tradition and idea of the

---

[20]   M. Weber, *Economy and Society*, University of California Press, Berkeley, 1978 (German edition 1922), https://archive.org/stream/MaxWeberEconomyAndSociety/MaxWeberEconomyAndSociety_djvu.txt.

[21]   Qvortrup, 'Introduction', 14. 'The decline in the ability of élite-directed organizations such as parties, trade unions, and churches to achieve mass mobilization has provided the political space for the emergence of élite-directing social movements that are disposed to use methods of political action other than voting for political representatives', Hayward, 'The Populist', 22.

[22]   'Four principal virtues can be advanced briefly for the referendum. First, it disentangles issues that are confused in a "take it or leave it" party electoral programme and so provides a more accurate popular verdict. Second, the referendum campaign helps educate at least some of the electorate about the issues over which citizens are invited to make up their minds, although in a plebiscite the issues are deliberately obfuscated. Third, casting their votes in a referendum gives citizens a sense of direct participation in decisions, and so they acquire a greater identification with public policies. Fourth, it strengthens the electorate against their representatives, who may – like all élites – misrepresent their views. Four countervailing vices may be adduced to which referendums are prone. First, political problems are often interdependent and difficult to isolate, so attempts to deal with them piecemeal readily lead to divergent decisions and the inability to pursue consistent public policies. Second, referendums tend to highlight the inertia of public opinion, although Italy has recently provided a strong counter-example to habitual references to Swiss experience. Third, not merely are radical policies generally promoted by minorities, but the voters are not competent to decide complex issues and are susceptible to demagogic propaganda. Voters find it easier to judge the actions of their representatives retrospectively, by results. Fourth, recourse to direct democracy encourages the deferential politician who leads from behind. The cultivation of prevailing prejudices in pursuit of short-term popularity displaces courageous leadership that persuades the less well informed', Hayward, 'The Populist', 17.

constituent power developed during the revolutionary period.[23] The frequent use of the referendum during the presidency of General de Gaulle has induced some scholars to speak of 'Bonapartism',[24] an element which can be found even more recently in French history.[25]

Comparative lawyers and political scientists have reflected at length on the complicated relationship between referendums and representative democracy.[26] British lawyers have reclaimed the topic in light of the recent debate on Brexit, and EU law scholars have also developed a mass of literature on it due to the several examples of consultations that have taken place on European issues, starting with the referendum conducted in 1975, for instance.[27]

Morel has identified at least two research strands in the debate on referendums and argued:

> Theoretical accounts on referendums belong either to the constitutional debate or to democratic theory. What distinguishes the two debates in a rather precise way is the set of questions raised: while the classical, constitutional, debate questions the

---

[23] 'This seems by one reading at least to embody a restatement of the radical *pouvoir constituant* of the French body politic, returning us to the age-old paradox – does the constitution become the only source for any legitimate exercise of popular constitutional power or does popular sovereignty in France contain its own source of legitimacy? In other words, does Article 3 constitute mere recognition of popular sovereignty rather than legitimacy for it, acknowledging that a higher power vested in the people resides outside and above that of the constitution itself? But there is another element to the equation: the specific reference to the referendum in Article 3. Since the constitution explicitly invokes the referendum as the mode of expression of this power, a further question is begged: even if this higher power of the people above and beyond the constitution does indeed survive constitutional instantiation of lawful authority, are expressions of this power only legitimate when exercised through a referendum? In other words, it may be that the constitution cannot contain (as in circumscribe) the sovereignty of the people, but can it contain (as in facilitate) the vehicle for the exercise of this sovereignty. And if so, how and by whom may such referendums be triggered?', S. Tierney, *Constitutional Referendums: The Theory and Practice of Republican Deliberation*, Oxford University Press, 2012.

[24] F. Mitterrand, *Le Coup d'État permanent*, Plon, Paris, 1965, 27; S. Hazareesingh, 'De Gaulle, le mythe napoléonien, et la consécration de la tradition consulaire républicaine', *Cahiers Jaurès*, No. 3, 2008, 3.

[25] N. Hewlett, 'Nicolas Sarkozy and the Legacy of Bonapartism: The French Presidential and Parliamentary Elections of 2007', *Modern & Contemporary France*, No. 4, 2007, 405.

[26] Carré de Malberg, 'Considérations', Mirkine Guetzévitch, 'Le référendum'; P. V. Uleri, *Referendum e democrazia. Una prospettiva comparata*, Il Mulino, Bologna, 2003; Tierney, *Constitutional*; D. Lewis, *Direct Democracy and Minority Rights: A Critical Assessment of the Tyranny of the Majority in the American States*, Routledge, Abingdon, 2013; C. Schmitt, *Volksentscheid und Volksbegehren. Ein Beitrag zur Auslegung der Weimarer Verfassung und zur Lehre von der unmittelbaren Demokratie* De Gruyter, Berlin, 1927, in Italian, C. Schmitt, *Democrazia e liberalismo. Referendum e iniziativa popolare Hugo Preuss e la dottrina tedesca dello Stato*, Giuffrè, Milan, 2001.

[27] F. Mendez, M. Mendez, V. Triga, *Referendums and the European Union: A Comparative Inquiry*, Cambridge University Press, 2014. More recently: F. Mendez, M. Mendez, V. Triga (eds.), *Referendums on EU Matters*, Policy Department for Citizens' Rights and Constitutional Affairs, European Parliament's Committee on Constitutional Affairs 2017, www.europarl.europa.eu/RegData/etudes/STUD/2017/571402/IPOL_STU(2017)571402_EN.pdf. See also: E. Ö. Atikcan, 'The Puzzle of Double Referendums in the European Union', *Journal of Common Market Studies*, No. 5, 2015, 937.

issue of the compatibility of the referendum with representative democracy and the extent and modalities of its use, the democratic debate rather focuses on the democratic quality of the referendum and whether its extension could help to improve the quality of contemporary democracies.[28]

The ideal starting point of this debate is obviously the well-known exchange between Carré de Malberg and Mirkine Guetzévitch.[29] According to the former, the referendum is compatible with parliamentary systems,[30] especially if understood as a way of solving conflicts occurring between parliament and government and of limiting parliamentary almightiness.[31] According to the latter, the referendum implies a tension that could not be solved with the idea of rationalisation of parliamentarism.[32] This view is somewhat different than Mirkine Guetzévitch's earlier position, as observed by Morel.[33] Actually, the two scholars started with a common premise, that is, the anti-parliamentary flavour of the referendum.[34]

This debate is partly connected to the qualification of the referendum as an instrument of direct democracy. This position is quite widespread in the Italian debate, but there are important scholars who have rejected this view and see the referendum as a device for popular participation[35] on the basis of an interesting historical excursus. It is the case of those, for instance, who have stressed the necessary physical coexistence of people ('the assembled people' as Luciani wrote commenting on Rousseau)[36] as an essential connotation of direct democracy. Similar considerations have been shared by political scientists who argue that direct democracy does not exist as a modern form of government and is a misleading category,[37] and also in light of the continuity that exists between referendums and political competition. If comparative law offers a variety of typologies of referendum (constitutional, legislative, territorial, conventional, preventive, successive,

---

[28] L. Morel, 'Referendum' in M. Rosenfeld, A. Sajó (eds.), *The Oxford Handbook of Comparative Constitutional Law*, Oxford University Press, 2012, 502.

[29] Carré de Malberg, 'Considérations'; Mirkine Guetzévitch, 'Le référendum'.

[30] See also G. Guarino, 'Il referendum e la sua applicazione al regime parlamentare', *Rassegna di diritto pubblico*, No. 1, 1947, 30.

[31] Carré de Malberg, 'Considérations', 232.

[32] Mirkine Guetzévitch, 'Le référendum', 334. 'The discussion of the Russian constitutionalist focused in particular on a new variety of referendums and popular initiatives aimed at solving conflicts between the executive and the legislative, which could lead to the dissolution of parliament or the revocation of the head of the state. Mirkine Guetzévitch regarded this as contradictory with the trend toward a "rationalization" of parliamentarism, by means of a strengthening of executives, which he welcomed as the great novelty of these Constitutions', Morel, 'Referendum', 504.

[33] 'The author had, however, expressed a rather different position one year earlier, in *Les Constitutions de l'Europe nouvelle* (1930), where he wrote that "the referendum is the logical conclusion of the process of rationalization of parliamentarism"', Morel, 'Referendum', n. 9.

[34] M. Luciani, *Commentario della Costituzione. Art. 75 Referendum*, Zanichelli, Bologna, 2005, 33.

[35] Luciani, 'Il referendum', 163.

[36] Luciani, *Commentario*, 11; Luciani, 'Il referendum', 158. On that occasion, Luciani referred to J. J. Rousseau, *Il contratto sociale (The Social Contract)*, 1762, available at: www .earlymoderntexts.com/assets/pdfs/rousseau1762.pdf.

[37] Uleri, *Referendum*, 17.

mandatory, optional, advisory)[38] such a variety does not impede the finding of common concerns and trends. This does not deny the analytical validity of the distinction between experiences in which the referendum initiative belongs to constitutional bodies only and experiences in which the initiative is, so to speak, dispersed (as opposed to centralised/institutionalised) in civil society. In these contexts', referendums have been seen as a 'counter-power'[39] or a manifestation of the 'right of resistance'.[40]

4.3 HOW CONSTITUTIONS COORDINATE REFERENDUMS AND REPRESENTATIVE DEMOCRACY

In order to maximise the impact of the referendum on the life of the legal systems they govern, constitutions establish forms of limitation of the political risks connected to the referendum or strategies that have emerged over the years to challenge shared concerns. For instance, in an essay devoted to the Swiss[41] and American experiences, Auer recalled the American founding fathers' fear of 'pure democracy',[42] and in light of this he went on to explain the lack of referendums at federal level in the United States. These remarks do not come as a surprise if it is true, as Elster argued, that constitutions are frequently the product of violence and

---

[38] Volpi, 'Referendum (dir. cost)'. On territorial referendums in Italy see: M. Nicolini, 'Reforming the Territorial Constitution in Italy: Some Reflections on Durability and Change', in G. Abels, J. Battke (eds.), *Regional Governance in the EU Regions and the Future of Europe*, Elgar, Cheltenham, 2019, 106.

[39] S. Fois, 'Il referendum come "contropotere" e garanzia nel sistema costituzionale italiano', in E. Bettinelli, L. Boneschi (eds.), *Referendum, ordine pubblico, Costituzione*, Bompiani, Milan, 1978, 130.

[40] G. Volpe, 'Referendum abrogativo e diritto di resistenza', in Corte costituzionale (ed.), *Il giudizio di ammissibilità del referendum abrogativo*, Giuffrè, Milan, 1998, 284.

[41] 'Exploring the interaction between voters and the representative branches of government is helpful. It is necessary to take into account that the influence of the representative branches of government is considerably more pervasive than is acknowledged. Consider how the Federal Assembly may respond to popular initiatives for instance; the relationship is an iterative one. The Federal Assembly may submit a counter-proposal to popular initiatives, that is, partial revisions of the constitution requested by the citizenry (art. 139(5)). Whenever such initiatives take the form of a specific draft of a provision (as opposed to a general proposal) the Federal Assembly may decide to take up some or all of the concerns expressed by the initiative to form the basis of its own draft. The electorate then vote on the initiative and the counter-proposal at the same time (art. 139b(1)). In addition to the two questions about the two different proposals, the ballot also contains a third question where the electorate are asked to indicate a preference in case both drafts are accepted (art. 139b(2)). The value of this example is that it demonstrates that there is nothing particularly direct about democracy in Switzerland. Of course, there are more referendums in Switzerland than in, for example, the UK. But it is not the volume of referendums that makes the system distinctive, and it should not be understood to make it direct', L. Raible, L. Trueblood, 'The Swiss System of Referendums and the Impossibility of Direct Democracy', 2017, https://ukconstitutionallaw.org/2017/04/04/lea-raible-and-leah-trueblood-the-swiss-system-of-referendums-and-the-impossibility-of-direct-democracy/.

[42] A. Auer, 'L'esperienza del referendum in Svizzera e negli Stati Uniti', in M. Luciani, M. Volpi (eds.), *Referendum*, Laterza, Rome, 1992, 61, 64.

fear.[43] Obviously, the British experience is quite peculiar due to the only partially written nature of its constitutional sources[44] and to the relatively recent practice of an instrument which has been studied by eminent British lawyers such as Dicey.[45] Dicey analysed the issue in light of the well-known distinction between 'political sovereignty' and 'legal sovereignty'.[46] However there have been attempts to extend some of the considerations made with regard to Continental Europe[47] to the British case, and British constitutional lawyers have stressed that the UK peculiarity does not impede fruitful comparisons.[48] It is sufficient to compare, for instance, the Italian discussion about the advantages and disadvantages of referendums[49] with what was written by the Select Committee on the Constitution of the House of Lords some years ago.[50] Even though these cases are different, some of the arguments employed in this debate are identical, and it is no coincidence that the issue of the referendum has given new lifeblood to the need for a (further) codification of British constitutional law.[51] Another element of comparability is given by the common influence exercised by the EU. This also explains why the first important consultation held in the 1970s in the UK was on British membership of the European Economic Community. It is also known, historically, that referendums on European integration have often gone back for seconds: this happened in Ireland and Denmark, for

[43] J. Elster, 'Constitution-Making and Violence', *Journal of Legal Analysis*, No. 1, 2012, 7.

[44] See V. Bogdanor, *The People and the Party System: The Referendum and Electoral Reform in British Politics*, Cambridge University Press, 1981, 75.

[45] A. V. Dicey, 'Ought the referendum to be introduced into England?', *Contemporary Review*, No. 3, 1890, 531.

[46] A. V. Dicey, *Introduction to the Study of the Law of the Constitution*, St. Martin's Press, New York, 1959: 'At this point comes into view the full importance of the distinction already insisted upon between "legal" sovereignty and "political" sovereignty. Parliament is, from a merely legal point of view, the absolute sovereign of the British Empire, since every Act of Parliament is binding on every Court throughout the British dominions, and no rule, whether of morality or of law, which contravenes an Act of Parliament binds any Court throughout the realm. But if Parliament be in the eye of the law a supreme legislature, the essence of representative government is, that the legislature should represent or give effect to the will of the political sovereign, i.e. of the electoral body, or of the nation. That the conduct of the different parts of the legislature should be determined by rules meant to secure harmony between the action of the legislative sovereign and the wishes of the political sovereign, must appear probable from general considerations. If the true ruler or political sovereign of England were, as was once the case, the King, legislation might be carried out in accordance with the King's will by one of two methods. The Crown might itself legislate, by royal proclamations, or decrees; or some other body', in 2013 edition (*The Law of the Constitution*, Oxford University Press, 2013) edited by J. Allison; this passage can be found at 429.

[47] For instance, M. Calamo Specchia, 'Quale disciplina referendaria nel Regno Unito? Brevi note su di un approccio sistematico per un modello a-sistematico', in A. Torre, J. Frosini (eds.), *Democrazia rappresentativa e referendum nel Regno Unito*, Maggioli, Rimini, 2012, 146.

[48] P. Leyland, *Referendums, Popular Sovereignty, and the Territorial Constitution*, in R. Rawlings, P. Leyland, A. Young (eds.), *Sovereignty and the Law*, Oxford University Press, 2013, 145.

[49] Luciani, *Commentario*, 82.

[50] House of Lords. Select Committee on the Constitution 12th Report of Session 2009–10, *Referendums in the United Kingdom. Report with Evidence*, 2010, www.publications.parliament.uk/pa/ld200910/ldselect/ldconst/99/99.pdf.

[51] Leyland, *Referendums*.

instance, with regard to the ratification of some European treaties.[52] In the case of the EU, the 'referendum on sovereign powers' (*referendum sui poteri sovrani*), as described by Baldassarre, has been trialed[53] and, here again, it is possible to recall the different uses of the instrument. Within the almost seventy referendums held on European matters,[54] scholars have identified at least four groups: 1) 'membership referendums'; 2) 'treaty revision referendums'; 3) 'policy referendums'; and 4) 'third-country referendums'.[55] Within these four groups, it is possible to find other sub-typologies based on the reasons that have led to the consultation and the subject of the question.[56] All this confirms not only the topicality of the issue but also the multi-functional nature of this device in European and comparative constitutional law.

Even in the UK, concerns about the use of the referendum have not been absent. There is legislative discipline which governs the use of this tool,[57] although it is not easy to understand what the formula 'constitutional matters' means. Indeed, although it is unquestioned that 'referendums undoubtedly have a constitutional role to play',[58] in this context, as Bogdanor said, 'the problem is that in Britain constitutional issues can easily arise out of seemingly non-constitutional legislation'.[59] Not to mention that 'without clear rules referendums can be manipu-lated politically'.[60] The report of the Select Committee on the Constitution of the House of Lords gave an important contribution to this debate. First, it offered an

---

[52] Atikcan, 'The Puzzle'.

[53] A. Baldassarre, 'Il referendum» costituzionale', *Quaderni costituzionali*, No. 2, 1994, 235.

[54] 'To date there have been 60 referendums on EU-related matters making the referendum a key feature of the European integration process since the 1970s', Mendez, Mendez, Triga (eds.), *Referendums on EU Matters*, 8.

[55] Mendez, Mendez, Triga (eds.), *Referendums on EU Matters*.

[56] 'Referendums on EU matters vary considerably in terms of (1) their functional properties or type and (2) the reasons for calling them. Taking into account these two dimensions is crucial to understanding the dynamics of EU-related referendums. There are four main types of EU-related referendum: (1) membership referendums (which can be divided between the frequently deployed accession referen-dum and the rarely used withdrawal referendum); (2) treaty revision referendums, which were generated by all six main rounds of treaty revision from the SEA to Lisbon; (3) policy referendums, which are held by EU Member States on an EU-related policy matter but are neither about membership nor treaty revision; (4) third-country referendums, which are held on the topic of European integration by states that are neither EU Member States nor are they Candidate States voting directly on an accession treaty. There are three broad categories of motives for referendums on EU matters which operate under distinct decisional logics: (1) the logic of constitutionality where referendums are either clearly constitutionally mandatory or at least considered to be; (2) the logic of appropriateness where the overriding rationale for deployment of a referendum is due to legitimacy concerns; (3) the logic of partisan calculus where the referendum is held for partisan motives whether to boost the popularity of an incumbent leader or to mediate divisions within a political party', Mendez, Mendez, Triga (eds.), *Referendums on EU Matters*, 19.

[57] 'The Election Commission is placed under a duty to advise on the intelligibility of any referendum questions and the legislation also establishes control over donations and expenses and many other issues. However, no clear rules have emerged to determine under what precise constitutional conditions referendums can be held', Leyland, *Referendums*, 145.

[58] Leyland, *Referendums*, 146.

[59] Bogdanor, *The People*, 183.

[60] Leyland, *Referendums*, 146.

account of the pros[61] and cons[62] in the use of the referendum; second, it recalled some of the fundamental constitutional issues that would require the holding of a referendum (to abolish the Monarchy; to leave the European Union; for any of the nations of the UK to secede from the Union; to abolish either House of Parliament; to change the electoral system for the House of Commons; to adopt a written constitution; and to change the UK's system of currency).[63]

There are, finally, two other considerations that make the referendum fascinating to comparative lawyers: the fact that many constitutional lawyers have changed their minds about this instrument,[64] which confirms its very complex nature and, above all, the chameleonic essence of this tool. The first consideration can be explained in light of the fact that it is always necessary to look at it from the systemic impact that it might have on the context of representative democracy. This partly explains the changing position of Dicey, a point Weill has explored in a very important article which revolved around the reasons for this (apparent) departure from the principle of parliamentary sovereignty.[65]

Many criticised Dicey for this change of mind; others have tried to find continuity in his thought by stressing the parliamentary disappointment that caused it.[66]

This was due to the Parliament Act 1911 which had removed, in Dicey's own words, '[the] last effective constitutional safeguard'[67] by recognising the supremacy of the House of Commons over the House of Lords and creating a system in which the majority of the Commons 'can arrogate to itself that legislative omnipotence which of right belongs to the nation'.[68] In other words, according to Dicey, referendums could compensate the new institutional scenario after the weakening of the House of Lords. Because of the fact that the British institutional equilibrium had

---

[61] 'That referendums enhance the democratic process'; 'that referendums can be a "weapon of entrench-ment"'; 'that referendums can "settle" an issue'; 'that referendums can be a "protective device"'; 'that referendums enhance citizen engagement'; 'that referendums promote voter education'; 'that voters are able to make reasoned judgments'; 'that referendums are popular with voters'; 'that referendums complement representative democracy', House of Lords, Select Committee on the Constitution 12th Report of Session 2009–10; on this, see Leyland, *Referendums*, 13.

[62] Among others: 'That referendums are a tactical device'; 'that referendums are dominated by elite groups'; 'that referendums can have a damaging effect on minority groups'; 'that referendums are a conservative device'; 'that referendums do not "settle" an issue'; 'that referendums fail to deal with complex issues'; 'that referendums tend not to be about the issue in question'; 'that voters show little desire to participate in referendums'; 'that referendums are costly'; 'that referendums undermine representative democracy', House of Lords, Select Committee on the Constitution 12th Report of Session 2009–10; on this, see Leyland, *Referendums*, 16.

[63] House of Lords, Select Committee on the Constitution 12th Report of Session 2009–10, Leyland, *Referendums*, 27.

[64] I already mentioned the case of Mirkine Guetzévitch, but see also A. V. Dicey *infra*.

[65] R. Weill, 'Dicey Was Not Diceyan', *Cambridge Law Journal*, No. 2, 2003, 474, 481.

[66] Weill, 'Dicey', 475.

[67] A. V. Dicey, 'The Parliament Act 1911 and the Destruction of All Constitutional Safeguards', in W. Anson, F. E. Smith, W. de Broke (eds.), *Rights of Citizenship: A Survey of Safeguards for the People*, Frederick Warne, London, 1912, 81.

[68] Dicey, *The Parliament*, 91.

changed, Dicey's point was necessary to involve the people in the 'constitutional changes'.

The referendum also has a chameleonic nature, as it can serve different purposes and be activated in different manners, depending on the jurisdiction taken into account for the comparative analysis.

It is sufficient here to notice what has happened in the UK, where in 1981 Bogdanor defined the referendum as a 'conservative device':

> The referendum is generally seen as an instrument of popular sovereignty, an institutional expression of the doctrine that political authority derives from the people. Yet, as the history of the debate in Britain shows, the urge towards popular participation or self-government has not played a very important part in its advocacy. On the contrary, since first proposed by Dicey, the referendum has been suggested primarily as a means of checking disagreeable legislation [. . .] It has been, in the words of Beaverbrook, 'not a spear but a shield', an adjunct to representative government and not a replacement for it.[69]

This explains why referendums 'could serve to increase its [the government's] power', and it is no coincidence that over recent years the debate has focused on how to regulate them to avoid possible abuses. Confirmation of this intuition came in the 1990s when referendums were used as an instrument to enfranchise the leadership from the internal influences of the party and to create a direct connection with the people. This has led to forms of plebiscitary drift.[70]

These considerations also clarify why the referendum – once defined by Bogdanor as a 'conservative device' – became part of the reformist season later, during the Blair government, for instance.[71]

Finally, all the procedural caveats surrounding the holding of a referendum matter; while many perceive that the only significant difference between the Scottish and Catalan referendums was the unilateral nature of the latter, what really makes the Catalan scenario inconsistent with the domestic constitutional framework is the fact that the Spanish Autonomous Communities have no competence to call these types of referendums, as laid down in Article 149.1.32 of the Spanish Constitution.[72] This might appear to be a procedural element, but it affects the substance of the issue even more than the generic content of Article 2 of the Spanish Constitution, according to which 'The Constitution is based on the indissoluble unity of the Spanish Nation'.[73]

---

[69] Bogdanor, *The People*, 69.
[70] A. Torre, Il referendum nel Regno Unito: radici sparse, pianta rigogliosa, in A. Torre, J. Frosini (eds.), *Democrazia rappresentativa e referendum nel Regno Unito*, Maggioli, Rimini, 2012, 11, 73.
[71] G. Carboni, 'I referendum mai realizzati e ancora da realizzare', in A. Torre, J. Frosini (eds.), *Democrazia rappresentativa e referendum nel Regno Unito*, Maggioli, Rimini, 2012, 399, 401.
[72] Article 149.1.32 of the Spanish Constitution: '1. The State shall have exclusive competence over the following matters [. . .]: 32. Authorization of popular consultations through the holding of referendums'.
[73] Article 2 of the Spanish Constitution.

4.4 HOW POPULISTS UNDERSTAND THE REFERENDUM

As discussed previously, the obsession of populist movements with the 'politics of immediacy'[74] inevitably results in questioning many of the instruments of representative democracy and in emphasising the importance of instruments of direct and participatory democracy. This explains the importance that referendums play in the populist agenda as a tool for charismatic leaders who have direct contact with the people (a concept frequently employed, but scarcely developed, as Canovan pointed out in 2004).[75] Frequently, the attack on representative institutions and the emphasis on referendums are taken as two sides of the same coin, since they are both emanations of that lack of mediation that political scientists frequently portray as one of the pillars of populism.[76] As Canovan pointed out: 'New Populists often call for issues of popular concern to be decided by referendum, by-passing professional politicians and leaving decisions to the people'.[77] Referendums also galvanise the dichotomous approach frequently endorsed by populists in their constant appeals to the people understood as a monolithic entity, in the sense that they tend to represent a part of the people as the people:

> Reporting on the High Court judgement regarding Article 50, the pro-Brexit press emphatically evoked a stark populist dichotomy: 'The judges vs. the people' was the front headline of the normally austere *The Daily Telegraph*; while the *Daily Mail* went one further with 'Enemies of the People' under the front-page photograph of the three High Court judges.[78]

References to the necessity of calling a referendum to amend the constitution were also present in the strategy endorsed by Marine Le Pen during the presidential electoral campaign in 2017 in order to restore the superiority of national law over the international obligations of France, especially with regard to duties stemming from EU membership.[79]

A massive use of referendums and the need for a grand constitutional reform are elements that have characterised the recent history of the *Front National* (now *Rassemblement National*), which has proposed a referendum to reintroduce the death penalty and on other very sensitive issues.[80] However, the *Front National*'s populism also presents elements of continuity with the past (and similar

---

[74] L. Corrias, 'Populism in a Constitutional Key: Constituent Power, Popular Sovereignty and Constitutional Identity', *European Constitutional Law Review*, No. 1, 2016, 6, 12.

[75] M. Canovan, 'Populism for PoliticalTtheorists?', *Journal of Political Ideologies*, 3, 2004, 241.

[76] Y. Mény, Y. Surel, *Populismo e democrazia*, Il Mulino, Bologna, 2004.

[77] Canovan, 'Populism', 241, 242.

[78] M. Freeden, 'After the Brexit Referendum: Revisiting Populism as an Ideology', *Journal of Political Ideologies*, No. 1, 2017, 1, 7.

[79] J. Patard, 'Le référendum constitutionnel de Marine Le Pen: Moi présidente, je rétablirai la supériorité du droit national!', 2017, www.lepetitjuriste.fr/droit-constitutionnel/referendum-constitutionnel -de-marine-pen-moi-presidente-retablirai-superiorite-droit-national/; T. Fournier, 'From Rhetoric to Action: A Constitutional Analysis of Populism', *German Law Journal*, No. 3, 2019, 362, 376.

[80] Fournier, 'From Rhetoric', 378.

considerations can also be made – regardless of the different constitutional frame – for the Italian context).

Referendums are also unpredictable, and the Hungarian case is very telling of that. Orbán called a referendum on the so-called EU migrant quotas, which was held on 2 October 2016. This referendum was the apex of a long racist and anti-refugee campaign orchestrated by the media close to Orbán. On that occasion, Hungarian people were asked to answer the following question: 'Do you want the European Union to be entitled to prescribe the mandatory settlement of non-Hungarian citizens in Hungary without the consent of parliament?'. Ninety-eight per cent of those who voted rejected the EU's quotas, but in spite of the declarations released after the referendum, the consultation did not achieve the necessary turnout (50%).[81] Nevertheless, as often happens with populists, Orbán presented the result as a great message sent to Brussels and announced possible reforms to 'remove the necessity for 50% of the country's voters to participate in a referendum for it to be valid'.[82] It has been said that Orbán's real intent was to influence domestic politics, and thus he probably managed to achieve his goal. At the same time, the Hungarian context confirms how risky and unpredictable referendums are, as they can act as a boomerang against those who have supported their call. Not by coincidence, while commenting upon this event, Halmai argued that the Hungarian government is a form of authoritarian populism.[83]

4.5 THE ITALIAN DEBATE FROM A COMPARATIVE PERSPECTIVE

Referendums have played an important role in Italian constitutional law; this can be argued even whilst looking at the genesis of the constitutional system, since it was through the so-called institutional referendum held in 1946 that Italy became a Republic. The Italian case is also interesting from a constitutional law perspective for several reasons. It responds to a long-standing debate in continental Europe about how to reconcile direct and representative democracy. To confirm this, it is sufficient to look at the discussion in the Constituent Assembly, in which Costantino Mortati – later justice of the Italian Constitutional Court and eminent constitutional lawyer – proposed constitutionalising different types of referendums (advisory, binding, deliberative) to be triggered by different institutional actors and by the people. In his view, the referendum was a stimulus to keep institutions in touch with their citizens.[84] However, there were three elements to be carefully considered: 1)

---

[81]   J. Culik, 'Hungary's Invalid Refugee Referendum Dents Viktor Orbán's Anti-EU "Revolution"', 2016, https://theconversation.com/hungarys-invalid-refugee-referendum-dents-viktor-orbans-anti-eu-revolution-66424.

[82]   Culik, 'Hungary's'.

[83]   Halmai, 'The Coup against Constitutional Democracy: The Case of Hungary', 2018, https://me.eui.eu/gabor-halmai/wp-content/uploads/sites/385/2018/06/Chapter-15-Halmai-Hungary.pdf.

[84]   C. Mortati, 'Relazione alla II Sottocommissione', 3 September 1946, www.nascitacostituzione.it /05appendici/01generali/00/02/06-mortati.htm;

the turnout; 2) the deliberative quorum; and 3) the number of proponents necessary to trigger the procedure. Finally, Mortati also warned of the necessity to inform the people in order to foster awareness and ensure they were sufficiently educated on the issue to make a decision. This proposal was only partly accepted by the rest of the Constituent Assembly.

The Italian case is particularly interesting as – unlike in other countries – the Italian Constitution permits referendums both at the state and regional levels. Moreover, the abrogative referendum as regulated by the Italian Constitution has been described as a *unicum* in comparative law.[85] The relevant constitutional provisions are the following: Articles 75, 123, 132 and 138.[86] Article 123 is about regional fundamental charters ('Statuti') and provides for the holding of a referendum on these Statuti 'if one-fiftieth of the electors of the Region or one-fifth of the members of the Regional Council so request within three months from its publication' (Art. 123). Article 132 examines a referendum on the possible 'merger between existing Regions' or 'the creation of new Regions having a minimum of one million inhabitants'. The constitutional amendment procedure is governed by Article 138, which provides for the possibility of submitting laws amending the constitution or other constitutional laws 'when, within three months of their publication, such request is made by one-fifth of the members of a House or five hundred thousand voters or five Regional Councils'.

Article 138 also clarifies that the 'law submitted to referendum shall not be promulgated if not approved by a majority of valid votes. A referendum shall not be held if the law has been approved in the second voting by each of the Houses by a majority of two-thirds of the members'. This is what Italian scholars call 'constitutional referendum'.

The recent attempts at reforming the Italian Constitution[87] have reserved a central role for constitutional referendums; suffice to mention here the referendum on Renzi's reform held in 2016. Unlike Salvini and Conte, Renzi has never defined himself as populist but, as suggested by Blokker, amongst others, his behaviour in the campaign for the referendum on constitutional reform and his general

---

F. Rosa, 'Art. 75', in F. Clementi, L. Cuocolo, F. Rosa, G. E. Vigevani (eds.), *La Costituzione italiana*, Vol. II, Il Mulino, Bologna, 2018, 116, 117.

[85] Rosa, 'Art. 75', 116.

[86] See also Article 87 about the power of the President of the Republic to call a general referendum in the cases provided for by the constitution. Of special mention is the only EU-related referendum in Italy, which was held in 1989. It regarded the transformation of the European Communities into a European Union with a European parliament entitled to draft a constitution for Europe. The outcome was highly positive. This referendum is understood as special and advisory in nature. In this respect, a specific constitutional law was adopted (constitutional law 2/1989) since this kind of referendum was understood to be different from those governed by the Italian Constitution; A. Barbera, A. Morrone, *La Repubblica dei referendum*, Il Mulino, Bologna, 2003, 102–3.

[87] F. Politi, 'Il procedimento di revisione della Costituzione Repubblicana. La funzione di garanzia dell'art. 138 Cost. e il ricorso a procedimenti alternativi della forma di governo e tutela dei valori costituzionali', in V. Baldini (ed.), *La Costituzione e la sua revisione*, Pisa University Press, 2014, 87.

conduct recall populist rhetoric. This is particularly true if one thinks of the way in which Renzi tried to dichotomise 'the vote between those that want to modernise Italy – a reform that will "bring Italy into the future" – and the "conservatives" that supposedly cling to a (corrupt) past'.[88] This narrative accompanied the formation of the *Lega–MoVimento 5 Stelle* government. According to Renzi, those who voted against the constitutional reform should be accused of indirectly making this new populist wave in Italy possible, by creating a narrative that links the 'no' vote to his constitutional reform to the victory of 5 *Stelle* in the subsequent general election. The situation is obviously more complex.

Stepping back to the abrogative referendum, this instrument is governed by Article 75, which reads:

> A general referendum may be held to repeal, in whole or in part, a law or a measure having the force of law, when so requested by five hundred thousand voters or five Regional Councils. No referendum may be held on a law regulating taxes, the budget, amnesty or pardon, or a law ratifying an international treaty. Any citizen entitled to vote for the Chamber of Deputies has the right to vote in a referendum. The referendum shall be considered to have been carried if the majority of those eligible has voted and a majority of valid votes has been achieved.

Here, we have a fundamental difference between the constitutional and abrogative referendum: while Article 75 provides for two types of *quorum* – a structural/participatory one and a deliberative one – Article 138 only provides for a deliberative *quorum* without making the validity of the result conditional upon a minimum turnout. This has triggered an interesting debate, as Article 138 was designed for micro-reforms but, since the 1990s, it has been used either to carry out[89] or to propose grand constitutional reforms and sometimes deviations from the procedure designed by Article 138 have been established by constitutional laws. This is the case of constitutional law 1/1997, which established a bicameral parliamentary committee on constitutional reforms ('Bicamerale D'Alema'), in particular by transforming the constitutional referendum from a possibility – if requested according to the terms of Article 138 – into a necessary part of the procedure.

According to some scholars,[90] this would alter the nature of the constitutional referendum, understood by the constitution as a means to preserve minorities (it is 'oppositive' in nature), which would be transformed by constitutional law 1/1997 into a 'confirmative' referendum. The project drafted by the bicameral commission was

---

[88] P. Blokker, '"Vote Yes for a Safe Italy" or "Vote No to Defend the Constitution": Italian Constitutional Politics between Majoritarianism and Civil Resistance', 2016, https://verfassungsblog.de/italy-constitution-referendum-renzi-blokker/.

[89] This was the case of constitutional law 3/2001, which reshaped Title V of the second part of the constitution.

[90] R. Romboli, 'Il referendum costituzionale nell'esperienza repubblicana e nelle prospettive di riforma dell'Article 138 Cost.', in A. Pisaneschi, L. Violini (eds.), *Poteri, garanzie e diritti a sessanta anni dalla Costituzione: scritti per Giovanni Grottanelli de' Santi*, Giuffrè, Milan, 2007, 573.

later abandoned and the new procedure designed by constitutional law 1/1997 was never implemented.

However, the use of Article 138 in cases of grand reforms has inevitably had an impact on the homogeneity of the question submitted to the reform, since voters have been asked (in 2001, 2006 and 2016) to vote either 'yes' or 'no' on particularly heterogeneous and complex questions.

Concerning participation in the constitutional referendums held thus far, in 2001 the turnout was very low, at 34.05 per cent, while it increased in both 2006 (52.46%) and 2016 (65.48%). In the case of the 2020 constitutional referendum the turnout decreased again (53.84%).

The constitutional frame, however, is not exhaustive; in fact, in the history of the Italian Republic the first referendums at national level were activated only after the entry into force of law 352/1970, which complements the constitutional picture by designing the procedure, the conditions and the temporal limitations according to which requests for referendums can be presented.[91] Additionally, it gave the central office of the *Corte di Cassazione* the power to verify compliance with the legislative requirements (i.e., validity and number of signatures).

Moreover, by means of constitutional law 1/1953, a new fundamental competence was given to the Italian Constitutional Court, which is charged with verifying the permissibility of referendums requested by Article 75. Originally, the *Corte costituzionale* understood its role within a narrow perspective by verifying whether the law subject to referendum belonged to exceptions mentioned by Article 75. Later, however, it went beyond this duty by giving a fundamental contribution to the 'rationalisation' of the referendum.[92] For instance, in judgment 16/1978, the Italian Constitutional Court referred to a number of further limitations that can be inferred from the principles governing the system and the very nature of the referendum.[93] In this way the *Corte costituzionale* paved the way for a series of decisions that have insisted on the homogeneity and clarity of the question and on the need to limit the risk of destabilisation inherent in the improper use of the instrument:

> For example, the Court has disallowed requests for referenda in which a single question incorporates several distinct items to be abrogated, thus precluding voters from independently exercising their judgment with respect to each component of the referendum. Likewise, the Court has blocked requests for referenda aimed at abrogating laws the content of which is in some way bound by the Constitution, or which cannot be amended without revising the Constitution itself. A referendum is not permitted if it amounts to an attempt to introduce new legal provisions by

---

[91] This law was passed by the Italian parliament after a long period of reluctance. It is no coincidence that scholars have written of an unwritten anti-referendum convention (*convenzione antireferendaria*) to describe this political attitude. See E. Bettinelli, 'Itinerari della razionalizzazione della convenzione antireferendaria', *Politica del diritto*, No. 5, 1978, 513 and Barbera, Morrone, *La Repubblica*.

[92] Barbera, Morrone, *La Repubblica*, 63; Bettinelli, 'Itinerari', 513.

[93] Corte costituzionale, decision 16/1978, www.cortecostituzionale.it.

rewriting a legislative text rather than an attempt to simply eliminate existing provisions. Nor may a referendum seek to repeal laws required by international or Community obligations, to avoid giving rise to international responsibility on the part of the State without parliamentary approval.[94]

Thanks to this case law,[95] the Italian Constitutional Court has also contributed to guaranteeing the space reserved for political institutions[96] by minimising the risk of collisions between direct and representative democracy. As mentioned previously, referendums have always played an important role in Italian constitutional law, covering particularly sensitive issues[97] that divided the country (the divorce and abortion referendums held, respectively, in 1974 and 1981, for instance), and contributing to reshaping the institutional system. An example of the latter is of course the referendum on the electoral system in 1993. This referendum contributed to a fundamental shift towards a majoritarian system that seemed to favour the emergence of elements of a bipolar political system in Italy before the start of a long reform period, in which different electoral systems were approved by the Italian parliament. Its impact on the institutional system is due to the abrogative nature of referendums in accordance with Article 75, and to the possibility of partial abrogative referendums, that is, referendums on portions of laws. The latter may result in manipulative referendums, since they erase only part of the original provision. In this way, it is not only the letter of the provision that changes (as it can be partially cancelled, thanks to the abrogative force of law of the referendum) but also its content. This explains why abrogative referendums are generally considered as sources of law (provided with the same force of law as the laws that they repeal) by Italian constitutional scholars, since their employment makes it possible to contribute to the law-making process. This also explains why referendums are risky.

It is no coincidence that, in a pivotal book published in 2003, Barbera (current Justice of the Italian Constitutional Court) and Morrone defined Italy as the *Republic of the referendums*.[98] These authors have identified different seasons in the history of the Italian Republic by showing the chameleonic nature of this instrument, which has sometimes served a crucial role in the fight for civil rights promoted by the *Partito Radicale*, while in other periods it has worked as a stimulus for parliament or a form of contestation or counter-power, understood as a means of

---

[94] Italian Constitutional Court, *The Italian Constitutional Court*, 2019, www.cortecostituzionale.it /documenti/download/pdf/The_Italian_Constitutional_Court.pdf.

[95] See also Corte costituzionale, decisions 30/1981, 31/1981, 8/1995, 27/1997, www.cortecostituzionale.it; Rosa, 'Article 75', 120.

[96] This can be found even with regard to other types of referendums, like consultative referendums held at the regional level. See Corte costituzionale, decision 118/2015, www.cortecostituzionale.it.

[97] G. Santomauro, 'Referendum as an Instrument of "Policy Change" on a Crucial Bioethical Issue: A Comparative Case Study on Abortion in Italy and Ireland', in *Nomos. Le attualità del diritto*, No. 1, 2019, 1–37.

[98] Barbera, Morrone, *La Repubblica*.

questioning the establishment.[99] Constitutional scholars in Italy are still debating about what happens to the legislation previously in force when a statute is repealed due to an abrogative referendum. Furthermore, in light of the Constitutional Court case law,[100] the automatic restoration of the legislation previously in force seems to be excluded. Another issue regards whether it is forbidden for the legislator to re-introduce the legislation repealed by a referendum. Since it is prohibited to repeat a referendum which has been rejected in the previous five years (Art. 38 of law 352/1970), scholars have argued that a similar temporal limitation should be imposed on parliament, but the issue is still being debated.[101] Over the last twenty years, a meagre turnout has characterised rounds of consultations and triggered an interesting debate about whether to reform abrogative referendums. A new stimulus to this discussion has been prompted by the activism of the Five Star Movement.

The short (but intense) experience of government of the *Lega* and Five Star Movement coalition was characterised by constant reference to the need for change. It is no coincidence that the government declared itself the 'government of change'[102] (*il governo del cambiamento*). It is interesting to look at the constitutional reforms proposed by the first Conte (to distinguish it from the second Conte executive)[103] government.[104]

Apart from the reduction of the number of parliamentarians – which was confirmed by the constitutional referendum in 2020 and which will be analysed in Chapter 5 – the most interesting proposals are those connected to the enhancement of direct democracy. In this sense, it is necessary to heed the popular initiative[105] with the introduction of a type of legislative referendum (*referendum propositivo*), that is, a referendum on a legislative initiative, if parliament does not deal with and approve said popular initiative within a reasonable term (18 months), provided that

---

99   Rosa, 'Article 75', 121.

100   Corte costituzionale, decision 13/2012, www.cortecostituzionale.it.

101   Luciani, *Commentario*, 680.

102   See the 'Summary of the contract for the government of change' signed by Five Star Movement and *Lega*: www.ilblogdellestelle.it/2018/05/summary_of_the_contract_for_the_government_of_change_in_italy.html.

103   Supported by the Five Star Movement, the Democratic Party (PD), the Free and Equal Party (LeU) and the new political force created by Matteo Renzi, *Italia Viva*.

104   I am not going to offer an overview of all of the constitutional reforms proposed, as I shall focus on those proposed by exponents of the majority: https://www.camera.it/temiap/documentazione/temi/pdf/1104514.pdf. There is an entire section devoted to that in the 'Nota di aggiornamento del DEF 2018', http://www.mef.gov.it/inevidenza/documenti/NADEF_2018.pdf.

105   Currently, Article 71 of the Italian Constitution reads: 'Legislation may be introduced by the Government, by a Member of Parliament and by those entities and bodies so empowered by constitutional amendment law. The people may initiate legislation by proposing a bill drawn up in sections and signed by at least fifty-thousand voters'.

the Constitutional Court declares the referendum permissible.[106] These proposals clearly look at Switzerland; in particular, the legislative referendum is inspired by Article 139b of the Swiss Constitution, which provides for a simultaneous referendum on a popular initiative and its counter-proposal.[107] This does not come as a surprise, Fraccaro, former Minister for Parliamentary Relations and Direct Democracy during the first Conte government, openly declared his admiration for Switzerland in an interview, saying that 'The Swiss system is our beacon: it is the one we prefer and the one that inspires us the most'.[108] Switzerland is notoriously the 'promised land' of direct and participatory democracy and its constitution provides for different types of referendums.[109] However, the importance acquired by the referendum in the Swiss system can also be explained in light of the particular features that characterise its constitutional order: its directorial form of government,[110] in which there is no proper relationship of confidence between the Federal Council and the Federal Assembly, and the lack of judicial review of legislation for federal laws. These are just two elements that make Switzerland special and they have somehow been compensated by an evident use of instruments of direct democracy, which can be used as a stimulus for the political system and in order to remedy the risk of institutional paralysis.[111] This context is very far from the features of the Italian constitutional system, which has a parliamentary form of government. These differences inevitably make the possibility of a legal transplant[112] more difficult.

Indeed, these potential reforms have been criticised since they would risk altering the equilibrium between direct and representative democracy by introducing a sort of 'concurrent and alternative popular legislative power'.[113] These words stress the anti-parliamentary flavour that inspired this proposal. This chapter does not aim to offer an exhaustive analysis of this proposal, which is just the tip of the iceberg. There are also a number of technical points that can be made in this regard: first, Article 139b of the Swiss Constitution refers to a 'popular initiative requesting a partial revision of the Federal Constitution in specific terms' (which is governed by Art.

---

[106]   D'Uva et al., A. C. n. 1173, http://documenti.camera.it/leg18/pdl/pdf/leg.18.pdl.camera .1173.18PDL0028960.pdf.

[107]   Raible, Trueblood, 'The Swiss System'.

[108]   My own translation. For the interview see: S. Fenazzi, 'Per M5S, quello svizzero è il "modello faro" di democrazia diretta', 20 June 2016, https://bit.ly/2SMkqlz.

[109]   See Articles 138–42 for instance.

[110]   D. Popović, *Comparative Government*, Elgar, Cheltenham, 2019, 196. On the Swiss system see also: A. Lijphart, 'Consociational Democracy', *World Politics*, No. 2, 1969, 207.

[111]   Pallante, *Contro la democrazia diretta*, 119.

[112]   On legal transplants: A. Watson, *Legal Transplants: An Approach to Comparative Law*, Scottish Academic Press, Edinburgh 1974; O. Kahn-Freund, 'On Uses and Misuses of Comparative Law', *Modern Law Review*, No. 1, 1974, 1; P. Legrand, 'The Impossibility of Legal Transplants', *Maastricht Journal of European and Comparative Law*, No. 1, 1997, 111.

[113]   A. Morrone, 'L'iniziativa popolare propositiva: per una democrazia plebiscitaria contro la democrazia rappresentativa?', 2018, www.federalismi.it/nv14/editoriale.cfm?eid=499. My own translation.

139), while the proposal advanced in Italy concerns legislative proposals. Second, and the most problematic aspect of this sort of legislative referendum, is the fact that according to the original proposal, it was possible to activate a referendum even if parliament had adopted a different text. Indeed, according to the original text of the proposal, in cases of 'non-merely formal changes' it was possible to have a ballot on the original proposal and the new text passed by parliament. According to the initial draft, the people could be asked to decide on two different texts, and this would have inevitably rendered the referendum question heterogeneous. Fortunately, major changes were introduced to the original proposal during the parliamentary process, above all thanks to the pressure exercised by the *Partito democratico*. These changes have partly tamed the problematic aspects of this proposal.

For instance, the most recent version of the text excludes such a ballot and now states that if the chambers approve the popular proposal with amendments that are not merely formal, the referendum will be called on the proposal presented, unless the promoters of the initiative decide to give up their original proposal. The proposal approved by the chambers will be promulgated if the one subject to a referendum is not approved. Another important element of this proposal is represented by the turnout threshold, which was not mentioned in the original version; this was a response to one of the mottos of the Five Star Movement: 'Zero quorum, more democracy'.[114] The new draft amendment states that the referendum shall be considered to have been carried if a majority of valid votes has been achieved 'provided that it is higher than a quarter of those entitled to vote'. The same quorum is also extended to abrogative referendums pursuant to Article 75 of the Italian Constitution. As said, this debate about whether and how to reform referendums has been fed by the very low turnout that characterised rounds of consultations over the last twenty years. This partly explains the changes proposed by the Five Star Movement, in particular, those concerning lowering the turnout in cases of 'legislative referendums' and 'abrogative referendums'. Scholars have expressed concerns about this,[115] and it is useful to recall that, originally, the proposal did not provide for a minimum turnout threshold. Another interesting element that acknowledges the important case law of the Italian Constitutional Court is the latest version of the draft amendment to Article 71, which has incorporated some of the further limitations inferred by the court in recent years and codified some implicit limits to the referendum.

It seems, thus, that the parliamentary arena has tamed the most controversial aspects of this reform, although many ambiguous points remain.[116] However, since

---

[114] R. Fraccaro, 'Referendum senza quorum: decide chi partecipa. Per riconquistare la sovranità servono cittadini attivi', 29 May 2016, www.riccardofraccaro.it/referendum-senza-quorum-decide-chi-partecipa-per-riconquistare-la-sovranita-servono-cittadini-attivi/.

[115] Morrone, 'L'iniziativa'; G. Grasso, 'La balestra di Guglielmo Tell e l'iniziativa legislativa popolare. Note minime a proposito del disegno di legge costituzionale in materia di iniziativa legislativa popolare e di referendum', 2019, https://bit.ly/3zzyUWt.

[116] Morrone, 'L'iniziativa'.

the end of the first Conte government the future of these proposals has been unclear. In any case, given that the Five Star Movement is one of the most important political forces in parliament even after the end of the second Conte government, these issues are, in theory, still relevant.

4.6 WHAT COMPARATIVE CONSTITUTIONAL LAW CAN TEACH US

This book maintains that comparative constitutional law is a laboratory for those who want to find powerful arguments to challenge the constitutional counter-narrative advanced by populists. This also applies to the politics of immediacy. Coming back to mimetism, the Five Star Movement tends to present the necessity to strengthen the dose of direct democracy as a way to galvanise the constitutional potential already present in the Italian Constitution, making the people really sovereign, as suggested by the first part of Article 1 of the constitution cited by Conte in his speech at the United Nations.[117] To those who warn about the possible impact on the institutions of representative democracy, the Five Star Movement countered that the proposed reforms would not automatically affect them, but this is uncertain and here the risk of parasitism emerges. The issue is complex, but in order to prepare the terrain for the last part of the book, where I shall look at the necessary balance between the need to preserve the untouchable constitutional core and the necessity of renovating the constitutional pact, and in order to filter the claims made by populists, it is necessary to recall the essence of the comparative law lesson about the referendum.

The final part of this chapter revolves around three main points. The first one is the idea of the referendum as a graft transplanted into contexts of constitutional representative democracy:

> This is because referendums are not just one person, one vote expressions of democracy, but also typically one-time events. They thus represent a departure from the usual structural principle of the democratic process, with its cyclical repetition of elections for representatives. Moreover, unlike regularly scheduled elections, referendums do not offer built-in options for holding campaigners accountable or deciding on a change of course. Referendums are usually one-directional: They irreversibly alter the status quo, not necessarily for the best. They thus leave voters with few alternatives if they experience 'buyer's remorse,' or realize that they have voted on the basis of misleading information or unrealistic policy proposals.[118]

Constitutional lawyers are aware of the risks of abuse in the case of referendums. This approach can be justified in light of the political risks connected to excessive use of the referendum. In other words, referendums, if used as a full alternative to the instruments and institutions representative of democracy, risk creating parallel channels of

---

[117]   See Chapter 1.
[118]   Topaloff, 'The Rise', 128, 135.

legitimation which could destabilise and delegitimise parliaments. Indeed, what populists do is make the people competitors of their own representatives.

Should we despair at this point? Actually, recent empirical research confirms that referendums can also be used as a democratic safeguard.[119] This confirms the chameleonic nature of this instrument and the importance of constitutional procedures. Indeed, in order to prevent the political risks connected to the referendum, constitutions (even in contexts provided with partly written constitutions, for instance, the UK) come up with solutions designed to strike a balance between representative and direct/participatory (depending on how scholars understand referendums) democracy.[120]

The second point I would like to make is about the artificial concept of majority:

> A majority is not something you will find in nature. It is an artifact of law. You need legal rules to determine who counts, and in which way. You need legal safeguards of liberty, equality and diversity of opinion. You also need legal rules to determine what the majority will be able to do, which necessarily implies that the majority gets told what she is not allowed to do. In short, you need constitutional law.[121]

It is possible to find confirmation of this in comparative law. Both the Clarity Act in Canada and Schedule I of the Good Friday Agreement give political actors an important role in detecting the existing majorities. The Clarity Act was a follow up to the secession reference, specifically the part in which the Canadian Supreme Court outlined that: 'In this context, we refer to a "clear" majority as a qualitative evaluation. The referendum result, if it is to be taken as an expression of the democratic will, must be free of ambiguity both in terms of the question asked and in terms of the support it achieves'.[122]

In light of this, the Clarity Act listed some factors that should be taken into account by the House of Commons to verify *a posteriori* the existence of a majority:

> Factors for House of Commons to take into account
> (2) In considering whether there has been a clear expression of a will by a clear majority of the population of a province that the province cease to be part of Canada, the House of Commons shall take into account (a) the size of the majority of valid votes cast in favour of the secessionist option; (b) the percentage of eligible voters voting in the referendum; and (c) any other matters or circumstances it considers to be relevant.[123]

---

[119] M. Qvortrup, 'Two Hundred Years of Referendums', in M. Qvortrup (ed.), *Referendums Around the World*, Palgrave, London, 2018, 263, 271.

[120] Luciani, 'Il referendum', 163.

[121] M. Steinbeis, 'Majority Is a Legal Concept', 2017, http://verfassungsblog.de/majority-is-a-legal-concept/.

[122] Reference Re Secession of Quebec [1998] 2 SCR 217.

[123] An Act to give effect to the requirement for clarity as set out in the opinion of the Supreme Court of Canada in the Quebec Secession Reference SC 2000, c. 26, http://laws-lois.justice.gc.ca/eng/acts/c-31.8/page-1.html.

This caused a harsh reaction in Quebec.[124] A similar role, albeit to be played in the phase before the holding of a referendum, is granted to the secretary of state by Schedule I of the Good Friday Agreement:[125]

1. The Secretary of State may by order direct the holding of a poll for the purposes of section 1 on a date specified in the order.
2. Subject to paragraph 3, the Secretary of State shall exercise the power under paragraph 1 **if at any time it appears likely to him that a majority of those voting would express a wish that Northern Ireland should cease to be part of the United Kingdom and form part of a united Ireland** [emphasis added].
3. The Secretary of State shall not make an order under paragraph 1 earlier than seven years after the holding of a previous poll under this Schedule.

These two examples show that the majority is not a neutral or easy concept; on the contrary, it is an artificial one which can be built through political and legal decisions, for instance by excluding or including particular groups of people in the right to vote. This is why procedural caveats are important, since they contribute to ensuring the preservation of that core of untouchable values that constitutionalism must defend.

Finally, the third point lies at the heart of the alleged tension between formal and substantive democracy or, better still, between democracy and majority rule. This point has been clarified – once again – in the aforementioned Reference Re Secession of Quebec by the Canadian Supreme Court in 1998, when it said:

Democracy, however, means more than simple majority rule. Constitutional jurisprudence shows that democracy exists in the larger context of other constitutional values [. . .] Canadians have never accepted that ours is a system of simple majority rule. Our principle of democracy, taken in conjunction with the other constitutional principles discussed here, is richer [. . . .] While it is true that some attempts at constitutional amendment in recent years have faltered, a clear majority vote in Quebec on a clear question in favour of secession would confer democratic legitimacy on the secession initiative which all of the other participants in Confederation would have to recognize [. . .] However, it will be for the political

---

[124] P. Dumberry, 'The Secession Question in Quebec', *Diritto pubblico comparato ed europeo*, No. 2, 2015, 357, 361.

[125] 'ANNEX A 1. (1) It is hereby declared that Northern Ireland in its entirety remains part of the United Kingdom and shall not cease to be so without the consent of a majority of the people of Northern Ireland voting in a poll held for the purposes of this section in accordance with Schedule 1.

(2) But if the wish expressed by a majority in such a poll is that Northern Ireland should cease to be part of the United Kingdom and form part of a united Ireland, the Secretary of State shall lay before Parliament such proposals to give effect to that wish as may be agreed between Her Majesty's Government in the United Kingdom and the Government of Ireland', The Northern Ireland Peace Agreement. The Agreement reached in the multi-party negotiations, 10 April 1998, http://peacemaker.un.org/sites/peacemaker.un.org/files/IE%20GB_980410_Northern%20Ireland%20Agreement.pdf.

actors to determine what constitutes 'a clear majority on a clear question' in the circumstances under which a future referendum vote may be taken.[126]

Within the principles recalled by the Canadian Court, there is also the protection of minorities. Although the Canadian Court focussed on linguistic minorities in that case, the language used throughout the Reference allows it to be connected to a broader concept of minority as clarified by the court itself by insisting on the distinction between democracy and majority rule (para. 63). From that and other passages, we can understand that democracy cannot be used as a 'trump card' to alter the untouchable core that characterises (liberal) constitutional systems, since there are values that cannot be decided by the majority in democratic systems.

This is why, in my view, these inspirational words pronounced by the Canadian Supreme Court confirm the strong counter-majoritarian nature of constitutionalism as such.[127] When applied to referendums, this means that the good reasons inducing the introduction and fostering of direct democracy have to be balanced with other values that are connected to the need to protect the untouchable core of constitutional democracies. After all, as Kelsen pointed out, 'the concept of a majority assumes by definition the existence of a minority, and thus the right of the majority presupposes the right of a minority to exist. From this arises perhaps not the necessity, but certainly the possibility, of protecting the minority from the majority. This protection of minorities is the essential function of the so-called basic rights and rights of freedom, or human and civil rights guaranteed by all modern constitutions of parliamentary democracies'.[128]

---

[126]   Reference Re Secession of Quebec [1998] 2 SCR 217.
[127]   C. Pinelli, 'The Populist Challenge to Constitutional Democracy', *European Constitutional Law Review*, No. 1, 2011, 5, 15. On the counter-majoritarian difficulty see: A. Bickel, *The Least Dangerous Branch*, Yale University Press, New Haven, 1986.
[128]   H. Kelsen, 'On the Essence and Value of Democracy', in A. J. Jacobson, B. Schlink (eds.), *Weimar: A Jurisprudence of Crisis*, University of California Press, Berkeley, 2000, 84, 100.

5

The Assault on Representative Democracy as the Other Side of the Politics of Immediacy

5.1 ANTI-PARLIAMENTARISM AND POPULISM: AN INTRODUCTION

'We will open up Parliament like a can of tuna fish'.[1] This is what Grillo said before the general election of 2013, when the Five Star Movement obtained its first representatives in the parliament. In the rhetoric of the movement, direct democracy is frequently understood as inevitably enriched by the use of new technology and in the long run, according to the Five Star Movement, this will reduce the centrality of parliaments.[2] This emphasis on online democracy has induced political scientists to classify the *MoVimento 5 Stelle* as one of the most telling examples of a 'digital party'.[3]

In their emphasis on the idea of politics of immediacy, populists inevitably target parliaments as the venue of the elite and the arena where bad compromises are reached. Generally speaking, populism and representative politics have a paradoxical relationship:

---

[1] 'Grillo presenta le liste: "Apriremo il Parlamento come una scatola di tonno"', 11 January 2013, www1 .adnkronos.com/IGN/News/Politica/Grillo-presenta-le-liste-Apriremo-il-Parlamento-come-una-scatola-di-tonno_314071018512.html. My own translation.

[2] 'On the basis of such beliefs, the recourse to its people's voice is rather frequent and comes about with a variety of tools, in most cases structured through the computer platform that the Movement provides and manages in order not to lose contact with its basis of members and militants', M. Damiani, 'Citizen Democracy: New Politics in New Participation Models', in M. Anselmi, P. Blokker (ed.), *Multiple Populisms Italy as Democracy's Mirror*, Routledge, Abingdon, 2019, 181, 191.

[3] 'The digital party, or alternatively the "platform party", to indicate its adoption of the platform logic of social media, is to the current informational era of ubiquitous networks, social media and smartphone apps – what the mass party was to the industrial era or the cynically professionalised "television party" was during the post–Cold War era of high neoliberalism [...] The digital party is a "platform party" because it mimics the logic of companies such as Facebook and Amazon of integrating the datadriven logic of social networks in its very decision-making structure; an organisation that promises to use digital technology to deliver a new grassroots democracy, more open to civil society and the active intervention of ordinary citizens. It is "data hungry" because, like internet corporations, it constantly seeks to expand its database, the list, or "stack", of contacts that it controls. The digital party is also a start-up party, reminiscent of "unicorn companies" such as Uber, Deliveroo and Airbnb, sharing their ability to grow very rapidly', P. Gerbaudo, *The Digital Party: Political Organisation and Online Democracy*, Pluto Press, London, 2019, 4–5.

Populism is a feature of representative politics. The tenacity of and tensions within European representative democratic practices, ideas and institutions mean that contemporary Europe provides fertile territory for populism. From Bové to Haider to Berlusconi and Bossi via Chevènement and Fortuyn, politicians, movements and parties have used populism to great effect to challenge the functioning of representative democracy in contemporary Europe while at the same time championing the virtues of representation. This tells us something (or some things) about the shortcomings or inherent difficulties of representative politics, and it tells us something about populism.[4]

If for Taggart, populism is 'a feature of representative politics', at the same time the personalisation of politics that characterises populism is inevitably at odds with the constraints posed by the system of checks and balances and suffers from the 'legendary' centrality of parliaments. This has been noted by Taggart himself, who added that 'Populists have often relied on charismatic leaders. This means that in the very form of authority, they are expressing a rejection of more bureaucratised, regularised and constrained forms of leadership'.[5] Not by coincidence, '[p]opulism strongly emphasises the role of strong executive leadership and its ability to reach out to the people'.[6]

The anti-parliamentary flavour that characterises populism is, in general, confirmed in the Italian case, where it has also found fertile terrain in the anti-party-ism that, as we saw in Chapter 2, has been a feature of the post–WWII political scenario. This anti-parliamentary and anti-institutional feature has different explanations. It is frequently accompanied by that sense of moral superiority often found in populist movements which is connected to the dichotomous opposition: (honest) people versus the (corrupt) elite. A confirmation of this can be found in the constitutional reform passed by the Italian Parliament (and later confirmed by a constitutional referendum) by which the number of deputies was reduced to 400 (from 630) and that of senators to 200 (from 315) as of the next legislature.

Indeed, the recently approved reform on the reduction in the number of representatives is characterised by a punitive approach to institutions in the name of a relatively small economic saving. It is not the first time that the number of representatives has been changed,[7] but the reasons for this are questionable. Italy is not an exception if one takes comparative law seriously.[8]

4   P. Taggart, 'Populism and Representative Politics in Contemporary Europe', *Journal of Political Ideologies*, No. 3, 2004, 269, 269.

5   Taggart, 'Populism', 276.

6   G. Delledonne, 'Populism and Government: Continuity and Paradoxes in the Yellow-Green Experiment', in G. Delledonne, G. Martinico, M. Monti, F. Pacini (eds.), *Italian Populism and Constitutional Law: Strategies, Conflicts and Dilemmas*, Palgrave, London, 2020, 135, 148.

7   E. Rossi, 'Il numero dei parlamentari in Italia, dallo Statuto albertino ad oggi', in E. Rossi (ed.), *Meno parlamentari, più democrazia? Significato e conseguenze della riforma costituzionale*, Pisa University Press, 2020, 17.

8   G. Delledonne, 'Un'anomalia italiana? Una riflessione comparatistica sul numero dei parlamentari negli altri ordinamenti', in E. Rossi (ed.), *Meno parlamentari, più democrazia? Significato e conseguenze della riforma costituzionale*, Pisa University Press, 2020, 55.

Scholars have identified many grounds for criticism of the reform, which have been outlined in some appeals signed by academics:[9]

1. The reform would debase the role of parliament and reduce its representative-ness, without offering any appreciable advantages either in terms of the efficiency of democratic institutions or in terms of saving public expenditure.
2. The reform presupposes that national representation can be absorbed in the representation of other elective bodies (European Parliament, regional councils, city councils), against the case law of the Constitutional Court, which stated that 'only the Parliament is the seat of the national political representation, which impresses on its own functions a typical and unattainable characterization'.[10]
3. The reform would disproportionately and unreasonably reduce the representation of territories.[11]
4. The reform would not eliminate but, on the contrary, exacerbate the problems of what is called 'perfect bicameralism'.
5. The reform appears to be inspired by a 'punitive' logic towards parliamentarians, confusing the quality of the representatives with the role of the representative institution itself.

Point 4 is especially crucial in my view, as this kind of reform does not fix the real issue of Italian parliamentarism: its 'perfect' bicameralism, that is, the fact that the chambers have the same powers and that every law has to be passed – in an identical text – by both chambers. This inevitably renders the law-making process slow and ineffective.[12] It should be noted that originally, the Italian Constitution provided for a variable number of deputies and senators depending on the size of the Italian population. This was changed in 1963 after the approval of a constitutional law,[13] which established the number of 630 members in the Chamber of Deputies and 315 members in the Senate for about 51 million inhabitants. The current Italian population exceeds 60 million.

While the questionable 2016 Renzi–Boschi constitutional reform project had at least the merit of being organic, trying to reduce the size of and at the same time make parliament representative, this element is not present in the 2020 approved reform. This is perhaps the most striking difference between this attempt to reduce the numbers of members of the houses and the previous reform bills, which were accompanied by other novelties. Scholars have also pointed out the impact of this

---

[9]   For instance V. Baldolini, 'Referendum, 183 costituzionalisti dicono No', 24 August 2020, https://bit.ly/35F3hNv; 'Referendum, 183 costituzionalisti dicono No'; see also M. Siclari, 'Taglio parlamentari, accolgo l'appello. I tre motivi perché voto no', 10 August 2020, https://bit.ly/3qcalum.

[10] Corte costituzionale, decision 106/2002, www.cortecostituzionale.it. My own translation.

[11] For instance, Liguria, Abruzzo and Calabria. See M. Sesto, 'Taglio parlamentari, ecco come si restringe il Senato. La Lombardia è la regione che perde più seggi', Il Sole 24 Ore, 28 agosto 2020, https://bit.ly/3gIJvpu.

[12] Delledonne, 'Un'anomalia italiana?'.

[13] Namely constitutional law 2/1963, available at: https://bit.ly/2Skygvm.

reform on the supermajorities necessary in the joint parliamentary sessions requested by the Italian Constitution for the election of constitutional judges, the president of the Republic and the members of the High Council of the Judiciary.[14] Especially with regard to the election of the president of the Republic, the role acquired by the 'delegates from every Region' – who participate in the election according to Article 83 of the constitution – would increase decisively.[15] Moreover, this reform has an impact on the functioning of parliamentary committees and should be followed up by a series of legislative innovations; otherwise, the margin for political minorities in the functioning of the houses will be affected.[16] In other words, as Paolo Carrozza powerfully stated, 'it is not only a matter of numbers'.[17] It is perhaps too early to judge this reform. Very much will depend, as aforementioned, on the legislative follow up. If the Five Star Movement can go beyond a merely quantitative approach (i.e., an approach that has a strategy to cut costs) to the issue of reforms, then this might trigger an unprecedented season of reforms, as suggested by some members of the *Partito democratico*, which agreed to support the reform when the second Conte government was created.[18] Italy needs a season of reforms, but the premise must be the centrality of the parliament and respect of minorities. Otherwise, this reform risks being very dangerous.

I shall go back to the content of this reform in the last chapter, but for the purpose of this part, I would like to stress the merely quantitative approach of this reform. Germs of this approach to constitutional (and other types of) reforms can be found even earlier.[19]

The parliamentary approval of the reform was presented by the Five Star Movement as a victory, as part of a broader strategy to tackle elitism and wasteful

---

[14] P. Carrozza, 'È solo una questione di numeri? Le proposte di riforma degli artt. 56 e 57 Cost. per la riduzione dei parlamentari', *Diritto pubblico comparato ed europeo*, special issue, 2019, 88; G. Tarli Barbieri, 'La riduzione del numero dei parlamentari: una riforma opportuna? (ricordando Paolo Carrozza)', *Le Regioni*, No. 2, 2019, 375.

[15] Article 83, Constitution of Italy: 'The President of the Republic is elected by Parliament in joint session.
      Three delegates from every Region elected by the Regional Council so as to ensure that minorities are represented shall participate in the election.
      Valle d'Aosta has one delegate only.
      The election of the President of the Republic is by secret ballot with a majority of two thirds of the assembly. After the third ballot an absolute majority shall suffice'. On this, see: E. Vivaldi, 'Prime considerazioni sulla legge costituzionale di riduzione del numero dei parlamentari', 2020, www.giurcost.org/LIBERAMICORUM/vivaldi_scrittiCostanzo.pdf.

[16] Tarli Barbieri, 'La riduzione del numero dei parlamentari', 387.

[17] Carrozza, 'È solo una questione di numeri?', 88.

[18] See, for instance, S. Ceccanti, 'Referendum, perché Sì. Votare per il taglio dei parlamentari è una decisione da riformisti veri. Ve lo spiego in cinque punti', *Il Foglio*, 13 August 2020, www.ilfoglio.it /politica/2020/08/13/news/referendum-perche-si-330990/?underPaywall=true. Ceccanti is a member of the Chamber of Deputies and professor of public comparative law.

[19] A. M. Russo, 'El Ordenamiento Regional Italiano En La Espiral Centralizadora De La Crisis: ¡Todo Cambia Para Que Nada Cambie!', *Cuadernos Manuel Giménez Abad*, No. 6, 2013, 9.

spending, which needs to be followed by the reduction in parliamentary allowances as suggested by Di Maio and Taverna before the constitutional referendum.[20]

This approach is very telling of the attack against the members of the parliament seen as professionals of politics, who are accused of abusing parliamentary privileges. Sometimes this anti-parliamentarism supported by populists can be explained in light of the necessity to give a voice to the excluded, the underdogs. In this sense 'the underlying idea that populists often give voice to concerns that are not adequately taken up in the democratic process is undoubtedly compelling. However, it is more correct to conclude from this observation that populism operates as a symptom which signals that something is going wrong in the representative process'.[21]

In the case of the Five Star Movement, this anti-institutional flavour has been accompanied by emphasis on the opportunities offered by new technologies in terms of popular participation and direct democracy.[22] For the purpose of this chapter, I shall look at how the Five Star Movement portrays the role of the parliament and their intents, by examining some declarations or interviews given by Grillo and the other gurus of the movement, Gianroberto and Davide Casaleggio. Indeed, as we will see in this and the next chapter, a private company, *Casaleggio Associati*, has developed a crucial role in the history of the movement. Before launching the *Rousseau* platform (*infra*), which is evoked in the *statuto* (the basic charter of a political party) of the Five Star Movement, *Casaleggio Associati* also managed Beppe Grillo's blog.

On 5 June 2021, the paths of the Five Star Movement and *Rousseau* officially parted, following Davide Casaleggio's announcement that he was leaving the movement.[23] The decision was taken after a long clash between the two souls of the Movement and between former Prime Minister Conte and Casaleggio on the transfer of members' data by *Rousseau*, with the intervention of the Italian Data Protection Authority.[24]

There are many anecdotes that can be cited in order to explain the anti-politics flavour of the Five Star Movement. From his blog, for instance, Grillo invited his fans and followers to join him in some public meetings held in several squares for the 'so called V-Day, where "V" stood for the Italian expression *Vaffanculo*/"f*** you

---

[20] 'M5S non si accontenta: "Se vince il Sì poi tagliamo anche gli stipendi dei parlamentari"', 13 September 2020, https://bit.ly/3iXaK2j.

[21] S. Rummens, 'Populism as a Threat to Liberal Democracy', in C. Rovira Kaltwasser, P. Taggart, P. Ochoa Espejo, P. Ostiguy (eds.), *The Oxford Handbook of Populism*, Oxford University Press, 2017, 554, 563.

[22] E. De Blasio, M. Sorice, 'Technopopulism and Direct Representation', in P. Blokker, M. Anselmi (eds.), *Multiple Populisms: Italy as Democracy's Mirror*, Routledge, Abingdon, 2020, 127.

[23] L. Mari, 'M5S, Casaleggio lascia il Movimento: "Nemmeno mio padre lo riconoscerebbe. Se si cerca legittimazione in tribunale la democrazia interna è fallita"', 5 June 2021, www.repubblica.it/politica/2021/06/05/news/m5s_rousseau_dati-304277205/.

[24] 'Garante privacy: "Entro 5 giorni Rousseau consegni i dati al Movimento"', 1 June 2021, www.garanteprivacy.it/web/guest/home/docweb/-/docweb-display/docweb/9591994.

all" directed at Italian politicians'.[25] This is very telling of the populist jargon employed by the *MoVimento 5 Stelle* in their political battle.

5.2 REPRESENTATIVE DEMOCRACY AND THE FIVE STAR MOVEMENT

This book is based on the conviction that there is no absolute and pure idea of democracy. The history of this concept is too long, and as Salvadori, among others, masterfully recalled, democracy has 'many faces'.[26] In his *'Crucifige!' e la democrazia*, Zagrebelsky, former president of the *Corte costituzionale*, also underlined the polysemic nature of the idea, identifying different understandings (dogmatic, sceptical and critical) of democracy.[27] I believe the importance of the debate that we are rediscovering in this crucial phase consists, after all, as Ginsburg and Huq wrote, in realising that: 'an effort to understand democratic decline must start with a threshold question that is more difficult than first appears: What, precisely, do we mean by democracy?'.[28]

To understand the role of parliaments and the future of representative democracy in the narrative advanced by the Five Star Movement, it is necessary to start with an article that Davide Casaleggio wrote in *Corriere della Sera* in 2019,[29] in which he presented what he called the seven brief paradoxes of democracy.

As we have seen, on 5 June 2021, Davide Casaleggio announced the break between *Rousseau* and the Five Star Movement. However, at the time of writing, the Five Star Movement has not yet found an alternative to Casaleggio's platform although they have recently approved a new *statuto* where Rousseau is not mentioned.

Moreover, this rupture does not necessarily transform the nature of the Movement. Indeed, it is likely that another platform will be chosen, but certainly

---

[25] E. Trerè, V. Barassi, 'Net-authoritarianism? How Web Ideologies Reinforce Political Hierarchies in the Italian 5 Star Movement', *Journal of Italian Cinema & Media Studies*, No. 3, 2015, 287, 291.

[26] M. Salvadori, *Democrazia. Storia di un'idea tra mito e realtà*, Donzelli, Rome, 2016, 483.

[27] G. Zagrebelsky, *Il 'Crucifige!' e la democrazia. Il processo di Gesú Cristo come paradigma dei diversi modi di pensare la democrazia*, Einaudi, Turin, 1995, 10. See also H. Kelsen, *Vom Wesen und Wert der Demokratie*, Mohr, Tübingen, 1929 (Italian translation, Essenza e valore della democrazia, Giappichelli, Turin, 2004).

[28] T. Ginsburg, A. Z. Huq, *How to Save a Constitutional Democracy*, University of Chicago Press, 2018, 7. On the challenges posed to constitutional law by authoritarian populisms, see the considerations by Jakab and Schweber: 'Therefore, the third wave of autocratization does not simply deliver a new set of questions for constitutional lawyers; it also motivates us to rethink the methods of constitutional scholarship. Purely doctrinal analyses are likely to become less attractive—in certain countries perhaps much less attractive—than before. And analyses combining legal-doctrinal and political science methods, like the ones in the present volume, are likely to gain further popularity in the future', A. Jakab, H. Schweber, 'Editorial: Constitutional Decline, Constitutional Design, and Lawyerly Hubris', *Constitutional Studies*, special issue, 2020, 1, 3.

[29] D. Casaleggio, '7 brevi paradossi della democrazia', *Corriere della Sera*, 17 September 2019, www.corriere.it/politica/19_settembre_17/06-politico-t7ccorriere-web-sezioni-29ff88c4-d8bb-11e9-a64f-042100a6f996.shtml.

the split from *Rousseau* represents a potential turning point in the history of the movement.

However, in order to understand what *Rousseau* has represented for the Five Star Movement, it is worth remembering the importance it has had over the years. For these reasons, and because of the influence that Casaleggio still exerts on many of the movement's supporters, I believe it is important to start from this document, which well describes the *MoVimento 5 Stelle*'s approach to democracy.

The first paradox described by Casaleggio tries to reverse the traditional relationship between electors and their representatives that we have come to know over the history of democracy. While, as we saw in the previous chapter, referendums and other instruments of direct and participatory democracy are seen as grafts transplanted onto contexts of representative democracy, according to Casaleggio, by contrast, '[t]he elector should always decide, except when only his representative can do so. Almost always the opposite happens [. . .] Whenever possible, it is important that the electors are the ones who decide'.[30] Casaleggio, goes on to state that 'mistaking direct democracy for tyranny "is like saying that Ghandi was a dangerous undemocratic subversive"'.[31] After questioning the way in which contemporary constitutionalism understands the relationship between direct and representative democracy, Casaleggio explains how we should give more weight to direct democracy. In his view we should accept what new technologies have delivered, overcoming our scepticism and increasing the participation of the people in the most important decisions. This can be made possible thanks to the opportunities (e.g., online consultations) offered by the Internet, for example, his own platform *Rousseau*, named after the Swiss philosopher known as the champion of direct democracy.

The second paradox of democracy states that:

> The medium is the message when you communicate, it is a simple tool when you participate [. . .] Technology has always evolved faster than culture, but we have always adapted quickly.[32]

This statement is linked to the techno-utopian democracy advanced by the Five Star Movement, as we will see later in this chapter by recalling the *Gaia* project, for instance.

The third paradox has to do with political parties. As we saw in Chapter 2, the Italian context, especially after World War II, has always been characterised by a strong hostility towards particracy[33] and in this sense, as Urbinati has suggested 'anti-party-ism' is seen as a structural component of Italian democracy.[34] The Five

---

[30] Casaleggio, '7 brevi', my own translation.

[31] Casaleggio, '7 brevi', my own translation. It was actually a quotation from a book written by his father G. Casaleggio, *Insultatemi!*, Adagio eBook, Milan, 2013.

[32] Casaleggio, '7 brevi', my own translation.

[33] D. Ragazzoni, '"Particracy". The Pre-populist Critique of Parties and Its Implications', in P. Blokker, M. Anselmi (eds.), *Multiple Populisms: Italy as Democracy's Mirror*, Routledge, Abingdon, 2020, 86.

[34] N. Urbinati, 'Anti-party-ism as a structural component of Italian democracy', in P. Blokker, M. Anselmi (eds.), *Multiple Populisms: Italy as Democracy's Mirror*, Routledge, Abingdon, 2020, 67.

Star Movement retrieves this feeling and builds upon the post-*Tangentopoli* protest against traditional political parties. Two other elements in their 'menu' are an anti-pluralism and an anti-establishment approach, which lead to the presentation of political parties as both factors of fragmentation in the direct relationship with the people, and intimately corrupt forces. This explains his third paradox according to which 'those who support the party model as an instrument of democracy are the ones who complain about low representation compared to the voters of the movements'.[35] While political parties are considered closed and hierarchical (the Five Star Movement has refused to call itself a party), 'movements are inclusive, they do not require fees to register and give the power to decide on important issues to the members themselves'.[36]

The fourth paradox is called the 'paradox of the mute decision-maker' and is all about the importance of the debate, which is crucial to explaining fundamental choices and engaging voters. Casaleggio wrote that 'we are more concerned about who votes "wrongly" than explaining our reasons'. These lines are understandable and call for more transparency. However, there is subsequently a passage that reveals the temporal element discussed previously, while presenting the risks of instantaneous democracy: 'When we argue that there is not enough time to allow the vote, we are just saying that we have not made enough effort to involve people in the choice process when it was appropriate to do so. Institutional short circuits such as Brexit, or journalistic short circuits such as Trump's election campaign, always arise from this mechanism'.[37] I think this passage is telling of the fact that when presenting his own view of democracy, Casaleggio probably neglects the risks of information disorder[38] that may (dis)orientate the vote.

The fifth paradox is about the relationship between experts, decision-makers and voters. Here the so-called 'intelligentsia' is compared to a football coach who thinks he is the striker of the team: 'Experts can explain the issue (e.g. the risks of nuclear power) and the impact it will have on our lives, but the final decision (e.g. whether or not to take that risk) must be made by the community if possible'.[39] Again, this point is per se reasonable and can be seen as a reaction to another de-politicisation factor:

---

[35] Casaleggio, '7 brevi', my own translation.

[36] Casaleggio, '7 brevi', my own translation.

[37] Casaleggio, '7 brevi', my own translation.

[38] C. Wardle, H. Derakhshan, 'Information Disorder: Toward an Interdisciplinary Framework for Research and Policy Making', *Council of Europe report DGI(2017)09*, 2017, https://firstdraftnews .org/wp-content/uploads/2017/10/Information_Disorder_FirstDraft-CoE_2018.pdf?x40896. The authors identify three types of information disorder: 'Dis-information. Information that is false and deliberately created to harm a person, social group, organization or country. Mis-information. Information that is false, but not created with the intention of causing harm. Mal-information. Information that is based on reality, used to inflict harm on a person, organization or country', Ivi, 20. See also: *A Multi-dimensional Approach to Disinformation: Report of the Independent High Level Group on Fake News and Online Disinformation*, 2018, https://op .europa.eu/en/publication-detail/-/publication/6ef4df8b-4cea-11e8-be1d-01aa75ed71a1.

[39] Casaleggio, '7 brevi', my own translation.

technocracy. At the same time, these considerations must be contextualised. They have become topical in times of COVID-19. One of the Five Star Movement members, Paola Taverna, the current deputy president of the Italian Senate, has revealed her proximity to the 'no vax' position. In Italy,[40] this is in line with one of the characteristic features of contemporary populism. According to the populist narrative, experts are normally targeted as part of the establishment and are seen, in a way, as a source of limitation of the full space of political decision requested by populist leaders.

At the same time, there is no linear link between science and populism, since also technocracy (like populism), seen as a degeneration, contributes to de-politicising the debate:

> Populism and technocracy have been treated, by some observers, as correlative and related to one another. Jan-Werner Müller, for instance, has recently suggested that they are 'mirror images of each other.' 'Technocracy' he writes 'holds that there is only one correct policy solution; populism holds that there is only one authentic will of the people [...] In a sense, therefore, both are curiously apolitical. For neither technocrats nor populists is there any need for democratic debate' (Müller, 2016). This depiction is reminiscent of a characterization already proposed by Vivienne Schmidt of populism as a form of 'politics without policy' and technocracy as 'policy without politics' (Schmidt, 2006). Indeed, some recent commentators have even gone as far as to suggest that in many advanced western democracies the old opposition between left and right is increasingly being replaced by a new structuring opposition between populism and technocracy.[41]

In particular, in the Italian case, the 2018 general election success of *Lega* and the Five Star Movement gave a new boost to this debate, since '[i]n their electoral campaigns, both parties had trenchantly opposed the vaccination policy, repeatedly raising pseudoscientific objections, to MMR (measles, mumps, and rubella) injections in particular'.[42]

Turning back to Casaleggio's democratic paradoxes, the sixth paradox is called the 'subversive participant' and is about citizens' participation and involvement:

> Those who complain about the lack of respect for institutions, on the other hand, openly support the fact that the same decisions have so far been taken by a small management group rather than by the members.[43]

---

[40] G. Rodriquez, 'Dai "marchi pe 'e bestie", alle "processioni a casa de mi cugino" per poter contrarre malattie esantematiche. I vaccini secondo Paola Taverna (M5S)', 7 August 2018, www .quotidianosanita.it/governo-e-parlamento/articolo.php?articolo_id=64805.

[41] C. Bickerton, C. Invernizzi Accetti, 'Populism and Technocracy', in C. Rovira Kaltwasser, P. Taggart, P. Ochoa Espejo, P. Ostiguy (eds.), *The Oxford Handbook of Populism*, Oxford University Press, 2017, 326, 326–7. The authors refer to the following work: V. Schmidt, *Democracy in Europe: The EU and National Polities*, Oxford University Press, 2006.

[42] Tomasi, 'Populism, Science', 226–7.

[43] Casaleggio, '7 brevi', my own translation.

Here again, these reflections about anti-party-ism make party leaders – and 'not the institutions'[44] – the real target of this critique. However, this statement should be read together with other declarations delivered to the press in which Casaleggio himself openly spoke of an inevitable overcoming of representative democracy.[45] This is probably a symptom of the fact that the Five Star Movement itself has been changing its original polemical target since it became the political majority in power. The target is not the parliament, seen as a can of tuna fish that should be opened – as suggested by Grillo in the sentence quoted at the beginning of this chapter – but a space still dominated by a corrupt elite. Again, not by coincidence, the Movement has refused to define itself as a party. We will see in the next chapter that it is part of a communication strategy. However, this has not impeded judges applying many of the norms directed at political parties to the Five Star Movement.

The final paradox is perhaps the most ambiguous one. At first sight, the first part of the paradox is not divisive at all, as it reads: 'A voting community unites even if it has different opinions'.[46] This looks like a call to respect pluralism and the subsequent lines of Casaleggio's article also push for more digital innovation and for a true digital citizenship. However, later Casaleggio adds: 'a community which does not enable voting splits up and drives away those who think differently'.[47] This line can be interpreted in different ways. Of course, voting is part of the very idea of democracy, but this passage also reflects the reductionist attitude of the Five Star Movement, which tends to neglect the substantive side of the notion of democracy. The mantra 'let us vote' has been repeated by other populist forces, especially after the fall of the first Conte government.[48] This kind of reading has been supported by the usual reference to a part of Article 1 of the Italian Constitution according to which 'sovereignty belongs to the people'.[49] This reasoning proposed by, inter alia, Salvini and Meloni neglects the important role granted to the president of the Republic according to Article 88 of the Italian Constitution, that is, the power to dissolve the parliamentary chambers.[50] Indeed, Italy has a parliamentary form of government, and the relationship between parliament and government must be supported by the existence of confidence

---

[44] Casaleggio, '7 brevi', my own translation.

[45] 'Davide Casaleggio: "Il Parlamento? In futuro forse non sarà più necessario"', *Corriere della Sera*, 23 July 2018, https://bit.ly/2UjK7tW.

[46] Casaleggio, '7 brevi', my own translation.

[47] Casaleggio, '7 brevi', my own translation.

[48] 'Salvini in Senato: "Basta trionfalismi, siamo la maggioranza nel Paese, lasciateci parlare"', 22 July 2020, www.agi.it/politica/news/2020-07-22/salvini-senato-mes-9230606/.

[49] See for instance the intervention of Giorgia Meloni, the leader of *Fratelli d'Italia* at the end of the consultations with President Sergio Mattarella. Here is the video: 'Consultazioni, Giorgia Meloni: per Fratelli d'Italia unico sbocco è ritorno alle urne', 28 August 2019, https://bit.ly/2SdX7AO.

[50] Article 88 Italian Constitution, 'The President of the Republic, having heard the Presidents of the Houses, may dissolve Parliament or even only one House. The President of the Republic cannot exercise said right during the last six months of the presidential mandate, unless said period coincides in full or in part with the last six months of Parliament'.

(Art. 94 of the Italian Constitution).[51] However, the lack of confidence connecting a certain majority stemming from the elections and the parliament does not automatically lead to the dissolution of the chambers if another majority in parliament is possible. As elsewhere, the relationship between the government and the parliament is also governed by unwritten norms, including customary practices and conventions.[52] The formation of government in Italy is indeed only partially governed by Article 92 of the Constitution, which reads:

> The Government of the Republic is made up of the President of the Council and the Ministers who together form the Council of Ministers. The President of the Republic shall appoint a President of the Council of Ministers, on whose proposal the President of the Republic shall appoint Ministers.

The actual process is much more complex and has been forged by non-written norms as well. First, there is a preparatory phase consisting in consultations, which are carried out – it is a constitutional practice – to identify the potential president of the Council in order to form a government that 'must receive the confidence of both Houses of Parliament'.[53] The consultations are activated even in case of a crisis of government due to the loss of confidence or the resignation of the government in power. This confirms that in parliamentary forms of government, the dissolution of parliament is an *extrema ratio*.

In deciding on whether to dissolve the chambers or not, and this is the function of these consultations with the 'Presidents of the Houses', the president of the Republic tries to verify whether there is the possibility of forming a new political majority in parliament. This is a very important power, which has been limited by paragraph 2 of the same provision reading that it: 'may not exercise such right during the final six months of the presidential term unless said period coincides in full or in part with the final six months of parliament'.[54]

---

[51] Article 94 Italian Constitution: 'The Government must receive the confidence of both Houses of Parliament.
  Each House grants or withdraws its confidence through a reasoned motion voted on by roll-call.
  Within ten days of its formation the Government shall come before Parliament to obtain confidence.
  An opposing vote by one or both the Houses against a Government proposal does not entail the obligation to resign.
  A motion of no-confidence must be signed by at least one-tenth of the members of the House and cannot be debated earlier than three days from its presentation'.

[52] G. U. Rescigno, 'Prassi, regolarità, regole, convenzioni costituzionali, consuetudini costituzionali, consuetudini giuridiche di diritto pubblico', *Osservatorio sulle fonti*, No. 2, 2018, 1.

[53] Article 94, Italian Constitution and Article 1, p. 3, law no. 400/88. 'The Italian government is appointed and sworn in by the President of the Republic, but must then win an explicit ex post investiture vote in both the Chamber of Deputies and the Senate. In both chambers the voting rule is simple majority. Despite these provisions, minority governments have been a common feature of Italian politics', F. Russo, 'Government Formation in Italy: The Challenge of Bicameral Investiture', B. E. Rasch, S. Martin, J. A. Cheibub (eds.), *Parliaments and Government Formation: Unpacking Investiture Rules*, Oxford University Press, 136.

[54] Article 88(2) of the Italian Constitution.

The president of the Republic 'may' indeed dissolve the chambers, but is not obliged to do so if another parliamentary majority is possible. This was also the case after the end of the partnership between *Lega* and the *MoVimento 5 Stelle* because, as we have seen, they were not allied during the electoral campaign. The argument frequently used by *Lega* and *Fratelli d'Italia*, according to which accepting another Conte government led to an electoral betrayal, does not stand up, because the *Partito democratico* received more votes than the *Lega* during the 2018 elections in spite of the more recent electoral success of the *Lega* in the European elections. Something similar was argued by *Lega* and *Fratelli d'Italia* with reference to the birth of the Draghi government. Later *Lega* changed its mind and agreed to support the new government.

The case of Draghi, however, was also partially different. On that occasion, the president of the Republic insisted on the pandemic context that made the vote dangerous. To this element, the lack of electoral reform after the constitutional reform must be added. The forces in support of the constitutional reform, in fact, recognised the need for electoral reform after the reduction of the number of MPs. The pandemic context – mentioned by President Mattarella – and the lack of follow-up on electoral law are the elements that led Mattarella to take the Draghi option. What was needed, in Mattarella's words, was 'a government in the fullness of its functions'.[55]

This debate is also interesting to verify another constant element of the populist approach to constitutions: instrumentalism. Indeed, when the second Conte government was formed the Five Star Movement did not join *Lega* and *Fratelli d'Italia* in this reading of Article 1 of the Italian Constitution for opportunistic purposes, since they were already in office. To remedy this, they built on the German example[56] and made the formation of a new coalition with the *Partito democratico* conditional upon the results of an online vote. A similar online consultation was organised on the decision on whether to support the Draghi government. As noted by many commentators, in so doing, they created an additional procedural burden in the procedure of formation of government. Casaleggio found counter-arguments to face this criticism:

> The real paradox is who, for fear of changing habits, prefers to think that innovation is dangerous regardless. Digital citizenship actually brings a new dimension of participation in the life of one's community. There will be limits that we should imagine, but also tools that we will have to build and new rights that we should affirm in order to allow, without discrimination, everyone to participate in order to share their value.[57]

---

[55] 'Sergio Mattarella annuncia: incarico a Mario Draghi, no elezioni anticipate', 2 February 2021, www .youtube.com/watch?v=uSeLmozgWSc.

[56] Also, Casaleggio referred to the consultation held in Germany in 2018. 'In 2018 in Germany, the SPD party, in order to confirm the government contract with Merkel's CDU, had its members vote; 239,000 people gave their consent by mail', Casaleggio, '7 brevi', my own translation.

[57] Casaleggio, '7 brevi', my own translation.

What is wrong with that? The procedure followed to justify the new alliance with the Conte government partly deviated from the constitutional wording but, above all, it occurred by relying on an online consultation carried out by using a private platform (the *Rousseau* platform), which had also suffered from cyberattacks thus revealing itself as a non-reliable instrument.[58] This goes to the heart of the problem. Democracy is not only about voting, but it is about giving citizens the right to vote after having given them the chance and the time to gather necessary information and knowledge. This is an essential guarantee to ensure the freedom of the vote, namely to protect the vote from the interference of information disorder.

Indeed, it is impossible to deny that the Internet offers and launches new challenges, as expressed by Davide Casaleggio in a brief speech at a meeting organised at the United Nations.[59] Digital identity, digital education and access to the Internet are undoubtedly three important goals of an ambitious and potentially revolutionary agenda. However, little space is devoted in Casaleggio's speeches to the risks of the Internet. This is a strange absence in the aftermath of the explosion of the Cambridge Analytica scandal and in light of the cyberattacks suffered by the *Rousseau* platform.

This platform has been of crucial importance for the success of the Five Star Movement as Davide Casaleggio wrote in another article published in the *Washington Post*:

> The platform that enabled the success of the Five Star Movement is called Rousseau, named after the 18th century philosopher who argued politics should reflect the general will of the people. And that is exactly what our platform does: it allows citizens to be part of politics. Direct democracy, made possible by the Internet, has given a new centrality to citizens and will ultimately lead to the deconstruction of the current political and social organizations. Representative democracy – politics by proxy – is gradually losing meaning [...] Our goals are ambitious: We plan to get to a million active members. The movement's North Star is the participation of its members. They are the ones who determine the most important decisions the movement has to make and the direction it will take. Our slogan – 'Participate, don't delegate!' – is what guarantees our continuing success in the future. And our hope is that we will provide a model for renovating democracy everywhere by giving it back to the citizens.[60]

'Giving back' is a crucial concept here,[61] which leads us back to the politics of immediacy and the idea of instantaneous democracy already analysed in Chapter 4.

---

[58] G. Jones, A. Cinelli, 'Hacking Attacks: A Pre-election Setback for Italy's 5-Star Movement', 5 October 2017, www.reuters.com/article/us-italy-politics-5star-idUSKBN1CA1TM.

[59] The video of the whole speech is available at: 'Davide Casaleggio all'ONU. Testo e video integrale del discorso', 1 October 2019, www.affaritaliani.it/politica/davide-casaleggio-all-onu-per-promuovere-la-cittadinanza-digitale-628599.html.

[60] D. Casaleggio, 'A top leader of Italy's Five Star Movement: Why we won', *The Washington Post*, 19 March 2018, www.washingtonpost.com/news/theworldpost/wp/2018/03/19/five-star/.

[61] F. Pallante, *Contro la democrazia diretta*, Einaudi, Turin, 2020, 59–60.

What is politics for the Five Star Movement? Gianroberto Casaleggio was the creator of a short video, called *Gaia – The Future of Politics*,[62] in which he imagined a future world divided into two main blocks: the Western world characterised by direct democracy and free access to the Internet, and the Eastern world characterised by the spread of 'Orwellian dictatorships'.[63] This video is very telling of the kind of world imagined by the Five Star Movement and says a lot about their idea of politics. In this video, 2054 (namely, 14 August 2054) is described as the date of birth of a new world where conflicts (ideological, religious, territorial, racial) no longer exist, where every citizen is subject 'to the same law'.

> One of the core ideas of the Gaia project is the inherent immorality of any power, whether economic (financial above all else), ideological, religious or political [...] Its narrative recalls those of millenarians: after a catastrophic war, in 2054 a new society arises where digital identities replace the physical and human spheres, and people are constantly connected via the web. The prophecy outlines the onset of Gaia, a worldwide transparent government system where secret societies are banned, and any citizen is able to become president. In Gaia, political parties, religions, ideologies disappear so that man may truly become the master of his own destiny. Gaia offers a solution to two fundamental questions in politics: the incompetence of citizens and the problems that arise out of collective decision-making. Collective knowledge rests on the assumption that collective intelligence aggregates the knowledge of many to form an unbiased and, in many cases, accurate opinion. Collective decisions are deemed by definition superior to individual ones.[64]

Gaia is the name of this future world government, supposedly created after the first world elections on the Internet, where 'secret organizations are banned'[65] and 'every human can become president and control the actions of the government through the net'.[66]

In the background, the perennial contestation of representative institutions and parties, in particular parties and ideologies, will disappear in Gaia. This view implies an optimistic approach to technologies and again perhaps neglects possible shortcomings. A further example of this approach can be found in another video produced by Casaleggio Associati: *Prometeus – The Media Revolution*,[67] describing a society where 'Individuals are expected to share private experiences through technologies to enhance human communicability. Unfiltered communication,

---

[62] The full video is available at the following link: 'Gaia – The Future of Politics', 21 October 2008, www.youtube.com/watch?v=sV8MwBXmewU.

[63] 'Gaia – The Future of Politics'.

[64] L. Corso, 'When Anti-Politics Becomes Political: What Can the Italian Five Star Movement Tell Us about the Relationship Between Populism and Legalism', *European Constitutional Law Review*, No. 3, 2019, 462.

[65] 'Gaia – The Future of Politics'.

[66] 'Gaia – The Future of Politics'.

[67] 'Prometeus – The Media Revolution', 6 June 2007, www.youtube.com/watch?v=xj8ZadKgdCo.

free flows of information and enhanced accessibility will result in augmented collective knowledge. Web citizens will get things right'.[68]

Having tested the techno-utopian character of the Five Star Movement agenda, it is time to go back to our current world. In Casaleggio and the Five Star Movement's evocation of the opportunities offered by digital citizenship and e-participation, there is instead almost nothing about the risk of innovation. In the next section, I shall offer an overview of the impact of the Five Star Movement on the legislative and non-legislative functions of the Italian parliament once in office.

5.3 A FIRST ASSESSMENT OF THE IMPACT OF THE FIVE STAR MOVEMENT ON THE ACTIVITY OF THE ITALIAN PARLIAMENT

In 1975, Polsby[69] described the Italian Parliament as one of the strongest worldwide, but in the 1990s the situation started changing and, as elsewhere, the parliament was marginalised:

> It is in this context that the marginalization of the parliament in the system of government has gradually occurred. Every government, though with a different intensity, more or less oriented towards populism, has abused decree-laws, has shortened parliamentary debates and has made use of 'maxi-amendments', composed of one article and a thousand commas and replacing the entire text of a bill, coupled with a confidence vote. These tools have become a routine in parliament. To some extent, the populist tone of the political struggle has never disappeared since the 1990s. While, luckily, not every government in office has promoted anti-élites and anti-pluralist discourses, elements like the personalization of politics and the engagement in a permanent electoral campaign have never abandoned the Italian political landscape, for example, also during Renzi's government (2014–2016), as the possible reasons behind the defeat of 'his' constitutional reform at the referendum held on 4 December 2016 show.[70]

Parliaments are seen by populists as obscure and slow. This has been a mantra, which was also present in Berlusconi's rhetoric and was one of the rationales behind the 2016 failed constitutional reform proposed by Renzi. These elements have somehow been picked up by the Five Star Movement. Generally speaking, 'Populism is, by definition, against everything that appears to make public decisions less "easy", thus making the lawmaking process as one of its natural targets. In fact, the essence of the legislative procedure is not to make the decision instant but

[68] Corso, 'When Anti-Politics Becomes Political', 469.
[69] N. W. Polsby, 'Legislatures', in F. I. Greenstein, N. W. Polsby (eds.), *Handbook of Political Science*, Vol. V, Addison-Wesley, Reading, 1975, 257.
[70] C. Fasone, 'Is There a Populist Turn in the Italian Parliament? Continuity and Discontinuity in the Non-legislative Procedures', in G. Delledonne, G. Martinico, M. Monti, F. Pacini (eds.), *Italian Populism and Constitutional Law: Strategies, Conflicts and Dilemmas*, Palgrave, London, 2020, 41, 43.

subject it to a series of intermediate steps. Hence, a populist movement clashes with it once it enters the parliament'.[71]

Surprisingly (or perhaps not surprisingly), once in power the Five Star Movement did not revolutionise the way in which the parliament works. Indeed, empirical research shows an evident continuity between the first Conte government and its predecessors, especially with regard to the pathological elements in the relationship between parliament and executive.[72] The political forces in office seemed to be more concentrated on the visibility than on the substance of the lawmaking process:

> The XVIII parliamentary term has so far created a number of laws almost identical to the previous one, in the same period: 70 in the first year of the last term (2013–2014) and 69 in this one, up to the time of the resignation of the first Conte government in August 2019. Since the beginning of the XVIII parliamentary term (March 23, 2018), 30 decree-laws have been issued (4 deliberated by the Gentiloni government and 26 by the first Conte government) with 23 of these being turned into law.[73]

Especially at the beginning of the first Conte government, a partial innovation was represented by the increase in the approval of laws triggered by a parliamentary initiative, in particular from parliamentarians belonging to the political majority. At the same time there was a strategic use of decree-laws, especially for 'communicative purposes'.[74] This leads us to an important factor that characterised the Conte governments: the spectacularisation of legislative politics and the electoral use of the legislative activity. This is in line with the permanent electoral campaign and mobilisation that traditionally characterise populisms. The parliament was called on to approve 'cover-measures' (*provvedimenti copertina*), called thus 'since the first page is the only one which actually exists at the moment of approval'. In these cases, 'the act lacks all the normative content and is a resolution "on nothing"'.[75] In other words, these measures are mere propaganda and totally irrelevant from a legal point of view.[76]

[71]   F. Pacini, 'Populism and Law-Making Process', in G. Delledonne, G. Martinico, M. Monti, F. Pacini (eds.), *Italian Populism and Constitutional Law: Strategies, Conflicts and Dilemmas*, Palgrave, London, 2020, 119, 120.

[72]   N. Lupo, 'Populismo legislativo?: continuità e discontinuità nelle tendenze della legislazione italiana', *Ragion pratica*, No. 1, 2019, 251.

[73]   Pacini, 'Populism', 125.

[74]   Pacini, 'Populism', 126. On this see also: G. Lasorella, 'Aggiornamenti e sviluppi in tema di programmazione dei lavori, tra decreti-legge e maggioranze variabili', in V. Lippolis, N. Lupo (eds.), *Il Parlamento dopo il referendum costituzionale (Il Filangieri. Quaderno 2015–2016)*, Jovene, Naples, 2017, 53; G. Di Cosimo, 'Fonti normative del Governo: molti problemi e tre modi per affrontarli', *Osservatorio sulle fonti*, No. 3, 2016, 1, 2.

[75]   Pacini, 'Populism', 127. See also A. Di Chiara, 'Due prassi costituzionalmente discutibili: delibere del Governo "salvo intese" e pubblicazione tardiva dei decreti legge', *Osservatorio sulle fonti*, No. 1, 2019, 1, 3.

[76]   Di Chiara, 'Due prassi', 22.

There were embarrassing situations, for example when the then leader of the Five Star Movement, Luigi Di Maio, generically accused 'someone' of having altered the content of a decree-law on fiscal matters, arguing that a controversial tax amnesty had been introduced by what Di Maio called 'a little hand' after the approval by the Council of Ministers.[77] Emergency measures were announced but only published after several days. This is again in line with an approach that prefers announcements over substance. As for the other legislative measures at the disposal of the government, namely the delegated legislative decrees, the ones that were approved and published 'were mainly "inherited" from the previous parliamentary term, when the corresponding delegating provisions had been enacted. Furthermore, in 32 cases these legislative decrees are just transposing European Union legislation'.[78] Finally, another instrument used by the Conte governments was the block (also known as 'maxi') amendment, which 'consists of a government amendment, whilst examination of a bill is about to be concluded, which completely replaces the bill in question, and also integrates it with provisions that have nothing to do with the original bill'.[79]

This instrument has a negative effect in terms of both accountability and of quality of the legislative output. It is a technique by which the majority de facto deprives the parliament of important spaces for bargaining. This happens especially when this instrument is coupled with the abuse of another tool, the *questione di fiducia*,[80] an instrument by which the government may request a confidence vote[81] on a measure which it deems fundamental to its agenda. If the parliament wants to question that provision this will lead to the end of the government. As is evident, this is a powerful strategy to put pressure on the parliament to reduce its margin of intervention. Make no mistake, both this kind of confidence vote and the blocked amendments were present before the advent of the Five Star Movement, thus this political force has not really been innovative in their use.

A group of senators also brought a case before the Constitutional Court to defend their parliamentary prerogatives, but the Constitutional Court delivered a decision characterised by great deference towards the political branch, admitting the possibility of reviewing the violation of the parliamentary rules only in exceptional cases of evident character.[82] However, a particular strategy that was frequently adopted

---

[77] He referred to a 'little hand' which had altered the original text. See: A. Carconi, 'Di Maio e la "manina", proviamo a capirci qualcosa', 18 October 2018, www.ilpost.it/2018/10/18/condono-di-maio/.

[78] Pacini, 'Populism', 1269.

[79] S. Vassallo, 'Government Under Berlusconi: The Functioning of the Core Institutions in Italy', *West European Politics*, No. 4, 2007, 692, 702.

[80] G. Pistorio, *Maxi-emendamento e questione di fiducia. Sottotitolo. Contributo allo studio di una prassi illegittima*, ES, Naples, 2018.

[81] This instrument, unlike the motion of confidence and no confidence (Art. 94 Italian Constitution) is not provided for by the Italian Constitution, but it is governed by a statutory source, namely law 400/1988 and by the internal rules of the chambers: Article 116 of the rules of the Chamber of Deputies and Article 161 of the rules of the Senate.

[82] Corte costituzionale, order 17/2019, www.cortecostituzionale.it; more recently see also order 60/2020, www.cortecostituzionale.it.

during the second Conte government is the so-called *approvazione salvo intese*. This refers to the approval of decree-laws and bill proposals by the Council of Ministers "'subject to further agreements", while it is formally a final approval. With this expression, we refer to the hypotheses in which is reached a political understanding in principle among the Council of Ministers, yet not fully translated into regulatory provisions'.[83] In other words, by this formula a measure is approved in its general outline, but the government is taking more time to define its details.

Sometimes measures approved by the Council of Ministers with this formula had still not been published a month after the (in theory) final approval. This is the case of a decree-law about some measures in the field of public procurement and tenders (so called *sblocca cantieri*). In that instance, the president of the Republic intervened, and the publication occurred after a new approval of the final text by the Council of Ministers.[84] The use of this mechanism is linked to the politics of announcements that frequently characterises populist governments. However, again, the roots of this tool can be traced back to the action of previous governments, for instance the Monti government.[85]

However, 'as Walter Bagehot [...] taught long ago, the centrality of parliament has, with the exception of the finance law, little to do with lawmaking'.[86] That is why it is necessary to look at its non-legislative functions to offer a comprehensive view of the situation. As we saw in Chapter 2, one of the main features of the Five Star Movement is penal populism and this has inevitably given blood to its anti-privilege narrative, which results in questioning some instruments functional to the preservation of parliamentary tasks, namely the parliamentary allowance[87] and inviolability.[88] These instruments are normally presented by populist leaders as individual privileges, but they are 'functional immunities, instrumental in assuring the good functioning—against corruptive practices—and the stable composition of the institution. The same goes for some attempts to overcome or revise the

---

[83]   Pacini, 'Populism', 127.

[84]   'The political clash between Lega and the Five Star Movement was harsh. It had been approved by the Council of Ministers on March 20, 2019. Interestingly, after almost a month it had not yet been published, in spite of being an emergency decree! Hence, an unprecedented, complete re-approval was therefore necessary on April 18, 2019 also because of the pressure of the President of the Republic', Pacini, 'Populism', 128.

[85]   M. A. Cortelazzo 'Le parole della neopolitica – Salvo intese', 2019, www.treccani.it/magazine/lingua_italiana/articoli/parole/Neopolitica14.html.

[86]   G. Pasquino, 'The State of the Italian Republic', *Contemporary Italian Politics*, No. 2, 2019, 195.

[87]   Article 69 of the Italian Constitution: 'Members of Parliament shall receive an allowance established by law'.

[88]   Article 68 of the Italian Constitution: 'Members of Parliament cannot be held accountable for the opinions expressed or votes cast in the performance of their function. In default of the authorisation of his House, no Member of Parliament may be submitted to personal or home search, nor may he be arrested or otherwise deprived of his personal freedom, nor held in detention, except when a final court sentence is enforced, or when the Member is apprehended in the act of committing an offence for which arrest flagrante delicto is mandatory'. See the considerations made in Chapter 2 about the legacy of *Tangentopoli*.

prohibition of a binding mandate for MPs'.[89] The emphasis on the politics of announcement and the spectacularisation of politics (apparently) led to revitalising some 'traditional instruments of parliamentary oversight, like committees of enquiry and parliamentary questions, as part of the strategy of political propaganda'.[90] Such a strategy inevitably changed the nature of these instruments, which were used to target and combat political opponents. Other instruments of parliamentary law were tested by populists once in power, such as the parliamentary committees of inquiry or question time. In Italian constitutional law parliamentary committees of inquiry may either be unicameral or be bicameral (in this second case they are established by passing a law), and their composition responds to a proportional representation.[91] The practice developed in the history of the Italian Republic shows they have not worked to protect parliamentary minorities, but have been used by the majorities to serve their interests, and indeed normally the chairmanship is traditionally in favour of the political majority both in the case of bicameral and unicameral committees (with some limited exceptions).[92]

Looking at the current legislative term, in the case of the parliamentary committee of enquiry established by law[93] on the banking and financial system, the broad understanding of its mandate and the dose of penal populism present in the Five Star Movement's rhetoric have caused concerns about the relationship with the judiciary.[94]

The use of social media has also given a new role to question time. Indeed:

> [T]he increasing use of the question time and the fact that it has eventually become more 'entertaining', also using social media, like in the practice of Fratelli d'Italia, does not necessarily conclude that these developments improve the quality of parliamentary oversight as long as they only serve to echo the political strategy of a party without adding substantive contents to the scrutiny.[95]

The abuse of social media and the search for visibility by the members of populist forces has de facto affected the quality of the parliamentary activity in the name of

---

[89] Fasone, 'Is There a Populist', 46. On the development of these committees in Italy, see: A. Pace, *Il potere di inchiesta delle assemblee legislative: Saggi*, Giuffrè, Milan, 1973.

[90] Fasone, 'Is There a Populist', 70.

[91] Article 82 of the Italian Constitution: 'Each House of Parliament may conduct enquiries on matters of public interest.
  For this purpose, it shall detail from among its members a Committee formed in such a way so as to represent the proportionality of existing Parliamentary Groups. A Committee of Enquiry may conduct investigations and examination with the same powers and limitations as the judiciary'.

[92] M. Malvicini, G. Lauri, 'Le commissioni parlamentari di inchiesta: recenti sviluppi e osservazioni alla luce della prassi', 2016, https://bit.ly/3qg1OXf; Fasone, 'Is There a Populist', 70.

[93] Law no. 28/2019, www.camera.it/leg18/1099?shadow_organo_parlamentare=3176.

[94] Over the years there have been several conflicts between parliamentary committees of inquiry and the judiciary, and the Italian Constitutional Court has even been called to solve these disputes, frequently invoking the principle of sincere cooperation. See Corte Costituzionale, decision 241/2007.

[95] Fasone, 'Is There a Populist', 57.

a sort of fake transparency at all costs,[96] which has distracted the Parliament from its ordinary tasks. It is no coincidence that Article 64 of the Constitution reads that parliamentary 'sittings are public; however, each of the Houses and Parliament in joint session may decide to convene a closed session'. Even Article 72 of the Constitution refers to the rules of procedures of the houses, by establishing that such 'rules shall establish the ways in which the proceedings of Committees are made public'.[97] In other words, these norms confirm that there might be cases where parliamentary activity needs informality and to strike a difficult balance between transparency and efficiency. With the advent of the Internet and the abuse of social media platforms by members of the parliament, the institution has lost 'to a certain extent, the monopoly of the information over its activities and is bound to compete with a series of sources of information, potentially every single MP, that escape its institutional control'.[98] This fragmentation has led to the proliferation of several counter-narratives about how institutions really work and why they are corrupt. In this way, populist forces have contributed to delegitimising the role of the parliament once again.

5.4 FINAL REMARKS

Populism can contribute to weakening the position of national parliaments, but the roots of the crisis of parliamentary institutions can be found elsewhere. The crisis of parliaments started soon after World War II,[99] and it is not directly connected to the EU integration[100] process or to populism. They have contributed to it but are not its cause. Normally the EU is blamed because it has never renounced its

---

[96] 'In the name of "transparency at any cost", populist forces and their MPs tend to use the Internet and social media to break parliamentary rules. With this regard, in violation of the rules of procedure that makes summary reports the ordinary device to ensure the visibility of committee meetings in both Houses, from time to time MPs of the 5SM have provided streaming via Facebook or other social media of the committee meetings they are participating in. The streaming of committee meetings, however, may pose a series of problems to the good functioning of parliamentary procedures. Indeed, it can impair the quality of the preliminary analysis (istruttoria) and the negotiation preceding the decision. The closed venue of a parliamentary committee is expected to favour the in-depth and specialized examination of the issue at stake without the interference of the public, with a view to enhance the authenticity of the discussion and the achievement of a political compromise. The high degree of informality, which features the work of Italian parliamentary committees and that follows from the fact that usually they do not meet in public, is beneficial for the committees' deliberative process', Fasone, 'Is There a Populist', 54.

[97] Article 72 of the Italian Constitution.

[98] Fasone, 'Is There a Populist', 53. More in general, see: P. Carnevale, D. Chinni, 'To Be or Not to Be (Online)? Qualche considerazione sul rapporto fra web e organi costituzionali', 2019, www .giurcost.org/LIBERAMICORUM/carnevale&chinni_scrittiCostanzo.pdf.

[99] G. Pasquino, L. Pelizzo, *Parlamenti democratici*, Il Mulino, Bologna, 2006, 15; F. Pacini, 'Dall'autorità della legge all'autorevolezza delle Assemblee', *Quaderni costituzionali*, No. 1, 2015, 9.

[100] Although it has had an impact on the role of national parliaments: T. Raunio, S. Hix, 'Backbenchers Learn to Fight Back: European Integration and Parliamentary Government', *West European Politics*, No. 4, 2000, 142.

intergovernmental dynamics. Indeed, Intergovernmentalism is still an important component of EU constitutional dynamics,[101] even more so after the adoption of the anti-austerity measures as we saw in Chapter 3. However, comparative studies[102] demonstrate that Europeanisation in this field has not necessarily affected the role of national parliaments, since they have improved their scrutiny powers or, at least, benefitted (indirectly) from the fewer margins left to the executive due to the role acquired by supranational actors (especially the Commission) and technical and independent bodies, such as the fiscal councils. In sum, the so-called crisis of parliaments is a broader phenomenon with roots in the emergence of super-specialised policies and the emphasis on efficiency that has favoured the executive as a rule maker. Against this background, the EU has given a new role to national parliaments, especially after the Lisbon Treaty came into force, and empirical research demonstrates that even the measures adopted at the national level in light of the TSCG (Treaty on Stability, Coordination and Governance in the Economic and Monetary Union) have a limited margin of manoeuvre for the executives favouring, in some cases, a new space for the legislatures.[103]

In this chapter, I explored the impact of populism on the role of the Italian Parliament. First I tried to sum up how Casaleggio and the Five Star Movement understand democracy, and then I looked at the findings of some recent research[104] on the influence of the Conte governments on the legislative and non-legislative functions of the Italian Parliament. The electors of the Five Star Movement are probably only relatively interested in these techno-utopian aspects of Casaleggio's thinking. This is indirectly confirmed by the electoral volatility of their voters, illustrated by the loss of votes of the Five Star Movement in the regional elections held in September 2020. However, in order to understand why the Internet is so important to their functioning it was essential to recall Casaleggio's understanding of politics. The colossal electoral loss suffered in the regional elections held in September 2020 and the progressive institutionalisation of the Five Star Movement have led to a much less prominent role for Casaleggio and the *Rousseau* platform, as we will see in Chapter 6.[105]

As we have seen, the impact of the Five Star Movement has not been staggering and that is why I see a lot of continuity between the pre-Conte situation and the current legislature; this is confirmation that the Italian Parliament is paying the price

[101]   J. H. H. Weiler, 'The Community System: The Dual Character of Supranationalism', *Yearbook of European Law*, 1981, 267.

[102]   E. Griglio, N. Lupo, 'Parliamentary Democracy and the Eurozone Crisis', *Law and Economics Yearly Review*, No. 2, 2012, 313, 340.

[103]   Griglio, Lupo, 'Parliamentary democracy', 340.

[104]   Pacini, 'Populism'; Fasone, 'Is There a Populist'.

[105]   'M5S a rischio scissione dopo il post di Casaleggio sul Blog: cosa sta succedendo', 5 October 2020, www
.fanpage.it/politica/m5s-a-rischio-scissione-dopo-il-post-di-casaleggio-sul-blog-cosa-sta-succedendo/.

for a crisis that started several years ago and for other reasons. At the same time, the increasing use of the *approvazione salvo intese* technique and the lack of parliamentary centrality due to the COVID-19 emergency are two important novelties that have marginalised the Italian chambers. Perhaps even more evident was the impact of populist forces on the non-legislative functions of parliament, especially on its expressing and informing functions. The COVID-19 crisis and the inevitable centralisation of power in favour of the executive[106] gave new blood to the leadership of Giuseppe Conte, who has decided to manage the crisis directly, by reaching Italians through Facebook instead of using traditional media. During the lockdown, Italians were following his video messages, normally scheduled after dinner. In these speeches, he communicated directly with Italians by announcing urgent measures whose content frequently remained unclear for some days. Indeed, measures were announced and explained but then officially approved and published in the Official Gazette of the Republic one or two days later. This contributed to confusion and disorder. Masses escaping from Milan's railway station – images of which were broadcast on Italian and foreign television channels[107] – was instigated by the announcement of very restrictive measures which came into effect only some hours later. As written in the Introduction, the crisis was mainly managed by decrees of the president of the Council of Ministers (DPCM); these are measures that are administrative in nature established by the Code of Civil Protection, a legislative source which provides for special powers in cases of emergency.[108] Over the ensuing months, the parliament has reacquired some of its importance, and the government has used decree-laws, which require the conversion of the parliament. After the second wave of contagion, which affected some members of the parliament, the debate about how to allow members of the parliament to vote remotely restarted. Currently, this is not allowed and it will probably be necessary to amend the internal rules of the chambers to do this.[109]

Conte also evolved as a political character: first, he was depicted as a low-profile figure chosen by the leaders of *Lega* and the Five Star Movement, and later, before

---

[106] E. Longo, M. Malvicini, 'Il decisionismo governativo: uso e abuso dei poteri normativi del Governo durante la crisi da COVID-19', 2020, www.federalismi.it/nv14/articolo-documento.cfm?Artid=44237.

[107] M. Johnson, D. Ghiglione, 'Coronavirus in Italy: "When we heard about the lockdown we rushed to the station"', *Financial Times*, 8 March 2020, www.ft.com/content/27458814-6159-11ea-a6cd-df28cc3c6a68.

[108] Decreto Legislativo 1/2018, www.gazzettaufficiale.it/eli/id/2018/1/22/18G00011/sg.

[109] 'Article 64, third paragraph, of the Italian Constitution establishes that "The decisions of each House and of Parliament are not valid if the majority of the members is not present, and if they are not passed by a majority of those present, unless the Constitution prescribes a special majority". It has been argued that the presence, for the purposes of calculating both the legal number (structural quorum), and the majority to deliberate (functional quorum), needs to be physical presence, and that therefore it must be considered in contrast with this provision whatever measure that authorizes a virtual or "remote" presence', N. Lupo, 'Perché non è l'art. 64 Cost. a impedire il voto "a distanza" dei parlamentari. E perché ammettere tale voto richiede una "re-ingegnerizzazione" dei procedimenti parlamentari', 2020, www.osservatorioaic.it/images/rivista/pdf/2020_3_02_Lupo.pdf. In that essay Lupo tried to question this reading of Article 64.

his resignation, he became the guarantor of the new political majority by developing a more direct relationship with public opinion and stakeholders.

However, during his two governments Conte questioned the significance of parliament in different ways. For instance, he discussed and presented some very foggy ideas about how to relaunch Italy in an alternative forum, pompously called *États généraux*. Finally, real power was managed in the Council of Ministers, the meetings of which are closed to the public. If we consider the Five Star Movement's emphasis on transparency, this sounds like a paradox indeed.

6

The Return of the Imperative Mandate?

6.1 OBJECTOCRACY AND POLITICAL MEDIATION

In this chapter, I shall undertake an in-depth analysis of how in-office Italian populists understand parliaments. Before going into the technicalities of constitutional law however, it is necessary to frame the issue in a broader perspective and mention the kind of politics that the Five Star Movement has in mind.

To define the politics of the Five Star Movement, Urbinati coined the term 'objectocracy', a word which refers to their claim to a '"true" or "objective" assessment of problems against opinionated media and established journalism. The myth of objectivity was, from the beginning, a distinctive mark of the movement and, as mentioned above, a possible implication of anti-partyism'.[1] This intuition was later developed by other scholars, who stressed that 'by construing themselves as the finders of ad hoc solutions to specific problems, M5S representatives undercut the very possibility of an ideological confrontation between competing visions of society'.[2]

Politics, for Grillo, is essentially vain ideological contention and, as seen in the previous chapter, in the new world order called *Gaia*, Gianroberto Casaleggio imagined a world without political parties. This is consistent with objectocracy. If it is possible to find and apply an objective truth, why should we waste time in political discussions?[3] It is no coincidence that for populists 'political mediation appears as a source of inefficiency and corruption'.[4] To a certain extent the same applies to technocrats. However, technocracy and populism differ on the role of experts and the importance of competence. As suggested:

[1] N. Urbinati, 'The Italian Five Star Movement for Foreigners', 2018, www.rivistailmulino.it/news/newsitem/index/Item/News:NEWS_ITEM:4272.

[2] L. Corso, 'When Anti-Politics Becomes Political: What Can the Italian Five Star Movement Tell Us about the Relationship between Populism and Legalism', *European Constitutional Law Review*, No. 3, 2019,469.

[3] J. W. Müller, *What Is Populism?* University of Pennsylvania Press, Philadelphia, 2017, 97.

[4] C. Bickerton, C. Invernizzi Accetti, 'Populism and Technocracy', in C. Rovira Kaltwasser, P. Taggart, P. Ochoa Espejo, P. Ostiguy (eds.), *The Oxford Handbook of Populism*, Oxford University Press, 2017, 330.

Objectocracy must not be confused with the dominion of experts. It rather results from collective knowledge. It does not predicate the prominence of will over reason and feeds on the delusion of perfect reason. Such a truth is procedural rather than substantive. It is tied to the idea that the decisions and assessments made by a large, generally heterogeneous group of people achieve results that compare with those of experts. Government is thus no longer dependent on competency. Decisions will henceforth be outsourced to crowdsourcing platforms. The Weberian concept of a politics that requires commitment and vocation is adroitly subverted.[5]

Indeed, populism is at the opposite of the very idea of procedural legitimacy because the truth may not be part of political competition and bargaining.[6] Following this reasoning, if political mediation is inefficient and if political discussion is a waste of time, the conclusion is that political parties are just factors of political fragmentation and paralysis and that professional politicians are not needed, as per the logic 'everyone is worth one' (*uno vale uno*), meaning that every member of the political community has the same value.

As we have seen, the constitutional reform proposals that have been started by the *MoVimento 5 Stelle* have focused on the reduction in the number of members of parliament and the introduction of a legislative referendum (*referendum propositivo*). As seen in Chapter 5, the message behind the first reform is evidently an attack on the headquarters of the supposed elite, which is targeted as the source of economic waste.[7] The second proposal has not yet been approved and was discussed in Chapter 4, but it is as telling of the populist approach as that concerning the reduction in the number of members of parliament. Both of these reforms respond to the idea of democracy endorsed by Davide Casaleggio in a speech given on the occasion of a workshop organised at the United Nations[8] and in his article on the seven paradoxes of democracy, which was duly analysed in the previous chapter.[9] In this chapter, it is sufficient to underline the strong support for direct democracy and the frontal attack on the actors of traditional politics, namely political parties and parliamentary arenas. On this basis, the former minister Riccardo Fraccaro[10] has denounced classic representative democracy as insufficient and stressed the need for more direct democracy, especially with the advent of new technologies.

---

[5]   L. Corso, 'When Anti-Politics Becomes Political', 470.

[6]   C. Bickerton, C. Invernizzi Accetti, 'Populism and Technocracy', 330.

[7]   M. Bassini, 'Rise of Populism and the Five Star Movement Model: An Italian Case Study', *Italian Journal of Public Law*, No. 1, 2019, 302, 314.

[8]   The speech can be watched at the following link: 'Davide Casaleggio all'ONU per promuovere la Cittadinanza Digitale', 1 October 2019, www.affaritaliani.it/politica/davide-casaleggio-all-onu-per-promuovere-la-cittadinanza-digitale-628599.html.

[9]   D. Casaleggio, '7 brevi paradossi della democrazia', 17 September 2019, www.corriere.it/politica/19_settembre_17/06-politico-t7ccorriere-web-sezioni-29ff88c4-d8bb-11e9-a64f-042100a6f996.shtml.

[10] C. Bertini, 'Riccardo Fraccaro: meno onorevoli e più referendum. In cinque leggi il piano di riforme', 11 September 2018, https://bit.ly/3dccnFH. See R. Fraccaro, 'La democrazia integrale', 19 June 2018, https://ricerca.repubblica.it/repubblica/archivio/repubblica/2018/06/19/la-democrazia-integrale32.html.

The debate regarding how representatives are chosen and what can (or cannot) be done to ensure their compliance with their mandate is crucial. The Five Star Movement has occasionally suggested methods other than elections to find representatives, namely lottery draws. Grillo himself authored a short piece in 2018 in which he proposed a citizens' senate to challenge what he called 'the greatest scam of politics: making us believe that we need politicians'.[11] Grillo referred to a book by Henning[12] in the piece and claimed that a lottery would make 'parliament truly representative of society, it would mean the end of politicians and politics as we have always thought of it'.[13]

However, looking at the agenda of the Five Star Movement we can also identify another solution: the abolition of the free parliamentary mandate.[14] As the Venice Commission stated, 'imperative mandate is generally awkward for Western democracies. The constitutions of many countries explicitly prohibit imperative mandate'.[15] At the same time, scholars have argued that '[p]opulists' claim to the imperative mandate can be understood as a [. . .] sign of the dissatisfaction of a huge part of the population with a kind of democracy in which those in power are increasingly distant from the governed',[16] which – again – lies at the very core of the perception of a functioning democracy.

The return of the imperative mandate is thus not consistent with the legacy of post–WWII, as we will see, but it is coherent with Five Star Movement's idea of the institutions. Indeed, in their logic, institutions 'are reduced to neutral transmission channels vested with the task of carrying the voice of social protesters without interference. Parliaments are required to vote mostly on Bills proposed by citizens, referenda become more frequent, deputies cannot shift from one political group to another'.[17] While, as we will see in the last chapter, there are populist claims that can be filtered and adjusted to make constitutional democracy better than it is, the abolition of the free parliamentary mandate radically challenges the very idea of representation and may not be tolerated from a constitutional point of view. Over the next few pages, I shall first recall the importance of the prohibition of the imperative

---

[11] G. Grillo, 'Il più grande inganno della Politica: farci credere che servano i politici', 27 June 2018, www.beppegrillo.it/il-piu-grande-inganno-della-politica-e-farci-credere-che-servano-politici/. My own translation.

[12] B. Henning, *The End of Politicians: Time for a Real Democracy*, Unbound Digital, Johnson City, 2017. See also B. Manin, *The Principles of Representative Government*, Cambridge University Press, 2010, 8; N. Urbinati, L. Vandelli, *La democrazia del sorteggio*, Einaudi, Turin, 2020.

[13] G. Grillo, 'Il più grande inganno'. My own translation.

[14] The abolition of the free parliamentary mandate is, for instance, also evoked in the 'contract for government' signed between the Five Star Movement and the *Lega*, available at: https://download .repubblica.it/pdf/2018/politica/contratto_governo.pdf. My own translation.

[15] The European Commission for Democracy through Law (Venice Commission), 'Report on the Imperative Mandate and Similar Practices', 2009, www.venice.coe.int/webforms/documents/default .aspx?pdffile=CDL-AD(2009)027-e.

[16] M. Tomba, 'Who's Afraid of the Imperative Mandate?', *Critical Times*, No. 1, 2018, 108, 114.

[17] L. Corso, 'When Anti-Politics Becomes Political', 471.

mandate in the history of constitutionalism and then examine how the Five Star Movement has proposed overcoming this principle. As always, coherently with the comparative method, I shall frame the first part of the chapter by looking at experiences other than the Italian one.

6.2 A 'CORNERSTONE OF EUROPEAN DEMOCRATIC CONSTITUTIONALISM'

The *MoVimento 5 Stelle* is interesting to comparative constitutional lawyers, as it calls into question 'the well-established, constitutional law category of representative democracy and accordingly, the role and responsibilities of traditional political parties'.[18] The particular understanding of democracy advanced by the Five Star Movement is at odds with many fundamental principles of the Italian Constitution, such as the principle of the free mandate for parliamentarians. The prohibition of the imperative mandate has been defined as the 'cornerstone of European democratic constitutionalism' by the Venice Commission.[19] The debate surrounding the prohibition of the imperative mandate (expressly established by, among others, Article 67 of the Italian Constitution,[20] Article 38(1) of the German Basic Law[21] and Article 27 of the French Constitution)[22] is directly linked to another feature of populism, namely the idea that representatives must respond immediately to the demands of the people with almost no autonomy in performing their public function, as though bound by a specific contract.

Many of these post–WWII constitutions, as always, looked at the laboratory represented by the Weimar Constitution, in particular by Article 21 thereof, which actually used the term 'people' instead of 'nation' in its wording.[23] The return of the mandatory mandate risks reducing representation to a private law scheme, and the narrative is confirmed in the idea of the 'contract for government'[24] signed between the Five Star Movement and the *Lega*. The idea of a contract is not entirely new,

---

[18] Bassini, 'Rise of Populism', 303.

[19] The European Commission for Democracy through Law (Venice Commission), 'Report on the Imperative Mandate'. 'The 2009 European Commission's report did not come out of the blue. The Commission was formed because of the restoration of the imperative mandate by parties and movements seeking to limit the so-called "floor crossing" practice, whereby representatives would shift factions or political parties once elected', Tomba, 'Who's Afraid', 114.

[20] Article 67 of the Italian Constitution: 'Each Member of Parliament represents the Nation and carries out his duties without a binding mandate'.

[21] Article 38(1) of the German Basic Law: 'Members of the German Bundestag shall be elected in general, direct, free, equal and secret elections. They shall be representatives of the whole people, not bound by orders or instructions and responsible only to their conscience'.

[22] Article 27 of the French Constitution: 'No Member shall be elected with any binding mandate. Members' right to vote shall be exercised in person. An Institutional Act may, in exceptional cases, authorize voting by proxy. In that event, no Member shall be given more than one proxy'.

[23] Article 21 of the Weimar Constitution: 'The delegates are representatives of the whole people. They are subject only to their own conscience and are not bound by any instructions'.

[24] For recent work on this concept, see: F. Di Marzio, *La politica e il contratto. Dalla affermazione dei valori alla negoziazione degli interessi*, Donzelli, Rome, 2018.

since Berlusconi also presented and signed the famous 'contract with the Italians' on a well-known talk show (*Porta a Porta*) on 8 May 2001. Although in Berlusconi's case this idea of contract was not necessarily accompanied by a similar attack on the principle of free parliamentary mandate, his actions demonstrate that these forms of populism did not emerge completely out of the blue. In addition, the very idea of a 'contract' – according to the populist rhetoric of the Five Star Movement – implies that there is a need to overcome the prohibition of the imperative mandate or at least to mitigate it by insisting on party discipline or pecuniary sanctions.[25]

These phenomena respond to the idea of democracy endorsed by Davide Casaleggio in the previously discussed speech given at a workshop organised by the United Nations and in his short piece on the paradoxes of democracy.[26] Casaleggio's words stress his strong support for direct democracy and reveal his frontal attack on the actors of traditional politics, namely political parties and parliamentary arenas. In this section, I will recall the debate on the importance of the free parliamentary mandate for the purpose of representative democracy.

In a nutshell, it is possible to argue that the free mandate is an essential requirement to fulfil political representation that should be understood as differing from the private law mandate. Imperative mandates were the rule in the Middle Ages, for instance, in the *Cortes* of the Kingdom of Castilla and León.[27] Deputies of these cities had to follow the detailed instructions given to them before each session, and they had to 'take oaths neither to vary from their instructions nor to overstep their mandates and this act was officially sanctioned by a public notary'.[28] As we will see, representation can be seen as a fiction, giving the idea of the existence of a unitary and abstract body behind the elected people: the nation. According to this idea, those that have been elected do not have to follow the instructions of their local electors because they represent the nation.

This happened in the eighteenth century, when 'democracy was generally associated with the gathering of citizens in assemblies and public meeting places, on the presumption that it was exclusively suited to small scale societies. Rousseau believed Geneva to be the ideal place for democracy, and even Montesquieu, although favourable to federal solutions, conceived republics only to be of small dimensions. The invention of representative democracy reversed this presumption'.[29] In the

---

[25] G. Grasso, 'Mandato imperativo e mandato di partito: il caso del MoVimento 5 Stelle', 2017, www
.osservatorioaic.it/images/rivista/pdf/Grasso%20Definitivo.pdf.

[26] Casaleggio, '7 brevi paradossi della democrazia'.

[27] A. M. Holden, 'The imperative mandate in the Spanish Cortes of the Middle Ages', *American Political Science Review*, No. 4, 1930, 886; also recalled in the Venice Commission's reports: The European Commission for Democracy through Law (Venice Commission), 'Report on the Imperative Mandate'. See also R. Scarciglia, *Il divieto di mandato imperativo: contributo a uno studio di diritto comparato*, CEDAM, Padua, 2005, 55.

[28] The European Commission for Democracy through Law (Venice Commission), 'Report on the Imperative Mandate'.

[29] C. Pinelli, 'The Populist Challenge to Constitutional Democracy', *European Constitutional Law Review*, No. 1, 2011, 5, 8.

Considerations on the Government of Poland, Rousseau understood the imperative mandate to be an adequate instrument against corruption and to guarantee democracy.[30]

Rousseau – who not incidentally was one of the alleged sources of the Five Star Movement and whose name was used for their online platform – was a supporter of this type of democracy rather than the representative type.

Famously, Rousseau wrote that sovereignty 'can't be represented, for the same reason that it can't be alienated; what sovereignty essentially is is the general will, and a will can't be represented [...]. The people's deputies, therefore, can't be its representatives: they are merely its agents, and can't settle anything by themselves'.[31] Since sovereignty cannot be alienated, deputies are actually mere commissaries and they are bound by the imperative mandate.

The legacy of Rousseau is still with us,[32] especially for those who understand representative democracy as 'at best, an instrumental substitute for stronger forms of democracy'.[33] This idea is present in the debate and has been challenged by Plotke, among others, who believes representation is democracy. Indeed, in his own words, '[r]epresentation is not an unfortunate compromise between an ideal of direct democracy and messy modern realities. Representation is crucial in constituting democratic practices'.[34]

Discussions about the origin of the free parliamentary mandate normally start by quoting Burke's speech to the electors of Bristol in 1774, in which he powerfully distinguished between representatives and ambassadors, a distinction which has become crucial in the modern theory of representation. Burke's speech was seminal, particularly if one remembers that at that time many constitutions still admitted the imperative mandate. Indeed, according to the constitution of Massachusetts, dated 1780, delegates 'of this commonwealth to the congress of the United States [...] shall have commissions under the hand of the governor, and the great seal of the commonwealth; but may be recalled at any time within the year'.[35] According to Burke, instead, overcoming the imperative mandate is essential in order to have proper parliaments:

> To deliver an opinion, is the right of all men; that of constituents is a weighty and respectable opinion, which a representative ought always to rejoice to hear; and which he ought always most seriously to consider. But authoritative instructions; mandates issued, which the member is bound blindly and implicitly to obey, to

[30] J. J. Rousseau, *Considérations sur le gouvernement de Pologne et sur sa réformation projetée*, 1772, www.espace-rousseau.ch/f/textes/considerations_pologne.pdf.

[31] J. J. Rousseau, *The Social Contract*, 1762, www.earlymoderntexts.com/assets/pdfs/rousseau1762.pdf.

[32] M. Goldoni, 'Rousseau's Radical Constitutionalism and Its Legacy', in M. Dowdle and M. Wilkinson (eds.), *Constitutionalism Beyond Liberalism*, Cambridge University Press, 2017, 227.

[33] N. Urbinati, M. Warren, 'The Concept of Representation in Contemporary Democratic Theory', *Annual Review of Political Science*, 2008, 387, 388.

[34] D. Plotke, 'Representation Is Democracy', *Constellations*, No. 1, 1997, 19, 19.

[35] Constitution of Massachusetts 1780, Chapter IV, www.nhinet.org/ccs/docs/ma-1780.htm.

vote, and to argue for, though contrary to the clearest conviction of his judgment and conscience,– these are things utterly unknown to the laws of this land, and which arise from a fundamental mistake of the whole order and tenor of our constitution.

Parliament is not a congress of ambassadors from different and hostile interests; which interests each must maintain, as an agent and advocate, against other agents and advocates; but Parliament is a deliberative assembly of one nation, with one interest, that of the whole; where, not local purposes, not local prejudices, ought to guide, but the general good, resulting from the general reason of the whole. You choose a member indeed; but when you have chosen him, he is not member of Bristol, but he is a member of parliament.[36]

However, while today we normally link the idea of representation to the abandonment of the imperative mandate, it is possible to say that Burke's view is just one of the possible theories of representation. This then explains why even leading scholars such as Kelsen – who understood representation to be a fiction[37] – for instance, expressed doubts about the free parliamentary mandate, and why the issue of the imperative mandate returns in a cyclical manner. This overview, as suggested by the Venice Commission, confirms that there are different theories of representation:

There is no single theory of representation. Different theories are based on particular ideologies and create several models of representation (trusteeship model, delegate model, mandate model and resemblance model). The trusteeship model is based on Edmund Burke's notion of representation. For Burke, representation is a moral duty: those with education and understanding should act in the interests of those who are less fortunate. Once elected, representatives should act independently on the grounds that the electors do not know their best interests. A similar view was expressed by J. S. Mill. His assumption was that, although all individuals have a right to be represented, not all political opinions are of equal value. He proposed a system of plural voting in which four or five votes would be given to holders of learned diplomas and degrees, two or three to managerial workers, and a single vote to ordinary workers. The delegate model is inspired by Thomas Paine, who believes that politicians are bound by the instructions they receive from those they represent and that there is a need for regular contact between representatives and their constituents through regular elections and short mandates. Supporters of the 'delegate model' are in favour of recall as well as of people's initiatives and

---

[36]   E. Burke, 'Speech to the Electors of Bristol', 3 November 1774, https://press-pubs.uchicago.edu/founders/documents/v1ch13s7.html.

[37]   H. Kelsen, *Vom Wesen und Wert der Demokratie*, Mohr, Tübingen, 1929, Italian translation *Essenza e valore della democrazia*, Giappichelli, Turin, 2004, 76. Another interesting case is the so called 'Czecoslovakian clause', namely Article 13b of the electoral law of Czechoslovakia (law 125/1920); G. Damele, 'Vincoli di mandato dei parlamentari e carattere democratico dei partiti. Spunti a partire dall'articolo 160 della Costituzione portoghese', 2017, www.forumcostituzionale.it/wordpress/wp-content/uploads/2016/06/damele.pdf; S. Curreri, *Democrazia e rappresentanza politica. Dal divieto di mandato al mandato di partito*, Firenze University Press, 2004, 141–2.

referendums for more control over politicians. The mandate model is based on the idea that a party gains a popular mandate that authorises it to carry out whatever programmes it supported during the election campaign. The resemblance model suggests that only those who come from a particular group can represent it and its interests.[38]

As always, populists rely on the ambiguity of the concepts belonging to the toolbox of constitutional theory. Indeed, as with the concept of democracy, populists benefit from this conceptual ambiguity in order to advance a constitutional counter-narrative. Scholars distinguish between representation understood as a mandate (*Vertretung*), and representation as an incarnation (*Repräsentation*),[39] the former being provided by private law, and the latter by public law.[40] The prohibition of the imperative mandate and the modern concept of representation are frequently conceptualised as a product of the Glorious Revolution in the UK and the French Revolution (although elements of it can be found back in the 14th century),[41] and flourished afterwards in a context characterised by the absence of mass political parties and before the progressive extension of suffrage. This caveat is very important, and I will come back to this throughout the chapter.

This debate is also useful to appreciate the chameleonic nature of the free parliamentary mandate. According to another historical reconstruction, the free parliamentary mandate was born as an instrument at the disposal of the sovereign to limit the fragmentation of power and only later became an instrument defending parliamentary sovereignty:[42]

The imperative mandate was banned as an obstacle to the concentration of power in the hands of the state [. . .] the practice of the imperative mandate had already been opposed by the monarchy. In June 1789, Louis XVI opposed the mandates of the

---

[38] The European Commission for Democracy through Law (Venice Commission), 'Report on Democracy, Limitation of Mandates and Incompatibility of Political Functions', 2013, www .venice.coe.int/webforms/documents/default.aspx?pdffile=CDL-AD(2012)027rev-e.

[39] For this distinction see, among others: G. Leibholz, *Das Wesen der Repräsentation und der Gestaltwandel der Demokratie im 20. Jahrhundert*, De Gruyter, Berlin, 1966 [1929]. Scholars have sometimes read this distinction as a dichotomy. For a critical overview, see: H. Hofmann, G. Pégny, Y. Sintomer, 'Le concept de représentation: un problème allemand?' *Raisons politiques*, No. 2, 2013, 79; S. Staiano, *La rappresentanza*, 2017, www.rivistaaic.it/images/rivista/pdf/4.%203_2017_Staiano_ .pdf.

[40] Concerning the way in which public lawyers have used and changed private law concepts, see: L. Pegoraro, 'Le categorie civilistiche e il parassitismo metodologico dei costituzionalisti nello studio del diritto comparato', *Annuario di diritto comparato e di studi legislativi*, 2013, 305.

[41] E. Rinaldi, 'Divieto di mandato imperativo e disciplina dei gruppi parlamentari', 2017, www .costituzionalismo.it/download/Costituzionalismo_201702_637.pdf. See also: R. Scarciglia, *Il divieto di mandato imperativo*, 33; A. Fontana, 'L'evoluzione storica del mandato imperativo, dal medioevo allo Statuto albertino', in P. Caretti, D. Morisi, G. Tarli Barbieri (eds.), *Il divieto di mandato imperativo: un principio in discussione*, Seminario di studi e ricerche parlamentari 'Silvano Tosi', Florence, 324, 327.

[42] L. Principato, 'Il divieto di mandato imperativo, da prerogativa regia a garanzia della sovranità assembleare', 2012, www.rivistaaic.it/images/rivista/pdf/Principato.pdf.

representatives of the three orders gathered in the National Assembly: 'His Majesty declares that in subsequent meetings of the États généraux he will not suffer cahiers or mandats to ever be regarded as imperative: they must be considered as mere instructions entrusted to the conscience and free opinion of the deputies who will make their decision'. The cahiers de doléances were indeed instructions through which the États, thanks to their authority, bound their representatives. The king, freeing the members of the Assembly from mandates, made them 'free' from all restrictions and all authority that was not that of the monarch himself.[43]

After the French Revolution, representation and free mandate developed an ambiguous relationship that was functional to guarantee the unity of the nation. The fundamental decision to vote *par tête* instead of *par ordre* was a decisive moment, although even earlier it was clear that a rigid application of the imperative mandate could lead to never-ending discussions and institutional paralysis.[44]

Two documents are particularly vital at this stage: the *Declaration on the establishment of the National Assembly*, stating that: 'representation is one and indivisible'[45] and the motion on the imperative mandates (*motion sur les mandats impératifs*),[46] which established the overcoming of the imperative mandate as a consequence of 'the primacy of a representative body of almost the entire population but it does not imply absolute freedom of choice for the representatives'.[47] In the French Constitution of 1791, the prohibition of the imperative mandate was codified in Article 7 of Section III.[48] With the National Convention of 1792, scholars[49] have also stressed the emergence of another fundamental shift: the emergence of a primitive concept of responsiveness according to which the representatives were asked to send periodic reports to their electors to give them the possibility of controlling their elected representatives. According to this approach, the imperative mandate did not have a private law nature. In actual fact, this reconstruction seems

---

[43] Tomba, 'Who's Afraid', 111.
[44] A. Fontana, 'L'evoluzione storica', 333.
[45] E. Sagan, *Citizens & Cannibals: The French Revolution, the Struggle for Modernity*, Rowman and Littlefield, Lanham, MD, 2001, 98.
[46] 'Motion de M. Talleyrand, évêque d'Autun sur les mandats impératifs, lors de la séance du 7 juillet 1789', available at: www.persee.fr/doc/arcpa_0000-0000_1875_num_8_1_4629_t2_0200_0000_8.
[47] 'Motion de M. Talleyrand', my own translation.
[48] Sect. III, Article 7 of the French Constitution 1791: 'The representatives selected in the department shall not be the representatives of one particular department, but of the entire nation, and no instructions can be given them'.
[49] Rinaldi, 'Divieto di mandato imperativo'. She traces accountability back to the contribution of Robespierre. M. Robespierre, *Discours sur le gouvernement représentatif*, 1793, https://archive.org /details/discourssurlegouoorobe/page/26/mode/2up (Italian translation, Sul governo rappresentativo, Manifestolibri, Rome, 1995, 36). See also G. Azzariti, *Cittadini, partiti e gruppi parlamentari: esiste ancora il divieto di mandato imperativo?*, in Associazione italiana dei costituzionalisti (ed.), *Partiti politici e società civile a sessant'anni dall'entrata in vigore della Costituzione*, Jovene, Naples, 2009, 177. Contra A. M. Citrigno and D. Moschella, 'Quale futuro per il divieto di mandato imperativo?', 2018, http://bpr.camera.it/bpr/allegati/show/CDBPR17-1932. N. Zanon, *Il libero mandato parlamentare. Saggio critico sull'art. 67 della Costituzione*, Giuffrè, Milan, 1991, 122.

to neglect that in a speech given on 10 May 1793, Robespierre himself advocated for the recall of representatives to avoid both 'absolute democracy' and 'representative despotism'.[50] Moreover, according to the Venice Commission, during the Commune of Paris, 'the experiment closest in time with imperative mandate', '[d]elegates to the council governing Paris had to report to their electors and they could be recalled by them if they did not stand by their original mandates'.[51] This confirms the importance of the French Revolution as a laboratory for those interested in comparative law and constitutional theory.

Nowadays, however, the prohibition of the imperative mandate has changed its nature again and there are other reasons for its justification: to avoid the institutional paralysis caused by the political heterogeneity characterising current societies and, above all, to give representatives the necessary margin of autonomy to decide on complex issues.[52]

Clearly, contemporary societies are much more pluralist and complex than the French one at that time, and so the debate continues:

> In modernity, the imperative mandate is usually rejected on the basis of two arguments, one technical, the other logical. In the first argument, the decision-making time of the imperative mandate is considered too long, while the state is seen as tending to accelerate decision-making, even at the cost of a loss of democracy. According to the second argument, in the era of the nation-state it is the nation as a whole that must be represented, and no other sovereign realities.
>
> If a parliament is the deliberative assembly of one whole nation, the representation of the unity of the nation is not compatible with the imperative mandate, which is instead the expression of local sovereign assemblies and districts. Indeed, in almost all European constitutions, the imperative mandate is explicitly forbidden, for the deputies do not represent their party or particular interests but the nation as a whole.[53]

Scholars have identified different forms of imperative mandates depending on the legal basis in question: a constitutional provision, a statutory one, an agreement or a convention.[54] The contemporary world is divided into experiences with regard to the adoption of the imperative mandate. In Europe, the imperative mandate does not belong to the texts of any constitution.[55]

---

[50] Robespierre, *Sul governo rappresentativo*.

[51] The European Commission for Democracy through Law (Venice Commission), 'Report on the Imperative Mandate'.

[52] A. Morelli, *Rappresentanza politica e libertà del mandato parlamentare*, ES, Naples, 2018, 33.

[53] Tomba, 'Who's Afraid', 112.

[54] Zanon, *Il libero mandato parlamentare*.

[55] Perhaps with the exception of Article 81.6 of the constitution of Ukraine: 'The authority of People's Deputies of Ukraine terminates simultaneously with the termination of authority of the Verkhovna Rada of Ukraine.
      The authority of a People's Deputy of Ukraine terminates prior to the expiration of the term in the event of [. . .] 6) his or her failure, as having been elected from a political party (an electoral bloc of political parties), to join the parliamentary faction representing the same political party (the same electoral bloc of political parties) or his or her exit from such a faction'. See the European

In the last century, only a select few communist countries codified the imperative mandate; the Bulgarian Constitution of 1971 is one example.[56] On other continents, instead, the imperative mandate in the form of a recall is well known. For instance, Article 77 of the Chinese Constitution provides that: 'Deputies to the National People's Congress are subject to the supervision of the units which elected them. The electoral units have the power, through procedures prescribed by law, to recall deputies whom they elected'.[57] In communist countries, however, the political actors who make these decisions are not 'the electors, but the party',[58] although sometimes this is not evident from the wording of the constitution.[59] However, forms of the imperative mandate are also known in some Western democracies. It is the case of the recall at state level in the United States and in Germany. With regard to the *Bundesrat*, Article 51(1) states that 'The Bundesrat shall consist of members of the Land governments, which appoint and recall them. Other members of those governments may serve as alternates'. On the other hand, Article 38(1), as we have seen, prohibits the imperative mandate in the *Bundestag*. This is due to the fact that the *Bundesrat*, as the German Constitutional Court itself stated,[60] is not a senate, but rather a federal council of the governments of the *Länder*. This also explains why under Article 51(2) of the German Basic Law 'the votes of each Land must be cast as a block'.[61] The other exception is given by the recall procedure in the United States, which 'allows citizens to remove and replace a public official before the end of a term of office'.[62] As for the grounds justifying recall, here scholars differentiate between models, depending on the accuracy of the provision. Recall per se is different from impeachment (a judicial proceeding resulting from a crime being committed), since, as the constitution of Michigan confirms, it is a political

---

Commission for Democracy through Law (Venice Commission), 'Report on the Imperative Mandate'.

[56] Article 67 of the constitution of Bulgaria of 1971.

[57] Article 77 of the constitution of the People's Republic of China.

[58] The European Commission for Democracy through Law (Venice Commission), 'Report on the Imperative Mandate'.

[59] This is the case of the Cuban Constitution, for instance. Its Article 101 reads: 'The organs of the State are formed and develop their activities upon the foundation of the principles of socialist democracy, which are expressed in the following rules:

    a. All the representative organs of State power are elected and renewable;

    b. The people monitor the activity of the State organs, their leaders, functionaries, representatives, and delegates, in accordance with that which the law prescribes;

    c. Elected representatives have the duty to periodically release required documentation regarding the performance of their duties and may be removed from office at any moment [omissis]'.

[60] German Constitutional Court (BVG) 37, 363, 380/1974.

[61] The European Commission for Democracy through Law (Venice Commission), 'Report on the Imperative Mandate'. Article 51(2) of the German Constitution: 'Each Land shall have at least three votes; Länder with more than two million inhabitants shall have four, Länder with more than six million inhabitants five and Länder with more than seven million inhabitants six votes'.

[62] The European Commission for Democracy through Law (Venice Commission), 'Report on the Imperative Mandate'.

process.[63] The recall of representatives is possible at the local level in Canada and Japan, for instance.[64] More recently, there has been a debate on whether to introduce forms of recall in both Australia and the United Kingdom.[65] In the UK, the Recall of MPs Act 2015 was approved but it provides for a particular case of recall to replace members of parliament who have been sentenced or convicted for certain crimes[66] or excluded from the House of Commons. It can be triggered by the speaker. Finally, another relevant area is Latin America, in which the instrument of recall has been widely codified by the domestic systems. For instance, Article 72 of the constitution of Venezuela[67] also provides for the recall of the president of the Republic. On the basis of this provision, in 2004 there was a referendum attempt to remove President Hugo Chávez, but it failed.

Contrasting with recall and the cases of imperative mandate that have already been analysed are the so-called anti-defection clauses, such as Article 160 of the Portuguese Constitution:

Members of the Assembly of the Republic shall lose their seat in the event that:

---

[63] Section 8 of the constitution of Michigan: 'Laws shall be enacted to provide for the recall of all elective officers except judges of courts of record upon petition of electors equal in number to 25 percent of the number of persons voting in the last preceding election for the office of governor in the electoral district of the officer sought to be recalled. The sufficiency of any statement of reasons or grounds procedurally required shall be a political rather than a judicial question'.

[64] The European Commission for Democracy through Law (Venice Commission), 'Report on the Imperative Mandate'.

[65] A. Twomey, 'Second Thoughts – Recall Elections for Members of Parliament', Sydney Law School Research Paper No. 11/55, 2011, https://papers.ssrn.com/sol3/papers.cfm?abstract_id=1922393.

[66] Section 1, paras. 3 and 4, of the Recall of MPs Act 2015: '(3) The first recall condition is that—
(a) the MP has, after becoming an MP, been convicted in the United Kingdom of an offence and sentenced or ordered to be imprisoned or detained, and
(b) the appeal period expires without the conviction, sentence or order having being overturned on appeal. Sections 2 to 4 contain more about the first recall condition.
(4) The second recall condition is that, following on from a report from the Committee on Standards in relation to the MP, the House of Commons orders the suspension of the MP from the service of the House for a specified period of the requisite length'.

[67] Article 72 of the Venezuelan Constitution: 'All magistrates and other offices filled by popular vote are subject to revocation.
Once half of the term of office to which an official has been elected has elapsed, a number of voters constituting at least 20% of the voters registered in the pertinent circumscription may extend a petition for the calling of a referendum to revoke such official's mandate.
When a number of voters equal to or greater than the number of those who elected the official vote in favor of revocation, provided that a number of voters equal to or greater than 25% of the total number of registered voters have voted in the revocation election, the official's mandate shall be deemed revoked, and immediate action shall be taken to fill the permanent vacancy in accordance with the provided for in this Constitution and by law.
The revocation of the mandate for the collegiate bodies shall be performed in accordance with the law.
During the term to which the official was elected, only one petition to recall may be filed'.

a) They become subject to any of the disqualifications or incompatibilities provided for by law;
b) They do not take up their seat in the Assembly, or they exceed the number of failures to attend laid down in the Rules of Procedure;
c) They register as members of a party other than that for which they stood for election;
d) They are convicted by a court of any of the special crimes for which political officeholders may be held liable, which they commit in the exercise of their functions and for which they are sentenced to such loss, or they are convicted of participating in organisations that are racist or display a fascist ideology.

Members of the Assembly of the Republic may resign their seat by means of a written declaration.

Article 160 of the Portuguese Constitution is frequently confused with norms admitting the imperative mandate, and even the Five Star Movement frequently evokes this provision, while advocating the introduction of a binding mandate,[68] but scholars have stressed some important differences.[69]

First, there are two other provisions of the same constitution that explicitly exclude the imperative mandate, namely Articles 152[70] and 155,[71] especially the latter, which states that '[m]embers of the Assembly of the Republic shall exercise their mandates freely'. Second, although Article 151 of the Constitution[72] recognises the crucial role of political parties[73] in a system characterised by unicameralism and

---

[68] For instance, in the 'contract for government' signed between the Five Star Movement and the Lega, available at: https://download.repubblica.it/pdf/2018/politica/contratto_governo.pdf.

[69] On Portugal, see: R. Orrù, 'Divieto di mandato imperativo e anti-defection laws: spunti di diritto comparato', *Diritto pubblico comparato ed europeo*, No. 4, 2015, 1099; Damele, 'Vincoli di mandato'.

[70] Article 152 of the Portuguese Constitution: 'The law may not set limits on the conversion of votes into seats by requiring a minimum national percentage of votes cast.
      Members of the Assembly of the Republic represent the whole country and not the constituencies for which they are elected'.

[71] Article 155 of the Portuguese Constitution: 'Members of the Assembly of the Republic shall exercise their mandates freely and shall be guaranteed the conditions needed to exercise their functions effectively, particularly those needed for the indispensable contact with registered electors and for ensuring that the latter are regularly kept informed.
      The law shall regulate the circumstances in which the absence of Members from official acts or proceedings that do not concern the Assembly of the Republic, due to Assembly sittings or missions, constitutes justified grounds for adjourning the said acts or proceedings.
      Public entities are under a duty, as laid down by law, to cooperate with Members of the Assembly of the Republic in the exercise of their functions'.

[72] Article 151 of the Portuguese Constitution: 'Nominations are submitted by political parties as laid down by law. Parties may submit nominations individually or in coalition, and the lists may include citizens who are not registered members of the respective parties.
      No one may be a candidate for more than one constituency of the same nature, with the exception of the national constituency when one exists. No one may appear on more than one list'.

[73] According to Article 51(5) of the Portuguese Constitution: 'Political parties must be governed by the principles of democratic transparency, organisation and management, and participation by all their members'.

a proportional electoral system,[74] there is nothing in Article 160 which obliges representatives to follow binding instructions from their electors and that provides for sanctions in case of violations of these instructions. Third, the loss of the seat is not automatic. Indeed, if the representatives decide to leave their party but do not join a 'party other than that for which they stood for election', they may retain their seat. This is possible since representatives can decide to serve as independents (*deputado independente*) after leaving their party.[75] The loss of the seat is declared by the *Assembleia da República* and it is possible to go before the Constitutional Court to oppose this decision.[76]

This makes Article 160 a powerful anti-defection clause. In Spain, a similar result has been pursued via other means. Indeed, in Spain the prohibition of the imperative mandate is enshrined in Article 67[77] and anti-defection norms can be found in the parliamentary rules of procedure, for instance, in Article 23(2) and Article 27 of the rules of the Spanish Congress.[78]

6.3 ARTICLE 67 OF THE ITALIAN CONSTITUTION: GENESIS AND CURRENT ISSUES

Article 67 of the Italian Constitution was approved without overly extensive discussions in the Constituent Assembly.[79] It is included in a series of provisions aimed at defining the status of the members of parliament.[80] This confirms that the prohibition of the imperative mandate is not only functional to the defence of the institution, but also to the preservation of the necessary autonomy of the member of parliament in question, an autonomy which is crucial to facilitate decision-making on complex matters in a highly pluralistic society.

Article 67 should be read together with Article 49, which is devoted to political parties.[81] Article 49 of the Italian Constitution reads: 'Any citizen has the right to

---

[74] Morelli, *Rappresentanza politica*, 76.

[75] Damele, 'Vincoli di mandato'.

[76] Morelli, *Rappresentanza politica*, 75.

[77] Article 67 of the Spanish Constitution: '1. No person may be a member of both Houses simultaneously, or be a representative in the Assembly of an Autonomous Community and a Deputy to Congress at the same time.

2. The members of the Cortes Generales shall not be bound by a compulsory mandate.

3. Meetings of members of Parliament which are held without having been called in the statutory manner shall not be binding on the Houses, and members may not exercise their functions therein nor enjoy the privileges deriving from their office'.

[78] The relevant norms can be found here: www.congreso.es/portal/page/portal/Congreso/Congreso/Hist_Normas/Norm/Reglam/Tit2.

[79] Zanon, *Il libero mandato parlamentare*, 212.

[80] C. Martinelli, 'Libero mandato e rappresentanza nazionale come fondamenti della modernità costituzionale', 2018, www.federalismi.it/nv14/articolo-documento.cfm?Artid=36456; L. Ciauro, 'Art. 67', in R. Bifulco, A. Celotto, M. Olivetti (eds.), *Commentario alla Costituzione*, Vol. II, UTET, Turin, 2006, 1289.

[81] P. Ridola, 'Partiti politici', *Enciclopedia del diritto*, Vol. XXXII, Giuffrè, Milan, 66; C. Esposito, 'I partiti nella Costituzione italiana', in C. Esposito, *La Costituzione italiana. Saggi*, Cedam, Padua, 1954, 215.

freely establish parties to contribute to determining national policies through democratic processes'. The importance accorded to political parties is not necessarily in conflict with the prohibition of the imperative mandate. As scholars stressed, these two provisions can be read as the outcome of a balance struck by the Constituent Assembly.[82] Article 67[83] tries to protect both the parliament and its members from different possible sources of interference: territorial interests, lobbies and economic groups.[84] At the same time, with the emergence of mass political parties, Article 67 needs to be framed in a triangular relationship: elected, electors and political parties.[85] Political parties are at the same level since they are fundamental actors in the selection of candidates, but they could become sources of external constraint affecting the autonomy of the member of parliament; Article 67 thus offers a shield. As we will see, this does not exclude the possibility that parties and political groups in the parliament[86] give guidelines to their members or even sanction them; this is possible and frequently provided for in the respective internal rules of organisation. What is not possible is recalling the elected member, or, in other words, imposing the automatic loss of their seat, because this would give political parties 'absolute power over the elected in their list'.[87]

One of the most important constitutional lawyers – Costantino Mortati – while serving as a member of the Constituent Assembly, proposed a different version of the provision: 'Deputies represent the nation as a whole'.[88] He was slightly 'sceptical'[89] of this provision and aware of the growing role acquired by new mass political parties. Other members insisted on adding an explicit prohibition of the imperative mandate (for instance, Mannironi). Later (on 23 October 1946), on Mortati's proposal, the second sub-commission decided to extend this formula to members of the Senate[90] and this led to the final wording.[91]

---

[82] Martinelli, 'Libero mandato'.

[83] Ciaurro, 'Art. 67'.

[84] Rinaldi, 'Divieto di mandato imperativo', 155.

[85] P. Ridola, 'Divieto del mandato imperativo e pluralismo politico', in *Studi sulle fonti normative e altri temi di vario diritto in onore di Vezio Crisafulli*, Vol. II, Cedam, Padua, 1985, 679, 696.

[86] Political groups are defined as the parliamentary projection of political parties in the parliaments. The Standing Orders of each House provide for the minimum numbers of members for these groups; A. Pizzorusso, *I gruppi parlamentari come soggetti di diritto: pagine di un saggio giuridico*, Pacini Mariotti, Pisa, 1969.

[87] C. Pinelli, 'Libertà di mandato dei parlamentari e rimedi contro il Transfughismo', 2018, www.federalismi.it/nv14/articolo-documento.cfm?Artid=36498. My own translation.

[88] Atti dell'Assemblea Costituente, session held 19 September 1946, www.nascitacostituzione.it/03p2/01t1/s1/067/index.htm?art067-003.htm&2. My own translation.

[89] J. Mazzurri, 'La genesi del divieto ex art. 67 Cost. nel periodo costituente e brevi note sulle vicende della norma nei principali tentativi di riforma della Carta', in P. Caretti, D. Morisi, G. Tarli Barbieri (eds.), *Il divieto di mandato imperativo: un principio in discussione*, Seminario di studi e ricerche parlamentari 'Silvano Tosi', Florence, 339, 343.

[90] See the report at the following link: www.nascitacostituzione.it/03p2/01t1/s1/067/index.htm?art067-003.htm&2.

[91] See the report at the following link: www.nascitacostituzione.it/03p2/01t1/s1/067/index.htm?art067-003.htm&2.

Commentators have also discussed the relationship between the concept of the nation as enshrined in Article 67 and that of people mentioned elsewhere, for instance in Article 1. From the conceptual point of view, they are certainly distinguishable concepts,[92] but for the purpose of the constitution, this is not clear. Indeed, scholars have debated this,[93] stressing the risks of understanding 'nation' and 'people' as two potentially conflicting terms, in the case, for instance, of the emergence of a secessionist party in the country. Ciaurro identified three phases in the drafting of Article 67.[94] Initially the issue of the imperative mandate was not present in the draft, although later it emerged and part of the provision of the *Statuto Albertino* – the old constitution of the Kingdom of Italy[95] – was taken into account as a model. Finally, in the third phase, it was decided to 'streamline' the wording of the provision and this led to the final version. Italy has experienced different attempts at grand constitutional reforms since 2001. Still, the prohibition of the imperative mandate has not been put at stake by these attempts. A minor exception is represented by the failed Boschi–Renzi constitutional reform in 2016, which included an important differentiation between the members of the Chamber of Deputies and those of the Senate, in an amendment to Article 55 of the Constitution. Indeed, in the bill while the free mandate applied to the members of parliament,[96] the reform read that only the members of the Chamber of Deputies represented the nation, while the Senate represented territorial institutions.[97]

However, there have been other attempts aimed at amending Article 67 only.[98] More recently, for instance, in the 17th legislature, Vito Crimi, a Five Star Movement senator, proposed amending Article 67 as follows: 'Each Member of Parliament represents the nation and exercises his or her functions with the constraint of a popular mandate. Members of Parliament and senators who, during the legislature, join a parliamentary group other than the one for which they were elected, shall be declared lapsed and barred from future nominations'.[99] This

---

[92] For an overview, see: V. Crisafulli, D. Nocilla, 'Nazione', in *Enclopedia del diritto*, Vol. XXVII, Giuffrè, Milan, 1977, 814; P. Carrozza, 'Nazione', in *Digesto discipline pubblicistiche*, Vol. X, UTET, Turin, 1995, 126.

[93] On this debate, see: V. Crisafulli, 'Partiti, Parlamento, Governo', in V. Crisafulli, *Stato Popolo Governo. Illusioni e delusioni costituzional*, Giuffrè, Milan, 1985, 209; C. De Fiores, 'Sulla rappresentazione della Nazione. Brevi note sul divieto di mandato imperativo', *Diritto e società*, No. 1, 2017, 19; Morelli, *Rappresentanza politica*, 83; Rinaldi, 'Divieto di mandato imperativo', 155.

[94] Ciaurro, 'Art. 67'.

[95] Article 41, Statuto Albertino: 'The Deputies represent the Nation in general, and not only the provinces in which they were elected. No imperative mandate can be given to them by the Electors', my own translation.

[96] Article 8 of the constitutional amendment bill (DDL n. 1429-D amending Article 67), Italian Constitution, available at: www.senato.it/service/PDF/PDFServer/BGT/00955273.pdf. My own translation.

[97] Article 1 of the DDL n. 1429-D amending Article 55, Italian Constitution, available at: www.senato.it/service/PDF/PDFServer/BGT/00955273.pdf. My own translation.

[98] C. Fasone, 'Is There a Populist Turn in the Italian Parliament? Continuity and Discontinuity in the Non-legislative Procedures', in G. Delledonne, G. Martinico, M. Monti, F. Pacini (eds.), *Italian Populism and Constitutional Law: Strategies, Conflicts and Dilemmas*, Palgrave, London, 2020, 41, 48.

[99] Ddl 2759 Bill, https://parlamento17.openpolis.it/atto/documento/id/400317. My own translation.

proposal was highly problematic for both methodological and substantive reasons. It clearly took the Portuguese model into account but conflated an anti-defection clause with the source of a binding popular mandate. According to some scholars, Article 67 belongs to the unamendable part of the constitution covered by the concept of 'republican form' included in Article 139.[100] In fact, in the most important essay written on this topic in Italy, Zanon clarified that not all the content of Article 67 belongs to the unamendability clause, 'only its core', which consists of the freedom of the representatives from instructions and commands provided with efficacy and the impossibility of being recalled before the term of office expires.[101] The Constitutional Court intervened to stress the importance of Article 67, in its judgment 14/1964,[102] in which it clarified that:

> Article 67 [. . .] is aimed at ensuring the freedom of the members of Parliament. The prohibition of the imperative mandate implies that the member of Parliament is free to vote according to the guidelines of his party, but he is also free to escape from them; no norm could legitimately provide for consequences for the member of Parliament for the fact that he voted against the party's guidelines.[103]

More recently, Zanon himself wrote of a 'second youth of Article 67'[104] in light of decision 1/2014 on electoral law, in which the *Corte costituzionale* made Article 67 part of its yardstick to review the validity of the law in order to protect not only the role of single parliamentarians, but also the parliamentary dialectic. Article 67 is one of those 'constitutional principles according to which the Houses of Parliament are the exclusive locus for "national political representation" (Art. 67)'.[105]

Going back to the constitutional amendment bill proposed by the Five Star Movement, it is interesting to look at the words used by Senator Crimi when presenting the content of this constitutional reform proposal to the Senate in the 17th legislature. As always, here one can find the opportunistic use of constitutional law as one of the strategies employed by populists:

> The prohibition of mandatory mandate, in the Constituent [Assembly's] vision, meant that the parliamentarian, as representative of the entire nation, was guaranteed autonomy and freedom from influence in the exercise of the mandate itself. In the course of the history of the Republic, however, this prohibition has progressively transformed itself into a form of irresponsibility of individual deputies and senators

---

[100] Zanon, *Il libero mandato parlamentare*, 328.
[101] Zanon, *Il libero mandato parlamentare*, 328.
[102] Corte costituzionale, decision 14/1964.
[103] Corte costituzionale, decision 14/1964. My own translation.
[104] N. Zanon, 'La seconda giovinezza dell'art. 67 della Costituzione', 2014, www.forumcostituzionale.it /wordpress/images/stories/pdf/documenti_forum/giurisprudenza/2014/0007_nota_1_2014_zanon. pdf; see also: V. Tonti, 'Vincolo di mandato e democrazia diretta : verso un superamento del Parlamento?', in G. Allegri, A. Sterpa, N. Viceconte (eds.), *Questioni costituzionali al tempo del populismo e del sovranismo*, ES, Naples, 2019, 93.
[105] Corte costituzionale, decision 1/2014, English translation available at: www.cortecostituzionale.it /documenti/download/doc/recent_judgments/1-2014_en.pdf.

before the electoral body, in the sense of a pathological misrepresentation of the concept of political coherence and an alteration of the democratic balances sanctioned by the voters, as well as, in the final analysis, the popular sovereignty referred to in Article 1 of the Constitution [. . .] From a pragmatic point of view, therefore, Article 67 of the current Constitution risks offering an undeserved and blatant cover for shifting political alliances, which urgently needs to be overcome if we want to recover the profound sense of the bond between the holders of elected public office and those for whom they are candidates and who elected them at the fundamental moment of the democratic game. In modern democracies, voters choose between opposing sides that present distinct options to the electoral body, which cannot be misrepresented *ex post* for long without damaging democracy itself. Moreover, other legal systems, including European ones, provide for the restriction of the mandate of parliamentarians; it is well known that Article 160 of the Portuguese Constitution of 1976 states that a Member of Parliament shall lose his or her mandate simply if he or she resigns from the parliamentary group of his or her party and at the same time joins the group of another political faction. The experiences of 'popular recall' in other democratic systems are also well known.[106]

As such, one can thus infer that from a correct diagnosis of the problem (transfufugism), the wrong solution is derived. The Five Star Movement is correct in identifying transfugism as one of the main issues of the Italian political system,[107] but the abolition of the free parliamentary mandate is not a solution proportional to the higher goal. It would be sufficient to introduce – and this has partly been done, as we will see – some anti-defection clauses at either the constitutional or primary level. To remedy transfugism, which has traditionally caused instability in Italy, in 2017 the rules of the procedure of the Senate were amended, providing for a new Article 14

---

[106] 'Disegno di legge n. 2759. Relazione', available at: www.senato.it/japp/bgt/showdoc/17/DDLPRES/0/1021649/index.html?part=ddlpres_ddlpres1-relpres_relpres1. My own translation.

[107] '[C]ertain degree of constraint on the representative mandate is indeed instrumental to the operation of Parliaments. It is not by chance that, beyond the populistic discourse on the need to restore a binding mandate for MPs in front of the voters, for the sake of abiding to their preferences, the debate on the limitation of the free mandate typically arises in constitutional systems, like Italy since the mid-1990s, featured by high level of parliamentary "transfugism" (transfughismo parlamentare), that is the likelihood and the inclination of MPs to change political group or party once or several times since the electoral moment. In general, the limitation of the free mandate is tolerated, though with a number of guarantees, to protect competing constitutional values that deserve protection in the legal system, like ensuring governmental stability and the well-ordered functioning of parliamentary procedures. Those limitations can take the form of constitutional clauses, for example, Article 160 of the Portuguese Constitution (Scarciglia 2005; Orrù 2015), of provisions in the parliamentary rules of procedure, for example, Arts. 23.2 and 27 of the rules of Spanish Congress (Caretti et al. 2019: 1–70), or the balance between free mandate and other constitutional principles can be struck by case law, depending on where in the Parliament the limitation has occurred. For example, in the Wüppesahl case decided by the German Constitutional Tribunal in 1989, the court held that the norm of the rule of procedures foreseeing the automatic loss of the seat in a parliamentary committee for MPs who had exited their group, becoming non-attached members, was unconstitutional as it violated the principle of free mandate. In Italy parliamentary "transfugism" is a serious issue, whose solution is not eased by the instability of the electoral legislation', Fasone, 'Is There a Populist Turn in the Italian Parliament?', 46–7.

which 'allows the formation of a group only if it represents a political party or movement—also resulting from the aggregation of several parties and movements—that competed with their own candidates under the same symbol for seats in the Senate obtaining that at least some of them were elected'.[108] Unfortunately, this clause has already been circumvented given its broad interpretation by the president of the Senate. Indeed, *Italia Viva*, the new force created by Renzi after he left the *Partito democratico*, managed to create a political group in the Senate instead of joining the mixed group (*gruppo misto*).[109] This was possible thanks to a senator who had been elected as a member of the socialist party, who then joined Renzi and his new force, thus giving birth to a new political group: *Italia Viva/PSI* (which stands for *Partito socialista italiano*). In a similar way, before the birth of the Draghi government, Conte's supporters set up a movement called *Italia23*. They also used the logo of the MAIE (*Movimento Associativo Italiani all'Estero*, in English the Associative Movement of Italians Abroad) and created a new parliamentary group called *Europeisti Maie Centro democratico* (which immediately dissolved afterwards as we saw).

The frustration of Article 14 of the Senate's rules of procedure has given new lifeblood to this debate. In a way, the constitutional amendment bill presented in the 17th legislature aimed to solve the issue but went far beyond what was necessary both by questioning the imperative mandate and, even going beyond the Portuguese model, by making it impossible for offending members of parliament to be candidates in subsequent elections.

6.4 A PARTY IN DISGUISE: HOW TO UNDERSTAND THE FIVE STAR MOVEMENT FROM A LEGAL POINT OF VIEW

In an article published in 2017, Voßkuhle – former president of the German Constitutional Court – identified different tensions between populism and constitutionalism; the imperative mandate is one of these.[110] The attack on the free parliamentary mandate is part of a broader battle of a party which is clearly anti-establishment. Traditional political parties are another target of populist attack. In Italy, this battle has found a favourable context, as we saw in Chapter 2 when analysing the roots of anti-party-ism.[111] As discussed, another

---

[108] Fasone, 'Is There a Populist Turn in the Italian Parliament?', 47. Article 14, para. 4, Rules of Procedure of the Senate: 'Indeed, Art. 14 par. 4, states that "Each Group must be composed of at least ten Senators and must represent a political party or movement, including those resulting from the aggregation of several political parties or movements, which has presented its own candidates with the same mark in the Senate elections [...]"'.

[109] In both the Chamber of Deputies and the Senate, it is possible to join the so-called mixed group (*gruppo misto*), which comprises all the deputies or senators who do not belong to any other parliamentary group.

[110] A. Voßkuhle, 'Demokratie und Populismus', *Der Staatt*, No. 1, 2018, 119.

[111] N. Urbinati, 'Anti-party-ism as a Structural Component of Italian Democracy', in P. Blokker, M. Anselmi (eds.), *Multiple Populisms: Italy as Democracy's Mirror*, Routledge, Abingdon, 2020, 67.

vital source of anti-party-ism was *Tangentopoli*, a wide-ranging scandal which radically changed the Italian political system and the image of politicians. The Five Star Movement relies on these different waves of anti-party-ism. It does not define itself as a political party and did not ask for inclusion in the national register of political parties.[112] Initially, it defined itself as a 'non-association' provided with a 'non-statute' (*non-statuto*). As aforementioned, the *statuto* is the fundamental charter of a political party in Italy. Like elsewhere, political parties are not public law institutions but rather private associations in Italian constitutional law. It is no coincidence that political parties are governed by Article 49, which is included in the first part of the constitution and in particular in the section devoted to political rights. Although according to Article 49 of the Italian Constitution, parties are expected 'to contribute to determining national policies through democratic processes', this requirement has only been partially implemented in spite of reforms that have tried to do just that.[113] For instance, law 96/2012 requires that a political party's *statuto* is compatible 'with democratic principles in the internal organization, most notably with regard to the selection of candidates, the respect of internal minorities and the protection of the rights of party members'.[114] This is also the case in law 13/2014, an important reform passed during the Letta government, which abolished the direct public financing of political parties. To gain access to indirect public contributions,[115] parties have to comply with certain requirements established therein, in order to guarantee a democratic organisation.[116] The Five Star Movement has refused to apply for the indirect public financing provided for by these norms, but one should not forget that its parliamentary groups benefit from public funding from the budget of both the Chamber of Deputies and the Senate.[117]

---

[112] National register of political parties recognised pursuant to Decree-Law no. 149 of 28 December 2013, converted into law, with amendments, by Law no. 13 of 21 February 2014, available at: www .parlamento.it/1067.

[113] On this debate, see E. Caterina, 'L'attuazione del metodo democratico all'interno dei partiti politici: analisi della normativa vigente e spunti per una legge sui partiti', *Democrazia e diritto*, 2016, 61.

[114] Article 5 Law 96/2012, my own translation.

[115] These indirect contributions are 2x1000 and tax benefits on private contributions. See F. Mat, N. Caranti, 'The Funding of Politics in Italy', 2019, www.balcanicaucaso.org/eng/Projects2/ESVEI/ News-Esvei/The-funding-of-politics-in-Italy-197740/The-funding-of-politics-in-Italy.

[116] 'Article 3 of Law no. 13/2014, in turn (included in a specific section on "Internal democracy, accountability and transparency"), provides a comprehensive description of the content of party statutes, including: rights and duties of party members; modalities of participation in the party's political activities; criteria to ensure the representation of minorities in nonexecutive bodies; disciplinary measures applicable to party members; criteria for the selection of candidates running for European, general and local elections', M. Bassini, 'Rise of Populism and the Five Star Movement Model: An Italian Case Study', in G. Delledonne, G. Martinico, M. Monti, F. Pacini (eds.), *Italian Populism and Constitutional Law: Strategies, Conflicts and Dilemmas*, Palgrave, London, 2020, 216.

[117] 'Anche il Movimento 5 stelle riceve finanziamenti pubblici', 6 May 2019, www.openpolis.it/anche-il-movimento-5-stelle-riceve-finanziamenti-pubblici/.

The topic of political parties in the Italian constitutional system deserves an entire monograph, but for the purpose of this book, I shall limit myself to some general considerations, going beyond those in Chapter 2. Relying on the excellent works available in English by Bassini[118] and De Petris,[119] it is possible to find confirmation of the importance of the *Rousseau* platforms in the life of the movement. Things have been evolving rapidly since Davide Casaleggio's departure, but even today its importance cannot be denied. The first important aspect is the dynamic and chameleonic identity of this force. At the beginning, as said, the Five Star Movement defined itself not only as a non-party but also as a non-association provided with a *non-statuto*.[120] This phase has partly been overcome with the reform of the *non-statuto*, which is now called *statuto*.[121] Moreover, Article 1 now explicitly defines the Five Star Movement as an association. The *Rousseau* platform is indeed mentioned in the *statuto* approved at the end of 2017 while it is not recalled in the new statute approved in 2021. In order to guarantee transparency and legitimacy, this provides that any Italian citizen who does not belong to other parties and who has not been expelled from the Movement may join the Movement at no cost. The *Rousseau* platform is used to choose lists of candidates through a complex procedure of online primary elections.[122] Online consultations are also used for 'debating the approval or repeal of bills (or again, for deciding whether an MP must be excluded from the Movement); and the direct involvement of the constituents in a range of activities'.[123]

This also explains the terminology used by the Movement. Once elected, they are mere spokespeople (*portavoci* in Italian), and this is consistent with their view of politics, as we have seen. Now, as we also saw in the previous chapter, these kinds of procedures, in order to be wholly inclusive and open, need to comply with some basic security requirements. Those who are elected are required to contribute to the funds of the Movement, which, coherently with its nature, has decided not to ask for indirect public funds, although recently even some big names of the Movement have not complied with this requirement.[124] As observed in the previous chapter, *Rousseau* has revealed itself as unsafe, as it suffered from different cyberattacks, and

---

[118] Bassini, 'Rise of Populism', in *Italian Populism*.

[119] A. De Petris, 'Programs, Strategies and Electoral Campaigns of the Five Stars Movement in Italy. A Brand New Party Model or an "Anti-Party" State of Mind?', in A. De Petris, T. Poguntke (eds.), *Anti-Party Parties in Germany and Italy*, Luiss University Press, Rome, 2015, 125.

[120] De Petris, 'Programs, Strategies'.

[121] Actually, in theory it is still possible to distinguish two different movements: one called *movimento* and the other *MoVimento*, which is instead an association with a *statuto*. See L. Gori, *Le elezioni primarie nell'ordinamento costituzionale*, ES, Naples, 2018, 132.

[122] For details, see: L. Mosca, C. Vaccari, A. Valeriani, 'How to Select Citizen Candidates: The Five Star Movement's Online Primaries and Their Implications', in A. De Petris, T. Poguntke (eds.), *Anti-Party Parties in Germany and Italy*, Luiss University Press, Rome, 2015, 114.

[123] Bassini, 'Rise of Populism', in *Italian Populism*, 208.

[124] A. Carli, 'Rimborsi M5s, per probiviri irregolari oltre 45 parlamentari', 7 January 2020, www .ilsole24ore.com/art/m5s-vertice-probiviri-morosi-dodici-parlamentari-non-presentano-rendiconti-gennaio-2019-ACS4jBAB.

the online consultations are far from transparent.[125] Moreover, research suggests that the alleged horizontality of the Movement has remained a myth,[126] since 'the technological fetishism of the Net as an autonomous political agent has enabled Grillo and Casaleggio to conceal their authoritarian practices'.[127] This observation leads us back to the issue of the internal structure of the Five Star Movement and to the many threats that this political force presents to the parliamentary mandate.

Once projected onto the parliamentary dimension, the Five Star Movement confirmed its problematic nature. Indeed, in the internal rules of its political group in both the Chamber of Deputies and the Senate, it included a very problematic provision (Art. 21, para. 5) stating that: '[a]ny MP who leaves the parliamentary group because of either his/her exclusion or voluntary withdrawal or resignation based on political disagreement shall pay a fine amounting to Euro 100,000.00 to the Five Star Movement by ten days'.[128] This provision echoes the wording of the code of conduct applicable to the Five Star Movement members of the European Parliament, which also 'provides voters with the power to recall a member of the European Parliament if a "serious infringement" occurs'.[129] These internal rules also use the word 'contracts', signed by the president of the parliamentary group and its members, to refer to the signature of an agreement whereby elected parliamentarians have accepted to undertake duties stemming from their membership. What is the nature of these contracts? There are two main options: they could be either void as they conflict with an imperative norm,[130] namely Article 67 of the constitution, or simply not enforceable.[131] Relevant case law also confirms the hierarchical structure of the Five Star Movement. For instance, once the movement's leadership decided to exclude certain members from the list of candidates because they had violated the *statuto* and the code of conduct by creating a secret group on Facebook to foster discussion and exchange ideas. They were expelled in an email signed by 'the staff of Beppe Grillo'. As a consequence, they were not allowed to participate in the online primaries for some local elections. They brought the case before the Court of Naples[132] and the judge decided to suspend the expulsion of these members because it should have been decided by the assembly according to the relevant norms of the Civil Code, unless otherwise provided for by the *statuto*. This decision is relevant,

---

[125]   Bassini, 'Rise of Populism', in *Italian Populism*, 208.
[126]   Bassini, 'Rise of Populism', in *Italian Populism*, 211–12.
[127]   E. Trerè, V. Barassi, 'Net-authoritarianism ? How Web Ideologies Reinforce Political Hierarchies in the Italian 5 Star Movement', *Journal of Italian Cinema & Media Studies*, No. 3, 2015, 287, 299.
[128]   Translation by Bassini, 'Rise of Populism', in *Italian Populism*, 210.
[129]   Translation by Bassini, 'Rise of Populism', in *Italian Populism*, 209.
[130]   According to Article 1418 of the Civil Code: 'or are, at least, voidable (Ciaurro 2006: 1292). Indeed, it being patently in violation of Article 67 Const. the relevant clause can be annulled by the Constitutional Court, most likely by means of a conflict of attribution', Fasone, 'Is There a Populist Turn in the Italian Parliament', 50.
[131]   On this debate, see: Zanon, *Il libero mandato parlamentare*, 291.
[132]   Court of Naples, order of 14 July 2016, affirmed by the Court of Naples, 18 April 2018, no. 3773. See Bassini, 'Rise of Populism', in *Italian Populism*, 212.

because at that time the Court considered the Five Star Movement a political party and thus applied the norms of the Civil Code devoted to the associations to it. A confirmation of the applicability of the Civil Code to the Five Star Movement can be found in other cases, and therefore, despite the attempt to avoid the label of a party, the Five Star Movement cannot escape the relevant norms of the Civil Code. One such case is the decision of the Court of Genoa, which blocked the decision of Beppe Grillo to invalidate the result of the online primary elections in his capacity as guarantor of the Five Star Movement. Indeed, Grillo had decided to invalidate and replace one of the winners of the online elections with another candidate. The Court of Genoa noticed that this exceeded the powers of the guarantor and once again applied the norms of the Civil Code.[133] Grillo's decision had later been ratified by an online consultation but this was not enough to justify the decision of the guarantor. The importance of Grillo, especially in the first part of the life of the movement, confirms the populist nature of the MoVimento 5 Stelle. Indeed, as pointed out by Barber:

> In contrast to a properly functioning political party, the populist party is little more than a personality cult. The populist leader treats political parties – even those that have helped her gain power – like other constitutional institutions. Their existence as a matter of form may play a part in the populist constitution, but their substance is eroded. The populist party, where it exists, is a radically deviant instance of a political party, one which is failing to fulfill its function in the constitution.[134]

In conclusion, in the previous two chapters, we saw the essential elements of the anti-establishment agenda of the Five Star Movement, in particular the arguments employed against the parliament. This is in line with its populist nature.[135] In order to preserve constitutional democracy and political representation, it is necessary to defend the free mandate of the members of parliament, especially in light of the unclear and non-transparent organisation of the Five Star Movement.

---

[133] Court of Genoa, order of 10 April 2017.

[134] N. Barber, 'Populist Leaders and Political Parties', *German Law Journal*, special issue 2, 2019, 129, 137.

[135] The Five Star Movement is, however, part of a broader phenomenon, which finds its roots in a typically anti-politics culture that has always characterised Italy (see Chapter 2) and that has also retrieved elements from some post-*Tangentopoli* rhetoric, including some aspects of penal populism, which have not been examined in this book. This is further evidence of the heterogeneity of the movement. However, this book is not about the Five Star Movement as such, but deals with the problematic relationship between populism and post–WWII constitutionalism, of which Italy is a prime example.

7

Filtering Populist Claims to Fight Populism: Final Remarks

It is now time to draw some normative conclusions from this Italian journey.

Throughout this book, I have maintained that populism and constitutionalism, and in particular post–WWII constitutionalism (of which Italy is a prime example, as seen in Chapter 2) cannot be reconciled, due to the exclusionary, holistic and majoritarian nature of populism. As we saw in Chapter 1, this does not mean that populism and constitutionalism cannot have something in common, namely the importance of emotional reactions and the distrust of political power. In this sense, scholars who say that an antithetical reading of constitutionalism and populism is not enough are right. However, analogies cannot be extended further. Nevertheless, populists are interested in constitutional law. As Mudde argued, populists tend to have an opportunistic approach to constitutionalism,[1] and this is part of what Blokker called instrumentalism.[2] My point differs from that made by Blokker as I have argued against the possibility of populist constitutionalism, because of the strong counter-majoritarian and pro-integration nature of constitutionalism. At the same time, constitutional law is part of the language of populist forces when they are in power. Starting with this consideration, I explored the tricky relationship between constitutionalism and populism with the Italian case in mind. Is there such a thing as a populist theory of constitutional interpretation? I argued that this is not the case; the populist approach to constitutionalism is merely one of convenience. In order to

[1] 'While the relationship between populism and constitutionalism is fairly clear in theory, populists have taken a broad variety of approaches to constitutions in practice. In general, populists-in-opposition approach constitutions opportunistically; when the constitution supports their point, they will revere it, but if it opposes their idea, they will deny its importance. Similarly, their position towards constitutional judges is purely opportunistic. Depending upon the usefulness of their ruling, a judge is branded as one of "the people" or a member of "the elite". Populists-in-power are similarly opportunistic, clinging to the "sacred" constitution whenever it serves their purpose, and criticizing or even changing it when it does not. The opportunistic position of populists-in opposition toward constitutions is nowhere as visible as in the United States, where the Constitution is both an instrument and a symbol', C. Mudde, 'Are Populists Friends or Foes of Constitutionalism?', 2013, www.fljs.org /content/are-populists-friends-or-foes-constitutionalism.

[2] P. Blokker, 'Populism as a Constitutional Project', *International Journal of Constitutional Law*, No. 2, 2019, 537, 540–1.

investigate the way in which populists tend to read constitutions, I introduced two strategies: mimetism and parasitism. The former refers to the way in which populists try to conceal their majoritarian claims behind the words of the constitution; the latter to the actual plan to alter the equilibrium between the majoritarian and counter-majoritarian parts of the constitution, to change the axiological hierarchies on which the constitution is based. Indeed, by treating democracy as the mere rule of the majority populists claim that democracy should prevail over the other elements of the constellation, namely the rule of law and the protection of minorities.

When applied to the Italian case, this reveals the preference of populists for two constitutional provisions: Article 1 and Article 11 of the Italian Constitution.

In Article 1, populists pay particular attention to the sentence which states 'sovereignty belongs to the people'. We also saw in this reading – and here parasitism enters the scene – that they tend to omit the remaining part of the provision, according to which sovereignty 'is exercised by the people in the forms and within the limits of the Constitution'. This omission is tactical and reveals that for populists, constitutions are straitjackets that frustrate the democratic principle. This view of democracy is based on a methodological reduction of a complex concept. It is no coincidence that Article 1 is also used to question all the counter-majoritarian devices present in the post–WWII constitutional toolbox: the judicial review of legislation is just the most famous example of this trend.

Since I purposely decided not to enter the well-explored terrain of what populism is by giving a definition, the book follows a different strategy. Instead of defining populism *ex ante*, I looked at some elements that have been traced back (via identification) to the core of any populist force: identity politics, politics of immediacy and extreme majoritarianism.

In Chapter 2, I explained why Italy is an ideal case to explore the reasons populism is at odds with the essence of what we called post–WWII constitutionalism, and offered the necessary historical background to understand why the country has been characterised by several waves of populism. In Chapter 3, I explored the way in which populist sovereignists read Article 11 of the Italian Constitution to question EU integration, depicted – by both right-wing and left-wing populists – as a constitutional *coup d'état*. The texts of some academic sovereignists in Italy were analysed to stress all the inconsistencies and false dichotomies used and built by populists to question EU integration. The EU is seen as the main source of technocratic choices that has deprived Italians of their sovereignty. To question this point, I first showed that the principle of sovereignty, as understood by Article 11, is still preserved and defended by the Italian Constitutional Court. This is the essence of the so-called counter-limits doctrine, which is still alive and kicking. Second, I debunked the sovereignist reading of Article 11 by putting the Italian case in the context of the group of post–WWII constitutions based on the principle of constitutional openness to the international community. In light of these considerations, the alleged dichotomy between the EU treaties and the Italian Constitution does not exist. There might be a dialectic between them, for there have been and will be interpretive conflicts between the Court of Justice of the European Union (CJEU) and national constitutional courts. This means that the EU treaties and the Italian Constitution do not represent a dichotomy at all, as they can be reconciled. This opposition is based on an anti-European approach, which was one of the very few points in common between the *MoVimento 5 Stelle* and the *Lega*, and was still present in the second Conte government, as the debate on the European Stability Mechanism confirms. In Chapter 4, I looked at the politics of immediacy and the use of the referendum. I first underlined the multi-functional nature of this instrument and the risks of instrumentalisation. I then moved to the constitutional amendment bill advanced by the Five Star Movement aimed at introducing a new propositive referendum on the basis of the Swiss model. I argued that the very first proposal was hardly compatible with the constitution and highlighted some problematic elements present in the latest version. In Chapters 5 and 6, I looked at the institutional impact of this kind of instantaneous democracy advanced by the Five Star Movement. I first recalled the importance that the *Rousseau* platform has (to some extent also after Casaleggio's exit from the *MoVimento*) for the movement – as we saw, it also figured in the movement's official charters and documents – and the consequent techno-utopian approach of the *grillini* (supporters of Beppe Grillo as they are called in Italy). Having clarified the kind of democracy and politics that the Five Star Movement has advanced, I looked at the ways in which populists have influenced the activity of the parliament. We saw elements of continuity in the first Conte government despite the announcements made by the *Lega* and *5 Stelle*, while the second Conte government was inevitably affected by the COVID-19 crisis, which has contributed to the progressive marginalisation of the Italian Parliament and the growing personalisation and spectacularisation of politics. While the *Partito democratico* probably supported the birth of the second Conte government in order to tame the Five Star Movement, this plan failed and Renzi took advantage of this when he triggered the crisis in the second Conte government. Finally, in Chapter 6, I looked at the other side of the coin, that is, immediacy: the attempt made by the Five Star Movement to overcome the free parliamentary mandate, either directly – with some constitutional amendment bills – or indirectly, by introducing problematic sanctions that contrast with the core of Article 67 of the Italian Constitution.

However, it would be unfair to conclude that we cannot learn anything from the latest round of Italian populism. While I have maintained that with its extreme majoritarianism and its idea of instantaneous democracy populism represents a threat to the equilibria of constitutional democracy, this does not add up to the conclusion that all the claims advanced by populist movements cannot be filtered to make them compatible with the essence of Italian (and post–WWII) constitutionalism.

In so doing, my approach is similar – but not identical, as we will see – to that proposed by Alterio in her seminal article published in *Global Constitutionalism*, in which she convincingly distinguished between two approaches to populism: a reactive approach and a structural approach. In her words:

[S]ome scholars present what I call a 'reactive approach' to populism. As an intuitive response, they propose to hamper popular participation by avoiding plebiscites, referendums, or any other kind of public engagement. The idea is to close the political (and constitutional) system in order to protect it from backlashes or populist attacks. In this approach, Constitutional Courts and judicial review play a crucial role. [...] it is possible to respond to populism from a 'structural point of view'. This approach considers that the emergence of populism has its roots in the multifaceted crisis of political representation which has identifiable institutional correlates. Hence, to resist populism, public law should take into account the lack of responsiveness and accountability of representative systems. This article puts forward a proposal in that direction; it advances a response to populism in the form of new institutional design that generates strong participatory mechanisms to appropriate 'the popular'. In this manner, public law can repair (and occupy) the cracks that allow the discursive strategy of populism.[3]

Building upon this intuition, as I wrote at the beginning of this book, we should make a distinction between populist claims that could be pushed forward by either populist or non-populist forces, and populism as such. This distinction is the outcome of a contamination of the political register, which has induced even non-populist forces to sometimes make populist arguments in order to compete with populists and thus deprive them of some of their electors. This is, of course, a negative consequence of this new wave of populism.

Keeping this distinction in mind and building upon the comparative reconstruction of some of the instruments and concepts of constitutional law analysed in previous chapters, in this final chapter I shall try to analyse some points recently made by Italian populists that could be tamed, filtered and channelled in order to make constitutional democracy better. For the sake of clarity, these points have been at the heart of the Five Star Movement but also of other political forces in the past. In this sense, apart from the Internet dimension, the Five Star Movement has not really been innovative, as we will see. However, it has had the merit of mobilising people better than other political leaders did in the past. Its success in the constitutional referendum on the reduction of the number of members of parliament is a confirmation of that, in my view. It would be naïve to think that the new populist wave ended in Italy with the start of the Draghi government. This makes these conclusions still useful and topical.

The Internet is also a political resource, but safeguards are necessary.

The Five Star Movement – in its intrinsic heterogeneity – is right in insisting on the potential of the Internet for the democracy of tomorrow. New technologies offer

---

[3] A. M. Alterio, 'Reactive vs Structural Approach: A Public Law Response to Populism', *Global Constitutionalism*, No. 2, 2019, 270, 273.

interesting ideas for redefining the relationship between democracy and constitutionalism and perhaps even for overcoming that noble but ambiguous concept, that is, the constituent power. The Icelandic experience of the so-called 'crowdsourced constitution' has attracted the attention of many comparative lawyers, despite its substantial final failure due, inter alia, to the contradictions and ambiguities that the process experienced.[4]

So, Davide Casaleggio was right when, in his already mentioned speech at the United Nations,[5] he identified three priorities: digital identity, digital education and access to the Internet.

Access to the Internet, in particular, is necessary to improve the exercise of some of our fundamental rights (right to vote, right of assembly) and to enrich our set of rights. Online voting undoubtedly offers interesting indicators, but this must happen with the necessary safeguards that are functional to preserving not only the validity of the consultation, but also users' personal data. I have already referred to the cyberattacks suffered by the *Rousseau* platform, for which it received a fine of 50,000 euros by the Italian data protection authority. After this fine, the Rousseau Association attacked the authority saying that 'the authority in Italy is unfortunately driven by an ex-deputy of an opposition group' and later Casaleggio added that 'this is obviously a way to attack, politically, the [Rousseau] system'.[6] The president of the Italian authority was at that time Antonello Soro, who had been elected to the Italian parliament some years earlier in the lists of the *Partito democratico*. When the fine was imposed, the first Conte government was still in office. Soro reacted to the attack with a brief press release in which he rejected the accusation of partiality.[7] This episode is very telling of the risks of the Internet and reminds us of what Bobbio wrote about 'computer-cracy'.[8] By that, Bobbio[9] meant the risks that excessive online participation could create, namely electoral apathy:

> The price one has to pay for the efforts of a few is often the indifference of many. Nothing threatens to kill democracy more than an excess of democracy.[10]

---

[4] H.Landemore, *We, All of the People. Five Lessons from Iceland's Failed Experiment in Creating a Crowdsourced Constitution*, 2014, https://slate.com/technology/2014/07/five-lessons-from-icelands-failed-crowdsourced-constitution-experiment.html.

[5] The speech can be found at the following link: www.affaritaliani.it/politica/davide-casaleggio-all-onu-per-promuovere-la-cittadinanza-digitale-628599.html.

[6] See the declarations released to *Politico* and available here: L. Cerulus, '5Stars Defend Their Digital Democracy in Face of Privacy Sanction', 19 April 2019, www.politico.eu/article/davide-casaleggio-5stars-rousseau-platform-lashes-out-over-political-motivated-data-protection-fine/.

[7] 'Piattaforma Rousseau: Soro risponde a Casaleggio', 6 April 2019, www.garanteprivacy.it/web/guest/home/docweb/-/docweb-display/docweb/9102895.

[8] N. Bobbio, *Il futuro della democrazia*, Einaudi, Turin, 1984, 13.

[9] Bobbio, *Il futuro della democrazia*. On the relationship between direct and representative democracy in Bobbio, see: E. Grosso, 'Democrazia diretta e democrazia rappresentativa nel pensiero di Norberto Bobbio', 2015, https://bit.ly/2Sz4vHg.

[10] Bobbio, *Il futuro della democrazia*, 14, my own translation.

Against this background, online participation cannot completely replace representative democracy because it would work against integration, by producing the atomisation[11] and individualisation of civil society. The Five Star Movement, and in particular former Minister Fraccaro,[12] sometimes refers to the idea of 'integral democracy', understood as real democracy, or the democracy of the people. The irony here is that integral democracy is a concept used by Bobbio, who actually gave it a very different understanding.[13] In Fraccaro's words:

> The Government's institutional reform programme aims to bridge the gap between public decisions and the will of the people within a framework that not only respects but enriches institutional pluralism. For this reason, the discipline of the propositive referendum [**referendum on a legislative proposal**] will have to provide for a process capable of enabling citizens' dialogue with the parliamentary institutions [...] We want to implement integral democracy, in which people and institutions can both participate in the formation of decision-making mechanisms as happens in the most advanced systems. Only by dividing powers and responsibilities between parliament and citizens will it be possible to avoid the drifts of technocracy and ungovernability in the name of active participation.[14]

For Bobbio, integral democracy was understood as 'a continuum between the extremes of direct democracy and of representative democracy, which are therefore not alternatives, but both necessary according to different needs and situations'.[15] In other words, while according to Fraccaro direct democracy and representative democracy participate in the decision-making mechanism, according to Bobbio these two forms of democracy can certainly cooperate and be reconciled, but they have different functions and scopes of operability. This means that the role of institutions is not only crucial but cannot be replaced by the exercise of direct democracy.

This must be clarified once again. In representative democracy, the role of the so-called elites is necessary in particular political parties. The Five Star Movement has almost realised this, I think. Initially, it defined itself as a non-association and a non-party. Over the years, it has accepted its definition as an association with a *statuto*, and recently it has overcome another taboo by forming electoral alliances with other political parties after an online consultation on the *Rousseau* platform. This decision was a game changer, because previously the Five Star Movement had always denied

[11]   F. Pallante, *Contro la democrazia diretta*, Einaudi, Turin, 2020, 85.

[12]   R. Fraccaro, 'Perché serve colmare il gap fra istituzioni e volontà popolare', 9 agosto 2018, www .ilsole24ore.com/art/perche-serve-colmare-gap-istituzioni-e-volonta-popolare–AEhzbyXF.

[13]   As pointed out by A. Mozzo, 'Ascesa dei leader e presidenzializzazione dei governi: la corrosione della democrazia nasce dal "cuore" dello Stato', 2020, www.opiniojuris.it/presidenzializzazione-ascesa-leader/#_ftn11.

[14]   R. Fraccaro, 'Perché serve colmare il gap fra istituzioni e volontà popolare', 9 August 2018, www .ilsole24ore.com/art/perche-serve-colmare-gap-istituzioni-e-volonta-popolare–AEhzbyXF. My own translation, emphasis added.

[15]   Bobbio, *Il futuro della democrazia*, 41, my own translation.

the possibility of alliances like this. Even though it formed the first Conte government together with *Lega*, one should not forget that during the electoral campaign *Lega* was in coalition with *Forza Italia* and *Fratelli d'Italia* while the Five Star Movement had decided to run alone. This is also an important signal that once in power the Five Star Movement is perhaps being tamed by the political system. Scholars have shown that different ideas of democracy seem to coexist in the Five Star Movement in a confusing manner (direct democracy, deliberative democracy and even a bit of representative democracy).[16] The Five Star Movement had a similar turning point when it allowed members to respond to the invitation of traditional media, to participate in talk shows, for instance, or give interviews, when this was initially forbidden. Indeed, not everything can be done on the Internet only. The original idea, that TV is dead,[17] has been overcome. The Internet is the future, undoubtedly, but the Five Star Movement has understood that there must also be life beyond it. At the same time, as the lockdown showed, Italy desperately needs to reduce its digital divide in order to make Internet access, and the right to it, effective and widespread. Against this background, it has been said that the right to the Internet should be understood as a fundamental good. This is a long-standing issue which has been discussed globally at least since 2005, the year of the World Summit on the Information Society held in Tunis.[18] At the same time, as research proves,[19] the Internet needs to be better governed to guarantee that it can foster – rather than frustrate – a proper exchange of views, freedom of expression and access to good information, all elements that do not flourish naturally on the web.

Participative (Structural) Quorum is Necessary. It Can be Reduced, but not Cancelled.

Concerning the referendum, one of the political battles of the Five Star Movement has been to annul the so-called structural quorum for abrogative referendums governed by Article 75 of the Italian Constitution. As we saw in Chapter 4, this view was also present in one of the constitutional amendment bills advanced by the movement and then partly amended thanks to the influence of parliamentary debate with the other political forces. Even among academics there has been a long

---

[16] A. Floridia, R. Vignati, 'Deliberativa, diretta o partecipativa? Le sfide del Movimento 5 stelle alla democrazia rappresentativa', *Quaderni di sociologia*, No. 65, 2014, https://journals.openedition.org /qds/369. On deliberative democracy, see: Jane J. Mansbridge, *Beyond Adversary Democracy*, Basic Books, New York, 1980 and J. S. Fishkin, *Democracy and Deliberation: New Directions for Democratic Reform*, Yale University Press, New Haven, 1991.

[17] 'Le condizioni M5S per mandare i big in tv. Pd: vietano il confronto', 30 March 2017, www .repubblica.it/politica/2017/03/30/news/le_condizioni_m5s_per_mandare_i_big_in_tv_pd_vieta no_il_confronto-161757515/.

[18] With the debate on a possible Bill of Rights of the Internet. S. Rodotà, 'Una Costituzione per Internet?', *Politica del diritto*, No. 3, 2010, 337.

[19] C. Sunstein, *#republic: Divided Democracy in the Age of Social Media*, Princeton University Press, 2017; C. Sunstein, *The Filter Bubble: What the Internet Is Hiding from You*, Penguin Press, London, 2011.

discussion about the nature of the participative quorum in light of recent trends characterised by lower participation in popular consultation. The participative quorum has been described as an anachronism,[20] but I do not share this view. As has been suggested heretofore, the rationale of Article 75 of the Italian Constitution is based on the presumption of the efficacy of the law that the promoting committee wishes to abrogate.[21] Thus, the burden is on the supporters of the referendum to mobilise and convince a majority to repeal a certain law, and not the other way round. Against this background, the participative quorum is a safeguard to impede a low majority of voters from repealing a law passed by a broad majority in parliament.[22] This is also what emerges from the preparatory works of the Constituent Assembly. So, if eliminating the participative quorum does not make any sense, we could reflect instead on the possibility of lowering such a quorum, but maintain the onus on the supporters of the referendum. Participation – if coupled with deliberation – is key to overcoming passivity. Indeed, it has been argued that 'under a democratic model exclusively sustained and driven by elections, citizens are encouraged to remain passive'.[23] However, if the issue is represented by a lack of participation, the solution is not to cancel the quorum but perhaps to favour a propaedeutic discussion by also using the opportunities offered by e-democracy. Instead of giving the people the illusion of making decisions for themselves by replacing institutions, we should channel criticism, transforming 'mounting distrust into an active democratic virtue'[24] to create pressure on elected representatives, thus contributing to critical discussion and fostering a sense of belonging.

The European Union is not the Product of a Coup d'état. The EU is part of our Constitutional Pact and a Vehicle of Constitutional Improvement.

As we saw in Chapter 3, there is no dichotomy between national constitutionalism and EU treaties. The EU is not comparable to the level of democracy achieved at the domestic level thus far, but it should be taken into account that it does not intend to replace the state as the primary guarantor of fundamental rights. Thus, when considering the democratic nature or lack thereof of the EU, we should consider its complementarity to the state level. The EU has also improved, especially after the Lisbon Treaty, which marked its 10th anniversary in 2019, and which made the Charter of Fundamental Rights of the EU binding. A dialectic is possible within the EU, as Article 4.2 TEU and the case law of national constitutional courts show. At the same time, the EU also offers new paths to improve national democracy.

---

[20] A. Ciancio, 'Il quorum di partecipazione nel referendum abrogativo. (Causa ed effetti di un anacronismo)', *Politica del diritto*, No. 4, 1999, 676.

[21] M. Betzu, P. Ciarlo, A. Deffenu, 'Per il mantenimento del quorum strutturale nel referendum abrogativo', 2018, https://bit.ly/2TaCgyS.

[22] A. Di Giovine, *Democrazia diretta e sistema politico*, Cedam, Padua, 2001, 89.

[23] A. Alemanno, *Lobbying for Change: Find Your Voice to Create a Better Society*, Icon Books, London, 2017, 37.

[24] Alemanno, *Lobbying for Change*, 103.

Measures that attack the independence of the judiciary, that centralise the power of the executives in office, that restrict the freedom of the press and that close universities – scenarios that might have seemed impossible in Europe only a few years ago – are instead the disconcerting reality today in countries like Hungary and Poland.

How can we deal with this retreat in terms of constitutional guarantees and what role can the European Union play?

For many years now, the EU has been facing a multi-faceted crisis:[25] economic and financial, institutional, and value-based. Today, a number of Member States are evidently paying attention to the full permanence of the primary values of the Union: respect for dignity and human rights, democracy and the rule of law. As is well known, the EU treaties provide for the possibility of sanctions, to be decided following a complex procedure, in the event of a serious and persistent breach by a Member State of the EU's values as enshrined in Article 2 TEU.

European integration is now not only about purely economic matters, and, above all, this cooperation does not accept the loss of guarantees that protect fundamental rights. All this demonstrates once again the centrality of the issue of respect for rights on the EU's agenda. It also confirms the added value that European law gives to the protection of fundamental rights which, in theory, are already guaranteed by national constitutions. Constitutionalism, understood as a philosophical–political phenomenon, cannot be reduced to its state epiphany, but is enriched by the contribution made by EU law, which provides further arguments to limit and channel the claims of political power into procedural paths. In this scenario, European constitutionalism is not based on the denial of the state or national constitutionalism; on the contrary, as Milward has also pointed out,[26] the state is and remains a fundamental actor of government. However, European constitution-alism adds value to the achievements of the state experience over time, offering extra protection for the system of fundamental rights, especially when it is the state that contradicts the values of democracy and neglects the teaching of post–WWII constitutionalism from which our constitutions and the European Union are derived.

In other words, this confirms that today the EU is the main antidote to the new wave of populism (either authoritarian or otherwise) that has developed in some of its Member States. Indeed, the current wave of anti-Europeanism has also been caused by the austerity policy adopted at the European level to address the previous financial crisis.

Social justice in Europe can be improved but within the European integration process. In this sense, the debate on the European Stability Mechanism is also one about the kind of democracy we have in mind. Too often, we exclude the

---

[25] A. Menéndez, 'The Existential Crisis of the European Union', *German Law Journal*, No. 5, 2013, 453.
[26] A. Milward, *The European Rescue of the Nation-State*, University of California Press, Berkeley, 1992.

importance of inter-generational justice, which should be taken into account as an essential element of any constitutional reflection on this topic. Suffice it to think of the exchange between Jefferson and Madison, for instance. Who owns the constitution? Who owns the Earth?[27] For those who believe in the European integration process as a constitutional phenomenon, these lines by Poiares Maduro still have a lot to say:

> The freedom to do things that the current members of the political community acquire by incurring on large budget deficits may limit the democratic freedom of deliberation for future generations. I say may, because, in effect, budget deficits may also bring benefits for future generations depending on how productively the money is employed. The democratic problem remains however: one current generation decides for another (particularly, because we cannot be certain that the current members of a political community will base their decisions on the interests of the future members of that political community instead of their own immediate needs). This can be presented as a democratic malfunction, a democratic externality in generational terms. Also, in this case, EU law can be presented as an instrument of external constitutional control on national democratic processes. EU law exercises many other such forms of external constitutional discipline and reform over national democratic processes.[28]

Returning to the rule of law crisis in the EU, if it is true that Article 7 TEU has been a sleeping giant, it is also true that the CJEU has remedied that by adapting the infringement procedure to comply with cases of violation of values. Thanks to this, the CJEU has recognised the breach of EU values committed by Poland, Hungary and other countries in many cases.[29] In other cases, the CJEU tried to preserve the independence of the national judiciary, confirming in this way the important role of EU law in the preservation of constitutional values and safeguards.[30]

The same can be said with regard to the refugee crisis and the inefficiency of the Dublin system, which was strategically used by *Lega*, in particular by Salvini, who served as interior minister in the first Conte government.[31]

---

[27] See the powerful arguments used by Jefferson: T. Jefferson, 'To James Madison Paris', 6 September 1789, www.let.rug.nl/usa/presidents/thomas-jefferson/letters-of-thomas-jefferson/jefl81.php.

[28] M. Poiares Maduro, 'Passion and Reason in European Integration', 2010, https://papers.ssrn.com/sol3/papers.cfm?abstract_id=1709950.

[29] Among others, see CJEU, C-78/18 – Commission v. Hungary (Transparence associative), ECLI:EU:C:2020:476; CJEU, C-715/17 – Commission v Poland (Mécanisme temporaire de relocalisation de demandeurs de protection internationale), ECLI:EU:C:2020:257. For an overview, see: R. Mańko, *Protecting the Rule of Law in the EU: Existing Mechanisms and Possible Improvements*, European Parliamentary Research Service, 2019, www.europarl.europa.eu/RegData/etudes/BRIE/2019/642280/EPRS_BRI(2019)642280_EN.pdf.

[30] For instance, CJEU, C-216/18 PPU, Minister for Justice and Equality v. LM, ECLI:EU:C:2018:586.

[31] Italy missed at least twenty-two meetings in the negotiation for the reform of the Dublin system according to the accusation made by Elly Schlein, member of the Partito Democratico in the European Parliament, the interview is available at: www.facebook.com/ellyschlein1/videos/238619856836691/. See also: 'La Lega ha davvero disertato i negoziati per riformare il Regolamento

The Parliamentary Mandate Must be Free, but We must find Solutions to Challenge Parliamentary Transfugism.

In Chapter 6, we saw that the prohibition of the imperative mandate is a common element of European constitutional law. Born in a different context, nowadays it serves to guarantee that margin of manoeuvre that representatives need to exercise their function, as the Italian Constitutional Court clarified. We also saw that, according to scholars, the parliamentary free mandate is part of the untouchable core of the Italian Constitution[32] and is thus covered by the 'republican form' concept under Article 139. In this sense, not even recall is possible. Forms of recall have been at the heart of the reformist agenda of Latin American populisms. Scholars, such as Alterio,[33] have written of a form of 'constitutional populism' while describing the constitutional provisions devoted to popular participation and other devices. Alterio mainly took the constitutional texts of Venezuela (1999), Ecuador (2008), and Bolivia (2009), into account. In these constitutions:

> Participation goes far beyond the constituent act or the election of representatives, since it perpetuates along the constitutional texts in areas such as the popular, legislative, and constitutional initiatives or the approving, consultative, recall, and abrogative referendums. It is also reflected in citizen control instances of public administration and in the recognition of forms of communitarian democracy developed by indigenous peoples. Finally, participation is not limited to formal institutions, but there are also mechanisms of informal participation such as neighbourhood assemblies, open councils, accountability committees, and citizens' observatories.[34]

As Alterio herself clarified, these mechanisms have sometimes proved to be extremely problematic[35] and are hardly compatible with the role they have in post–WWII constitutions, in Europe at least. However, in Zanon's view, not all of Article 67 can be considered unamendable,[36] so there is margin to amend its wording or to limit transfugism, which has been one of the causes of the Italian Republic's political instability.

This is a crucial battle that is currently at the heart of the agenda of the Five Star Movement, too. Indeed, one should not underestimate the set of solutions proposed by the Movement. Some of them are far from being naïve, as Fasone pointed out:

> While this measure is objectively problematic from a constitutional standpoint and the constitutional amendment bill on the popular binding mandate of MPs

---

di Dublino?', 20 September 2018, https://pagellapolitica.it/dichiarazioni/8104/la-lega-ha-davvero-disertato-i-negoziati-per-riformare-il-regolamento-di-dublino.

[32] N. Zanon, *Il libero mandato parlamentare. Saggio critico sull'art. 67 della Costituzione*, Giuffrè, Milan, 1991, 328.

[33] Alterio, 'Reactive vs Structural Approach'.

[34] Alterio, 'Reactive vs Structural Approach', 290.

[35] Alterio, 'Reactive vs Structural Approach', 290.

[36] Zanon, *Il libero mandato parlamentare*, 328.

presented in 2017 provides a distorted interpretation of what an accountable and responsive MP is expected to fulfil, limitations of the reach and the scope of the representative mandate may not appear as necessarily driven by the last populist wave. Indeed, further proposals strongly supported by the 5SM like the limit of two parliamentary mandates or the reduction of the number of seats in both Houses, eventually approved by the parliament, though for different reasons and arguments, had been discussed for decades. While the limit to representative mandates has eventually materialized at local level, for example, for consecutive mandates of mayors, the lowering of the number of the seats in parliament had been on the agenda since the 1990s, though being often linked to the reform of the bicameral system.[37]

Indeed, limitations to the representative mandate are allowed and can acquire different forms[38] and some of them are entirely compatible with the untouchable constitutional core. It is also true that the Five Star Movement has changed its view on this issue as well, and hence the decision to re-nominate Virginia Raggi for a second term as mayor of Rome is another turning point in the history of the movement.[39] Going back to transfugism: How can we solve it? We saw that the recent reform of the rules of procedure in the Senate did not impede the creation of a parliamentary group consisting of the *Italia Viva* parliamentarians (the new party created by Renzi) and Conte's supporters (*Europeisti Maie Centro democratico*), which blatantly breached these norms.

A good model offered by comparative law is the Portuguese one, which is enshrined in Article 160 of the constitution. Wrongly understood as a constitutionalisation of the imperative mandate, as we saw in Chapter 6, it is actually a sophisticated and proportional anti-defection clause that does not automatically imply the loss of the seat. Indeed, the figure of the *deputado independente* shows that the loss can be saved if the parliamentarian decides not to join another political force. Now, given the highly difficult amendability of the Italian Constitution, a much quicker path could be represented by the codification of this solution in the rules of the chambers. It should be more powerful than the recently amended Article 14 of the Rules of Procedure of the Senate and could represent an unsurmountable obstacle for transfugism.

It is not only a matter of numbers. Efficiency Requires a Different Bicameralism in Italy.

---

[37] C. Fasone, 'Is There a Populist Turn in the Italian Parliament? Continuity and Discontinuity in the XE "Non-legislative Procedures"', in G. Delledonne, G. Martinico, M. Monti, F. Pacini (eds.), *Italian Populism and Constitutional Law: Strategies, Conflicts and Dilemmas*, Palgrave, London, 2020, 41, 50.

[38] The European Commission for Democracy through Law (Venice Commission), 'Report on Democracy, Limitation of Mandates and Incompatibility of Political Functions', 2013, www .venice.coe.int/webforms/documents/default.aspx?pdffile=CDL-AD(2012)027rev-e.

[39] Virginia Raggi is an important figure of the Five Star Movement and has been mayor of Rome since 2016. The decision to re-nominate her for a second term has been seen as an exception to the fundamental rules of the movement.

The constitutional reform providing for the reduction in the size of the parliament, confirmed by a constitutional referendum in September 2020, was triggered by the Five Star Movement with a clear punitive intent. Suffice it to mention here the image of Di Maio and his men in *piazza Montecitorio* showing big (fake) scissors to cut the seats of the parliament[40] to celebrate the parliamentary vote supporting the constitutional amendment bill. As written in Chapters 5 and 6, the Five Star Movement sees the parliament as the venue of a lazy and corrupt elite. The reform was later backed by the *Partito democratico* as part of the deal to support the second Conte government. Not all members and voters of the *Partito democratico* – in spite of the words of its leader, Nicola Zingaretti – supported the referendum, but many top parliamentarians did, including constitutional law professor Stefano Ceccanti – currently a member of the Chamber of Deputies.

The reasons behind this support are different. First, this reform was seen as useful to break a taboo and to open a new season of reforms. Second, the reduction in the size of the parliament was also part of the 2016 Renzi–Boschi (rejected) constitutional reform. Third, even those who had doubts about the added value of this constitutional reform believed it could work if accompanied by other sub-constitutional reforms, including the change of the electoral law. This argument, in my view, is tricky, because it risks making a legislative statute the pivot of the system, thus reversing the normal hierarchical relationship between constitutional and legislative sources. Technically speaking this reform could work with the old electoral law, but this would create under-representation of some territories in Italy, as noted in Chapter 5, which is why a new electoral law is desirable. However, it will not be easy to find an agreement. The inadequacy of the current electoral law can be seen as one of the reasons that implicitly led the president of the Republic to opt for the Draghi government after the demise of the second Conte government.

Something similar can be said with regard to the amendment of the internal rules of the chambers. Such an amendment is also necessary with regard to the Senate, which risks functioning badly because of the reduction in its members, a prospect admitted even by those who supported the reform.[41]

It is worth recalling that another constitutional reform bill was presented to either complement or remedy the consequences of this approved amendment. It aims to amend Articles 57 and 83 of the constitution, concerning, respectively, the territorial basis for the election of the Senate of the Republic and the reduction in the number of regional delegates for the election of the president of the Republic.[42] The second reform is especially needed to counter-balance the greater weight acquired by the

---

[40] 'Taglio dei parlamentari, forbice gigante e striscione: i Cinquestelle festeggiano in piazza Montecitorio', 8 October 2019, https://bit.ly/2St4oNe.

[41] L. Gianniti, N. Lupo, 'Le conseguenze della riduzione dei parlamentari sui Regolamenti di Senato e Camera', *Quaderni costituzionali*, No. 3, 2020, 559.

[42] A.C. 2238, www.camera.it/leg18/126?tab=&leg=18&idDocumento=2238.

regional delegates in the election of the president of the Republic after the reduction in the size of the parliament, as we saw in Chapter 5.

If taken alone, this reform, confirmed by the constitutional referendum, does not solve the main issue at stake, namely the existence of two chambers with identical powers, which is the real Italian anomaly. In this sense, Italy needs a serious season of reforms, but the centrality of the parliament and the respect of minorities must be the premise. It might be argued that with the reduction in the size of the parliament the reformist agenda of the Five Star Movement is over and a new season in the life of the Movement will begin. This is not certain – especially after the end of the second Conte government. After all, that reform was part of a broader strategy, pushing for more direct democracy and less representative democracy. Recently, a new boost was given to another constitutional reform aimed at amending Article 58[43] of the Italian Constitution in order to reduce the voting age for the Senate from twenty-five to eighteen.[44] This is the second important reform passed by this parliament; hopefully the other constitutional reform bills proposed by the Five Star Movement – in particular that concerning the popular legislative initiative (Art. 71 of the Italian Constitution) – will be tamed by the non-populist component of the political majority.

Political Parties Have a Bad Reputation in Italy, but they have a crucial role according to the constitution. We should fight to Make Them More Democratic instead of Asking for Their Elimination.

In 2012, Gianroberto Casaleggio and Beppe Grillo wrote a short book entitled *Siamo in guerra. La rete contro i partiti per una nuova politica* (in English, 'We Are at War. The Network against Parties for a New Kind of Politics'), in which they expressed their profound distrust of political parties understood as the main actors of an old kind of politics. As the title suggests, political parties were seen as the enemy. We saw in Chapter 2 how this way of depicting political parties has long-standing causes and has been fed by *Tangentopoli*. The Five Star Movement has indeed retrieved many of these elements already present in Italian politics. However, as Article 49 of the Italian Constitution states, political parties have a privileged role in the contribution to the political life of the country. This provision has never been fully implemented, in spite of the Letta reform on the abolition of direct public funding of parties (see Chapter 6). *Lega* has always been a fully-fledged political party. Starting out as a sort

---

[43] Article 58, Italian Constitution: 'Senators are elected by universal and direct suffrage by voters who are twenty-five years of age. Voters who have attained the age of forty are eligible to be elected to the Senate'.

[44] Disegno di legge costituzionale A.S. 1440 'Modifiche all'articolo 58 della Costituzione, in materia di elettorato per l'elezione del Senato della Repubblica', www.senato.it/service/PDF/PDFServer/BGT/01121849.pdf.

of federation of territorial parties,[45] it has managed to reach out to a wider electorate by abandoning (apparently) the battle for the secession of the North from the rest of Italy, especially after Salvini became its leader. The Five Star Movement still refuses to define itself as a party, as we saw in Chapters 5 and 6. Nevertheless, even the nature of the *MoVimento 5 Stelle* has been changing. This is partly due to pragmatism and partly because it has been forced to adopt a document, formally called *statuto*, as the case law of Italian courts have constantly applied the normal provisions included in the Italian Civil Code for associations and political parties to the Movement. As a consequence, the *MoVimento 5 Stelle* has had to adapt to the requirements provided for by the law. The 2020 online vote on the possibility of forming alliances with other parties has broken a taboo, as has the acceptance of the renewal of the political mandate in case of re-election. There are still some anomalies in this political force. Its *statuto* mentioned *Rousseau* as the only platform in which it is possible to discuss and carry out online consultations, but we have seen that after the break between Casaleggio and the Five-Star Movement things will change. *Rousseau* was formally donated by *Casaleggio Associati*, Gianroberto and Davide Casaleggio's private company. In turn, waiting for inevitable developments after Casaleggio's departure, according to the rules for the selection of candidates for the Five Star Movement, the Movement's parliamentarians have to contribute to the Rousseau Association.[46] This confirmed the ambiguity and element of non-transparency in the life of the movement. It has also given birth to internal conflicts as some Five Star Movement members of parliament refused to pay the sums due according to the *statuto*, and Davide Casaleggio threatened to cut its services. These and other members of the Five Star Movement sitting in parliament claimed the necessity that the *Rousseau* platform be managed by the movement directly. In reaction, at the beginning of October 2020, Davide Casaleggio published a post entitled *Noi siamo Movimento* ('We Are Movement')[47] in which he attacked the Movement for its slow but evident transformation into a political party. In his thinking, the Five Star Movement cannot become a political party without betraying its nature and mission, which is to represent 'an alternative and innovative model to the twentieth-century model of party hierarchies'.[48] He then recalled some promises made by the Movement at its birth, especially the one stating 'we will never become a party, not only in terms of structure, but above all in terms of mentality'.[49] His post

[45] I. Diamanti, *La lega. Geografia, storia e sociologia di un nuovo soggetto politico*, Donzelli, Rome, 1993.

[46] 'Regolamento per la selezione dei candidati del Movimento 5 Stelle', Article 6: 'At the time of the application, each candidate undertakes, should their nomination be accepted and they be subsequently elected to the Chamber or Senate, to [...] make a monthly contribution of EUR 300 to maintain the technological platforms that support the work of the groups and individual members of parliament', my own translation. The rules are available at the following link: https://s3-eu-west-1.amazonaws.com/associazionerousseau/documenti/regolamento_parlamentarie2018.pdf.

[47] D. Casaleggio, 'Noi Siamo Movimento', 4 October 2020, www.ilblogdellestelle.it/2020/10/noi-siamo-movimento.html. My own translation.

[48] Casaleggio, 'Noi Siamo Movimento'. My own translation.

[49] Casaleggio, 'Noi Siamo Movimento'. My own translation.

highlighted the tension within the movement: on the one hand, we have those supporting the government and the struggle for the institutionalisation of the party, and on the other we have those supported by the base who do not want to renounce its penchant for contestation and mobilisation. If the movement became a party 'all the principles, values and pillars on which the identity of a movement of free citizens have been built as well as its beating heart of participation, which we must protect, would be lost'.[50]

Casaleggio's post predictably attracted huge criticism. The disagreement is a confirmation of the perhaps inevitable change that is occurring within the *MoVimento*. These tensions then led to the aforementioned break between Casaleggio and the Movement.

Traditional political parties also have to change so as to become more open and transparent. In this sense, the *Partito democratico* has partly responded to such needs by carrying out primary elections for the first time in Italy. At the same time, the absence of a uniform regulation for these acts of participation and the ambiguity of the first primary elections run by the *Partito democratico* have induced many scholars to be sceptical or at least cautious about these responses.[51] The Five Star Movement could play an important role in forcing political competitors to be more transparent, but it has to first abandon its project to destroy political parties if it wants to run the country again.

This list is not exhaustive, but it might represent a starting point. Populism belongs to the realm of possibilities in contemporary democracies. External and internal factors show that our constitutional democracies have been suffering a long-standing crisis, and populist movements have re-emerged and benefitted from that. Italy is not a system of militant democracy, as we saw in Chapter 2, so the only way of dealing with populist forces is combatting them at the level of political ideas to improve our current system. By adopting a reactive, rather than a merely defensive approach, constitutional democracies should be able to filter some of the claims adopted and exploited by populists to translate them into digestible and tolerable calls for changes in our systems. These claims should be tested and tamed provided that the untouchable core of our post–WWII constitutional systems is safeguarded. Indeed, we tend to conflate constitutional rigidity, which is one of the pillars of post–WWII constitutionalism, with the inability to change. On the contrary, constitutions need to be adaptive – without being flexible[52] – in order to endure. And as comparative law research shows, this is one of the requirements of successful constitutions.[53]

---

[50] Casaleggio, 'Noi Siamo Movimento'. My own translation.
[51] For an overview, see: L. Gori, *Le elezioni primarie nell'ordinamento costituzionale*, ES, Naples, 2018.
[52] On the distinction between flexible and rigid constitutions, see: J. Bryce, 'Flexible and Rigid Constitution', in J. Bryce, *Studies in History and Jurisprudence*, Vol. I, Clarendon Press, Oxford, 1901, 124.
[53] Z. Elkins, T. Ginsburg, J. Melton, *The Endurance of National Constitutions*, Cambridge University Press, 2009.

Bibliography

Abromeit, J., 'A Critical Review of Recent Literature on Populism', *Politics and Governance*, No. 4, 2017, 177

Abts, K., Rummens, S., 'Populism versus Democracy', *Political Studies*, No. 2, 2007, 405

Albert, R., *Constitutional Amendments: Making, Breaking, and Changing Constitutions*, Oxford University Press, 2019

Albert, R., Contiades, X., Fotiadou, A. (eds.), *The Foundations and Traditions of Constitutional Amendment*, Hart, Oxford, 2017

Albertazzi, D., 'Going, Going,... Not Quite Gone Yet? Bossi's Lega and the Survival of the Mass Party', *Contemporary Italian Politics*, No. 2, 2016, 115

Albertazzi, D., Giovannini, A., Seddone, A., '"No Regionalism Please, We Are Leghisti!" The Transformation of the Italian Lega Nord under the Leadership of Matteo Salvini', *Regional and Federal Studies*, No. 5, 2018, 645

Albertazzi, D., McDonnell, D., *Populists in Power*, Routledge, Abingdon, 2015

Alemanno, A., *Lobbying for Change: Find Your Voice to Create a Better Society*, Icon Books, London, 2017

Alterio, A. M., 'Reactive vs Structural Approach: A Public Law Response to Populism', *Global Constitutionalism*, No. 2, 2019, 270

Amoroso, D., 'Italy', in F. Palombino (ed.), *Duelling for Supremacy International Law vs. National Fundamental Principles*, Cambridge University Press, 2019, 184

Anastasia, S., Anselmi, M., 'Penal Populism in the Multi-populist Context of Italy', in P. Blokker, M. Anselmi (eds.), *Multiple Populisms: Italy as Democracy's Mirror*, Routledge, Abingdon, 2020, 164

Anderson, B., *Imagined Communities: Reflections on the Origin and Spread of Nationalism*, Verso, London, 1983

Anselmi, M., *Populism: An Introduction*, Routledge, Abingdon, 2018

Arato, A., 'How We Got Here? Transition Failures, Their Causes, and the Populist Interest in the Constitution', 2017, https://papers.ssrn.com/sol3/papers.cfm?abstract_id=3116219

Arato, A., 'Political Theology and Populism', *Political Theology*, No. 1, 2013, 143

Arditi, B., 'On the Political: Schmitt contra Schmitt', *Telos*, No. 142, 2008, 7

Arditi, B., 'Populism as a Spectre of Democracy: A Response to Canovan', *Political Studies*, No. 1, 2004, 135

Arendt, H., *The Origins of Totalitarianism*, Harcourt, Brace and Co., New York, 1951

Atikcan, E. Ö., 'The Puzzle of Double Referendums in the European Union', *Journal of Common Market Studies*, No. 5, 2015, 937

Auer, A., 'L'esperienza del referendum in Svizzera e negli Stati Uniti', in M. Luciani, M. Volpi (eds.), *Referendum*, Laterza, Rome, 1992, 61

Avbelj, M., 'The Right Question about the FCC Ultra Vires Decision', 2020, https://verfas sungsblog.de/the-right-question-about-the-fcc-ultra-vires-decision

Azzariti, G., 'Cittadini, partiti e gruppi parlamentari: esiste ancora il divieto di mandato imperativo?', in Associazione italiana dei costituzionalisti (ed.), *Partiti politici e società civile a sessant'anni dall'entrata in vigore della Costituzione*, Jovene, Naples, 2009, 177

Baldassarre, A., 'Il "referendum" costituzionale', *Quaderni costituzionali*, No. 2, 1994, 235

Baldassarri, M., 'The Resilient Governance of the EU: Towards a Post-democratic Society', in M. Baldassarri, E. Castelli, M. Truffeli, G. Vezzani (eds.), *Anti-Europeanism Critical Perspectives Towards the European Union*, Springer, Berlin, 2020, 77

Baraggia, A. (ed.), 'The Aftermath of the Italian General Election of March 4', 2018, https://bit .ly/3gLwjQK

Baraggia, A., Martinico, G., 'Who Is the Master of the Treaties? The Compact Theory in Karlsruhe', *Diritti Comparati*, 2020, www.diritticomparati.it/who-is-the-master-of-the-treaties-the-compact-theory-in-karlsruhe/

Barber, N., 'Populist Leaders and Political Parties', *German Law Journal*, special issue 2, 2019, 129

Barbera, A., Morrone, A. , *La Repubblica dei referendum*, Il Mulino, Bologna, 2003

Barra Caracciolo, L., *Euro e (o?) democrazia costituzionale. La convivenza impossibile tra costituzione e trattati europei*, Dike Giuridica Editrice, Rome, 2013

Bassini, M., 'Rise of Populism and the Five Star Movement Model: An Italian Case Study', *Italian Journal of Public Law*, No. 1, 2018, 302

Bassini, M., 'Rise of Populism and the Five Star Movement Model: An Italian Case Study', in G. Delledonne, G. Martinico, M. Monti, F. Pacini (eds.), *Italian Populism and Constitutional Law: Strategies, Conflicts and Dilemmas*, Palgrave, London, 2020, 216

Battini, M., *The Missing Italian Nuremberg*, Palgrave, London, 2007

Becchi, P., *Italia sovrana*, Sperling & Kupfer, Milan, 2018

Becchi, P., *Manifesto sovranista: per la liberazione dei popoli europei*, Giubilei Regnani, Cesena, 2019

Becchi, P., *Colpo di Stato permanente: Cronache degli ultimi tre anni*, Marsilio, Venice, 2014.

Becchi, P., Palma, G. , *Dalla Seconda alla Terza Repubblica. Come nasce il governo Lega-M5S*, Paesi edizioni, Rome, 2018

Berlin, I., 'To Define Populism', 1967, http://berlin.wolf.ox.ac.uk/lists/bibliography/bib111bLSE.pdf

Betlem, G., Nollkaemper, A., 'Giving Effect to Public International Law and European Community Law Before Domestic Courts. A Comparative Analysis of the Practice of Consistent Interpretation', *European Journal of International Law*, No. 3, 2003, 569

Betti, E., *Teoria generale della interpretazione*, Vol. II, Giuffrè, Milan, 1955

Bettinelli, E., 'Itinerari della razionalizzazione della convenzione antireferendaria', *Politica del diritto*, No. 5, 1978, 513

Betzu, M., Ciarlo, P., Deffenu, A., 'Per il mantenimento del quorum strutturale nel referendum abrogativo', 2018, https://bit.ly/2TaCgyS

Biagi, F., 'Plebiscite', The Max Planck Encyclopedia of Comparative Constitutional Law, 2017, https://oxcon.ouplaw.com/view/10.1093/law-mpeccol/law-mpeccol-e414

Biancalana, C., 'Four Italian Populisms', in P. Blokker, M. Anselmi (eds.), *Multiple Populisms: Italy as Democracy's Mirror*, Routledge, Abingdon, 2020, 216

Biancalana, C. (ed.), *Disintermediazione e nuove forme di mediazione. Verso una democrazia post-rappresentativa?*, Feltrinelli, Milan, 2018

Bianco, G., 'The New Financial Stability Mechanisms and Their (Poor) Consistency with EU Law', *EUI RSCAS* 2012/44, 2012, http://cadmus.eui.eu/handle/1814/23428

Bickel, A., *The Least Dangerous Branch*, Yale University Press, New Haven, CT, 1986

Bickerton, C., Invernizzi Accetti, C., 'Populism and Technocracy', in C. Rovira Kaltwasser, P. Taggart, P. Ochoa Espejo, P. Ostiguy (eds.), *The Oxford Handbook of Populism*, Oxford University Press, 2017, 330

Bignami, F., *EU Law in Populist times*, Cambridge University Press, 2019

Bin, R., 'L'interpretazione conforme. Due o tre cose che so di lei', 2015, www.rivistaaic.it/it/rivista/ultimi-contributi-pubblicati/roberto-bin/l-interpretazione-conforme-due-o-tre-cose-che-so-di-lei

Biondi Dal Monte, F. , Fontanelli, F., 'The Decisions No. 348 and 349/2007 of the Italian Constitutional Court: The Efficacy of the European Convention in the Italian Legal System', *German Law Journal*, No. 7, 2008, 889

Blanchard, M., 'Review: Mimesis, Not Mimicry', *Comparative Literature*, No. 2, 1997, 176

Blokker, P., 'Populism and Constitutional Reform. The Case of Italy', in G. Delledonne, G. Martinico, M. Monti, F. Pacini (eds.), *Italian Populism and Constitutional Law: Strategies, Conflicts and Dilemmas*, Palgrave, London, 2020, 11

Blokker, P., 'Populism as a Constitutional Project', *International Journal of Constitutional Law*, No. 2, 2019, 537

Blokker P., '"Vote Yes for a Safe Italy" or "Vote No to Defend the Constitution": Italian Constitutional Politics between Majoritarianism and Civil Resistance', 2016, https://verfassungsblog.de/italy-constitution-referendum-renzi-blokker/

Blokker, P., Anselmi, M., 'Introduction', in P. Blokker, M. Anselmi (eds.), *Multiple Populisms: Italy as Democracy's Mirror*, Routledge, Abingdon, 2020, 1

Blokker, P., Anselmi M. (eds.), *Multiple Populisms: Italy as Democracy's Mirror*, Routledge, Abingdon, 2020

Bobbio, N., *Contro i nuovi dispotismi: scritti sul berlusconismo*, Rome, Dedalo, 2008

Bobbio, N., *Il futuro della democrazia*, Einaudi, Turin, 1984

Bobbio, N., 'Sul fondamento dei diritti dell'uomo', in N. Bobbio, *L'età dei diritti*, Einaudi, Turin, 1997, 5

Bobek, M., Kosař, D., 'Report on the Czech Republic and Slovakia', in G. Martinico, O. Pollicino (eds.), *The National Judicial Treatment of the ECHR and EU Laws: A Comparative Constitutional Perspective*, Europa Law Publishing, Groningen, 2010, 133

Bogdandy, A., Sonnevend, P. (eds.), *Constitutional Crisis in the European Constitutional Area. Theory, Law and Politics in Hungary and Romania*, C. H. Beck-Hart-Nomos, Oxford, 2015

Bogdanor, V., *The People and the Party System: The Referendum and Electoral Reform in British Politics*, Cambridge University Press, 1981

Boom, S. J., 'The European Union after the Maastricht Decision: Will Germany Be the Virginia of Europe', *American Journal of Comparative Law*, No. 2, 1995, 177

Bordignon, F., 'Matteo Renzi: A "Leftist Berlusconi" for the Italian Democratic Party?', *South European Society and Politics*, No. 1, 2014, 1

Bressanelli, E., Natali, D. (eds.), *Contemporary Italian Politics*, special issue on Italian politics, No. 3, 2019

Brettschneider, C., 'Popular Constitutionalism contra Populism', *Constitutional Commentary*, No. 1, 2015, 81

Breuer, M. (ed.), *Principled Resistance to ECtHR Judgments – A New Paradigm?*, Springer, Berlin, 2019

Brubaker, R., 'Why Populism?', *Theory and Society*, No. 5, 2017, 357

Bruno, F., 'I giuristi alla Costituente: l'opera di Costantino Mortati', in U. De Siervo (ed.), *Scelte della Costituente e cultura giuridica*. II: *Protagonisti e momenti del dibattito costituzionale*, Il Mulino, Bologna, 1980, 59

Bryce, J., 'Flexible and Rigid Constitution', in J. Bryce, *Studies in History and Jurisprudence*, Vol. I, Clarendon Press, Oxford, 1901, 124

Buratti, A., Fioravanti, M. (eds.), *Costituenti ombra. Altri luoghi e altre figure della cultura politica italiana (1943-48)*, Carocci, Rome, 2010

Burke, E., 'Speech to the Electors of Bristol', 3 November 1774, https://press-pubs.uchicago.edu/founders/documents/v1ch13s7.html

Butler, D., Ranney, A. (eds.), *Referendums Around the World: The Growing Use of Direct Democracy*, AEI press, Washington, DC, 1994

Calamandrei, P., 'Cenni introduttivi sulla Costituente e i suoi lavori', in P. Calamandrei, A. Levi (eds.), *Commentario sistematico alla Costituzione italiana*, G. Barbèra, Florence, 1950, lxxxix

Calamandrei, P., Discorso sulla Costituzione, 1955, www.professionegiustizia.it/documenti/guide/piero_calamandrei_e_la_costituzione

Calamandrei P., 'La Costituzione e le leggi per attuarla', in AA.VV., *Dieci anni dopo: 1945-1955*, Laterza, Bari, 1955, now in *Opere giuridiche*, Vol. III, Morano, Naples, 1965, 553

Calamandrei, P., *Scritti e discorsi politici*, Vol. II, La Nuova Italia, Florence, 1966

Calamo Specchia, M., 'Quale disciplina referendaria nel Regno Unito? Brevi note su di un approccio sistematico per un modello a-sistematico', in A. Torre, J. Frosini (eds.), *Democrazia rappresentativa e referendum nel Regno Unito*, Maggioli, Rimini, 2012, 146

Calhoun, J. C., *A Disquisition on Government*, 1849, http://praxeology.net/JCC-DG.htm

Calise, M., *Il partito personale. I due corpi del leader*, Laterza, Rome, 2007

Canovan, M., *The People*, Polity, Oxford, 2005

Canovan, M., 'Populism for Political Theorists?', *Journal of Political Ideologies*, No. 3, 2004, 241

Canovan, M, Populism, Harcourt Brace Jovanovich, Oxford, 1981

Canovan, M., 'Trust the People! Populism and the Two Faces of Democracy', *Political Studies*, No. 1, 1999, 2

Carboni, G., 'I referendum mai realizzati e ancora da realizzare', in A. Torre, J. Frosini (eds.), *Democrazia rappresentativa e referendum nel Regno Unito*, Maggioli, Rimini, 2012, 399

Carnevale, P., Chinni, D., 'To Be or Not to Be (Online)? Qualche considerazione sul rapporto fra web e organi costituzionali', 2019, www.giurcost.org/LIBERAMICORUM/carnevale&chinni_scrittiCostanzo.pdf

Carré de Malberg, R. , 'Considérations théoriques sur la question de la combinaison du referendum avec le parlementarisme', in *Annuaire de l'Institut international de droit public*, Vol. II, PUF, Paris, 1931, 272

Carreira da Silva, F., Brito Vieira, M., 'Populism as a Logic of Political Action', *European Journal of Social Theory*, No. 4, 2019, 497

Carrozza, P., 'Nazione', in *Digesto discipline pubblicistiche*, Vol. X, UTET, Turin, 1995, 126

Carrozza, P., 'Constitutionalism's Post-modern Opening', in M. Loughlin, N. Walker (eds.), *The Paradox of Constitutionalism: Constituent Power and Constitutional Form*, Oxford University Press, 2007, 169

Carrozza, P., 'È solo una questione di numeri? Le proposte di riforma degli artt. 56 e 57 Cost. per la riduzione dei parlamentari', *Diritto pubblico comparato ed europeo*, special issue, 2019, 88

Cartabia, M., 'La ratifica del trattato costituzionale europeo e la volontà costituente degli Stati membri', 2004, www.forumcostituzionale.it

Cartabia, M., 'The Italian Constitution as a Revolutionary Agreement', in R. Albert (ed.), *Revolutionary Constitutionalism: Law, Legitimacy, Power*, Hart, Oxford, 2020, 313

Cartabia, M., *Principi inviolabili e integrazione europea*, Giuffrè, Milan, 1995

Cartabia, M., Weiler, J. H. H, *L'Italia in Europa*, Il Mulino, Bologna, 2000

Casaleggio, G., *Insultatemi!*, Adagio eBook, Milan, 2013

Cassese, A., 'Politica estera e relazioni internazionali nel disegno emerso alla Assemblea Costituente', in U. de Siervo (ed.), *Scelte della Costituente e cultura giuridica. I: Costituzione italiana e modelli stranieri*, Il Mulino, Bologna, 1980, 505

Cassese, A., 'Modern Constitutions and International Law', *Recueil des Cours*, 1985, 331

Cassina Wolff, E., 'CasaPound Italia: "Back to Believing. The Struggle Continues"', *Fascism*, No. 1, 2019, 61

Caterina, E., 'L'attuazione del metodo democratico all'interno dei partiti politici: analisi della normativa vigente e spunti per una legge sui partiti', *Democrazia e diritto*, No. 3, 2016, 61

Chalmers, D., Davies, G., Monti, G., *European Union Law: Cases and Materials*, Cambridge University Press, 2010

Cheli, E., 'Il problema storico della Costituente', *Politica del diritto*, No. 4, 1973, 485

Chiarelli, R., 'Il populismo nella Costituzione italiana', in R. Chiarelli (ed.), *Il populismo tra storia, politica e diritto*, Rubettino, Soveria Mannelli, 2015, 177

Choudhry, S., 'Civil War, Ceasefire, Constitution: Some Preliminary Notes', *Cardozo Law Review*, No. 5, 2012, 1907

Ciancio, A., 'Il quorum di partecipazione nel referendum abrogativo. (Causa ed effetti di un anacronismo)', *Politica del diritto*, No. 4, 1999, 676

Ciaurro, L., 'Art. 67', in R. Bifulco, A. Celotto, M. Olivetti (eds.), *Commentario alla Costituzione*, Vol. II, UTET, Turin, 2006, 1289

Citrigno, A.M., Moschella, D., 'Quale futuro per il divieto di mandato imperativo?', 2018, http://bpr.camera.it/bpr/allegati/show/CDBPR17-1932

Cloots, E., *National Identity in EU Law*, Hart, Oxford, 2015

Closa, C., 'A Critique of the Theory of Democratic Secession', in C. Closa, C. Margiotta, G. Martinico (eds.), *Between Democracy and Law: The Amorality of Secession*, Routledge, Abingdon, 2019, 49

Closa, C., Kochenov, D. (eds.), *Reinforcing Rule of Law Oversight in the European Union*, Cambridge University Press, 2016

Cocco, M., *Qualunquismo. Una storia politica e culturale dell'uomo qualunque*, Le Monnier, Florence, 2018

Colón-Ríos, J., *Weak Constitutionalism: Democratic Legitimacy and the Question of Constituent Power*, Routledge, Abingdon, 2012

Corrias, L., 'Populism in a Constitutional Key: Constituent Power, Popular Sovereignty and Constitutional Identity', *European Constitutional Law Review*, No. 1, 2016, 6

Corso, L., 'Populismo, limiti al potere e giudici costituzionali. Una lezione americana', *Ragion pratica*, No. 1, 2019, 211

Corso, L., 'What Does Populism Have to Do with Constitutional Law? Discussing Populist Constitutionalism and Its Assumptions', *Rivista di Filosofia del Diritto*, No. 2, 2014, 443

Corso, L., 'When Anti-Politics Becomes Political: What Can the Italian Five Star Movement Tell Us about the Relationship Between Populism and Legalism', *European Constitutional Law Review*, No. 3, 2019, 462

Cortelazzo, M. A., 'Le parole della neopolitica – Salvo intese', 2019, www.treccani.it/magazine/lingua_italiana/articoli/parole/Neopolitica14.html

Cragin, T., Salsini, L. A., *Resistance, Heroism, Loss World War II in Italian Literature and Film*, Rowman and Littlefield, Lanham, 2018

Crisafulli, V., Nocilla, D., 'Nazione', in *Enciclopedia del diritto*, Vol. XXVII, Giuffrè, Milan, 1977, 814

Crisafulli, V., 'Partiti, Parlamento, Governo', in V. Crisafulli, *Stato Popolo Governo. Illusioni e delusioni costituzionali*, Giuffrè, Milan, 1985, 209

Croce, B., *Per una nuova Italia. Scritti e discorsi (1943-44)*, Ricciardi, Naples, 1944

Culik, J., 'Hungary's invalid refugee referendum dents Viktor Orbán's anti-EU "revolution"', 2016, https://theconversation.com/hungarys-invalid-refugee-referendum-dents-viktor-orbans-anti-eu-revolution-66424

Curreri, S., *Democrazia e rappresentanza politica. Dal divieto di mandato al mandato di partito*, Firenze University Press, Florence, 2004

Damele, G., 'Vincoli di mandato dei parlamentari e carattere democratico dei partiti. Spunti a partire dall'articolo 160 della Costituzione portoghese', 2017, www.forumcostituzionale.it/wordpress/wp-content/uploads/2016/06/damele.pdf

Damiani, M., 'Citizen Democracy: New Politics in New Participation Models', in P. Blokker, M. Anselmi (eds.), *Multiple Populisms: Italy as Democracy's Mirror*, Routledge, Abingdon, 2019, 181

Dani, M., Menéndez, A. J., 'Soft-Conditionality through Soft-Law: le insidie nascoste del Pandemic Crisis Support', 2020, www.lacostituzione.info/index.php/2020/05/10/soft-conditionality-through-soft-law-le-insidie-nascoste-del-pandemic-crisis-support/

Dani, M., Mendes, J., Menéndez, A. J., Wilkinson, M., Schepel, H., Chiti, E., *At the End of the Law. A Moment of Truth for the Eurozone and the EU*, 2020, https://verfassungsblog.de/at-the-end-of-the-law

Dann, P., Engelhardt, M., 'The Global Administrative Order Through a German Lens: Perception and Influence of Legal Structures of Global Governance in Germany', *German Law Journal*, No. 7, 2011, 1371

De Blasio, E., Sorice, M., 'Technopopulism and Direct Representation', in P. Blokker, M. Anselmi (eds.), *Multiple Populisms: Italy as Democracy's Mirror*, Routledge, Abingdon, 2020, 127

de Cleen, B., 'Populism and Nationalism', in C. Rovira Kaltwasser, P. Taggart, P. Ochoa Espejo, P. Ostiguy (eds.), *The Oxford Handbook of Populism*, Oxford University Press, 2017, 342

De Felice, R., *Mussolini l'alleato. Vol. I. L'Italia in guerra, 1940-1943. Tomo I: Dalla guerra 'breve' alla guerra lunga*, Einaudi, Turin, 1990

De Felice, R., *Mussolini l'alleato. Vol. II. L'Italia in guerra 1940-1943. Tomo II: Crisi e agonia del regime*, Einaudi, Turin, 1990

De Felice, R., *Mussolini l'alleato. Vol. III. La guerra civile 1943-1945*, Einaudi, Turin, 1997

De Felice, R., *Mussolini il duce. Vol. I: Gli anni del consenso, 1929-1936*, Einaudi, Turin, 1974

De Felice, R., *Mussolini il duce. Vol. II: Lo stato totalitario 1936-1940*, Einaudi, Turin, 1981

De Felice, R., *Mussolini il fascista. Vol. I: La conquista del potere, 1921-1925*, Einaudi, Turin, 1966

De Felice, R., *Mussolini il fascista. Vol. II: L'organizzazione dello stato fascista, 1925-1929*, Einaudi, Turin, 1968

De Felice, R., *Mussolini il rivoluzionario, 1883-1920*, Einaudi, Turin, 1965

De Fiores, C., 'Sulla rappresentazione della Nazione. Brevi note sul divieto di mandato imperativo', *Diritto e società*, No. 1, 2017, 19

Degryse, C., 'The New European Economic Governance', *Working Paper European Trade Union Institute*, 2012/14, 2012, www.etui.org/Publications2/Working-Papers/The-new-European-economic-governance

Delfino, F., 'La democrazia "illiberale": il modello di democrazia "sovrana" in Russia e di democrazia "cristiana" in Ungheria. Origini, similitudini e divergenze', *Nuovi Autoritarismi e Democrazie (NAD)*, No. 2, 2019, 1

Delledonne, G., 'Un'anomalia italiana? Una riflessione comparatistica sul numero dei parlamentari negli altri ordinamenti', in E. Rossi (ed.), *Meno parlamentari, più democrazia? Significato e conseguenze della riforma costituzionale*, Pisa University Press, 2020, 55

Delledonne, G., 'Populism and Government: Continuity and Paradoxes in the Yellow-Green Experiment', in G. Delledonne, G. Martinico, M. Monti, F. Pacini (eds.), *Italian Populism and Constitutional Law: Strategies, Conflicts and Dilemmas*, Palgrave, London, 2020, 135

Delledonne, G., 'La Resistenza in Assemblea costituente e nel testo costituzionale italiano del 1948', *Historia Constitucional*, No. 1, 2009, 217

Del Vecchio, G., 'Les bases du droit comparé et les principes généraux du droit', *Revue internationale de droit comparé*, No. 3, 1960, 493

De Nardis, F., 'Depoliticization, Anti-politics and the Moral People', in P. Blokker, M. Anselmi (eds.), *Multiple Populisms: Italy as Democracy's Mirror*, Routledge, Abingdon, 2020, 49

De Petris, A., 'Programs, Strategies and Electoral Campaigns of the Five Stars Movement in Italy. A Brand New Party Model or an "Anti-Party" State of Mind?', in A. De Petris, T. Poguntke (eds.), *Anti-Party Parties in Germany and Italy*, Luiss University Press, Rome, 2015, 125

De Spiegeleire, S., Skinner, C., Sweijs, T., 'The Rise of Populist Sovereignism: What It Is, Where It Comes From and What It Means for International Security and Defense', *The Hague Centre for Strategic Studies (HCSS)*, 2017, https://bit.ly/3jqPeDe

de Vergottini, G., *Diritto costituzionale*, Cedam, Padua, 2004

De Witte, B., 'Using International Law in the Euro Crisis: Causes and Consequences', *ARENA Working Paper*, 4/2013, www.sv.uio.no/arena/english/research/publications/arena-working-papers/2013/wp4-13.pdf

Diamanti, I., *La lega. Geografia, storia e sociologia di un nuovo soggetto politico*, Donzelli, Rome, 1993

Diamanti, I., Lazar, M. , *Popolocrazia. La metamorfosi delle nostre democrazie*, Laterza, Rome, 2018

Dicey, A. V., *Introduction to the Study of the Law of the Constitution*, St. Martin's Press, New York, 1959

Dicey, A. V., 'Ought the Referendum to be Introduced into England?', *Contemporary Review*, No. 3, 1890

Dicey, A. V., 'The Parliament Act 1911 and the Destruction of All Constitutional Safeguards', in W. Anson, F. E. Smith, W. de Broke (eds.), *Rights of Citizenship: A Survey of Safeguards for the People*, Frederick Warne, London, 1912, 81

Di Chiara, A., 'Due prassi costituzionalmente discutibili: delibere del Governo "salvo intese" e pubblicazione tardiva dei decreti legge', *Osservatorio sulle fonti*, No. 1, 2019, 1

Di Cosimo, G., 'Fonti normative del Governo: molti problemi e tre modi per affrontarli', *Osservatorio sulle fonti*, No. 3, 2016, 1

Di Federico, G., *L'identità nazionale degli stati membri nel diritto dell'Unione europea. Natura e portata dell'art. 4, par. 2, TUE*, Editoriale Scientifica, Naples, 2017

Di Giovine, A., *Democrazia diretta e sistema politico*, Cedam, Padua, 2001

Di Giovine, A., 'Referendum e responsabilità politica', *Diritto Pubblico Comparato ed Europeo*, No. 3, 2005, 1214

Di Gregorio, A., 'La Russia e le elezioni europee', 2019, www.federalismi.it/nv14/articolo-documento.cfm?Artid=38721

Di Marzio, F., *La politica e il contratto. Dalla affermazione dei valori alla negoziazione degli interessi*, Donzelli, Rome, 2018

Donovan, M., Gilbert, M., 'Silvio Berlusconi and Romano Prodi', in E. Jones, G. Pasquino (eds.), *The Oxford Handbook of Italian Politics*, Oxford University Press, 2015, 394

Doyle, O., 'Populist Constitutionalism and Constituent Power', *German Law Journal*, special issue 2, 2019, 161

Dugin, A., *The Fourth Political Theory*, Arktos, London, 2012, 196

Dumberry, P., 'The Secession Question in Quebec', *Diritto pubblico comparato ed europeo*, No. 2, 2015, 357

Dumbrovsky, T., 'Federal Solution to the EU Internal Sovereignty Conundrum: The European Doctrine of the Czech Constitutional Court and the U.S. Compact Theory', in L. Tichy, T. Dumbrovsky (eds.), *Sovereignty and Competences of the European Union*, Charles University, Prague, 2010, 80

Dworkin, R., *Taking Rights Seriously*, Harvard University Press, Cambridge, MA, 1977

Eco, U., 'Ur-Fascism', *The New York Review*, 22 June 1995, www.nybooks.com/articles/1995/06/22/ur-fascism/

Elchardus, M., Spruyt, B., 'Populism, Persistent Republicanism and Declinism: An Empirical Analysis of Populism as a Thin Ideology', *Government and Opposition*, No. 1, 2016, 111

Elia, L., 'La commissione dei 75, il dibattito costituzionale e l'elaborazione dello schema di costituzione', in AA.VV., *Il parlamento italiano 1861-1988*, Vol. XIV, Nuova Cei, Milan, 1989, 128

Elia, L., 'Governo (forme di)', in *Enciclopedia del Diritto*, Vol. XIX, Giuffé, Milan, 1970, 657

Elkins, Z., Ginsburg, T., Melton, J., *The Endurance of National Constitutions*, Cambridge University Press, 2009

Ellwood, D. W., *L'alleato nemico. La politica dell'occupazione*, Feltrinelli, Milan, 1977

Elster, J., 'Constitution-Making and Violence', *Journal of Legal Analysis*, No. 1, 2012, 7

Esposito, C., 'I partiti nella Costituzione italiana', in C. Esposito, *La Costituzione italiana. Saggi*, Cedam, Padua, 1954, 215

European Commission for Democracy through Law (Venice Commission), 'Report on Democracy, Limitation of Mandates and Incompatibility of Political Functions', 2013, www.venice.coe.int/webforms/documents/default.aspx?pdffile=CDL-AD(2012)027rev-e

European Commission for Democracy through Law (Venice Commission), 'Report on the Imperative Mandate and Similar Practices', 2009, www.venice.coe.int/webforms/documents/default.aspx?pdffile=CDL-AD(2009)027-e

Fabbrini, F., 'Suing the BVerfG', 2020, https://verfassungsblog.de/suing-the-bverfg/#comments

Fabbrini, F., Pollicino, O., 'Constitutional Identity in Italy: Institutional Disagreements at a Time of Political Change', in C. Calliess, G. van der Schyff (eds.), *Constitutional Identity in a Europe of Multilevel Constitutionalism*, Cambridge University Press, 2019, 201

Faraguna, P., 'Unamendability and Constitutional Identity in the Italian Constitutional Experience', *European Journal of Law Reform*, No. 3, 2019, 329

Fasone, C., 'Constitutional Courts Facing the Euro Crisis. Italy, Portugal and Spain in a Comparative Perspective', Max Weber Programme MWP 2014/25, 2014, cadmus.eui.eu/bitstream/handle/1814/33859/MWP_WP_2014_25.pdf

Fasone, C., 'Is There a Populist Turn in the Italian Parliament? Continuity and Discontinuity in the Non-legislative Procedures', in G. Delledonne, G. Martinico, M. Monti, F. Pacini (eds.), *Italian Populism and Constitutional Law: Strategies, Conflicts and Dilemmas*, Palgrave, London, 2020, 41

Fasone, C., 'Quale è la fonte più idonea a recepire le novità del Trattato di Lisbona sui parlamenti nazionali?', *Osservatorio sulle Fonti*, No. 3, 2010, 1

Fenazzi, S., 'Per M5S, quello svizzero è il "modello faro" di democrazia diretta', 2016, www .swissinfo.ch/ita/ballottaggi-sindaci-in-italia_per-m5s-quello-svizzero-%C3%A8-il-modello-faro-di-democrazia-diretta/42239748

Fenoglio, B., *Johnny the Partisan*, Quartet Books, London, 1995

Filippetta, G., *L'estate che imparammo a sparare. Storia partigiana della Costituzione*, Feltrinelli, Milan, 2018

Finchelstein, F., *From Fascism to Populism in History*, University of California Press, Oakland, 2018

Fioravanti, M., 'Aspetti del costituzionalismo giacobino. La funzione legislativa nell'acte constitutionnel del 24 giugno 1793', *Historia del constitucionalismo*, No. 1, 2016, 123

Fishkin, J. S., *Democracy and Deliberation: New Directions for Democratic Reform*, Yale University Press, New Haven, CT, 1991

Floridia, A., Vignati, R., 'Deliberativa, diretta o partecipativa? Le sfide del Movimento 5 stelle alla democrazia rappresentativa', *Quaderni di sociologia*, No. 65, 2014, https://journals .openedition.org/qds/369

Focardi, F., *La rimozione delle colpe della seconda guerra mondiale*, Laterza, Rome, 2013

Fois, S., 'Il referendum come "contropotere" e garanzia nel sistema costituzionale italiano', in E. Bettinelli, L. Boneschi (eds.), *Referendum, ordine pubblico, Costituzione*, Bompiani, Milan, 1978, 130

Foley, M., *The Silence of Constitutions: Gaps, 'Abeyances', and Political Temperament in the Maintenance of Government*, Routledge, Abingdon, 1989

Fontana, A., 'L'evoluzione storica del mandato imperativo, dal medioevo allo Statuto albertino', in P. Caretti, D. Morisi, G. Tarli Barbieri (eds.), *Il divieto di mandato imperativo: un principio in discussione*, Seminario di studi e ricerche parlamentari 'Silvano Tosi', Florence, 2019, 324

Forcellese, T., 'L'uomo qualunque. L'idea dello "Stato amministrativo" alla Costituente', in A. Buratti, M. Fioravanti (eds.), *Costituenti ombra. Altri luoghi e altre figure della cultura politica italiana (1943-48)*, Carocci, Rome, 2010, 445

Fournier, T., 'From Rhetoric to Action: A Constitutional Analysis of Populism', *German Law Journal*, No. 3, 2019, 362

Freeden, M., 'After the Brexit Referendum: Revisiting Populism as an Ideology', *Journal of Political Ideologies*, No. 1, 2017, 1

Fusaro, D., *Glebalizzazione. La lotta di classe al tempo del populismo*, Rizzoli, Milan, 2019

Galli, C., *Sovranità*, Il Mulino, Bologna, 2019

Gallie, W. B., 'Essentially Contested Concepts', *Proceedings of the Aristotelian Society*, No. 1, 1956, 16

Galston, W., *Anti-Pluralism: The Populist Threat to Democracy*, Yale University Press, New Haven, CT, 2018

Gargarella, R., *Latin American Constitutionalism, 1810-2010: The Engine Room of the Constitution*, Oxford University Press, 2013

Gatti, C., *I demoni di Salvini. I postnazisti e la Lega Milano*, Chiarelettere, Milan, 2019

Gentile, E., *Chi è fascista? Gli italiani stanno tornando a essere fascisti?*, Laterza, Rome, 2019

Gentile, E., 'Le silence de Hannah Arendt: L'interprétation du fascisme dans Les origines du totalitarisme', *Revue d'histoire moderne et contemporaine*, 2008, 11

Gerards, J., 'The Irrelevance of the Netherlands Constitution, and the Impossibility of Changing It', *Revue interdisciplinaire d'études juridiques*, No. 2, 2016, 207

Gerbaudo, P., *The Digital Party: Political Organisation and Online Democracy*, Pluto Press, London, 2019

Germino, D. E., *The Italian Fascist Party in Power: A Study in Totalitarian Rule*, University of Minnesota Press, Minneapolis, 1959

Ghisalberti, C., *Storia costituzionale d'Italia 1848-1994*, Laterza, Rome, 2020

Giacché, V., *ANSCHLUSS. L'annessione: L'unificazione della Germania e il futuro dell'Europa*, Imprimatur, Reggio Emilia, 2013

Giacché, V., *Costituzione italiana contro trattati europei. Il conflitto inevitabile*, Imprimatur, Reggio Emilia, 2015

Giannini, G., *La folla. Seimila anni di lotta contro la tirannide*, Il Faro, Rome, 1945

Gianniti, L., Lupo N., 'Le conseguenze della riduzione dei parlamentari sui Regolamenti di Senato e Camera', *Quaderni costituzionali*, No. 3, 2020, 559

Ginsburg, T., Simpser, A. (eds.), *Constitutions in Authoritarian Regimes*, Cambridge University Press, 2014

Ginsburg, T., Huq, A. Z., *How to Save a Constitutional Democracy*, Chicago University Press, 2018

Ginsburg, T., Lansberg-Rodriguez, D., Versteeg, M., 'When to Overthrow Your Government: The Right to Resist in the World's Constitutions', *UCLA Law Review*, No. 5, 2013, 1184

Giuliani, A., 'Le disposizioni sulla legge in generale. Gli articoli da 1 a 15', in P. Rescigno (ed.), *Trattato di diritto privato. Premesse e disposizioni preliminari*, Vol. I, UTET, Turin, 1999, 379

Goldoni, M., 'Rousseau's Radical Constitutionalism and Its Legacy', in M. Dowdle, M. Wilkinson (eds.), *Constitutionalism Beyond Liberalism*, Cambridge University Press, 2017, 227

Gori, L., *Le elezioni primarie nell'ordinamento costituzionale*, ES, Naples, 2018

Grabenwarter, C., 'Constitutional Resilience', 2018, https://verfassungsblog.de/constitutional-resilience/

Graber, M., Levinson, S., Tushnet, M. (eds.), *Constitutional Democracy in Crisis?*, Oxford University Press, 2018

Grasso, G., 'La balestra di Guglielmo Tell e l'iniziativa legislativa popolare. Note minime a proposito del disegno di legge costituzionale in materia di iniziativa legislativa popolare e di referendum', 2019, https://bit.ly/3zzyUWt

Grasso, G., 'Mandato imperativo e mandato di partito: il caso del MoVimento 5 Stelle', 2017, www.osservatorioaic.it/images/rivista/pdf/Grasso%20Definitivo.pdf

Gregor, A. J., *The Ideology of Fascism: The Rationale of Totalitarianism*, Free Press, New York, 1969

Gregorio, M., *Parte totale. Le dottrine costituzionali del partito politico in Italia tra Otto e Novecento*, Giuffrè, Milan, 2013

Griglio, E., Lupo, N., 'Parliamentary Democracy and the Eurozone Crisis', *Law and Economics Yearly Review*, No. 2, 2012, 313

Grossi, P., *A History of European Law*, Blackwell, Malden, 2010

Grosso, E., 'Democrazia diretta e democrazia rappresentativa nel pensiero di Norberto Bobbio', 2015, https://bit.ly/2Sz4vHg

Guarino, G., 'Il referendum e la sua applicazione al regime parlamentare', *Rassegna di diritto pubblico*, No. 1, 1947, 30

Guarino, G., 'The "Truth" about Europe and the Euro. A Second Essay', *Nomos. Le attualità del diritto*, No. 2, 2014, 25

Guastini, R., *Le fonti del diritto. Fondamenti teorici*, Giuffrè, Milan, 2010

Guazzarotti, A., 'Sovranità e integrazione europea', 2017, www.rivistaaic.it/it/rivista/ultimi-contributi-pubblicati/andrea-guazzarotti/sovranit-e-integrazione-europea

Guazzarotti, A., 'Very Unkind Things about the German Constitutional Court's Rebellion against the ECJ in the Quantitative Easing Case', 2020, https://verfassungsblog.de/very-unkind-things-about-the-german-constitutional-courts-rebellion-against-the-ecj-in-the-quantitative-easing-case/

Hailbronner, M., Landau, D. (eds.), 'Constitutional Courts and Populism', 2018, www.iconnectblog.com/2017/04/introduction-constitutional-courts-and-populism/

Halmai, G., 'Abuse of Constitutional Identity. The Hungarian Constitutional Court on Interpretation of Article E) (2) of the Fundamental Law', *Review of Central and East European Law*, No. 1, 2018, 23

Halmai, G., 'The Coup against Constitutional Democracy: The Case of Hungary', 2018, https://me.eui.eu/gabor-halmai/wp-content/uploads/sites/385/2018/06/Chapter-15-Halmai-Hungary.pdf

Halmai, G., 'Is There Such Thing as "Populist Constitutionalism"? The Case of Hungary', *Fudan Journal of the Humanities and Social Sciences*, No. 3, 2018, 323

Hayward, J., 'The Populist Challenge to Élitist Democracy in Europe', in J. Hayward (ed.), *Elitism, Populism, and European Politics*, Oxford University Press, 1996, 10

Hazareesingh, S., 'De Gaulle, le mythe napoléonien, et la consécration de la tradition consulaire républicaine', *Cahiers Jaurès*, No. 3, 2008, 3

Henning, B., *The End of Politicians: Time for a Real Democracy*, Unbound Digital, Johnson City, 2017

Hewlett, N., 'Nicolas Sarkozy and the Legacy of Bonapartism: The French Presidential and Parliamentary Elections of 2007', *Modern & Contemporary France*, No. 4, 2007, 405

Heydt, C., *Moral Philosophy in Eighteenth-Century Britain. God, Self, and Other*, Cambridge University Press, 2017

Hofmann, H., Pégny, G., Sintomer, Y., 'Le concept de représentation: un problème alle-mande?', *Raisons politiques*, No. 2, 2013, 79

Holden, A. M., 'The Imperative Mandate in the Spanish Cortes of the Middle Ages', *American Political Science Review*, No. 4, 1930, 886

House of Lords, Select Committee on the Constitution 12th Report of Session 2009–10, *Referendums in the United Kingdom. Report with Evidence*, 2010, www.publications.parliament.uk/pa/ld200910/ldselect/ldconst/99/99.pdf

Howse, R., 'Epilogue: In Defense of Disruptive Democracy – A Critique of Anti-populism', *International Journal of Constitutional Law*, No. 2, 2019, 641

Hüppauf, B., 'Camouflage and Mimesis: The Frog between the Devil's Deceptions, Evolutionary Biology, and the Ecological Animal', *Paragrana Internationale Zeitschrift für Historische Anthropologie*, No. 1, 2015, 132

Independent High level Group on fake news and online disinformation, 'A multi-dimensional approach to disinformation. Report of the independent High level Group on fake news and online disinformation', 2018, https://op.europa.eu/en/publication-detail/-/publication/6ef4df8b-4cea-11e8-be1d-01aa75ed71a1

Jakab, A., 'What Can Constitutional Law Do against the Erosion of Democracy and the Rule of Law? On the Interconnectedness of the Protection of Democracy and the Rule of Law', *Constitutional Studies*, special issue, 2020, 5

Jakab, A., Schweber, H., 'Editorial: Constitutional Decline, Constitutional Design, and Lawyerly Hubris', *Constitutional Studies*, special issue, 2020, 1

Jakab, A., Kochenov, D. (eds.), *The Enforcement of EU Law and Values*, Oxford University Press, 2017

Jefferson, T., 'To James Madison Paris', 6 September 1789, www.let.rug.nl/usa/presidents/thomas-jefferson/letters-of-thomas-jefferson/jefl81.php

Jones, E., 'Not Hamilton but Madison: Diversity Makes for a Better Union', 2020, www.iiss.org /blogs/survival-blog/2020/05/europe-diversity-politics-covid-19

Kahn-Freund, O., 'On Uses and Misuses of Comparative Law', *Modern Law Review*, No. 1, 1974, 1

Kaletsky, A., 'Europe's Hamiltonian Moment', 2020, www.project-syndicate.org/commentary/ french-german-european-recovery-plan-proposal-by-anatole-kaletsky-2020-05

Kelemen, R. D., Pech, L., 'Why Autocrats Love Constitutional Identity and Constitutional Pluralism. Lessons from Hungary and Poland', *Reconnect Working Paper*, No. 2, 2018, https:// reconnect-europe.eu/wp-content/uploads/2018/10/RECONNECT-WorkingPaper2-Kelemen -Pech-LP-KO.pdf

Keller, H., Stone Sweet, A. (eds.), *A Europe of Rights: The Impact of the ECHR on National Legal Systems*, Oxford University Press, 2009

Kelsen, H., *General Theory of Law and State*, Russell and Russell, New York, 1945

Kelsen, H., 'On the Essence and Value of Democracy', in A. J. Jacobson, B. Schlink (eds.), *Weimar: A Jurisprudence of Crisis*, University of California Press, Berkeley, 2000, 84

Kelsen, H., *Vom Wesen und Wert der Demokratie*, Mohr, Tübingen, 1929 (Italian translation, *Essenza e valore della democrazia*, Giappichelli, Turin, 2004)

Kosař, D., Sipulova, K., 'How to Fight Court-Packing?', *Constitutional Studies*, No. 1, 2020, 133

Kramer, L., *The People Themselves: Popular Constitutionalism and Judicial Review*, Oxford University Press, 2004

Krastev, I., *After Europe*, University of Pennsylvania Press, Philadelphia, 2017

Krastev, I., '"Sovereign Democracy", Russian-Style', *Insight Turkey*, No. 4, 2006, 113

Kriesi, H., 'The Populist Challenge', *West European Politics*, No. 2, 2014, 361

Krisch, N., *Beyond Constitutionalism: The Pluralist Structure of Postnational Law*, Oxford University Press, 2010

Krugman, P., *End This Depression Now!*, W. W. Norton & Company, New York, 2012

Kuo, M. S., 'Against Instantaneous Democracy', *International Journal of Constitutional Law*, No. 2, 2019, 554

Laclau, E., *On Populist Reason*, Verso, London, 2005

Landau, D., 'Abusive Constitutionalism', *UC Davis Law Review*, No. 1, 2013, 189

Landau, D., 'Populist Constitutions', *The University of Chicago Law Review*, No. 5, 2018, 521

Landemore, H., 'We, All of the People. Five Lessons from Iceland's Failed Experiment in Creating a Crowdsourced Constitution', 2014, https://slate.com/technology/2014/07/five-lessons-from-icelands-failed-crowdsourced-constitution-experiment.htm

Lasorella, G., 'Aggiornamenti e sviluppi in tema di programmazione dei lavori, tra decreti-legge e maggioranze variabili', in V. Lippolis, N. Lupo (eds.), *Il Parlamento dopo il referendum costituzionale (Il Filangieri. Quaderno 2015-2016)*, Jovene, Naples, 2017, 53

Ledeen, M., 'Renzo De Felice and the Controversy over Italian Fascism', *Journal of Contemporary History*, No. 4, 1976, 269

Lefort, C., *Democracy and Political Theory*, University of Minnesota Press, Minneapolis, 1988

Legrand, P., 'The Impossibility of Legal Transplants', *Maastricht Journal of European and Comparative Law*, No. 1, 1997, 111

Leibholz, G., *Das Wesen der Repräsentation und der Gestaltwandel der Demokratie im 20. Jahrhundert*, De Gruyter, Berlin, 1966 [1929]

Lewis, D., *Direct Democracy and Minority Rights: A Critical Assessment of the Tyranny of the Majority in the American States*, Routledge, Abingdon, 2013

Leyland, P., 'Referendums, Popular Sovereignty, and the Territorial Constitution', in R. Rawlings, P. Leyland, A. Young (eds.), *Sovereignty and the Law*, Oxford University Press, 2013, 145

Linz, J., *Totalitarian and Authoritarian Regimes*, Lynne Rienner, Boulder, CO, 2000

Lijphart, A., 'Consociational Democracy', *World Politics*, No. 2, 1969, 207

Livingston, A., 'Was the Fascist Era Really a "Parenthesis" for the Italian Legal System?', in S. Skinner (ed.), *Fascism and Criminal Law: History, Theory, Continuity*, Hart, Oxford, 2015, 85

Livingston, L., 'Understanding Hungary's Authoritarian Response to the Pandemic', 2020, www.lawfareblog.com/understanding-hungarys-authoritarian-response-pandemic

Loewenstein, K., 'Militant Democracy and Fundamental Rights, I', *American Political Science Review*, No. 3, 1937, 417

Loewenstein, K., 'Militant Democracy and Fundamental Rights, II', *American Political Science Review*, No. 4, 1937, 638

Lollini, A., Palermo, F., 'Comparative Law and the "Proceduralization" of Constitution-Building Processes', in J. Raue, P. Sutter (eds.), *Facets and Practices of State-building*, Martinus Nijoff, Leiden, 2009, 301

Longo, E., Malvicini, M., 'Il decisionismo governativo: uso e abuso dei poteri normativi del Governo durante la crisi da COVID-19', 2020, www.federalismi.it/nv14/articolo-documento.cfm?Artid=44237

Loo, A., 'John C. Calhoun's Concurrent Majority', 2016, theprincetontory.com/john-c-cal houns-concurrent-majority/

Louis, J. V., 'The Review of the Stability and Growth Pact', *Common Market Law Review*, No. 1, 2006, 85

Luciani, M., 'Antifascismo e nascita della costituzione', *Politica del diritto*, No. 2, 1991, 191

Luciani, M., 'L'antisovrano e la crisi delle costituzioni', *Rivista di diritto costituzionale*, No. 1, 1996, 124

Luciani M., *Commentario della Costituzione. Art. 75 Referendum*, Zanichelli, Bologna, 2005

Luciani, M., 'Introduzione', in M. Luciani, M. Volpi (eds.), *Referendum*, Laterza, Rome, 1992, 3

Luciani, M., 'Il referendum: questioni teoriche e dell'esperienza italiana', *Revista catalana de dret públic*, No. 2, 2008, 157

Lupo, N., '"Populismo legislativo?": continuità e discontinuità nelle tendenze della legislazione italiana', *Ragion pratica*, No. 1, 2019, 251

Lupo, N., 'Perché non él'art. 64 Cost. a impedire il voto "a distanza" dei parlamentari. E perché ammettere tale voto richiede una "re-ingegnerizzazione" dei procedimenti parlamentari', 2020, www.osservatorioaic.it/images/rivista/pdf/2020_3_02_Lupo.pdf.

Madison, J., 'The Structure of the Government Must Furnish the Proper Checks and Balances Between the Different Departments', 1788, www.constitution.org/fed/federa51.htm

Mair, P., 'Partyless Democracy', 2000, https://newleftreview.org/issues/II2/articles/peter-mair-partyless-democracy

Malvicini, M., Lauri, G., 'Le commissioni parlamentari di inchiesta: recenti sviluppi e osservazioni alla luce della prassi', 2016, https://bit.ly/36bVbMp

Manconi, L., Graziani, F., *Per il tuo bene ti mozzerò la testa. Contro il giustizialismo morale*, Einaudi, Turin, 2020

Manin, B., *The Principles of Representative Government*, Cambridge University Press, 2010

Manucci, L., 'Populism and the Media', in C. Rovira Kaltwasser, P. Taggart, P. Ochoa Espejo, P. Ostiguy (eds.), *The Oxford Handbook of Populism*, Oxford University Press, 2017, 467

Mansbridge, J. J., *Beyond Adversary Democracy*, Basic Books, New York, 1980

Manucci, L., Amsler, M., 'Where the Wind Blows: Five Star Movement's Populism, Direct Democracy and Ideological Flexibility', *Italian Political Science Review / Rivista Italiana di Scienza Politica*, No. 1, 2018, 109

Maranini, G., *Governo parlamentare e partitocrazia: lezione inaugurale dell'anno accademico 1949-1950*, Editrice Universitaria, Florence, 1950

Marchlewska, M., Cichocka, A., Panayiotou, O., Castellanos, K., Batayneh, J., 'Populism as Identity Politics: Perceived In-Group Disadvantage, Collective Narcissism, and Support for Populism', *Social Psychological and Personality Science*, No. 2, 2018, 151

Martinelli, C., 'Libero mandato e rappresentanza nazionale come fondamenti della modernità costituzionale', 2018, www.federalismi.it/nv14/articolo-documento.cfm?Artid=36456

Martinico, G., 'Constitutionalism, Resistance, and Openness: Comparative Law Reflections on Constitutionalism in Postnational Governance', *Yearbook of European Law*, 2016, 318

Martinico, G., 'National Courts and Judicial Disobedience to the ECHR: A Comparative Overview', in O. M. Arnardóttir, A. Buyse (eds.), *Shifting Centres of Gravity in Human Rights Protection: Rethinking Relations between the ECHR, EU, and National Legal Orders*, Routledge, Abingdon, 2016, 59

Martinico, G., 'Resentment, Populism and Political Strategies in Italy', 2019, https://verfas sungsblog.de/resentment-populism-and-political-strategies-in-italy/

Martinico, G., *Lo spirito polemico del diritto europeo. Studio sulle ambizioni costituzionali dell'Unione*, Aracne, Rome, 2011

Martinico, G., *The Tangled Complexity of the EU Constitutional Process: The Frustrating Knot of Europe*, Routledge, Abingdon, 2012

Martinico, G., Repetto, G., 'Fundamental Rights and Constitutional Duels in Europe: An Italian Perspective on Case 269/2017 of the Italian Constitutional Court and Its Aftermath', *European Constitutional Law Review*, No. 4, 2019, 731

Martinico, G., Pollicino, O., *The Interaction between Europe's Legal Systems: Judicial Dialogue and the Creation of Supranational Laws*, Elgar, Cheltenham, 2012

Marzal, T., 'Is the BVerfG PSPP Decision "Simply Not Comprehensible"? A Critique of the Judgment's Reasoning on Proportionality', 2020, https://verfassungsblog.de/is-the-bverfg-pspp-decision-simply-not-comprehensible/

Mat, F., Caranti, N., 'The funding of politics in Italy', 2019, www.balcanicaucaso.org/eng/Projects2/ESVEI/News-Esvei/The-funding-of-politics-in-Italy-197740/The-funding-of-politics-in-Italy

Mazzoleni, G., 'Populism and the Media', in D. Albertazzi, D. McDonnell (eds.), *Twenty-First Century Populism: The Spectre of Western European Democracy*, Palgrave, London, 2008, 49

Mazzurri, J., 'La genesi del divieto ex art. 67 Cost. nel periodo costituente e brevi note sulle vicende della norma nei principali tentativi di riforma della Carta', in P. Caretti, D. Morisi, G. Tarli Barbieri (eds.), *Il divieto di mandato imperativo: un principio in discussione*, Seminario di studi e ricerche parlamentari 'Silvano Tosi', Florence, 2019, 339

McDonnell, D., 'Silvio Berlusconi's Personal Parties: From Forza Italia to the Popolo della Libertà', *Political Studies*, No. 1 suppl., 2013, 217

McDonnell, D., 'A Weekend in Padania: Regionalist Populism and the Lega Nord', *Politics*, No. 2, 2006, 126

Mendez, F., Mendez, M., Triga, V., *Referendums and the European Union: A Comparative Inquiry*, Cambridge University Press, 2014

Mendez, F., Mendez, M., Triga, V. (eds.), *Referendums on EU Matters*, Policy Department for Citizens' Rights and Constitutional Affairs, European Parliament's Committee on Constitutional Affairs, 2017, www.europarl.europa.eu/RegData/etudes/STUD/2017/571402/IPOL_STU(2017)571402_EN.pdf

Menéndez, A., 'The Existential Crisis of the European Union', *German Law Journal*, No. 5, 2013, 453

Mény, Y. (ed.), _Les politiques du mimétisme institutionnel: la greffe et le rejet_, L'Harmattan, Paris, 1993

Mény, Y., Surel, Y., 'The Constitutive Ambiguity of Populism', in Y. Mény. Y. Surel (eds.), _Democracies and the Populist Challenge_, Palgrave, London, 2002, 1

Mény, Y., Surel, Y., _Populismo e democrazia_, Il Mulino, Bologna, 2004

Mesežnikov, G., Gyárfášová, O., Smilov, D. (eds.), _Populist Politics and Liberal Democracy in Central and Eastern Europe_, Institute for Public Affairs, Bratislava, 2008

Michel, H., Mirkine-Guetzévitch, B., _Les idées politiques et sociales de la Résistance_, Presses universitaires de France, Paris, 1954

Michelman, F., 'Populist Natural Law (Reflections on Tushnet's "Thin Constitution")', _University of Richmond Law Review_, No. 2, 2000, 461

Milward, A., _The European Rescue of the Nation-State_, University of California Press, Berkeley, 1992

Milza, P., 'Mussolini entre fascisme et populisme', _Vingtième Siècle. Revue d'histoire_, No. 56, 1997, 115

Mirkine-Guetzévitch, B., _Les Nouvelles tendances du droit constitutionnel_, Giard, Paris, 1931

Mirkine-Guetzévitch, B., 'Le référendum et le parlementarisme dans les nouvelles constitutions européennes', _Annuaire de l'Institut international de droit public_, Vol. II, PUF, Paris, 1931, 285

Mittelstraß, J., 'Complexity, Reductionism, and Holism in Science and Philosophy of Science', in V. Hösle (ed.), _Complexity and Analogy in Science: Theoretical, Methodological and Epistemological Aspects_, Acta 22, Pontifical Academy of Sciences, Vatican City, 2014, www.pas.va/content/dam/accademia/pdf/acta22/acta22-mittelstrass.pdf

Mitterrand, F., _Le Coup d'État permanent_, Plon, Paris, 1965

Molier, G., Rijpkema, B., 'Germany's New Militant Democracy Regime: National Democratic Party II and the German Federal Constitutional Court's "Potentiality" Criterion for Party Bans: Bundesverfassungsgericht, Judgment of 17 January 2017, 2 BvB 1/13, National Democratic Party II', _European Constitutional Law Review_, No. 2, 2018, 394

Monti, M., 'Italian Populism and Fake News on the Internet: A New Political Weapon in the Public Discourse', in G. Delledonne, G. Martinico, M. Monti, F. Pacini (eds.), _Italian Populism and Constitutional Law: Strategies, Conflicts and Dilemmas_, Palgrave, London, 177

Morel, L., 'Referendum', in M. Rosenfeld, A. Sajó (eds.), _The Oxford Handbook of Comparative Constitutional Law_, Oxford University Press, 2012, 502

Morelli, A., _Rappresentanza politica e libertà del mandato parlamentare_, ES, Naples, 2018

Morgan, E., _Inventing the People: The Rise of Popular Sovereignty in England and America_, W. W. Norton & Company, New York, 1989

Morrone, A., 'L'iniziativa popolare propositiva: per una democrazia plebiscitaria contro la democrazia rappresentativa?', 2018, www.federalismi.it/nv14/editoriale.cfm?eid=499

Mortati, C., _Lezioni sulle forme di governo_, Cedam, Padua, 1973

Mortati, C., 'Relazione alla II Sottocommissione', 1946, www.nascitacostituzione.it/05appendici/01generali/00/02/06-mortati.htm

Mosca, L., Vaccari, C., Valeriani, A., 'How to Select Citizen Candidates: The Five Star Movement's Online Primaries and Their Implications', in A. De Petris, T. Poguntke (eds.), _Anti-Party Parties in Germany and Italy_, Luiss University Press, Rome, 2015, 114

Mozzo, A., 'Ascesa dei leader e presidenzializzazione dei governi: la corrosione della democrazia nasce dal "cuore" dello Stato', 2020, www.opiniojuris.it/presidenzializzazione-ascesa-leader/#_ftn11

Mudde, C., 'Are Populists Friends or Foes of Constitutionalism?', 2013, www.fljs.org/content/are-populists-friends-or-foes-constitutionalism

Mudde, C., *The Far Right Today*, Polity Press, Cambridge, 2019

Mudde, C., 'Populism: An Ideational Approach', in C. Rovira Kaltwasser, P. Taggart, P. Ochoa Espejo, P. Ostiguy (eds.), *The Oxford Handbook of Populism*, Oxford University Press, 2017, 27

Mudde, C., 'The Populist Zeitgeist', *Government and Opposition*, No. 4, 2004, 541

Müller, J. W., 'Populism and Constitutionalism', in C. Rovira Kaltwasser, P. Taggart, P. Ochoa Espejo, P. Ostiguy (eds.), *The Oxford Handbook of Populism*, Oxford University Press, 2017, 590

Müller, J. W., *What Is Populism?*, University of Pennsylvania Press, Philadelphia, 2017

Musso, M., Maccaferri, M., 'At the Origins of the Political Discourse of the 5-Star Movement (M5S): Internet, Direct Democracy and the "Future of the Past"', *Journal Internet Histories Digital Technology, Culture and Society*, Nos. 1–2, 2018, 98

Negri, A., *Insurgencies: The Constituent Power and the Modern State*, University of Minnesota Press, Minneapolis, 1999

Nelken, D., 'Legitimate Suspicions? Berlusconi and the Judges', *Italian Politics*, No. 1, 2002, 112

Nenni, P., *Una battaglia vinta*, Edizioni Leonardo, Rome, 1946

Nicolini, M., 'Reforming the Territorial Constitution in Italy: Some Reflections on Durability and Change', in G. Abels, J. Battke (eds.), *Regional Governance in the EU Regions and the Future of Europe*, Elgar, Cheltenham, 2019, 106

Ochoa Espejo, P., 'Populism and the Idea of The People', in C. Rovira Kaltwasser, P. Taggart, P. Ochoa Espejo, P. Ostiguy (eds.), *The Oxford Handbook of Populism*, Oxford University Press, 2017, 607

Oklopcic, Z., *Beyond the People: Social Imaginary and Constituent Imagination*, Oxford University Press, 2018

Olivetti, M., 'Foreign Influences on the Italian Constitutional System', Paper submitted to the 6th World Congress of the International Association of Constitutional Law, Santiago de Chile, 2004, www.researchgate.net/publication/281241329_Foreign_Influences_on_the_Italian_Constitutional_System

Onida, V., *La Costituzione. La legge fondamentale della Repubblica*, Il Mulino, Bologna, 2007

Oomen, B., 'Strengthening Constitutional Identity Where There Is None: The Case of the Netherlands', *Revue interdisciplinaire d'études juridiques*, No. 2, 2016, 235

Orrù, R., 'Divieto di mandato imperativo e anti-defection laws: spunti di diritto comparato', *Diritto pubblico comparato ed europeo*, No. 4, 2015, 1099

Orsina, G., *Il berlusconismo: nella storia d'Italia*, Marsilio, Venice, 2013

Pace, A., *Il potere di inchiesta delle assemblee legislative: Saggi*, Giuffrè, Milan, 1973

Pacini, F., 'Dall'autorità della legge all'autorevolezza delle Assemblee', *Quaderni costituzionali*, No.1, 2015, 9

Pacini, F., 'Populism and Law-Making Process', in G. Delledonne, G. Martinico, M. Monti, F. Pacini (eds.), *Italian Populism and Constitutional Law: Strategies, Conflicts and Dilemmas*, Palgrave, London, 2020, 119

Painter, B. W. Jr., 'Renzo De Felice and the Historiography of Italian Fascism', *American Historical Review*, 1990, 391

Pajno, A., 'Il rispetto dei vincoli derivanti dall'ordinamento comunitario come limite alla potestà legislativa nel nuovo Titolo V della Costituzione', *Le Istituzioni del federalismo*, No. 5, 2003, 814

Paladin, L., 'Costituzione, preleggi e codice civile', *Rivista di diritto civile*, No. 1, 1993, 19

Paladin, L., *Per una storia costituzionale dell'Italia repubblicana*, Il Mulino, Bologna, 2004

Palermo, F., *La forma di stato dell'Unione europea. Per una teoria costituzionale dell'integrazione sovranazionale*, Cedam, Padua, 2005

Pallante, F., *Contro la democrazia diretta*, Einaudi, Turin, 2020

Palm, A., Barana, L., 'Italy's Migration Policy: A Self-Defeating Approach Spells Marginalisation in Europe', 2019, www.iai.it/en/pubblicazioni/italys-migration-policy-self-defeating-approach-spells-marginalisation-europe

Palombella, G., 'Illiberal, Democratic and Non-Arbitrary? Epicentre and Circumstances of a Rule of Law Crisis', *Hague Journal on the Rule of Law*, No. 1, 2018, 5

Pansa, G., *Il sangue dei vinti*, Sperling & Kupfer, Milan, 2003

Pasquino, G., 'The State of the Italian Republic', *Contemporary Italian Politics*, No. 2, 2019, 195

Passarelli, G., Tuorto, D., *Lega & Padania: storie e luoghi delle camicie verdi*, Il Mulino, Bologna, 2012

Pasquino, G., Pelizzo, L., *Parlamenti democratici*, Il Mulino, Bologna, 2006

Patard, J., 'Le référendum constitutionnel de Marine Le Pen: Moi présidente, je rétablirai la supériorité du droit national!', 2017, www.lepetitjuriste.fr/referendum-constitutionnel-de-marine-pen-moi-presidente-retablirai-superiorite-droit-national/

Paterniti, F., 'La riforma dell'art. 117, 1°Co. della Costituzione e le nuove prospettive dei rapporti tra ordinamento giuridico nazionale e Unione Europea', *Giurisprudenza costituzionale*, No. 3, 2004, 2101

Pavone, C., *A Civil War: A History of the Italian Resistance*, Verso, London, 2013

Pazé, V., 'Il populismo come antitesi della democrazia', *Teoria politica*, No. 1, 2017, 111

Pegoraro, L., 'Le categorie civilistiche e il parassitismo metodologico dei costituzionalisti nello studio del diritto comparato', *Annuario di diritto comparato e di studi legislativi*, 2013, 305

Penasa, S., 'The Italian Way to Migration: Was It "True" Populism? Populist Policies as Constitutional Antigens', in G. Delledonne, G. Martinico, M. Monti, F. Pacini (eds.), *Italian Populism and Constitutional Law: Strategies, Conflicts and Dilemmas*, Palgrave, London, 2020, 255

Perassi, T., *La Costituzione e l'ordinamento internazionale*, Giuffrè, Milan, 1952

Pereira Coutinho, F., 'Report on Portugal', in G. Martinico, O. Pollicino (eds.), *The National Judicial Treatment of the ECHR and EU Laws: A Comparative Constitutional Perspective*, Europa Law Publishing, Groningen, 2010, 351

Pertici, A., 'L'etica pubblica e la riforma sempre in-attesa del conflitto di interessi', 2016, www.gruppodipisa.it/8-rivista/1-andrea-pertici-l-etica-pubblica-e-la-riforma-sempre-in-attesa-del-conflitto-di-interessi

Peters, A., 'Compensatory Constitutionalism: The Function and Potential of Fundamental International Norms and Structures', *Leiden Journal of International Law*, No. 3, 2006, 579

Pezzini, B., Rossi, S. (eds.), *I giuristi e la Resistenza: Una biografia intellettuale del Paese*, Franco Angeli, Milan, 2016

Pierdominici, L., *The Mimetic Evolution of the Court of Justice of the EU: A Comparative Law Perspective*, Palgrave, London, 2020

Pinelli, C., 'The Formation of a Constitutional Tradition in Continental Europe since World War II', *European Public Law*, No. 2, 2016, 257

Pinelli, C., 'Libertà di mandato dei parlamentari e rimedi contro il Transfughismo', 2018, www.federalismi.it/nv14/articolo-documento.cfm?Artid=36498

Pinelli, C., 'I limiti generali alla potestà legislativa statale e regionale e i rapporti con l'ordinamento comunitario', *Il Foro italiano*, No. 5, 2001, 194

Pinelli, C., 'The Populist Challenge to Constitutional Democracy', *European Constitutional Law Review*, No.1, 2011, 5

Pinelli, C., 'The Rise of Populism and the Malaise of Democracy', in S. Garben, I. Govaere, P. Nemitz (eds.), *Critical Reflections on Constitutional Democracy in the European Union*, Hart, Oxford, 2019, 27

Pistorio, G., *Maxi-emendamento e questione di fiducia. Sottotitolo. Contributo allo studio di una prassi illegittima*, ES, Naples, 2018

Pizzorusso, A., *La Costituzione ferita*, Laterza, Rome, 1999

Pizzorusso, A., 'Disp. XII', in G. Branca, A. Pizzorusso (eds.), *Commentario della Costituzione*, Zanichelli, Bologna, 1995, 198

Pizzorusso, A., *I gruppi parlamentari come soggetti di diritto: pagine di un saggio giuridico*, Pacini Mariotti, Pisa, 1969

Plotke, D., 'Representation Is Democracy', *Constellations*, No. 1, 1997, 19

Poiares Maduro, M., 'Passion and Reason in European Integration', 2010, https://papers .ssrn.com/sol3/papers.cfm?abstract_id=1709950

Poiares Maduro, M., 'Some Preliminary Remarks on the PSPP Decision of the German Constitutional Court', 2020, https://verfassungsblog.de/some-preliminary-remarks-on-the-pspp-decision-of-the-german-constitutional-court

Poiares Maduro, M., 'Three Claims of Constitutional Pluralism', in M. Abvelj, J. Komárek (eds.), *Constitutional Pluralism in the European Union and Beyond*, Hart, Oxford, 2012, 67

Poli, E., *Forza Italia: strutture, leadership e radicamento territoriale*, Il Mulino, Bologna, 2001

Politi, F., 'Il procedimento di revisione della Costituzione Repubblicana. La funzione di garanzia dell'art. 138 Cost. e il ricorso a procedimenti alternativi della forma di governo e tutela dei valori costituzionali', in V. Baldini (ed.), *La Costituzione e la sua revisione*, Pisa University Press, 2014, 87

Pollicino, O., *L'allargamento ad est dell'Europa e rapporti tra Corti costituzionali e Corti europee. Verso una teoria generale dell'impatto interordinamentale del diritto sovranazionale?*, Giuffrè, Milan, 2010

Pollicino, O., 'The Italian Constitutional Court at the Crossroads between Constitutional Parochialism and Co-operative Constitutionalism. Judgments No. 348 and 349 of 22 and 24 October 2007', *European Constitutional Law Review*, No. 2, 2008, 363

Pollicino, O., 'Metaphors and Identity Based Narrative in Constitutional Adjudication: When Judicial Dominance Matters', 2019, https://blog-iacl-aidc.org/2019-posts/2019/2/27/meta phors-and-identity-based-narrative-in-constitutional-adjudication-when-judicial-dominance-matters

Polsby, N. W., 'Legislatures', in F. I. Greenstein, N. W. Polsby (eds.), *Handbook of Political Science*, Vol. V, Addison-Wesley, Reading, 1975, 257

Popelier, P., Lambrecht, S., Lemmens, K. (eds.), *Criticism of the European Court of Human Rights*, Intersentia, Antwerp, 2016

Popović, D., *Comparative Government*, Elgar, Cheltenham, 2019

Principato, L., 'Il divieto di mandato imperativo, da prerogativa regia a garanzia della sovranità assembleare', 2012, www.rivistaaic.it/images/rivista/pdf/Principato.pdf

Putin, V., 'Speech and the Following Discussion at the Munich Conference on Security Policy', 2007, http://en.kremlin.ru/events/president/transcripts/24034

Qvortrup, M., *A Comparative Study of Referendums: Government by the People*, Manchester University Press, 2002

Qvortrup, M., 'Introduction: Theory, Practice and History', in M. Qvortrup (ed.), *Referendums around the World*, Palgrave, London, 2018, 1

Qvortrup, M., 'Two Hundred Years of Referendums', in M. Qvortrup (ed.), *Referendums around the World*, Palgrave, London, 2018, 263

Ragazzoni, D., '"Particracy": The Pre-populist Critique of Parties and Its Implications', in P. Blokker, M. Anselmi (eds.), *Multiple Populisms: Italy as Democracy's Mirror*, Routledge, Abingdon, 2020, 86

Ragazzoni, D., 'The Populist Leader's Two Bodies: Bobbio, Berlusconi, and the Factionalization of Party Democracy', *Constellations*, No. 3, 2020, 213

Raible, L., Trueblood, L., 'The Swiss System of Referendums and the Impossibility of Direct Democracy', 2017, https://bit.ly/3jv3pY7

Raniolo, F., 'Forza Italia: A Leader with a Party', *South European Society and Politics*, No. 3–4, 2006, 439

Raunio, T., Hix, S., 'Backbenchers Learn to Fight Back: European Integration and Parliamentary Government', *West European Politics*, No. 4, 2000, 142

Rescigno, G. U., 'Prassi, regolarità, regole, convenzioni costituzionali, consuetudini costituzionali, consuetudini giuridiche di diritto pubblico', *Osservatorio sulle fonti*, No. 2, 2018, 1

Revelli, M., *Populismo 2.0*, Einaudi, Turin, 2017

Ridola, P., 'Divieto del mandato imperativo e pluralismo politico', in *Studi sulle fonti normative e altri temi di vario diritto in onore di Vezio Crisafulli*, Vol. II, Cedam, Padua, 1985, 679

Ridola, P., 'Partiti politici', in *Enciclopedia del diritto*, Vol. XXXII, Giuffrè, Milan, 66

Rinaldi, E., 'Divieto di mandato imperativo e disciplina dei gruppi parlamentari', 2017, www.costituzionalismo.it/download/Costituzionalismo_201702_637.pdf

Rizzo, M., *Il golpe europeo. I comunisti contro l'Unione*, Baldini Castoldi Dalai, Milan, 2012

Robespierre, M., *Discours sur le gouvernement représentatif*, 1793 https://archive.org/details/discourssurlegouoorobe/page/26/mode/2up (Italian translation, *Sul governo rappresentativo*, Manifestolibri, Rome, 1995)

Rodrik, D., 'Why Does Globalization Fuel Populism? Economics, Culture, and the Rise of Right-Wing Populism', 2020, https://drodrik.scholar.harvard.edu/publications/why-does-globalization-fuel-populism-economics-culture-and-rise-right-wing

Romboli, R., 'Il referendum costituzionale nell'esperienza repubblicana e nelle prospettive di riforma dell'art. 138 Cost.', in A. Pisaneschi, L. Violini (eds.), *Poteri, garanzie e diritti a sessanta anni dalla Costituzione: scritti per Giovanni Grottanelli de' Santi*, Giuffrè, Milan, 2007, 573

Rooduijn, M., 'The Nucleus of Populism: In Search of the Lowest Common Denominator', *Government and Opposition*, No. 4, 2014, 573

Rosa, F., 'Art. 75', in F. Clementi, L. Cuocolo, F. Rosa, G. E. Vigevani (eds.), *La Costituzione italiana*, Vol. II, Il Mulino, Bologna, 2018, 116

Rosanvallon, P., *Counterdemocracy: Politics in an Age of Distrust*, Cambridge University Press, 2008

Rossi, E., 'Il numero dei parlamentari in Italia, dallo Statuto albertino ad oggi', in E. Rossi (ed.), *Meno parlamentari, più democrazia? Significato e conseguenze della riforma costituzionale*, Pisa University Press, 2020, 17

Rousseau, J. J., *Considérations sur le gouvernement de Pologne et sur sa réformation projetée*, 1772, www.espace-rousseau.ch/f/textes/considerations_pologne.pdf

Rousseau, J. J., *The Social Contract*, 1762, www.earlymoderntexts.com/assets/pdfs/rousseau1762.pdf

Rovira Kaltwasser, C., Taggart, P., Ochoa Espejo, P., Ostiguy, P., 'Populism: An Overview of the Concept and the State of the Art', in C. Rovira Kaltwasser, P. Taggart, P. Ochoa Espejo, P. Ostiguy (eds.), *The Oxford Handbook of Populism*, Oxford University Press, 2017, 1

Roznai, Y., 'Negotiating the Eternal: The Paradox of Entrenching Secularism in Constitutions', *Michigan State Law Review*, No. 2, 2017, 253

Roznai, Y., *Unconstitutional Constitutional Amendments: The Limits of Amendment Powers*, Oxford University Press, Oxford, 2017

Rubio Llorente, F., *La forma del poder: estudios sobre la constitución*, CEPC, Madrid, 2013

Ruggeri, A., 'Dimensione europea della tutela dei diritti fondamentali e tecniche interpretative', 2009, www.federalismi.it/nv14/articolo-documento.cfm?Artid=14806

Ruggeri, A., 'Riforma del titolo V e giudizi di "comunitarietà" delle leggi', 2007, www.associazionedeicostituzionalisti.it/dottrina/ordinamentieuropei/ruggeri.html

Rummens, S., 'Populism as a Threat to Liberal Democracy', in C. Rovira Kaltwasser, P. Taggart, P. Ochoa Espejo, P. Ostiguy (eds.), *The Oxford Handbook of Populism*, Oxford University Press, 2017, 554

Ruotolo, M., 'L'incidenza della Costituzione repubblicana sulla lettura dell'art. 12 delle preleggi', in D. M. Cananzi, R. Righi (eds.), *Ontologia e analisi del diritto. Scritti per Gaetano Carcaterra*, Giuffrè, Milan, 2012, 1297

Rusconi, G. E., *Resistenza e postfascismo*, Il Mulino, Bologna, 1995

Russo, A. M., 'El Ordenamiento Regional Italiano En La Espiral Centralizadora De La Crisis: ¡Todo Cambia Para Que Nada Cambie!', *Cuadernos Manuel Giménez Abad*, No. 6, 2013, 9

Russo, F., 'Government Formation in Italy: The Challenge of Bicameral Investiture', in B. E. Rasch, S. Martin, J. A. Cheibub (eds.), *Parliaments and Government Formation: Unpacking Investiture Rules*, Oxford University Press, 2015, 136

Sadursky, W., *Poland's Constitutional Breakdown*, Oxford University Press, 2019

Sagan, E., *Citizens & Cannibals: The French Revolution, the Struggle for Modernity*, Rowman and Littlefield, Lanham, MD, 2001

Saiz Arnaiz, A., *La apertura constitucional al derecho internacional y europeo de los derechos humanos. El artículo 10.2 de la Constitución Española*, Centro de Estudios Políticos y Constitucionales, Madrid, 1999

Sajó, A., 'Emotions in Constitutional Design', *International Journal of Constitutional Law*, No. 3, 2010, 354

Sajò, A., 'From Militant Democracy to the Preventive State', *Cardozo Law Review*, No. 5, 2006, 2255

Salvadori, M., *Democrazia. Storia di un'idea tra mito e realtà*, Donzelli, Rome, 2016

Santomauro, G., 'Referendum as an Instrument of "Policy Change" on a Crucial Bioethical Issue: A Comparative Case Study on Abortion in Italy and Ireland', *Nomos. Le attualità del diritto*, No. 1, 2019, 1

Sartori, G., *Parties and Party Systems: A Framework for Analysis*, Cambridge University Press, New York, 1976

Scarciglia, R., *Il divieto di mandato imperativo: contributo a uno studio di diritto comparato*, CEDAM, Padua, 2005

Scheppele, K., 'Orban's Emergency', 2020, https://verfassungsblog.de/orbans-emergency/

Schmidt, V., *Democracy in Europe: The EU and National Polities*, Oxford University Press, 2006

Schmitt, C., *Democrazia e liberalismo. Referendum e iniziativa popolare Hugo Preuss e la dottrina tedesca dello Stato*, Giuffrè, Milan, 2001

Schmitt, C., *Volksentscheid und Volksbegehren. Ein Beitrag zur Auslegung der Weimarer Verfassung und zur Lehre von der unmittelbaren Demokratie*, De Gruyter, Berlin, 1927

Scholte, J., 'The Complacency of Legality: Constitutionalist Vulnerabilities to Populist Constituent Power', *German Law Journal*, special issue 3, 2019, 351

Schütze, R., 'Federalism as Constitutional Pluralism: "Letter from America"', in M. Avbelj, J. Komárek (eds.), *Constitutional Pluralism in the European Union and Beyond*, Hart, Oxford, 2012, 185

Scicluna, N., *European Union Constitutionalism in Crisis*, Routledge, Abingdon, 2015

Scicluna, N., 'Politicization without Democratization: The Impact of the Eurozone Crisis on EU Constitutionalism', 2013, https://bit.ly/3xkjRyc.

Selvaggi, N., 'Populism and Criminal Justice in Italy', in G. Delledonne, G. Martinico, M. Monti, F. Pacini (eds.), *Italian Populism and Constitutional Law: Strategies, Conflicts and Dilemmas*, Palgrave, London, 2020, 291

Shonfield, D., 'Claudio Pavone's classic history rescued the real history of the Italian resistance, and is still an essential counter to revisionist narratives, argues David Shonfield', 2014, www.counterfire.org/articles/book-reviews/16985-a-civil-war-a-history-of-the-italian-resistance

Somma, A., 'Europa, sovranità e ordine economico nel prisma delle teorie federaliste', *DPCE online*, No. 1, 2020, 427

Somma, A., 'Un sovranismo democratico per un nuovo europeismo', *MicroMega*, 2018, http://temi.repubblica.it/micromega-online/un-sovranismo-democratico-per-un-nuovo-europeismo/

Spadaro, A., 'Costituzionalismo versus populismo: sulla c.d. deriva populistico-plebiscitaria delle democrazie', in G. Brunelli, A. Pugiotto, P. Veronesi (eds.), *Scritti in onore di Lorenza Carlassare*, Vol. V, Jovene, Naples, 2009, 2007

Staiano, S., *La rappresentanza*, 2017, www.rivistaaic.it/images/rivista/pdf/4.% 203_2017_Staiano_.pdf

Stanley, B., 'The Thin Ideology of Populism', *Journal of Political Ideologies*, No. 1, 2008, 95

Stein, E., 'International Law in Internal Law: Toward Internationalization of Central-Eastern European Constitutions?', *American Journal of International Law*, No. 3, 1994, 427

Steinbach, A., 'The Mutualization of Sovereign Debt: Comparing the American Past and the European Present', *Journal of Common Market Studies*, No. 5, 2015, 1110

Steinbeis, M., 'Majority is a Legal Concept', 2017, http://verfassungsblog.de/majority-is-a-legal-concept/

Steuer, M., 'Militant Democracy on the Rise: Consequences of Legal Restrictions on Extreme Speech in the Czech Republic, Slovakia and Hungary', *Review of Central and East European Law*, 2019, 162

Streeck, W., *Buying Time: The Delayed Crisis of Democratic Capitalism*, Verso Books, London, 2014

Sturzo, L., 'La guerra, l'Italia e l'intervistato', in L. Sturzo, *Politica di questi anni. 1957-1959*, Zanichelli, Bologna, 1954, 144

Sunstein, C., *The Filter Bubble: What the Internet Is Hiding from You*, Penguin Press, London, 2011

Sunstein, C., 'Incompletely Theorized Agreements. Commentary', *Harvard Law Review*, No. 7, 1994, 1733

Sunstein, C., *#republic: Divided Democracy in the Age of Social Media*, Princeton University Press, 2017

Surkov, V. I., 'Nationalization of the Future: Paragraphs pro Sovereign Democracy', *Russian Studies in Philosophy*, No. 4, 2009, 8

Taggart, P., 'Populism and the Pathology of Representative Politics', in Y. Mény, Y. Surel (eds.), *Democracies and the Populist Challenge*, Palgrave, London, 2002, 62

Taggart, P., 'Populism and Representative Politics in Contemporary Europe', *Journal of Political Ideologies*, No. 3, 2004, 269

Taggart, P., 'Populism in Western Europe', in C. Rovira Kaltwasser, P. Taggart, P. Ochoa Espejo, P. Ostiguy (eds.), *The Oxford Handbook of Populism*, Oxford University Press, 2017, 248

Taguieff, P. A., *L'illusion populiste*, Berg International, Paris, 2002

Tarchi, M., *Italia populista. Dal qualunquismo a Beppe Grillo*, Il Mulino, Bologna, 2015

Tarchi, M., 'Italy: The Promised Land of Populism?', *Contemporary Italian Politics*, No. 3, 2015, 273

Tarchi, M., 'Populism Italian Style', in Y. Mény, Y. Surel (eds.), *Democracies and the Populist Challenge*, Palgrave, London, 2002, 120

Tarli Barbieri, G., 'La riduzione del numero dei parlamentari: una riforma opportuna? (ricordando Paolo Carrozza)', *Le Regioni*, No. 2, 2019, 375

Taussig, M., *Mimesis and Alterity*, Routledge, Abingdon, 1993

Telò, M., *Europe: A Civilian Power? European Union, Global Governance, World Order*, Palgrave, London, 2006

Tierney, S., *Constitutional Referendums: The Theory and Practice of Republican Deliberation*, Oxford University Press, 2012

Todorov, T., *Memory as a Remedy for Evil*, Seagull Books, Kolkata, 2010

Tomba, M., 'Who's Afraid of the Imperative Mandate?', *Critical Times*, No. 1, 2018, 108

Tonti, V., 'Vincolo di mandato e democrazia diretta: verso un superamento del Parlamento?', in G. Allegri, A. Sterpa, N. Viceconte (eds.), *Questioni costituzionali al tempo del populismo e del sovranismo*, ES, Naples, 2019, 93

Topaloff, L., 'The Rise of Referendums: Elite Strategy or Populist Weapon?', *Journal of Democracy*, No. 3, 2017, 127

Torre, A., 'Il referendum nel Regno Unito: radici sparse, pianta rigogliosa', in A. Torre, J. Frosini (eds.), *Democrazia rappresentativa e referendum nel Regno Unito*, Maggioli, Rimini, 2012, 11

Trerè, E., Barassi, V., 'Net-authoritarianism? How Web Ideologies Reinforce Political Hierarchies in the Italian 5 Star Movement', *Journal of Italian Cinema & Media Studies*, No. 3, 2015, 287

Tronconi, F., 'The Italian Five Star Movement during the Crisis: Towards Normalisation?', *South European Society and Politics*, No. 1, 2018, 163

Tushnet, M., 'Abolishing Judicial Review', *Constitutional Commentary*, No. 3, 2011, 581

Twomey, A., 'Second Thoughts – Recall Elections for Members of Parliament', Sydney Law School Research Paper No. 11/55, 2011, https://papers.ssrn.com/sol3/papers.cfm?abstract_id=1922393

Tyulkina, S., *Militant Democracy: Undemocratic Political Parties and Beyond*, Routledge, Abingdon, 2015

Uleri, P. V., *Referendum e democrazia. Una prospettiva comparata*, Il Mulino, Bologna, 2003

Urbinati, N., *Democracy Disfigured: Opinion, Truth, and the People*, Harvard University Press, Cambridge, MA, 2014

Urbinati, N., 'Democracy and Populism', *Constellations*, No. 1, 1998, 110

Urbinati, N., 'The Italian Five Star Movement for Foreigners', 2018, www.rivistailmulino.it/a/the-italian-five-star-movement-for-foreigners

Urbinati, N., *Me the People: How Populism Transforms Democracy*, Harvard University Press, Cambridge, MA, 2019

Urbinati, N., 'Populism and the Principle of Majority', in C. Rovira Kaltwasser, P. Taggart, P. Ochoa Espejo, P. Ostiguy (eds.), *The Oxford Handbook of Populism*, Oxford University Press, 2017, 571

Urbinati, N., Warren, M., 'The Concept of Representation in Contemporary Democratic Theory', *Annual Review of Political Science*, 2008, 387

Urbinati, N., Vandelli, L., *La democrazia del sorteggio*, Einaudi, Turin, 2020

Valditara, G., *Sovranismo. Una speranza per la democrazia di Valditara*, Book Time, Milan, 2017

Varriale, A., 'The Myth of the Italian Resistance Movement (1943-1945). The Case of Naples', *Kirchliche Zeitgeschichte*, No. 2, 2014, 383

Vassallo, S., 'Government Under Berlusconi: The Functioning of the Core Institutions in Italy', *West European Politics*, No. 4, 2007, 692

Vassallo, S., Passarelli, G., 'Centre-left Prime Ministerial Primaries in Italy: The Laboratory of the "Open Party" Model', *Contemporary Italian Politics*, No. 1, 2016, 12

Veca, S., *La priorità del male*, Feltrinelli, Milan, 2012

Veiga, F., González-Villa, C., Forti, S., Sasso, A., Prokopljevic, J., Moles, R., *Patriotas indignados*, Alianza, Madrid, 2019

Vermeule, A., *The Constitution of Risk*, Cambridge University Press, 2013

Vespa, B., *Perché l'Italia diventò fascista*, Mondadori, Milan, 2019

Vigevani, G. E., 'Origine e attualità del dibattito sulla XII disposizione finale della Costituzione: i limiti della tutela della democrazia', 2019, https://bit.ly/3AiOfuT

Volpe, G., 'Referendum abrogativo e diritto di resistenza', in Corte costituzionale (ed.), *Il giudizio di ammissibilità del referendum abrogativo*, Giuffrè, Milan, 1998, 284

Volpi, M., 'Referendum (dir. cost)', in *Digesto delle discipline pubblicistiche*, Vol. XII, UTET, Turin, 1997, 434

Volterra, S., 'La Costituzione italiana e i modelli anglosassoni con particolare riguardo agli Stati Uniti', in U. De Siervo (ed.), *Scelte della Costituente e cultura giuridica. I: Costituzione italiana e modelli stranieri*, Il Mulino, Bologna, 1980, 117

Voßkuhle, A., 'Demokratie und Populismus', *Der Staatt*, No. 1, 2018, 119

Waldron, J., 'The Core of the Case Against Judicial Review', *Yale Law Journal*, No. 6, 2006, 1346

Wardle, C., Derakhshan, H., 'Information Disorder: Toward an Interdisciplinary Framework for Research and Policy Making', *Council of Europe report DGI(2017)09*, 2017, https://first draftnews.org/wp-content/uploads/2017/10/Information_Disorder_FirstDraft-CoE_2018.pdf? x40896

Watson, A., *Legal Transplants: An Approach to Comparative Law*, Scottish Academic Press, Edinburgh, 1974

Weber, M., *Economy and Society*, University of California Press, Berkeley, 1978 (German edition 1922), https://archive.org/stream/MaxWeberEconomyAndSociety/ MaxWeberEconomyAndSociety_djvu.txt

Weiler, J. H. H., 'The Community System: The Dual Character of Supranationalism', *Yearbook of European Law*, 1981, 267

Weill, R., 'Dicey Was Not Diceyan', *Cambridge Law Journal*, No. 2, 2003, 474

Wind, M., *The Tribalization of Europe – A Defense of our Liberal Values*, Espasa Calpe, Madrid, 2019

Zagrebelsky, G., 'Una riflessione sulla democrazia', in Gruppo di Resistenza Morale (ed.), *Argomenti per il dissenso. Costituzione, democrazia, antifascismo*, Celid, Turin, 1994, 24

Zagrebelsky, G., *Il 'Crucifige!' e la democrazia. Il processo di Gesù Cristo come paradigma dei diversi modi di pensare la democrazia*, Einaudi, Turin, 1995

Zakaria, F., 'The Rise of Illiberal Democracy', *Foreign Affairs*, No. 6, 1997, 22

Zanon, N., *Il libero mandato parlamentare. Saggio critico sull'art. 67 della Costituzione*, Giuffrè, Milan, 1991

Zanon, N., 'La seconda giovinezza dell'art. 67 della Costituzione', 2014, www .forumcostituzionale.it/wordpress/images/stories/pdf/documenti_forum/giurisprudenza/ 2014/0007_nota_1_2014_zanon.pdf

Zolo, D., 'Teoria e critica dello Stato di diritto', in P. Costa, D. Zolo (eds.), *Lo Stato di diritto. Storia, teoria, critica*, Feltrinelli, Milan, 2003, 17

Zucca, L., 'Conflicts of Fundamental Rights as Constitutional Dilemmas', *STALS (Sant'Anna Legal Studies) Research Paper*, 16/2008, www.stals.santannapisa.it/sites/ default/files/stals_Zucca.pdf

ARTICLES FROM NEWSPAPERS

'Berlusconi: "Costituzione ideologizzata"', 7 February 2009, www.corriere.it/politica/09_feb braio_07/berlusconi_costituzione_bd1e8990-f53f-11dd-a70d-00144f02aabc.shtml

'Conte parla alla Camera: Fdi assente, Lega abbandona l'Aula', 17 June 2020, https://bit.ly /3dt4VpK

'Conte: "Rivendico natura populista del Governo"', 8 December 2018, www.ilgiornale.it /video/politica/conte-rivendico-natura-populista-governo-1622063.html

'La Costituzione è di ispirazione sovietica', 12 April 2003, www.repubblica.it/online/politica/ berluparla/torino/torino.html

'Davide Casaleggio: "Il Parlamento? In futuro forse non sarà più necessario"', 23 July 2018, https://bit.ly/2UjK7tW

'La democrazia integrale', 19 June 2018, https://ricerca.repubblica.it/repubblica/archivio/ repubblica/2018/06/19/la-democrazia-integrale32.html

'Garante privacy: "Entro 5 giorni Rousseau consegni i dati al Movimento"', 1 June 2021, https:// www.garanteprivacy.it/web/guest/home/docweb/-/docweb-display/docweb/9591994

'Governo: Di Battista contro Draghi, "l'apostolo delle élite"', 2 February 2021, www .affaritaliani.it/notiziario/governo_di_battista_contro_draghi_lapostolo_delle_elite-182844 .html

'Grillo presenta le liste: "Apriremo il Parlamento come una scatola di tonno"', 11 January 2013, https://bit.ly/3dB8g6c

'La Lega ha davvero disertato i negoziati per riformare il Regolamento di Dublino?', 20 September 2018, https://pagellapolitica.it/dichiarazioni/8104/la-lega-ha-davvero-disertato-i-negoziati-per-riformare-il-regolamento-di-dublino

'The many trials of Silvio Berlusconi explained', 9 May 2014, www.bbc.com/news/world-europe-12403119

'M5S a rischio scissione dopo il post di Casaleggio sul Blog: cosa sta succedendo', 5 October 2020, www.fanpage.it/politica/m5s-a-rischio-scissione-dopo-il-post-di-casaleggio-sul-blog-cosa-sta-succedendo/

'M5S non si accontenta: "Se vince il Sì poi tagliamo anche gli stipendi dei parlamentari"', 13 September 2020, https://bit.ly/3iXaK2j

'Riccardo Fraccaro: meno onorevoli e più referendum. In cinque leggi il piano di riforme', 11 September 2018, https://bit.ly/3gDm56c

'Salvini come Berlusconi: "Io ministro eletto dal popolo, i magistrati non lo sono"', 7 September 2018, www.ilfattoquotidiano.it/2018/09/07/salvini-come-berlusconi-io-ministro-eletto-dal-popolo-i-magistrati-non-lo-sono/4611540/

'Salvini in Senato: "Basta trionfalismi, siamo la maggioranza nel Paese, lasciateci parlare"', 22 July 2020, www.agi.it/politica/news/2020-07-22/salvini-senato-mes-9230606/

'Salvini per difendersi cita a sproposito la Costituzione: "La difesa della Patria è sacro dovere di ogni Cittadino"', 4 February 2020, https://bit.ly/3gL1qMm

'Taglio dei parlamentari, forbice gigante e striscione: i Cinquestelle festeggiano in piazza Montecitorio', 8 October 2019, https://bit.ly/2St4oNe

Baldolini, V., 'Referendum, 183 costituzionalisti dicono No', 24 August 2020, https://bit.ly /35F3hNv

Barber, L., Foy, H., Baker, A., 'Vladimir Putin: Liberalism Has "Outlived Its Purpose"', 28 June 2019, www.ft.com/content/670039ec-98f3-11e9-9573-ee5cbb98ed36

Bershidsky, L., 'Putin Ally's "Deep State" Twist Is Deep Russian People', 12 February 2019, www.bloomberg.com/opinion/articles/2019-02-12/russia-has-its-own-deep-state-it-s-called-deep-people

Bertini, C., 'Riccardo Fraccaro: meno onorevoli e più referendum. In cinque leggi il piano di riforme', 11 September 2018, https://bit.ly/3dccnFH

Calhoun, G., 'Europe's Hamiltonian Moment – What Is It Really?', 26 May 2020, www.forbes.com/sites/georgecalhoun/2020/05/26/europes-hamiltonian-moment–what-is-it-really/

Carli, A., 'Rimborsi M5s, per probiviri irregolari oltre 45 parlamentari', 7 January 2020, www.ilsole24ore.com/art/m5s-vertice-probiviri-morosi-dodici-parlamentari-non-presentano-rendiconti-gennaio-2019-ACS4jBAB

Casaleggio, D., 'Noi Siamo Movimento', 4 October 2020, www.ilblogdellestelle.it/2020/10/noi-siamo-movimento.html

Casaleggio, D., '7 brevi paradossi della democrazia', 17 September 2019, www.corriere.it/politica/19_settembre_17/06-politico-t7ccorriere-web-sezioni-29ff88c4-d8bb-11e9-a64f-042100a6f996.shtml

Casaleggio, D., 'A Top Leader of Italy's Five Star Movement: Why We Won', 19 March 2018, www.washingtonpost.com/news/theworldpost/wp/2018/03/19/five-star/

Cassese, S., 'Cassese: "La pandemia non è una guerra. I pieni poteri al governo non sono legittimi"', 14 April 2020, www.ildubbio.news/2020/04/14/cassese-la-pandemia-non-e-una-guerra-pieni-poteri-al-governo-sono-illegittimi/

Ceccanti, S., 'Referendum, perché Sì. Votare per il taglio dei parlamentari è una decisione da riformisti veri. Ve lo spiego in cinque punti', 13 August 2020, www.ilfoglio.it/politica/2020/08/13/news/referendum-perche-si-330990/?underPaywall=true

Cerulus, L., '5Stars Defend Their Digital Democracy in Face of Privacy Sanction', 19 April 2019, www.politico.eu/article/davide-casaleggio-5stars-rousseau-platform-lashes-out-over-political-motivated-data-protection-fine/

Fairless, T., 'After Firing Its Bazooka, ECB Could Reload to Fight Coronavirus', 29 April 2020, www.wsj.com/articles/after-firing-its-bazooka-ecb-could-reload-to-fight-coronavirus-11588155329

Fenazzi, S., 'Per M5S, quello svizzero è il "modello faro" di democrazia diretta', 20 June 2016, https://bit.ly/2SMkqlz

Fraccaro, R., 'La democrazia integrale', 19 June 2018, https://ricerca.repubblica.it/repubblica/archivio/repubblica/2018/06/19/la-democrazia-integrale32.html

Fraccaro, R., 'Perché serve colmare il gap fra istituzioni e volontà popolare', 9 agosto 2018, www.ilsole24ore.com/art/perche-serve-colmare-gap-istituzioni-e-volonta-popolare–AEhzbyXF

Fraccaro, R., 'Referendum senza quorum: decide chi partecipa. Per riconquistare la sovranità servono cittadini attivi', 29 May 2016, www.riccardofraccaro.it/referendum-senza-quorum-decide-chi-partecipa-per-riconquistare-la-sovranita-servono-cittadini-attivi/

Giubilei, F., 'Oggi tutti parlano di "sovranismo" ma (quasi) nessuno spiega che cosa sia', 11 December 2018, www.ilgiornale.it/news/spettacoli/oggi-tutti-parlano-sovranismo-quasi-nessuno-spiega-che-cosa-1614631.html

Grandesso, F., 'Black Smoke for Bersani, Dangerous Games for Italy!', 7 March 2013, www.neweurope.eu/article/black-smoke-bersani-dangerous-games-italy/

Grillo, G., 'Il più grande inganno della Politica: farci credere che servano i politici', 27 June 2018, www.beppegrillo.it/il-piu-grande-inganno-della-politica-e-farci-credere-che-servano-politici/

Hall, B., Arnold, M., Fleming, S., 'Coronavirus: Can the ECB's "Bazooka" Avert a Eurozone Crisis?', 23 March 2020, www.ft.com/content/a7496c30-6ab7-11ea-800d-da70cff6e4d3

Ignazi, P., 'Ora il Pd pensi ai più deboli', 5 August 2019, https://rep.repubblica.it/pwa/commento/2019/08/05/news/ora_il_pd_pensi_ai_piu_deboli-232905580/?ref=nrct-1

Johnson, M., Ghiglione, D., 'Coronavirus in Italy: "When we heard about the lockdown we rushed to the station"', 8 March 2020, www.ft.com/content/27458814-6159-11ea-a6cd-df28cc3c6a68

Kapoor, S., 'This Isn't Europe's "Hamilton" Moment', 22 May 2020, www.politico.eu/article/this-isnt-europes-hamilton-moment/

Kurz, S., 'The "Frugal Four" Advocate a Responsible EU Budget', 16 February 2020, www.ft.com/content/7faae690-4e65-11ea-95a0-43d18ec715f5

Le Nir, A., 'Italie: Giuseppe Conte ouvre des "états généraux" pour relancer le pays', 14 June 2020, www.rfi.fr/fr/europe/20200613-italie-giuseppe-conte-ouvre-etats-g%C3%A9n%C3%A9raux-relancer-le-pays

Maranini, G., 'Totalitarismo dei partiti', 28 July 1946, *L'Arno*

Mari, L., 'M5S, Casaleggio lascia il Movimento: "Nemmeno mio padre lo riconoscerebbe. Se si cerca legittimazione in tribunale la democrazia interna è fallita"', 5 June 2021, www.repubblica.it/politica/2021/06/05/news/m5s_rousseau_dati-304277205/

Mola, G., 'Berlusconi: "La mia biografia in tutte le famiglie italiane"', 11 April 2001, www.repubblica.it/online/politica/campagnacinque/libro/libro.html

Provenzani, F., '"La trappola della Germania per far accettare il MES all'Italia" (Paolo Becchi)', 7 May 2020, www.money.it/Piano-Germania-MES-Italia-Paolo-Becchi

Renzi, M., 'Renzi: Nessun filo rosso tra me e Salvini', 6 August 2019, www.repubblica.it/politica/2019/08/06/news/nessun_filo_rosso_tra_me_e_salvini-233001980/

Roberts, H., 'Salvini Occupies Italian Parliament in Lockdown Protest', 30 April 2020, www.politico.eu/article/matteo-salvini-coronavirus-occupies-italian-parliament-in-lockdown-protest/

Rodriquez, G., 'Dai "marchi pe 'e bestie", alle "processioni a casa de mi cugino" per poter contrarre malattie esantematiche. I vaccini secondo Paola Taverna (M5S)', 7 August 2018, www.quotidianosanita.it/governo-e-parlamento/articolo.php?articolo_id=64805

Sassoon, D., 'Claudio Pavone Obituary', 22 December 2016, www.theguardian.com/books/2016/dec/22/claudio-pavone-obituary

Sesto, M., 'Taglio parlamentari, ecco come si restringe il Senato. La Lombardia è la regione che perde più seggi', 28 agosto 2020, https://bit.ly/3gIJvpu

Siclari, M., 'Taglio parlamentari, accolgo l'appello. I tre motivi perché voto no', 10 August 2020, https://bit.ly/3qcalum

Index

25 April 1945, liberation day, 38, 44

Alfano, Angelino, 57
anti-defection clause, 158, 160
anti-Europeanism, 6, 63, 85, 178
anti-party-ism, 51, 125, 130, 166
approvazione salvo intese, 141, 145
armistice of Cassibile, 38
Assemblea Costituente, 38, 77, 79, 94, 161
Assembleia da República, 160
austerity, 73, 76, 178

Berlusconi, Silvio, 7, 21, 55–60
block amendment, 140
Bossi, Umberto, 54–5
Brexit, 102, 103, 131
Bribesville, 53
budget/budget rules, 73, 74, 78, 80, 86, 179
Bulgaria, 157
Bundesrat, 157
Bundesverfassungsgericht (German Constitutional Court), 35, 37, 45, 67, 71, 87, 88, 90, 157

Camera dei deputati (Chamber of Deputies), 3, 7, 114, 126, 162, 166, 168
Canada, 121
Canadian Supreme Court, 24, 121–3
Casaleggio Associati, 61, 128, 137, 184
Casaleggio, Davide, 99, 100, 128, 129–36, 148, 151, 174, 184
Casaleggio, Gianroberto, 61, 128, 137, 138, 144, 147, 168, 183, 184
CasaPound Italia (CPI), 44
Chamber of Deputies, 3, 7, 114, 126, 162, 166, 168
Chávez, Hugo, 158
Cinderella complex, 11
Civil Code (*codice civile*), 97, 168
Clarity Act, 121

codice civile. *See* Civil Code (*codice civile*)
committees of inquiry, 142
Common Man's Front (*qualunquismo*), 6, 29, 49, 50, 52
Community Law, 71, 80
constituent power, 20, 24, 28, 32, 47, 90, 100, 104, 174
constitutional amendment, 36, 46, 47, 82, 113, 122, 163, 165, 172, 176, 180, 182
Constitutional Court (*Corte Costituzionale*), 45, 79, 115, 129, 163
constitutional identity, 68–9, 84
constitutional openness, 37, 38, 47, 63, 77, 78, 84, 92, 96, 98, 171
constitutional pluralism, 4, 25, 48
constitutional politics, 59, 60
constitutional populism, 27, 180
constitutional reform, 57, 76, 80, 91, 111, 113, 114, 117, 125, 126, 135, 138, 148, 162, 163, 182, 183
constitutional rigidity, 33, 46, 185
constitutional silence, 5
constitutionalism
  abusive, 30
  as holism, 4
  European democratic, 150
  legal, 15, 18, 21, 26
  and memory of horror, 30
  political, 1, 15, 21, 28
  and populism, 10, 16
  post-WWII, 4, 7, 10, 15, 25, 26, 29, 32, 38, 46, 48, 77, 83, 91, 170, 171, 178
  weak, 24
Consulta (Italian Constitutional Court), 79, 81
Conte Government, First, Conte I, 2, 44, 117, 118, 120, 133, 135, 139, 172, 174, 176, 179
Conte Government, Second, Conte II, 1, 2, 7, 62, 117, 120, 127, 141, 172, 182, 183
contract for government, 150